PRAISE FOR *WAR AGAINST WAR*

A *New York Times* Editors' Choice Pick

"With his customary clarity and insight, Kazin draws our attention to the remarkable group of individuals who argued—eloquently and with great moral urgency—against intervention in World War I. They lost the debate, but a singular achievement of this deeply incisive book is to show the lasting resonance of their analysis and their fears, down to our present day."

—Fredrik Logevall, Pulitzer Prize–winning author of *Embers of War*

"Thrilling . . . . A well-researched and wonderfully written account of the American pacifist movement during World War I and its legacy in American history."

—*Los Angeles Review of Books*

"Michael Kazin's important history of American pacifism is a compelling cautionary tale. It not only provides an arresting history of a major American movement, it also reminds us of the false hopes that drew us into World War I, Vietnam, Iraq, and Afghanistan. The book should be required reading for aspiring military officers and every politician pronouncing on U.S. leadership around the globe."

—Robert Dallek, bestselling author of *An Unfinished Life*

"At a time when people tell veterans, 'Thank you for your service,' Michael Kazin reminds us of some largely forgotten people who deserve our thanks far more: those who tried to keep us out of the most terrible war the world had yet seen. The dissenters against American participation in the First World War are still a model for us, and Kazin evokes them with care and grace."

—Adam Hochschild, bestselling author of *To End All Wars*

"[A] fine, sorrowful history . . . A timely reminder of how easily the will of the majority can be thwarted in even the mightiest of democracies."

—*The New York Times Book Review*

"Well-written, carefully researched, and compelling scholarship. A dramatic read."

—*New York Journal of Books*

"Once again, Michael Kazin has written a book about the past that forces us to take another look at our present. *War Against War*, the story of the activists who opposed American entry into World War I, is a gem of historical analysis. Eloquently written, powerfully argued, fully documented, it introduces us to a remarkable and remarkably diverse cast of American characters and compels us to reexamine the most fundamental of questions: When is a war worth fighting?"

—David Nasaw, bestselling author of *The Patriarch*

"In this penetrating account of the women and men of a century ago, whom he calls the 'anti-warriors,' Michael Kazin brings off a skillful double play. First, he resurrects the memory of this varied and not so little band of sisters and brothers with both sympathy and critical detachment. Second, he illuminates attitudes and arguments that persist in underpinning and resisting America's 'great power' outreach. Anyone who cares about this country's role in the world should read this book."

—John Milton Cooper Jr., author of *Woodrow Wilson*

"Kazin . . . brings a fascinating perspective to the war that is still known as the Great War. . . . He convincingly argues that the U.S. decision to join the Allies was a turning point in history and one that reverberates today."

—*Los Angeles Times*

"*War Against War* is a magnificent book that gives opponents of American involvement in World War I, one of the most profoundly destructive

conflicts in human history, their due. In elegant and engaging prose, Michael Kazin tells a story about politics, morality, social forces, and a fascinating cast of personalities with power and clarity. This is a very important book, at once sobering and inspiring."
    —E.J. Dionne Jr., bestselling author of *Why the Right Went Wrong*

"[Kazin's] account of the failed but ardent movement that tried to prevent the country from joining [WWI] is impressive and moving."
    —*The Nation*

"Kazin's brilliant new book . . . lends credence to the old saying, "the past is a foreign country."
    —*Education and Culture*

"An astute account of the United States' futile struggle to stay out of WWI . . . Kazin's *War Against War* confirms his stature as one of the most astute historians of American 19th- and 20th-century social movements."
    —*Washington Independent Review of Books*

"[Kazin] has a mastery of his material and a readable style. [*War Against War*] richly deserves our attention."
    —*Currents*

"*War Against War*'s great strength is in laying out the pitfalls and fractures the pacifist movement confronted . . . while showing how it created a strong enough base, and a powerful enough critique to push back against U.S. entry for three years."
    —*In These Times*

"Kazin ends *War Against War* with a salute to those who search for peace. He deserves praise for portraying that quest with clear-eyed honesty and rigor. Maybe that kind of clarity could help keep us out of wars to come."
    —*Pittsburgh Post-Gazette*

ALSO BY MICHAEL KAZIN

*Barons of Labor: The San Francisco Building Trades
and Union Power in the Progressive Era*

The Populist Persuasion: An American History

America Divided: The Civil War of the 1960s (with Maurice Isserman)

A Godly Hero: The Life of William Jennings Bryan

American Dreamers: How the Left Changed a Nation

WAR
AGAINST
WAR

The American Fight for Peace,
1914–1918

MICHAEL KAZIN

SIMON & SCHUSTER PAPERBACKS

New York   London   Toronto   Sydney   New Delhi

Simon & Schuster Paperbacks
An Imprint of Simon & Schuster, Inc.
1230 Avenue of the Americas
New York, NY 10020

First Simon & Schuster trade paperback edition January 2018

SIMON & SCHUSTER PAPERBACKS and colophon are registered trademarks of
Simon & Schuster, Inc.

For information about special discounts for bulk purchases, please contact
Simon & Schuster Special Sales at 1-866-506-1949 or business@simonandschuster.com.

The Simon & Schuster Speakers Bureau can bring authors to your live event.
For more information or to book an event, contact the Simon & Schuster Speakers Bureau
at 1-866-248-3049 or visit our website at www.simonspeakers.com.

Interior design by Ruth Lee-Mui

Manufactured in the United States of America

1   3   5   7   9   10   8   6   4   2

The Library of Congress has cataloged the hardcover edition as follows:

Names: Kazin, Michael, 1948– author.
Title: War against war : the American fight for peace, 1914–1918 / Michael Kazin.
Description: New York : Simon & Schuster, 2017. | Includes bibliographical references and index.
Identifiers: LCCN 2016005355 (print) | LCCN 2016028651 (ebook) | ISBN 9781476705903
(hardback) | ISBN 9781476705910 (paperback) | ISBN 9781476705927 (E-Book)
Subjects: LCSH: World War, 1914–1918—United States. | Neutrality—United States—History—
20th century. | Peace movements—United States—History—20th century. | World War, 1914–
1918—Protest movements—United States. | World War, 1939–1945—Women—United States. |
Progressivism (United States politics) | United States—Politics and government—1913–1921. |
BISAC: HISTORY / United States / 20th Century. | HISTORY / Military / World War I. |
HISTORY / Modern / 20th Century.
Classification: LCC D619 .K39 2017 (print) | LCC D619 (ebook) | DDC 940.3/120973—dc23
LC record available at https://lccn.loc.gov/2016005355

ISBN 978-1-4767-0590-3
ISBN 978-1-4767-0591-0 (pbk)
ISBN 978-1-4767-0592-7 (ebook)

To My Fellow Dissentniks

CONTENTS

Introduction: Against a Great, Forgotten War   xi

PROLOGUE: A BETTER WORLD IN BIRTH?   1

1. **EVER WIDENING CIRCLES**   17
   August 1914 to May 1915

2. **CRY PEACE AND FIGHT PREPAREDNESS**   58
   May 1915 to May 1916

3. **KEEP US OUT**   112
   June 1916 to January 1917

4. **DO THE PEOPLE WANT WAR?**   146
   February 1917 to April 1917

5. **THE WAR—OR AMERICAN PROMISE: ONE MUST CHOOSE**   187
   April 1917 to November 1917

6. **A STRANGE SET OF CRIMINALS**   241
   December 1917 to December 1918

7. **LEGACIES**   275

Acknowledgments   293
Key Events   297

Abbreviations Used in Notes   305
Notes   307
Good Reading   359
Illustration Credits   363
Index   365

AGAINST A GREAT, FORGOTTEN WAR

"It is no longer questionable that modern war and the joy of existence are incompatible. War makes it impossible to live. It makes it impossible even to die for a noble purpose."

—Max Eastman, 1916[1]

This book is about Americans who tried to stop their nation from fighting in history's most destructive war and then endured the wrath of a government that punished them for refusing to change their minds. They came from a variety of backgrounds: wealthy and middle and working class, recent immigrant and "old stock," urban and rural, white and black, Christian and Jewish and atheist. They lived in every region of the country and belonged to every political party. Most wanted to make big changes in American society, although not always the same changes and not always by expanding the powers of the state. But they shared a profound revulsion toward the conflict that was taking the lives of millions of soldiers and civilians in Europe and the Middle East. In print and in person, they urged President Woodrow Wilson to help stop the carnage rather than joining one side in order to vanquish the other.

As "anti-militarists," they saw every war as a tragedy, a failure to resolve serious differences of interest and ideology. And the Great War was the most tragic conflict they had ever known. The major protagonists in 1914 were prepared to fight a war, but none wanted or expected to engage in anything like the long and unprecedentedly bloody one that ensued. On the late June day in Sarajevo when a Serbian terrorist murdered the archduke and archduchess of Austria-Hungary, authorities in the German port city of Kiel had just hosted a gala luncheon for a group of visiting officers from the British Royal Navy, whose ships lay peacefully at harbor. The British commander, reported London's *Sunday Times*, "thanked the German authorities" for their "splendid reception" and "spoke of his pleasure at renewing his acquaintance with old German naval friends." That evening, he and his wife dined "as the guests of the Emperor" on one of the Kaiser's favorite battleships. Six weeks later, all these people had become mortal enemies. They would remain so until November of 1918, after at least 15 million soldiers and civilians had died.[2]

The foes of militarism in the United States tried to prevent such horrors from occurring at all. Until the nation entered the conflict nearly three years later, they organized the largest, most diverse, and most sophisticated peace coalition to that point in U.S. history. Not until the movement to end the Vietnam War half a century later would there be as large, as influential, and as tactically adroit a campaign against U.S. intervention in another land. There has been none to rival it since. From 1914 to 1917, cosmopolitan Socialists and feminists worked closely with members of Congress from the small-town South and the agrarian Midwest. They mounted street demonstrations and popular exhibitions, founded such new organizations as the Woman's Peace Party and the American Union Against Militarism, attracted prominent leaders from the labor and suffrage movements, and ran peace candidates for local and federal office. For almost three years, they helped prevent Congress from authorizing a massive increase in the size of the U.S. Army, a step that, under the name of "preparedness," was advocated by some of the richest and most powerful men in the land—ex-president Theodore Roosevelt foremost among them.

Anti-war leaders met often in the White House with President Woodrow Wilson. Usually he assured them he also wanted the United States to remain neutral, so that he might broker an equitable peace. The relationship between articulate activists dedicated to stopping the Great War and creating a cooperative world order and a president who claimed to share their lofty goals was critical to the strategy the peace coalition followed. By arguing that they only wanted America's actions to live up to Wilson's rhetoric, the anti-militarists appealed to progressives in both parties. Until the president changed his mind in the early spring of 1917 and asked Congress to declare war, most members of the peace alliance took him at his word. In the end, their credulousness hindered their ability to oppose him forthrightly when that became necessary.

What the advocates of peace *were* able to achieve depended on a coalition of four major parts. One individual in each group spoke out most prominently for its grievances and visions. Morris Hillquit, a suave labor lawyer, played that role for the Socialist Party, then at the zenith of its historical influence, as well as for left-wing trade unionists. Crystal Eastman, a charismatic organizer with prodigious energy, spearheaded the efforts of feminists and liberal pacifists, many of whom were, like Jane Addams, famous and well connected. In the House of Representatives, the Majority Leader—Claude Kitchin from North Carolina—rallied dozens of his fellow Democrats to arrest the drift toward war and, at times, to oppose the president and leader of their own party. Over in the Senate, Robert La Follette of Wisconsin spoke out, with combative eloquence, for many like-minded Republicans from the Midwest and West who suspected that big businessmen with close ties to Great Britain were pushing the United States to enter the conflict. This combination of movement activists outside government and lawmakers doing their best to back up their efforts inside the halls of federal power gave the anti-war cause a breadth and influence neither contingent could have achieved alone.

These four leaders of the peace coalition did not agree about every key issue that roiled the nation. Kitchin opposed woman suffrage and was a stalwart defender of the Jim Crow laws that kept black people down. Only Hillquit was ready to abolish private enterprise. But all four believed that industrial corporations wielded too much sway over how Americans worked and what they earned, the taxes they had to pay, the officeholders they elected, and the future of the economy on which they depended. And all four were convinced that the men at the helm of American industry and finance (most of whom were Republicans) were eager to use war and preparations for war to augment their profits and power.[3]

The quartet of leaders and their fellow activists had many reasons to fight for peace, but "isolationism" was not among them. That sharply pejorative term, which became popular only in the 1920s, accurately describes neither the thought nor the actions of key participants in the peace coalition. Jane Addams presided over meetings with her sister feminists in Europe. Morris Hillquit sought to keep alive the ties of his Socialist Party to its comrades abroad. Senator Robert La Follette filled many a speech with praise for progressives in other countries who shared his hatred for militarism. Henry Ford chartered an ocean liner to transport himself and dozens of other activists across the Atlantic, where they lobbied neutral governments to embrace a peace plan they would press on the warring powers. These Americans, like most critics of the war elsewhere in the world, wanted to create a new global order based on cooperative relationships between nation states and their gradual disarmament. Militarism, they argued, isolated peoples behind walls of mutual fear and loathing.[4]

Until April 1917, this formidable coalition of idealists—or realists— did much to keep the nation at peace. They may even have had a majority of Americans on their side until just weeks before Congress, at

Wilson's behest, voted to declare war. To prevent that from happening, peace activists pressed for a national referendum on the question, confident that "the people" would recoil from fighting and paying the bills in order to help one group of European powers conquer another.

Once the United States chose to enter the fray, the president, with the aid of the courts, prosecuted opponents of the war with a ferocity neither his defenders nor his adversaries had expected. "The whole terrific force of the State is brought to bear against the heretics," wrote the critic Randolph Bourne. The persistence of anti-war sentiment was used to justify the creation of a large and pervasive federal apparatus of propaganda and repression, with both civilian and military officials at the controls. From Wilson on down, they resolved that their adversaries had to keep silent or suffer for their dissent.[5]

The U.S. decision to join the Allies was a turning point in world history. It altered the fortunes of the war and, quite likely, the course of the twentieth century. It foreclosed the possibility of a negotiated peace among belligerents exhausted by nearly three years of fighting. The American Expeditionary Force engaged in heavy combat in France for less than six months. But the fear that millions of fresh U.S. troops would alter the course of the war had led the Kaiser's generals to launch a series of last, desperate offensives in the spring of 1918 that pushed to the outskirts of Paris. When that campaign collapsed, Germany's defeat was inevitable.

How would the war have ended if the United States had *not* intervened? The carnage might have continued for another year or two until citizens in the warring nations, who were already protesting the endless sacrifices required of them, forced their leaders to reach a settlement. If the Allies, led by France and Great Britain, had not won a total victory, there would have been no punitive peace treaty like that completed at the Palace of Versailles in 1919, no reparations that helped bankrupt the Weimar Republic, no stab-in-the-back allegations by resentful Germans, and thus no rise, much less triumph, of Hitler and his National

Socialist Party. The next world war, with its fifty million deaths, would never have occurred.

But instead, the way the Great War ended touched off nearly thirty years of genocide, massacres, and armed conflict between and within nations, a period that the historian Eric Hobsbawm called "The Age of Catastrophe." The turmoil and bitterness of the war made it possible for the Bolsheviks to seize power in Russia, for Mussolini to wrest control in Italy, for the Japanese military to invade China, and for Hitler to begin his reign of terror in Germany. It also planted the seeds for wars that continue to rage. Witness the fate of the Sykes-Picot Treaty, the secret pact drawn up in 1916 by diplomats from Britain and France that mashed together Shiites, Sunnis, and Kurds in a new nation called Iraq.[6]

Following the Armistice, the United States became the most prosperous nation in history, the unofficial capital of the twentieth century. But for the rest of the world, the aftermath of the war was as tragic as the conflict itself. There would be no "peace without victory," as Wilson had grandly, if naïvely, demanded. The doughboys who helped win the war also made possible a peace of conquerors that stirred resentment on which demagogues and tyrants of all ideological stripes would feed.

The debate about whether the United States should have fought the Great War was thus among the most consequential in the nation's history. But, despite a wealth of good scholarship, few contemporary Americans are aware of it at all. In the United States, observes one prominent historian, World War I is "the forgotten war. . . . Considering the extent of the American contribution to the war, and its effect on American society, this is surprising." Although combatants in the Second World War and the Vietnam conflict are memorialized in large and popular sites on the National Mall, the men who fought in the Great War—and the fifty-three thousand who died in battle—have no such honor in stone on that quasi-sacred space. Alone among citizens of the former belligerent nations, Americans celebrate a holiday on the anniversary of the Armistice that makes no explicit reference to the war itself. When I ask students why Veterans Day happens to take place on November 11, hardly any know the answer.[7]

In Europe, however, the Great War remains "a tremendous, inescapable, collective experience." The remorseless suffering inspired countless monuments and a wealth of enduring art. The poetry of Wilfred Owen and Siegfried Sassoon, the novels of Erich Maria Remarque and Ford Madox Ford and Boris Pasternak, and Jean Renoir's film *La Grande Illusion* are among the most memorable reflections we have about human beings in extremis. But the sole work of distinction written by an American about the war is Ernest Hemingway's novel *A Farewell to Arms*. Its protagonist is not a U.S. soldier but a Yank who drove an ambulance for the Italian army and then deserted to neutral Switzerland.[8]

The consequences of the war for the United States help explain why it has dropped from public memory in the nation that played such a decisive role in the victory. The United States won the Great War but lost the peace, and the image of Woodrow Wilson has never recovered. In the absence of either a satisfying moral outcome (as with World War II) or an ignoble defeat (as in Vietnam), it does not seem so surprising that Americans are oblivious to the conflict of 1914–1918. It is easy to neglect a story whose only apparent lesson is to be cautious about leaping into murky waters with guns blazing.[9]

But the war the anti-militarists wanted to stop led to big changes in America as well as in the larger world. A grand cause that fails may, sometimes, matter as much as one that succeeds. That failure can mark, with a bright line, a moment when a people and their government might have avoided making a decision that fundamentally changed their society. The diverse assemblage of Americans who fought against plunging the country into combat in the trenches of France and Belgium and on the high seas made the last mighty attempt to prevent the establishment of a political order most Americans now take for granted, even if some protest it: a state equipped to fight numerous wars abroad while keeping a close watch on the potentially subversive activities of its citizens at home. Thus, although the anti-warriors of 1914–1918 were bent on creating a more peaceful and cooperative society, both at home and abroad, they were acting on an impulse that was, by definition, profoundly conservative.

Although the identity of the nation's enemies has changed often over the past century, the larger ends of America's policies have remained much the same: to make the world "safe for democracy," as its leaders define it. To achieve that purpose required another innovation of the Great War: a military-industrial establishment funded, then partly and now completely, by income taxes.

The surveillance state was also launched during the First World War, primarily to spy on U.S. citizens who sought to continue protesting the war and to persuade others to join them. The Bureau of Investigation (later renamed the FBI) took charge of enforcing the Espionage and Sedition Acts; Military Intelligence hired undercover agents to report on the "subversive" activities of black and radical organizations. This apparatus grew in size and power through the hot and cold wars of the past century and during the "war on terrorism" in this one.

While failing to stop the United States from declaring war in 1917, the peace coalition was enough of a worry for the Wilson administration that it initiated a process that, a century later, led to the federal government intercepting the records of phone calls made by millions of Americans. Perhaps it is fitting that it was foes of the Great War who created the organization we now know as the American Civil Liberties Union.

I should confess my sympathies at the outset: I wish the United States had stayed out of the Great War. Imperial Germany posed no threat to the American homeland and no long-term threat to its economic interests, and the consequences of its defeat made the world a more dangerous place. But, as a historian, it is not my task to reignite a debate that was won and lost a hundred years ago. I have sought instead to understand, empathetically but not uncritically, the ideas and actions of those Americans who thought their country should stay out of the war and who almost succeeded in that quest. Many of them wanted to change the world in fundamental ways. All of them wanted to stop its national rivalries from descending into continual bouts of mass slaughter. In neither case was their failure inevitable. Yet we still shudder at its consequences.

A BETTER WORLD IN BIRTH?

"The war against war is going to be no holiday excursion or camping party. The military feelings are too deeply grounded to abdicate their place among our ideals until better substitutes are offered than the glory and shame that come to nations as well as to individuals from the ups and downs of politics and vicissitudes of trade."

—William James, 1910[1]

Ever since the United States liberated the Filipinos from Spanish rule and then forced them, in a brutal conflict, to become American subjects, the philosopher William James had been worrying about the future of his country. Was it fated to become a militaristic empire, like the great powers of continental Europe? In the wake of victory over Spain in 1898, the ever-confident Theodore Roosevelt thundered, "By war alone can we acquire those virile qualities necessary to win in the stern strife of actual life." TR's martial feats in Cuba with his Rough Riders had turned him into an icon of "the strenuous life." A few years later, Roosevelt became a strenuous president, and an immensely popular one. His bellicose convictions, stiffened by Darwinian metaphors of "self-preservation," had, thought James, become all too common in the upper reaches of society. TR and his allies were deploying them in their campaign for a larger U.S. Navy. Some even floated the idea of conscripting young men into the army, a sharp break with the nation's peacetime history.[2]

Other prominent Americans were just as certain that warfare was a nightmarish vestige of a savage past from which enlightened men and women were gradually beginning to awaken. "We care less each day for the heroism connected with warfare and destruction," Jane Addams, the celebrated pioneer of social work, assured her readers, and we "admire more that which pertains to labor and the nourishing of human life." In 1910 Andrew Carnegie, the retired steel baron, took $10 million from his mammoth fortune to establish an "Endowment for International Peace," which would "render war impossible" by studying its causes and proposing rational, "scientific" ways to prevent it.[3]

Already there existed dozens of organizations, none as affluent as the Carnegie Endowment but all dedicated to the same purpose. They bore such hopeful names as the American Peace Society, the Universal Peace Congress, the National Peace Congress, the Universal Peace Union, the World Peace Foundation, and the Association for International Conciliation. The proliferation of like-minded groups had more to do with the desire of the well-born men who dominated them to run their own enterprises than with any sensible division of tasks or personnel. By combining public education, the arbitration and/or mediation of disputes, and a mutual preference for making profits instead of blowing up people and property, they were confident that the idiocy of war would soon become obvious to all. On occasion, even TR favored compromise over bloodshed. In 1906, after mediating an end to the Russo-Japanese War, the president was awarded the Nobel Peace Prize.

James sympathized with the would-be peacemakers, but he could not share their optimism. He maintained that war endured because it called on humanity's most virtuous impulses as well its most sadistic ones. It could not be vanquished with a sunny melange of up-to-date social science and statesman-like goodwill. It would require an alternative as honorable, as self-sacrificing, and as self-disciplined as the martial spirit that armed forces had instilled in young men since the dawn of written history. It would require "the moral equivalent of war." In February 1910, the great philosopher-psychologist, who had a weak heart, sent an essay with that title to the U.S. branch of the Association for International Conciliation. The group promptly distributed thirty thousand copies in pamphlet form and allowed two mass-circulation magazines to reprint it. Six months later, James was dead.[4]

His eloquent words of caution lived on. "Civilized man," wrote James—by which he primarily meant the citizens of Europe and the United States—"has developed a sort of double personality" about war. On the one hand, "no legitimate interest . . . would seem to justify the tremendous destructions which a war . . . would necessarily entail. It would seem that common sense and reason ought to find a way to reach agreement in every conflict of honest interests." Yet well-meaning citizens who point this out "fail to realize the full inwardness of the situation." Men of every nation were still willing, even eager, to fight—and most women supported them—because war seduced as well as horrified. It was a mark of "the *strong* life . . . of life *in extremis.*" In contrast, peace advocates appeared weak, soft, and ineffectual.[5]

James sketched out an idea about what *should* be that was less convincing than his analysis of what *was.* His alternative to war was a form of mandatory national service: draft "the whole youthful population" to spend a few years toiling, cooperatively, in pursuits from mining coal to washing dishes to digging tunnels. Such labor would, he surmised, help "our gilded youths . . . to get the childishness knocked out of them." But he failed to explain why such pursuits would appeal, morally or otherwise, to their ungilded counterparts who were already laboring for scant wages in mines and mills—much less to older workers who might lose their jobs to the new industrial conscripts.

James, who sympathized with the idea of socialism, did not neglect the stark economic inequalities of the modern world. Near the end of the essay, he lamented: "That so many men, by mere accidents of birth and opportunity, should have a life of *nothing* else but toil and pain and hardness and inferiority imposed upon them . . . *this* is capable of arousing indignation in reflective minds." Men trained to kill, James knew, often learned to sublimate such injuries of class. So the gap between outrage and solutions yawned wide, frustrating even his sublime intelligence to narrow.

A MOTLEY GATHERING OF PEACEMAKERS

If the anti-war activists whom James criticized were naïve, theirs was a remarkably pervasive condition. In 1912, William Hull, a devout Quaker and a history professor at Swarthmore College, compared the peace movement of his day to the abolitionists of the 1850s. Like the crusaders against slavery, peace groups were "aggressively on the offensive," uniting "great numbers" to marshal "a vast body of fact and argument and sentiment, economic, political and moral, in proof of the folly and wickedness of warlike preparations as a means of insuring national defense, and of warfare as a means of procuring international justice."[6] Hull hoped it would not take another terrible war to persuade the world to finally come to its senses.

In the United States, peace advocacy was indeed growing more popular, even fashionable, in the decade before the Great War. But its breadth belied a certain incoherence—and a potential weakness. Some activists called themselves—or were derided by their opponents as— "pacifists," a term that meant something quite different than it does today. First employed in 1901 (in French) at a Universal Peace Congress, it referred, rather vaguely, to anyone who put great faith in agreements that would further "the policy of avoiding or abolishing war," as the *Oxford English Dictionary* put it. Thus, Carnegie, James, and Addams were all "pacifists," although only the latter opposed any use of force to settle

disputes. Pacifism, at the turn of the twentieth century, meant the conviction that war and the sentiments that encouraged it should be and
could be eliminated. That belief did not override a preference for one
nation over another. Indeed, by 1915, many former "pacifists" would be
cheering for the Allies to defeat the Central Powers—and rooting for
their own country to take part in the fighting.[7]

While the idyll of world peace lasted, one could abhor war for many
different reasons and propose quite different ways to limit or abolish it.
Prominent statesmen, businessmen, and international lawyers sought to
replace global disorder with a new world system, regulated by commer-
cial empires. They led the major peace organizations and dominated the
debate about alternatives to war. Feminists, in contrast, preached the
duty to extend what Addams called "the kingdom of human kindness"
from neighbors to communities to nations to the world at large. Socialists and union leaders claimed that structures built on avarice were to
blame for militarism; to defeat the latter, one would have to challenge or
dismantle the foundation from which it sprang. Progressive lawmakers
in both major parties viewed preparations for war as a distraction from
the assault on corporate power and political corruption they believed
was vital to preserving American democracy.

At the dawn of the twentieth century, an impressive variety of world
leaders agreed that some kind of institution was needed to prevent and,
eventually, outlaw war. This yearning went as far back as Immanuel
Kant's 1795 sketch of a "federation of free states" that would guarantee
"perpetual peace." But the rapid build-up in Europe of sophisticated
land and sea weaponry lent the idea a certain urgency. In 1899, Tsar
Nicholas II and Queen Wilhemina of the Netherlands co-hosted a glit-
tering conference at The Hague where top officials from every major
power, and some minor ones, agreed to establish a Permanent Court
of Arbitration. Not until 1921 was the permanent World Court established in that Dutch city, by which time most of those crowned heads
and elected heads of state were no longer breathing.

In the United States, the elite wing of the peace movement sought to emulate the dignitaries at The Hague. At formal banquets and elaborately scripted meetings, four consecutive Republican secretaries of state—John Hay, Elihu Root, Robert Bacon, and Philander Knox—mingled with the presidents of Harvard, Columbia, and Stanford. No one attempted to match Carnegie's massive donations to the cause. But in 1906, as president of the New York Peace Society, the retired steel baron did manage to recruit the mining mogul Daniel Guggenheim, the sugar manufacturer John Craig Havemeyer, and George Perkins—a partner in J.P. Morgan's investment house—to help him run the organization. Hull bowed to such august allies when he dedicated his book to William Howard Taft, the sitting president. Taft's "magnificent efforts in behalf of international justice," claimed Hull, "have made him the leader in the world in the new peace movement."[8]

As befit a former and future judge, Taft put great faith in forging a legal path toward peace. In 1911, he declared that "a court of the nations" should be assembled to decide all international disputes. Unwilling to wait for the whole world to act, he started by negotiating arbitration treaties with Great Britain and France. Taft expected that men like him—accomplished, erudite, and compassionate—would respond to what he called the "moral awakening to the hideous wickedness of armed combat" with a new international code of justice that would be fair to and binding on all parties. Although the president was a mediocre orator, he still traveled around the country to promote his handiwork. But by the time the Senate took up his plan, the unpopularity of Taft's domestic policies had made him a political weakling. Lawmakers amended his treaties, stripping away the obligation for the United States to abide by them, and the president angrily refused to accept their "crippled" and "emasculated" changes.[9]

In retrospect, it is easy to be cynical about these efforts, which failed to prevent both the Great War and the two smaller Balkan conflicts that immediately preceded it. The Peace Society and its kindred groups signed up thousands of members by mixing diatribes against the inhumanity of combat with sober plans to adjudicate conflict. The Carnegie Endowment spent huge sums on studies of international law, court decisions, and munitions industries. But, like Taft's doomed treaties, all this knowledge and advocacy had no power to force anyone to do anything meaningful to create a more peaceful world. In 1936, the left-wing historian Merle Curti expressed his contempt for the impotent peace efforts of these otherwise powerful men and the equally comfortable Americans who wished them well. "No reform . . . demanded less sacrifice on the part of America's middle class," he wrote. "The support asked by the friends of peace from the fairly well-to-do was less likely to touch their purse and status than, for instance, the movement to curb the profits of business by subjecting it to thoroughgoing government regulation."[10]

But the sincerity of a conviction should not be judged by whether or not it threatens one's livelihood. Carnegie's plans for peace depended, fatefully, on the cooperation of famous, well-connected men like himself for whom peace was seldom a priority. However, for the seventy-five-year-old retired tycoon who had risen from poverty, that $10 million gift was the result of a lifelong passion. In the deed of trust to his Endowment, Carnegie fulminated, "Although we no longer eat our fellow men nor torture prisoners, nor sack cities killing their inhabitants, we still kill each other in war like barbarians. Only wild beasts are excusable for doing that in this, the twentieth century of the Christian era . . . .The nation is criminal which refuses arbitration."[11]

Such a nation would also be acting against its economic self-interest, or so several influential scholars and writers believed. A big war would disrupt the fast-growing and increasingly interdependent global marketplace, leaving the citizens of every belligerent state poorer in the process. But never fear, the distinguished economist John Bates Clark, later a top official at the Carnegie Endowment, assured delegates to a peace conference in 1901: "Parts of the world are already drawn

into such delicate relations that war encounters new and powerful obstacles. . . . We shall make ten-fold more difficult the breaking of ties
between nations."[12]

In 1910, Norman Angell, an English journalist who had spent six
years of his youth in the United States, made this practical argument
with great vigor and some hard evidence. His book, *The Great Illusion:
A Study of the Relation of Military Power to National Advantage*, drew
praise from a remarkable cross section of European and American readers and sold more than a million copies in seventeen languages. Businessmen and Socialists, progressives and conservatives all took comfort
in learning from Angell that citizens of such nations as Sweden and Belgium, with only tiny armies, had higher standards of living than Russia and Germany, which were expanding their already swollen armed
forces. Like William James, Angell acknowledged the seductiveness of
war. But he saw no need to offer a moral or psychological alternative to
it. He simply asked whether the preparations the big European nations
had been making for war—the "armed peace" of "slowly built warships
and forts, and slowly trained armies"—would ever lead to "more national well-being." In a world of booming commerce, militarism was an
ideology of men whose ideas had failed to change along with the evolution of material existence. Perhaps inevitably, one ecstatic reviewer
compared *The Great Illusion* to *The Origin of Species*.[13]

Of course, Angell had his critics, and they grew louder after the
Balkan wars of 1912 and 1913 appeared to refute his argument that
military power was "socially and economically futile." The Serbs, whose
victories in those conflicts almost doubled their national territory, certainly did not feel that way. "Who is the man foolish enough to say that
martial virtues do not play a vital part in the health and honor of every
people?" asked Winston Churchill to the cheers of a crowd in Sheffield.
In an appendix to his book, Angell responded, calmly, that he had never
denied that military conquerors reveled over their spoils. "It is not . . .
war which is the illusion, but its benefits" to future mankind.[14]

Womankind had never gained anything from the clash of armies, asserted most feminists. "Obviously," remarked Elizabeth Cady Stanton in 1872, "the woman's mission is to recognize the bond of humanity between all the peoples, the human solidarity deeper and prior to the national." In war and preparations for war, male aggression thrust itself into every sphere of civic life, slashing away at the compassionate vision that lay at the heart of her movement. [15]

Women in the abolitionist movement had first made this argument before the Civil War, coupling it with a fierce attack on the violence of male slaveholders. During the late nineteenth century, the Woman's Christian Temperance Union, the largest female organization to that point in U.S. history, bolstered it with a Department of Peace and Arbitration led by Hannah Johnston Bailey, a wealthy Quaker. Under her leadership and largesse, the WCTU published both a peace magazine for adults and one for children that denounced war toys and military drills in schools. Her department also sponsored an annual Peace Day in schools, at which "children's peace bands" performed pacifist songs. "It is the duty of the mother to prevent quarrels," Bailey asserted, "likewise to make peace where contentions exist."[16]

That feminism was in flower during the initial years of the twentieth century should have given women a major role in defining and directing the popular sentiment for peace. A united suffrage movement with some 2 million members lobbied dozens of state legislatures and tasted victory in California and Washington by 1912. That same year, the Progressive Party, which nominated Theodore Roosevelt for president, also endorsed votes for women—the first time a party with a serious chance at gaining the White House had taken that giant step. A growing infrastructure of settlement houses, women's labor unions, and middle-class women's clubs, both black and white, undergirded these advances. In Greenwich Village and other cosmopolitan enclaves, women dared to campaign for birth control, equal pay and reform of divorce laws, and even the right to have sex outside of marriage.

Yet their agitation for these causes left feminists little time or desire to participate in an anti-war movement dominated by men like Carnegie, Angell, and Taft. No peace society excluded women, and suffragists around the country rallied to promote the Hague conference and routinely declared their sympathy for anyone who had a promising idea for transcending armed conflict. But they were neither government officials, university presidents, nor reform-minded industrialists, and such members of the male elite tended to view the maternalist, often sentimental outlook of female activists with polite disdain. Charles W. Eliot, the retired president of Harvard who held a top post in the Carnegie Endowment, criticized calls for disarmament as "irritating to those in power." Sober research ought to replace "wholly ineffectual" demands to cease preparing for war. Most feminists took the hint.[17]

One who refused to step away from a grander pursuit of peace was Jane Addams, who somehow found time to speak and write nearly as much on this issue as she did on poverty, labor, and woman suffrage. Addams embraced the findings of modern social science, but she refused to allow humanitarian ideals to be brushed aside by haughty intellectuals like Eliot. In *Newer Ideals of Peace*, published in 1907, she argued that evolution toward a "higher imaginative pity" had already begun. She acknowledged, like James, that people would not soon give up the idea that "war is noble and necessary" and that boys would not easily abandon their fondness for guns. Yet, in multicultural cities and workplaces—and her own Hull House—ordinary men and women were learning to transcend a defensive patriotism and beginning to live "in the kingdom of human kindness." The more governments encouraged and funded programs of mutual aid, the less they would focus on military might.[18]

Addams knew a change so momentous would not occur either quickly or completely. Like James, she chided Leo Tolstoy and other absolute pacifists who preached an "older dovelike ideal" and waited, prophetically, for the rest of the world to see the light. In 1912, she seconded Roosevelt's nomination at the Progressive Party convention, even though he proposed building two new battleships a year. Still, she expressed a cautious optimism that a new, tolerant order would emerge as "simple people" of all countries grew accustomed to a world where interdependence was becoming the norm. "We may then give up war," she wrote, "because we shall find it as difficult to make war upon a nation at the other side of the globe as upon our next-door neighbor."[19] Like Stanton before her, Addams took the solidarity of female activists across borders for granted.

For Socialists, internationalism was, at least in theory, as essential as breathing. Few workers might actually believe, as Marx and Engels brashly declared in the *Communist Manifesto*, that they had no country. But they certainly had no reason, argued Marx's disciples, to fight in aggressive wars that would only benefit their capitalist exploiters. As Karl Liebknecht, a leading member of the German Social-Democratic Party (SPD), the largest of its kind in Europe, put it, the capitalist state "arms the people against the people itself." It forces workers "to become . . . enemies and murderers of their own class comrades and friends . . . murderers of their own past and future." Socialists did make one fateful exception to this ironclad doctrine: If their country were attacked, all citizens had a duty to defend it.[20]

But the comrades offered no guidance about how to stop wars of aggression from occurring or what to do once they began. So at the 1907 conference of the Socialist (or Second) International in Stuttgart, Germany, nine hundred delegates from dozens of nations debated for five days before they arrived at a rather cloudy consensus. The final resolution called for gradual disarmament through arbitration and the replacement of standing armies with popular militias. If war threatened, workers and their elected Socialist representatives in parliaments should "exert every effort . . . by the means they consider most effective" to prevent it. General strikes might have been one way to accomplish this, but the host SPD, afraid of jeopardizing its rising electoral fortunes, made sure the document excluded that option. To conclude on a bracingly radical note, a Russian delegate did persuade the congress to add the sentence: "In case war should break out . . . it is their duty to intervene in favor of its speedy termination and with all their powers to utilize the economic and political crisis created by the war to rouse the masses and thereby hasten the downfall of capitalist class rule." The delegate's name was Vladimir Ilyich Lenin. Less than a decade later, he would follow his own advice.[21]

American Socialists said little during the debate in Stuttgart. Their numbers did grow modestly during the early twentieth century, reaching a zenith of a hundred thousand members by 1912. But at the time of the Stuttgart gathering, they had not yet elected a single congressman (they would eventually elect two), and their pockets of strength in a few immigrant cities and industrial towns made the thought of toppling capitalism seem wildly utopian. The journalist Algie Simons, one of a handful of Americans at the conference, reported that the European delegates "seemed to act as though we . . . meant well—but we were not 'doing things'. . . . I rather believe they were right."[22]

Socialists in the United States were hardly that passive, but their activism rarely touched on issues of war and peace. They were dedicated union organizers, both within the reformist American Federation of Labor (AFL) and its rival, the revolutionary Industrial Workers of the World (IWW). They campaigned for municipal ownership of streetcars and other utilities and backed various reforms, from agrarian cooperatives to a graduated income tax to abolition of the electoral college. In 1912, the Socialist Party of America (the SPA) won almost a million votes for president, 6 percent of the total, and elected some 1,200 local officials across the land. In accepting his party's nomination, the former railroad union leader Eugene V. Debs denounced the "poverty, high prices, unemployment, child slavery . . . prostitution and insanity, suicide and crime" of the capitalist system. But he said not a word about either war or empire. Evidently, Debs had no fear that his nation's rulers might emulate the rapid build-up of military forces that was alarming his European comrades.[23]

Inside the unions, most leaders, whatever they thought about the evils of capitalism, took a similar stance—sympathizing with the peace movement's objectives—but not investing much time or influence to advance them. Samuel Gompers, the longtime president of the AFL, considered socialism an impossible ideal and accused its adherents of imperiling the progress American workers had made by turning all employers against them. But his hatred of militarism was as strong as that of any pacifist or Marxist.

Wars, thought Gompers, were the bane of civilized society, and he supported any serious effort to prevent them. Under his leadership, the AFL endorsed the 1899 Hague conference and sent representatives to several subsequent meetings in the United States that made grand pleas for arbitrating international disputes. Gompers even agreed to be a vice president of a Peace Congress organized in 1907 by Andrew Carnegie. He didn't stop with such anodyne endeavors: At least three different times between 1899 and 1907, Gompers suggested that wage earners should threaten a global general strike if war seemed imminent. "I look forward to the time when the workers will settle this question—by the dock workers refusing to handle goods that are to be used to destroy their fellow man, and by the seamen of the world . . . absolutely refusing to strike down their fellow man." Even the Socialists at Stuttgart had declined to go that far.[24]

Nearly every union in the AFL stood with him. In 1912, the United Mine Workers, whose members produced the prime source of energy for most factories and urban dwellings, resolved to strike "in the event of war." A few years earlier, a top AFL official from Colorado recommended that Congress fund an "annual peace budget" to promote amity with other nations. At a time when nearly half of all industrial wage earners were European immigrants or their children, the prospect of going to war against any of the continental powers was particularly

abhorrent. Most Irish-Americans, who held a large share of union offices, had no desire to fight alongside Great Britain; while Jews, Poles,
and other ethnic groups who had fled the Russian empire—the "charnel
house of nations"—felt even more strongly about any alliance with the
tsar. [25]

Yet few labor activists had much confidence in any of the peace initiatives touted by their social superiors. Gompers made clear he did
not think the United States should disarm unilaterally "when the world
is an armed camp outside." Echoing the Socialists, he and other labor
stalwarts thought the only sure way to stop wars between nations was
to nurture solidarity among their workers. In the meantime, they were
waging a war at home against anti-union bosses, judges who prohibited
boycotts and picketing, and the politicians who did their bidding.[26]

But in Congress, peace-minded representatives and senators could
not afford to ignore what they saw as a gradual but alarming rise in
militarism on high. As president, Roosevelt ardently promoted the objectives of the Navy League, founded in 1902 to "educate" both voters
and Congress about the need to build a larger and more technologi-
cally advanced force. While in office, TR signed bills authorizing the
construction of thirty-one new armed vessels, which gave the United
States the second largest fleet in the world—though still far behind the
size of Britain's Royal Navy. In 1907, during a brief war scare with Japan,
Congress acquiesced to the president's stern request that they immediately appropriate funds for two huge new battleships, known as dread-
noughts. The former Rough Rider made clear his hope that the United
States would soon construct a military second to none.

Most Democrats regarded that ambition as a reckless departure
from national tradition. In the 1900 campaign, under the leadership of
William Jennings Bryan, they had opposed the conquest of the Philippines, and since the days of Jefferson they had always viewed a standing
army as a threat to popular liberties, a monarchical excrescence that
self-governing Americans should spurn. To Bryan, who remained the

most popular Democrat in the country until Woodrow Wilson's nomination for president in 1912, Roosevelt's hankering for a bigger navy made him "a dangerous man for our country and for the world" and "a human arsenal, a dreadnought wrought in flesh and blood." It was imperative for his party to resist.[27]

Bryan's many disciples in Congress did make an effort. Over a hundred representatives, most of them Democrats, voted against funding TR's new battleships. In populist tones, they denounced the spending as a virtual subsidy to big industrialists, nearly all of whom were Republicans. A few GOP lawmakers from the Midwest joined the opposition and echoed those charges, while excising their partisan sting. Senator Moses Clapp of Minnesota called a larger navy "a menace to the peace of the Republic," and Robert La Follette of Wisconsin warned that military expansion was "a gigantic Wall Street gamble."[28]

But anti-militarists in Congress were ensnared in a dilemma. Nearly all endorsed the same reforms at home that Roosevelt was championing. During his second term, TR tried just as aggressively to enact changes that the conservative Republicans who ran Congress detested as he did to prepare the nation to fight a major war. So while opposing his plans to expand the armed forces, progressives in both parties cheered the president when he banned corporate donations to campaigns, curbed railroad fare abuses, blasted "malefactors of great wealth" for causing stock market panics, and condemned federal court judges for ruling against the rights of labor. For the moment, their passion for domestic change overshadowed their uneasiness about the expansion of the navy. George Norris, then a Republican congressman from Nebraska, later admitted he had silenced his doubts about Roosevelt's foreign and military policies because he stood for "so many reforms . . . which I thought American life needed badly." In 1906, the chairman of the Democratic Congressional Campaign Committee even urged voters to help TR—by electing more Democrats.[29]

"The vast body of people in every civilized land are being asked today," claimed William Hull in 1912, if they favor the "enormous and competitive increase of national armaments" or abolishing them, which would herald an epoch of "international peace." He believed "the leaders of thought and conscience" were steering the world toward "the happy conjunction of Peace and Justice."[30]

It was a beautiful prophecy, one rooted both in reason and the faith of religious liberals like himself. But most Americans were not reflecting on the question or even knew it was being posed. Outside the well-educated, well-fed, well-meaning circle to which Hull belonged and flattered, peace among the nations seemed a fine idea, yet a softly abstract one no amount of virtuous speeches, elite conferences, careful research, or moral proposals could achieve. A world war would turn the vision of world peace from an impossible dream into an urgent necessity.

ONE

EVER WIDENING CIRCLES

August 1914 to May 1915

"We must be impartial in thought as well as action, must put a curb upon our sentiments as well as upon every transaction that might be construed as a preference of one party to the struggle before another."

—President Woodrow Wilson, August 1914[1]

"As women, we are called upon to start each generation onward toward a better humanity. We will no longer tolerate without determined opposition that denial of the sovereignty of reason and justice by which war and all that makes for war today render impotent the idealism of the race."

—Woman's Peace Party, January 1915[2]

"The nation which stifles its martial spirit breeds a race of vassals. It has always been so. It always will be so."

—Representative Augustus Gardner
(R-Mass.), April 1915[3]

"The people of the United States have arrived at the parting of the ways. They will have to choose between embarking on an adventurous and exhausting policy of militarism or staking their future on a rigid determination to maintain peace and social progress."

—Morris Hillquit, April 1915[4]

WOMEN ON PARADE

One cloudy afternoon at the end of August 1914, some fifteen hundred women strode two miles down Fifth Avenue in a silent protest against the growing war in Europe. Many dressed in black to symbolize mourning; muffled drums intensified the mood. Ten times as many New Yorkers massed five deep along both sides of the wide boulevard, their own silence reflecting the solemn tone of the occasion. "I was more than surprised at the reverential attitude of the spectators," remarked Fanny Garrison Villard, the sixty-nine-year-old leader of the Women's Peace Parade. "It was only a feeble effort really, we have simply cast a pebble into the water. I hope there may be many ever widening circles that perhaps will make men realize what a crime it is to send thousands of husbands and fathers and sons to a useless slaughter."[5]

As the eldest daughter of the great abolitionist William Lloyd Garrison, Villard embodied the history of several intertwined crusades on the American left. Before 1914, she had agitated for suffrage and black rights, preaching, like her father, the gospel of absolute nonviolence— "a willingness to lose one's life in a good cause, while refusing to take the life of another." As the widow of railroad baron Henry Villard, Fanny could also help finance her cherished causes.[6]

In taking to the streets on August 29, Villard and her fellow activists were employing a tactic the anti-war movement had never used before. A change seemed urgent. The outbreak of war in Europe had exposed the legal paternalism of the existing peace groups—to which few of these women belonged—as an utter failure. Their male officials who had scorned female moralism as "ineffectual" now could only sputter their dismay at the mounting bloodshed with earnest editorials and private letters. The onset of war so shocked Andrew Carnegie that, as his wife, Louise, recalled, the once vigorous philanthropist "became an old man overnight . . . his face became deeply indented"; he lost his "zest for mere existence." The prime benefactor and entrepreneur of the prewar peace movement withdrew abruptly from what now seemed a pointless struggle. For the duration of the conflict, his Endowment for Peace funded hardly any peace initiatives at all.[7]

The exclusion of women from the inner, now passive circle of the prewar movement freed them to assemble a new kind of coalition. It drew from the remarkable variety of progressive initiatives then blooming in New York City, where, at least in reform circles, gender equality was more advanced than anywhere else in the country. Notable members of the parade committee included the pioneering social worker Lillian Wald; Frances Perkins, the industrial safety expert (and future secretary of labor); prominent unionists Rose Schneiderman and Leonora O'Reilly; suffrage leaders Carrie Chapman Catt and Harriot Stanton Blatch; and the popular feminist authors Charlotte Perkins Gilman, Gertrude Atherton, and Mary Beard.

Coverage of the women's protest in the big city's ardently competitive newspapers was lengthy and positive. The World noticed everything from the couture of the participants to the sight of Villard, walking by herself, "a gray-haired little lady . . . whose step was as steady for the whole length of the march as that of any younger woman in the line." Its arch-rival, the Journal, owned by William Randolph Hearst, displayed large photographs of several attractive, and wealthy, young marchers. The Times described the small contingents of African-American, Indian, Chinese, and French women—most of the latter were refugees—walking "not as nations, but as sorrowing women together" and mentioned that the display of any national flag—including the Stars and Stripes—was prohibited. The Socialist *Call* featured a contingent of "women comrades" who pinned red ribbons to their black dresses and published a poem the German-American feminist Meta Stern had composed for the occasion. The last lines predicted: "For the cannon will be silenced / And the bloody banners furled, / When, to guide the fate of mankind, / Come the women of the world."[8]

The internationalism of the prewar movement had been fashioned by men of economic substance and political title—most elected, a few inherited. The ethnic and social diversity of the women's parade revealed a bond of a more egalitarian kind. Villard's hastily organized committee dissolved just weeks after the march down Fifth Avenue. But the vision of mothers and daughters as the vanguard of a peaceful world—the antithesis of "isolationism"—continued to gain new converts. The following January it would take larger and more durable form as the Woman's Peace Party.

The feminist mode of activism developed alongside the more traditional style practiced by male politicians and dissidents on the left. While women like Fanny Villard spun visions of a more harmonious world in which mothers from every land would stop sons from killing other sons, their male counterparts fought over more immediate questions: whether to peddle munitions to belligerents and/or boost the size of the military. They proposed new laws to stop both actions and sought to win the battle for public opinion at home—while downplaying any desire they might have for a radical new order. In contrast, pacifist women, most of whom were still barred from voting, nurtured a community of idealists that spanned the Atlantic.

Not until the middle of 1915 would exponents of the two ways of making war against war unite in a common endeavor, muting while never abandoning their differences. Together they mounted an impressive challenge to Americans—whether ordinary men and women or members of the political and economic elite—who wanted the United States to tilt toward one side or the other in the European conflict. Their words and actions also helped stiffen President Wilson's resolve not to intervene.

A COMPROMISED NEUTRALITY
AND ITS DISCONTENTS

Behind the universal acclaim for the New York women's parade lay widespread revulsion at the war itself. "This dreadful conflict . . . came to most of us like lightning out of a clear sky," North Carolina congressman Robert Newton Page wrote that fall to his brother Walter Hines Page, the U.S. ambassador to Great Britain. "The horror of it all kept me awake for weeks, nor has the awfulness of it all deserted me, but at first it seemed a horrid dream." By September, French and British forces had stopped the German advance well short of Paris. Meanwhile, Russians battled the armies of Germany and Austria-Hungary for control of the Polish plains. On the Western Front, a bloody, exhausting stalemate set in, as the belligerents built opposing systems of trenches extending 475 miles from the North Sea to the Swiss border. The standoff—punctuated by spasmodic shelling and failed offensives that sacrificed tens of thousands of lives for a few kilometers of territory—would continue for nearly four more years.[9]

On August 19, Woodrow Wilson, who was mourning the death of his wife just two weeks earlier, released a short statement that expressed the sentiments of most of his fellow citizens. Recognizing that "the people of the United States are drawn from many nations, and chiefly from the nations now at war," the president urged them to stay "neutral in fact, as well as name." Otherwise, the "one great nation [still] at peace" would be unable to mediate the conflict—when and if it chose to do so. Two days later, Wilson wrote to Fanny Villard that he was "very glad" to support her parade, since it upheld the principle of impartiality. In

New York City, most immigrants from the belligerent countries obeyed Mayor John Mitchel's stern request to halt demonstrations of sympathy with their former homelands.[10]

Of course, even a plea by the president to "put a curb upon our sentiments" could not stop Americans of different ethnic backgrounds from rooting for one side or the other. The Irish-American nationalists of Clan na Gael hoped a British defeat would hasten the long-awaited freedom of their ancestral isle. Most Jews were convinced that no war fought by the military of Tsar Nicholas II—the world's most powerful anti-Semite—could ever be a just one. Few Scandinavian-Americans saw any reason to favor either the Allies or the Central Powers.

But the German invasion of Belgium on August 3, followed by the sacking and burning of the city of Louvain later that month, led many Americans to view the Kaiser's government as the war's sole culprit. Most metropolitan newspapers cheered the French and British efforts to revenge those "crimes," while also running occasional pieces that claimed Germany had acted in self-defense. The same day the *World* praised the women's march, it ran a large editorial cartoon depicting Marianne, the symbol of France, unsheathing her sword to stop German troops from approaching Paris. In London, Ambassador Page openly expressed his wish that "English civilization" would triumph over the "Prussian military autocracy." He raised no protest when, at the start of hostilities, the British cut the undersea cables linking the United States with Europe, ensuring that any direct dispatches from their enemies could be censored or destroyed before American readers could read them.[11]

Contrary to his public rhetoric, Woodrow Wilson's private sympathies were never truly in doubt. Anglophilia ran though the president's blood and his intellect. His mother hailed from the town of Carlisle in northern England, his first political heroes were the British statesmen Edmund Burke and William Gladstone, his most important scholarly work lauded parliamentary government as practiced in the United

Kingdom, and the Lake District was his favorite place on earth. On August 30, he confided to his closest advisor, Colonel Edward House, that "German philosophy was essentially selfish and lacking in spirituality." Wilson dreaded a German victory that "would change the course of our civilization and make the United States a military nation."[12]

But the president had no intention of asking Congress to send U.S. troops to prevent that from happening. He knew few Americans, whatever their views on the countries and the stakes involved, wanted to break with their nation's tradition of staying out of conflicts between other major powers. "This war is a calamity for Europe," wrote William Randolph Hearst in late August. The publisher predicted, quite accurately: "At the end of the war this country will be far ahead and Europe far behind. Peace will make this country pre-eminent, and that lesson will never be lost on the world." In any case, with roughly a hundred thousand troops and just eleven airplanes, the U.S. Army was hardly prepared to fight a major war. Nor were there enough ships in the merchant marine to transport them across the ocean. Far better to call for a speedy end to the bloody mess and, perhaps, help bring that about. Still, as Hearst implied, one could certainly do a good business with one or both sides while the killing lasted.[13]

Through the remainder of 1914 and the early months of 1915, the question of whether to profit from the Great War and how divided Americans along lines that foreshadowed later, more bitter debates. So did the beginnings of a dispute about whether the nation should build a much larger army and encourage or require young men to undergo military training—as much to school them in unselfish discipline as to protect their homeland from future attack. Members of the emerging anti-war coalition played a prominent role in all these debates.

When huge armies began to mobilize across the ocean, the American economy was in recession; about 12 percent of wage earners had no work at all, and many others scraped by with part-time jobs. The onset of conflict turned the downturn into a crisis. Panicked European investors cabled their Wall Street brokers to sell their securities, the very name of which had suddenly turned ironic. On the last day of July, the governors of the New York Stock Exchange, prodded by the financier J.P. Morgan Jr. and Secretary of the Treasury William McAdoo, shut the market down. It would not open again until four months later.

Meanwhile, there was a good deal of money to be made—at least potentially. But first, the Wilson administration had to resolve a critical question: Did the impartiality the president called for mean that banks could not lend money to belligerents and that companies could not make and sell goods to them, particularly the weapons and matériel of war? By 1914, the American economy had become increasingly dependent on foreign trade. "Upon its uninterrupted rhythm," reflected the historian Arthur Link, "depended the price that the southern planter would receive for his cotton and the western farmer for his wheat, the capacity at which steel mills would operate, indeed, whether the entire economy would prosper or decline."[14]

By late summer, it was clear the French and British would be the only realistic partners for American business, if and when commerce resumed. The Royal Navy controlled the sea lanes of the North Atlantic and was imposing an embargo in all but name on the North Sea, the only marine route for exports to Germany. What's more, nearly all the big American investment firms had close and long-standing ties to their counterparts in London and Paris.

At first, it appeared that Wilson and his top advisors would stay true to the president's words. They urged the British to abide by rules drafted two years earlier at an international conference in London that would have required its warships to allow Americans to conduct trade in non-military commodities with anyone they wished. Then, on August 15, Secretary of State William Jennings Bryan barred J.P. Morgan & Co.— the wealthiest firm on Wall Street—from giving a $100 million loan to France. "Money," intoned Bryan, "is the worst of contrabands—it commands everything else." The three-time Democratic candidate for president was an admirer of Leo Tolstoy, a pacifist icon, and had frequently addressed peace groups before the war. In his short time as secretary, Bryan had conceived and signed eighteen bilateral treaties with other nations in which each side agreed to submit any quarrel to an investigative tribunal—and, after doing so, begin no conflict for a "cooling-off period" of a full year. [15]

But soon law and economic necessity conspired to weaken both his and the president's resolve. The government could not legally prevent citizens of a neutral state from selling goods or lending money to a belligerent nation. So businessmen—from the iron and steel barons along the Great Lakes to the cotton planters of Dixie—clamored to ship their goods, usually in British-flag merchant ships, across the Atlantic. In October, Wilson allowed the National City Bank to extend $10 million in credits to France; Bryan did not object, on the grounds that a credit was different from a loan.

Before the year was over, the administration had abandoned even this superficial caveat. In November, Bethlehem Steel magnate Charles M. Schwab (whose grandparents on both sides had emigrated from Germany) signed a contract to deliver $50 million in arms to the Allies. On January 15, 1915, the mighty House of Morgan formally agreed to serve as the British government's exclusive purchasing agent in the United States. By war's end, the total cost to King and Country came to $3 billion; Morgan & Co. collected a tidy 1 percent commission on every sale. [16]

The Royal Navy's refusal to allow neutral ships to trade with Germany was a clear violation of international law. But the Wilson administration had neither the capacity nor the will to exert American rights against the largest fleet in the world; the State Department did issue occasional protests, but nothing more. In the journalistic cliché of the day, "Britain rules the waves and waives the rules." By late 1915, unemployment in the United States was down to 7 percent. "Let 'em shoot! It makes good business for us!" headlined a Nashville paper. Even most wage earners born in Germany and Austria-Hungary were glad to benefit from the manufacturing boom.[17]

Yet a healthy minority of Americans *did* reject the logic and morality of this deadly, if profitable, species of commerce. In Congress, several progressives from both parties demanded that all munitions should be produced by the federal government in order to "take the profits out of war." If that occurred, predicted Representative Clyde H. Tavenner, a Democrat from Illinois, "some of the very millionaire patriots who are now agitating for an ever and ever increased amount of armament" would start complaining about all the tax money being spent to prepare "for war in time of peace." A *Literary Digest* poll of newspaper editors from around the country found that nearly 40 percent favored an arms embargo. The strongest support came from small-town papers. In mid-February, thirty-six senators—mostly Republicans from the West and Midwest and Democrats from the South—voted against tabling an amendment to prohibit such exports. At the end of January 1915, advocates of the embargo met in Washington, D.C., to establish a new organization, the American Independence Union. Delegates pledged "to support only such candidates for public office, irrespective of party, who will place American interests above those of any other country."[18]

But the Union's flag-waving rhetoric could not mask the fact that it was essentially the creation of a large and well-organized lobby for the Kaiser's regime. The previous fall, the 2-million-member National German-American Alliance, funded largely by beer companies and headed by the civil engineer Charles John Hexamer, had launched its own embargo campaign. The idea quickly gained the support of several Teutonic congressmen as well as the governors of Pennsylvania and Texas. Politicians from every party in Wisconsin, where at least one-third of the residents claimed German heritage, signed on as well. Few if any of the campaign's backers knew that Count Johann von Bernstorff, the Kaiser's ambassador to Washington, was secretly helping to organize it. The trade in munitions, declared Wisconsin senator Robert La

Follette, had "but one purpose, and that is to sacrifice human life for private gain." The Independence Union aimed to give these sentiments a unified voice.[19]

The German-language press vigorously promoted the embargo, as did several periodicals edited by militant Irish republicans. During the winter of 1914–1915, this loose coalition drew audiences in the tens of thousands to halls in such midwestern cities as Chicago, Cleveland, and St. Louis—as well as in New York City, Philadelphia, and New Orleans. Together, Hibernian-Americans and German-Americans numbered more than 10 million inhabitants—about one-ninth of the U.S. population. If their leaders had united in support of the embargo, they could have turned aid to the Allies into a closely fought political issue. The British ambassador to the United States already feared, as he wrote to his superiors in February, that "something like a civil war" could erupt if Wilson openly abandoned his neutral stance.[20]

But champions of the embargo made no serious attempt to counter the doubts of a public that cheered the return of prosperity or of the majority in Congress that shunned an act that would have greatly boosted the prospect of a German victory. Hexamer certainly made no converts with widely reprinted speeches in which he condemned (in English) the "lick-spittle policy of our country" toward Great Britain and sneered that the stripes on the flag ought to be replaced with dollar signs. No prominent Irish-American—nearly all of whom were pro-Wilson Democrats—endorsed the embargo; neither did more than a handful of Catholic diocesan weeklies, whose combined circulation dwarfed that of papers edited by ardent republicans. So, by the spring of 1915, the only organized resistance to the arms trade with the Allies had all but collapsed.[21]

However, the debate about whether the United States should prepare for war was just beginning. Those favoring a larger military had a number of advantages. They could count on the self-interest of most of the nation's industrial corporations. They had a national organization:

the National Security League, founded in December 1914 and financed, in part, by such wealthy Americans as railroad owner Cornelius Vanderbilt, the financier Bernard Baruch, and steel magnate Henry
Clay Frick. The NSL packed its board with a variety of renowned figures: two former secretaries of war and a secretary of the navy, seventeen governors, the editors of such respected magazines as the *Outlook*
and *Scientific American*, and the inventor Thomas Alva Edison. Alton
Parker, the 1904 Democratic candidate for president, supplied a veneer
of bipartisanship to what was a largely Republican body. By the fall of
1915, the NSL boasted a staff of fifty in its New York City office and a
membership of fifty thousand, and it was well on its way to organizing
branches in every state.[22]

Theodore Roosevelt, who remained enormously popular despite
his loss in 1912, spoke out for the cause with his customary vigor. In
October, the Colonel, as he now liked to be known, told an audience of
Princeton students he had "seen plans of at least two empires now involved in the war to capture our great cities and hold them for ransom,
because our standing army is too weak to protect them." Soon TR was
promoting universal military training as a splendid means of making
America a more democratic society. With a draft, he enthused, "the son
of the capitalist and the son of the day laborer" would "eat the same
food, go on the same hikes, profit by the same discipline, and learn to
honor and take pride in the same flag." Senator Henry Cabot Lodge, a
prominent GOP voice on foreign policy, zestfully agreed with everything his best friend Colonel Roosevelt proposed.[23]

Yet in much of America, resistance to "militarism" ran wide and deep.
A traditional distaste for standing armies and foreign entanglements
mingled with a populist suspicion of the "war trust"—corporations
eager to produce munitions for domestic as well as overseas consumption. The ethnic groups that had spurned the Allies at the start of the war
recoiled at the campaign by the NSL and its allies—as did every major
labor union and, of course, the Socialist Party. In January, the *Literary*

Digest reported that, away from the two coasts, there was nearly as much sentiment against building "a stronger army and navy" as there was in favor of it. Within Wilson's cabinet, William Jennings Bryan warned against heeding the counsel of the NSL and its supporters.[24]

In Congress, an emerging coalition composed mainly of midwestern Republicans and southern Democrats like Claude Kitchin opposed any sizable increase in military strength. Kitchin, the unrivaled leader of anti-war Democrats in Congress until war was declared, was a true white son of Dixie who mingled together racist fears with a populist resentment against the wealthy barons of the North. He was born in 1869 and raised in the small town of Scotland Neck, a center of cotton plantations in the northeastern corner of North Carolina, where black people composed a majority of the population. Ideologically, Kitchin never really left it, although he would serve in Congress for twenty-two straight years.

Kitchin's father, Will, raised on a 475-acre plantation, had joined the Confederate Army soon after the attack on Fort Sumter. He rose to the rank of captain and fought at Chancellorsville and Gettysburg before being captured and imprisoned in the North. Because he refused to swear allegiance to the United States. Will Kitchin—or "Cap'n Buck" as he was known—remained in federal custody for six months after Lee had surrendered his sword to Grant. In 1878, running as a Democrat, he won a seat in Congress from the Second District by firing up the white minority with curses against the Republican "blood-suckers and political buzzards" who had "organized the colored man against his former masters" during Reconstruction. The party of the "blood-suckers" rallied to take back the seat two years later.[25]

At the end of the century, his son Claude regained it by fueling racist sentiments in both word and deed. Aided by the state's leading newspaper, he whipped up fear of black rapists in a transparent campaign to reestablish white political supremacy by any means necessary. "The

Anglo-Saxon will, sooner or later, reassert itself," the young Kitchin declared to a local party convention in 1898, "and awaken the State to an appreciation of that inexorable law of the universe . . . which declares that the FITTEST SHALL SURVIVE." That autumn, Kitchin, a tall and muscular figure, helped organize "White Supremacy Clubs" and rode with armed "Red Shirts" to warn black people not to bother exercising their constitutional rights. In 1900, as terror, real and threatened, kept most African Americans from going to the polls, North Carolina enacted an amendment to the state constitution that effectively barred them from voting in the future.[26]

That fall, the Democrats nominated Kitchin to Congress; he swept the Second District by more than ten thousand votes to become the youngest member of the new House. To protest the disenfranchisement of his people, the black Republican incumbent, George Henry White, had declined to run for reelection and moved his family to Washington, D.C. "I cannot live in North Carolina and . . . be treated as a man," he explained. It would be another seventy-two years before another African American was elected to Congress from a former Confederate state.[27]

But Claude Kitchin's politics were not driven by racism alone. "I have no guarantee that God has so endowed my little boy," he lamented during the 1900 campaign, "that when he grows up he will be able to make a living with the trusts stifling competition as they do." With no apparent fear of contradiction, Kitchin also denounced the U.S. war of conquest in the Philippines as an attempt to impose "government without consent of the governed." In expressing such anti-corporate and anti-imperialist rhetoric, he was siding with the majority of his national party and with William Jennings Bryan—its presidential nominee in 1896, 1900, and again in 1908.[28]

Bryanite Democrats from every region were determined to block the plans of northern financiers and factory owners—and the politicians who allegedly did their bidding—to accumulate power and riches on the backs of small farmers, little businessmen, and wage earners.

During the early twentieth century, southerners were a majority of the Democrats in Congress. Pillars of what one historian has called the party's "coalition of outsiders," they were perpetually wary of any move—in domestic or foreign policy—that would further an agenda they despised.

When Kitchin told a reporter, in 1904, that the Democrats should consider nominating a southerner for president, he melded his love for Dixie with his populist convictions: "Democracy, character and ability should be the [only] determining factors in the choice of a standard-bearer. Of course, in this event, the South would have a natural monopoly of candidates, but as we are opposed to monopoly, we would not take advantage of the situation."[29]

That ability to quip a controversial opinion suggests one reason why Kitchin gradually rose to leadership in the House. He battled the GOP on nearly every major issue but forced his adversaries to grin while they clashed. "Since my services here," Kitchin remarked in 1909, "I have met so many good Republicans that I have long since reached the conclusion that a Republican is never a danger to a Democrat except in elections and is never harmful to the public, except in office." When he turned serious, he could be masterful—blending legal reasoning, historical reflections, and melodramatic phrases in the same speech. Over six feet tall, stout, and with a prominent nose, he physically dominated most of his fellow congressmen too. Kitchin, observed one journalist, had a "shrewd face, salted liberally with conviction as well as sympathy and fun." That combination would be tested frequently once the Great War began.[30]

But Kitchin had to balance his principled opposition to preparedness with keeping the Democrats strong. The midterm election of 1914 had been a calamity for his party; it lost sixty seats in the House and emerged with just thirty-three more representatives than the GOP. After licking their wounds, one of the Democrats' first acts was to elect Kitchin majority leader as well as chairman of the Ways and Means

Committee, where all tax bills either got nurtured or died. Having just been lifted, at the age of forty-four, to the second highest post in the "people's chamber," Kitchin was not about to get branded a party renegade and throw it all away.[31]

Perched near the summit of power, the North Carolinian had to avoid taking any position that would endanger party unity or weaken the first Democratic president in almost two decades. Kitchin did give a few speeches warning generally about the perils of militarism. In February, he also voted unsuccessfully, with a majority of other Democrats, to build just one battleship a year instead of the two that the Navy Department requested. But he also whipped the members of his decreased majority to support every consequential piece of *domestic* legislation that Woodrow Wilson desired.

Amid this emerging struggle, the erstwhile academic in the White House sought to tamp down emotions and instill confidence in his leadership. "We are at peace with all the world," Wilson told the assembled lawmakers in his state of the union address that December. There was no "reason to fear that from any quarter our independence or the integrity of our territory is threatened." The United States could still rely on "a citizenry trained and accustomed to arms" instead of a standing army in the European style. "We shall not ask our young men to spend the best years of their lives making soldiers of themselves." Then, nearing the end of his address, in a swipe at Henry Cabot Lodge and other backers of a beefed-up military, the president said, "We shall not alter our attitude . . . because some amongst us are nervous and excited."[32]

The animosity was entirely mutual. A few weeks later, Lodge wrote to Roosevelt, "I heartily dislike and despise" Wilson and "live in hopes that he will be found out . . . for what he really is."[33] The senator and the president would never change their minds about one another.

On April 2, 1915, the conflict over preparedness landed on the stage of Carnegie Hall. Up for debate was the question: "Resolved, That the

Security of the Nation Requires an Increase of the Military Force of the United States." The antagonists that evening before a full crowd of three thousand in the ornate auditorium named after the retired philanthropist who paid for it were Augustus Peabody Gardner, a Republican congressman from Massachusetts and the son-in-law of Henry Cabot Lodge; and Morris Hillquit, a Jewish immigrant from Riga, Latvia, who had emerged as the Socialist Party's most influential spokesman about the Great War.

Hillquit—born in 1869 as Moishe Hillkowitz—converted to the gospel of a workers' world as a teenager in New York and never regretted it. He attended NYU Law School and began representing garment unions and their members who were injured on the job. Fluent in four languages, he was a natural choice to lead his party's delegation to meetings of the Second International, where he became friends with such prominent German leaders of the European Left as Karl Kautsky and August Bebel.[34]

In the center of the ideological hothouse that was American radicalism, Hillquit kept a cool, if uncharismatic, head. He predicted that socialism would eventually triumph in the United States as the party's share of the vote increased and workers realized that capitalists would never grant them the full value of their labor. Socialism, he promised, would create "a true democracy . . . in which all babes are born alike, and all human beings enjoy the same rights and opportunities."[35]

Some of his comrades thought Hillquit was rather too fond of the opportunities he had made for himself. They derided him as a "parlor socialist" who donned evening clothes to attend dinners given by wealthy progressives. Hillquit's legal practice was quite profitable, and his investments allowed him to rent, for two thousand dollars a year, an apartment on Riverside Drive where he and his wife, Vera, a first cousin, collected modern art. Hillquit helped to organize a union for actors in the Yiddish theater. But he seldom took in one of their performances.[36]

Hillquit's appearance helped advance his career. He bicycled to stay fit and sported a trim mustache and an ever-confident smile. An English leftist who met Hillquit in the mid-1890s remembered him as "a young man cleanly dressed who believed that washing himself was not a monopoly of the Hasidim . . . that a necktie can be tastefully tied and lying as it should, without breaking the principles of proletariat socialism."[37]

Hillquit's respectable image and calm eloquence helped him gain a hearing far outside the ranks of his own party, in venues that seldom featured an immigrant Jew from Eastern Europe. Besides contributing to a wide range of magazines and newspapers, he took part in several well-publicized debates about the merits of socialism with adversaries whose renown was greater than his. They included the president of Cornell University, the attorney general of New York State, one of the nation's most influential economists, and John Augustine Ryan, a leading Catholic theologian who later developed the concept of a "living wage." In the spring of 1914, Hillquit clashed with Samuel Gompers before the Commission on Industrial Relations, set up by Congress to look into "the underlying causes of dissatisfaction" in American workplaces. Hillquit articulated his opinions with earnest deliberation and light sarcasm—an attorney making the case for social transformation before a jury of thousands.[38]

Ever since war had broken out in Europe, Hillquit had persistently maintained that he and his fellow Socialists were the most reliable, most principled advocates of peace and neutrality. In December, he had composed his party's official statement on the war; as its representative to the Second International, he was in touch with European Socialists on both sides. "My party believes," he wrote in January, that "the most satisfactory solution of the great sanguinary conflict . . . lies in a draw, a cessation of hostilities from sheer exhaustion without deciding anything." Only then would it "become apparent to all the world that the heavy rivers of blood have flown for nothing." Only then would Americans and the people of other nations begin "to re-volt against the capitalist system which leads to such paroxysms of human madness."[39]

While making his case, the attorney had to rebut some mortify-ing evidence to the contrary. Just days after hostilities began in Europe, the majority of Socialist deputies in every belligerent nation save Italy had rallied behind their governments, voting to finance the war and urging every citizen to rally to their respective flags. Hillquit argued, along with his fellow comrades, that the war was precipitated by an arms race between imperialist powers. If the "Socialist parties in Eu-rope" had "been in control" instead of just a minority, they would, he claimed, have stopped the bloodshed. Still, he had to acknowledge that untold numbers of Europeans who had voted Red were now huddled in opposing trenches, waiting anxiously for the order to destroy one an-other. The resolutions made at Stuttgart in 1907 meant nothing as long as most Socialists believed they were fighting to defend their respective nations. Hillquit might still be certain that "the basic cause" of armed conflicts was "capitalism," aided by "the glorification of militarism . . . and the insidious dissemination of racial and national prejudices." But that did not explain why the largest Socialist parties in the world had failed to heed their own diagnosis.[40]

In Gardner, Hillquit was matched against an opponent who re-garded self-doubt as nearly an unpatriotic failing. A Harvard graduate and direct descendant of one of the first leaders of the Massachusetts Bay colony, Gardner devoted most of his political career to preparing his country for war—and enlisted to fight in two of them himself. He won a Distinguished Service Medal as a captain in the Spanish-American War and, in 1917, would resign a safe House seat to reenter the army. In 1914, he and his father-in-law had, in joint resolutions, urged Con-gress to create a special committee to investigate what they believed was the woeful state of national defense. Gardner called for doubling the size of the army to more than two hundred thousand men. Every

Democratic leader—from Woodrow Wilson on down—urged him to abandon the effort, which was clearly intended to embarrass the administration. But Gardner persisted, embarking on a cross-country tour to challenge the "preachers of national humility."[41]

That evening at Carnegie Hall, his language was as bellicose as his proposals. The debate was sponsored by the Rand School, an unofficial arm of the Socialist Party. So, at the outset, the pugnacious Gardner threw the crowd some raw ideological bait. "I am generally called a crook, somebody hired by the makers of armor plate," he began. "But I tell you I am here to advocate a few more dogs of war. . . . I don't much care what it costs."

For the next hour, Gardner stayed on the attack, vividly personifying his imagined nation of Caucasian warriors who should be ready and eager to take on any potential adversary. He scoffed at talk of arbitration and general disarmament and rejected the idea that Americans were "a peace-loving people." Our "peppery nation," Gardner asserted to laughter, "has had a fight every twenty-five years of its existence," but now "we have got a chip on each shoulder, and both arms in a sling." He made no apology for breaking treaties with the Indians—"A nation of ninety millions . . . cannot be kept back by a handful of savages"—and wanted to prepare America to fight a racial war against Japan as well as to battle Imperial Germany. Like Theodore Roosevelt, Gardner viewed a world-class military as not merely a practical necessity but one the lessons of history required: "It is the martial spirit which fights oppression in the only way that oppression ever yet was fought, by stout blows from strong arms, inspired by good stout hearts."[42]

Hillquit's rebuttal sounded at first like capitulation. If the United States were "in danger of becoming involved in war with a first-class foreign power," then it is indeed "woefully unprepared" and needs to build up its defenses. But he quickly added that Gardner's creed of "modern American militarism" was "based on a colossal fallacy." Then Hillquit made a set of arguments whose logical tone contrasted sharply with his opponent's entertaining bombast. If an unprepared nation invites attack, Hillquit asked, why did European nations "in full battle array" not avoid it? "They were ready for war—and they got their war," he answered soberly. "Their anti-war insurance turned out to be a bad case of over-insurance." The last remark, the stenographer noted, was met with "hearty applause."[43]

Knowing most of the crowd was now on his side (if it were not already), Hillquit drove home his larger arguments with the precision of a skilled and confident attorney. There is no good reason why Americans would want or need to engage in a war against an overseas power. The United States is mostly "self-sufficient," it has "no national grudges to settle," and neither Germany nor Japan could transport enough troops across an ocean to conquer it.[44]

Finally, Hillquit pivoted to a moral position he hoped would put every "militarist" on the defensive. The government, he pointed out, was already spending far more on the army and navy each year than it was to heal the casualties of "the actual daily war waged within the nation, the frightful and inhuman industrial war" that annually maimed or killed more than half a million American workers. It was thus Gardner's program that would truly put the nation at risk. Instead of lavishing more tax money on the apparatus of death, the state, insisted Hillquit, ought to devote a large share of its budget to building sanatoriums for TB victims, funding pensions for retired wage earners, and constructing factories for jobless toilers. The sponsors of the event left Gardner no time for a rebuttal.

Hillquit had adroitly introduced the two-step argument most anti-war activists would continue to articulate for the next two stressful years. The nation should not prepare to fight a war it had no need or ethical reason to wage. And the cost—in dollars and national priorities—would turn the United States into a militarized society. Yet, as William James might have counseled, to demand that the state spend a good deal more on welfare was not a convincing moral equivalent to war. Would-be peacemakers still lacked a powerful alternative to offer Americans willing to test their stout arms and hearts in future battles.

MEDIATING MOTHERS AND DAUGHTERS

During the early months of 1915, a new protest song was being played on Victrolas and sung in music halls across the land. The sheet-music version quickly sold a remarkable seven hundred thousand copies. Its lyrics began: "Ten million soldiers to the war have gone, / Who may never return again. / Ten million mothers' hearts must break / For the ones who have died in vain." Then, to a recorded accompaniment of bugles, came the chorus:

> *I didn't raise my boy to be a soldier,*
> *I brought him up to be my pride and joy.*
> *Who dares to place a musket on his shoulder*
> *To shoot some other mother's darling boy?*
> *Let nations arbitrate their future conflicts.*
> *It's time to lay the sword and gun away.*
> *There'd be no war today*
> *If mothers all would say,*
> *"I didn't raise my boy to be a soldier!"*[45]

For years, women in the peace movement had, in effect, been singing that tune. Leading activists like Fanny Villard and Jane Addams never confined themselves to maternalist rhetoric; like Morris Hillquit, they hated war because it jerked society away from the path of egalitarian change. But they did believe their motherly instincts made women, by nature, the more harmonious and humanitarian sex. As Charlotte Perkins Gilman wrote in 1911, "In warfare . . . we find maleness in its absurdist extremes." Feminists also understood that the wildly popular lyrics, written by the Canadian-born Alfred Bryan, neatly expressed a form of international solidarity whose appeal was more universal than the Socialist variety. The song's call for arbitration also echoed an idea pacifists of both genders had been promoting since the Gilded Age, now packed with a potent emotional charge.[46]

On the wings of these sentiments, three thousand American women flocked to the most impressive peace rally to that point in the nation's history. "War was formally declared on war," reported the *Washington Post* about the meeting that established the Woman's Peace Party on January 9 and 10, 1915, at the New Willard Hotel, two blocks from the White House.[47] Many of the participants already belonged to one or more of the female reform or charitable groups that were flourishing in an era when de Tocqueville's description of America as "a nation of joiners" was more accurate than ever before. They came from suffrage groups, temperance groups, teachers' groups, alumnae bodies, women's clubs, settlement houses, the Women's Trade Union League, the Woman's Committee of the Socialist Party, existing peace societies—and the Daughters of the American Revolution. They filled the hotel's cavernous ballroom, and five hundred would-be participants had to be turned away.[48]

The inspiration for this unprecedented gathering came largely from abroad—further proof that, from its start, the American anti-war movement was "isolationist" in neither word nor deed. The previous fall, Rosika Schwimmer and Emmeline Pethick-Lawrence—feminists from opposing belligerent powers—had embarked on a joint speaking tour to show Americans that European women yearned to stop the war and hoped to convince their sisters in the largest neutral nation to join them. Crystal Eastman helped organize Pethick-Lawrence's lecture in Carnegie Hall and urged her to meet with Jane Addams when she traveled to Chicago, to talk about forming an organization of feminists for peace.

For nearly two decades, Schwimmer, a thirty-seven-year-old Hungarian Jew, had spearheaded the suffrage movement in her country.

A talented journalist, passionate speaker, and exponent of female dress reform, she had managed, in September, to arrange a brief visit with Woodrow Wilson in the White House. By her account, the president politely agreed to consider her notion of meeting with the heads of other neutral countries; he left no comment for posterity about his encounter with a woman who wore neither a brassiere nor a corset under her brightly colored dress.

Pethick-Lawrence, a wealthy British citizen of forty-seven, was both a Socialist and a militant advocate of votes for women. She and her husband, Frederick, had merged their surnames when they married and retained separate bank accounts, an act that endeared them to feminists everywhere. On six occasions, Pethick-Lawrence's suffrage activism had landed her in prison; once she staged a hunger strike and had to endure forced feeding.[49]

The idea of giving birth to an all-female peace group flowed naturally from the suffrage work of these two dedicated campaigners. The Great War, Pethick-Lawrence argued, was the result of aggressive "male statecraft." "For this cataclysm," she asserted, "women bear no responsibility whatever." Because powerful men had failed to prevent it, they should "stand down" and let women "take the seat of judgment." Neither activist had children, but that did not prevent them from preaching a maternalist message. "Even women who are not physically mothers," explained Schwimmer, "feel all as the mothers of the human race." In December, the duo arrived in Chicago on their lecture tour. After several meetings with a local group headed by Jane Addams, they sent out a call for a national peace convention of American women.[50]

That Addams agreed to chair the gathering in Washington was probably vital to its success. Any American who read a daily newspaper knew her name; for many, she was "Saint Jane," a woman who, for decades, had devoted her great energy and subtle intellect to thoroughly altruistic purposes. "She was the most compassionate individual imaginable," testified Louis Lochner, a young peace activist from Chicago.

"With infinite patience she could listen to the underprivileged, the sick and needy, the spiritually dejected. . . . She never lost her temper." Addams was also a canny organizer who had a keen sense, trained by years of patient activism for a variety of causes, of how to coax her fellow reformers to work together for a higher end.[51]

Although Addams had been advocating peaceful solutions to war since the 1890s, the slaughter in Europe compelled her to devote more time to halting it than to anything else on her lengthy compassionate agenda. At first, she frowned on the idea of an organization that excluded men; she had always viewed her audience as bridging divides of gender as well as class, ethnicity, and nation. But Addams, like the suffrage leader Carrie Chapman Catt, was dismayed at the arrogance of the "great pacifists" who headed the prewar peace groups, confident that prosperous, law-abiding European nations would never seek to destroy each other. "When it was found that their conclusions were false and the great war came," Catt told the throng at the New Willard, "the women of this country . . . heard nothing from them—and they have heard nothing from the men of this country." So "they decided all too late to get together themselves."[52]

The meeting at the New Willard resembled a political convention, without the ritualistic parades and hackneyed oratory. Despite the name they adopted, the delegates neither planned to run nor endorse candidates for office. To call it a "party" wrapped the new group in a cloak of legitimacy; it implied that women *should* have all the political rights and power enjoyed by war-making men and would use the rights they did possess to stop what such men were doing.

The Reverend Anna Garlin Spencer opened the big meeting by reading the preamble she had written to the party's platform. A Unitarian who was the first woman of any denomination to be ordained in Rhode Island, the sixty-three-year-old Spencer had led a long career of social activism similar to that of Annis Eastman, Crystal's mother, who was also a liberal minister. Like Annis, Spencer was married to a minister less energetic than herself, and she lectured frequently about suffrage and the social gospel. In 1909, Spencer had also helped found the NAACP.

On this January afternoon, she took the podium to insist that a peaceful world depended upon the guidance of women. "As women, we are especially the custodian of the life of the ages. We will no longer consent to its reckless destruction." "As women," Spencer continued, we also "demand . . . a share in deciding between war and peace in all the courts of high debate—within the home, the school, the church, the industrial order, and the state." Not everyone who crowded into the New Willard favored woman suffrage. But given Spencer's logic, it had to be included in the platform of the new organization, and no one publicly objected.[53]

The prominent speakers who followed Spencer all echoed her arguments, adding urgent details of what one reporter called "the horrors of the present carnage and the resultant grief in many thousands of homes." Pethick-Lawrence predicted that, if given the chance, Europeans would vote against continuing the war begun by "international gamblers and degenerates." Schwimmer declared that, in the near future, women voters would "end all wars." Anna Howard Shaw—who headed the National American Woman Suffrage Association (NAWSA), the nation's largest suffrage group—said one man had asked her what peace-minded American women would do "if 50,000 German women came to this country to fight." She responded that the same number of her countrywomen would meet them at the dock, call them "sisters," and escort them to the Opera House "to reason with them and accomplish much more than man will by slaughter and murder." The delegates then elected a prominent set of officers to run the new party, including Fanny Villard, Anna Spencer, and Alice Thatcher Post, a well-known tax reformer and the wife of the assistant secretary of labor. Inevitably, Jane Addams was chosen as national "chairman"; she would preside over the national office in Chicago, her hometown.

The impressive size of the party's initial meeting and the respectability of its leaders did not obscure the audacity of its goals. These women
were "far from frivolous in either dress or countenance," as their first
historian put it.[54] In photos, few smiled, and their heavy dark clothes
and hair wrapped in tight buns and often stuffed under broad-brimmed
hats would have been appropriate for church. But they were demanding
a radical shift away from the world run by men, a change they hoped
would abolish war and the preparations for war forever.

They boldly aimed to transform the culture of belligerence as well as
to suggest new ways to undergird a new global order. To nudge human-
kind toward a glorious, if distant, future, activists called for educating
the young "in the ideals of peace," for the "democratic control of foreign
policies," and for the "removal of the economic causes of war." They
also proposed, as had some prewar pacifists, a "Concert of Nations" to
replace the geopolitics of power and the creation of "an international
police" to settle disputes between nations. Woodrow Wilson would later
make the last two institutions, under different names, the centerpieces
of his vision of a postwar world.[55]

But any hope of ending the current slaughter would require diplomacy at the highest level. To that end, the Woman's Peace Party advocated "the immediate calling of a convention of neutral nations in the
interest of early peace." Rosika Schwimmer had been talking up this
idea since arriving in the United States the previous fall. By the time
of the mass meeting at the New Willard, the new party had a detailed
proposal in hand, written by a twenty-three-year-old Canadian-born
Shakespeare instructor at the University of Wisconsin named Julia
Grace Wales.

Wales gave her ambitious plan the prosaic title "Continuous Mediation Without Armistice." It was designed to encourage neutral governments to do what belligerent ones would not do for themselves: propose
"principles favorable to the establishment of a permanent peace." Wales
imagined the creation of something resembling an ongoing college

seminar—but with the fate of the entire world at stake. The thirty-five existing neutral nations, or some portion of them, would send expert delegates to an international commission. As long as the war continued, that body would formulate ideas for a peace settlement and share them with the warring powers. After gathering responses, the commission would adjust its proposals and send them out again. Wales refrained from stipulating the terms of a just and lasting peace; the machinery of mediation would have to work that out. But the method itself, she argued, could be profoundly beneficial:

> The minimum gain would be the lifting of the programme of pacifism
> into the realm of serious political consideration. . . . It would focus the
> thought of the world at least momentarily on international righteous-
> ness. It would give a concrete expression to the inarticulate passion of
> all idealists both in the peaceful and the troubled lands. And if ever in
> the world's history there was dire need of such a common expression,
> it is now.[56]

Wales knew her plan would be criticized as naïve, depending as it did on the goodwill of savagely self-interested politicians. But with the optimism of like-minded peace activists whose numbers seemed to be growing, she claimed it was a practical way out of a stalemate that, every day, was killing and maiming thousands of men. Every warring nation "says that it is not to blame" and "was forced to fight in self-defence immediate or anticipatory." So why not let neutrals work diligently with these savage innocents to rescue them from mutual destruction? The Wisconsin legislature officially backed her plan and urged Congress to follow its lead. "The campaign of those individuals and groups who desire to ally themselves with our movement is already organized," Wales announced. "All they have to do is to importune their government to say yes."[57]

In the immediate aftermath of its founding, the Woman's Peace

Party seemed to validate that confidence. Local branches were quickly organized in Boston, Chicago, Philadelphia, San Francisco, St. Louis, Washington, D.C., and several small midwestern cities—as well as in New York City, where Crystal Eastman became its executive secretary. The national office printed and distributed tens of thousands of pieces of literature to grass-roots groups and foreign embassies. As international secretary, Rosika Schwimmer made contact with like-minded women in seventeen different countries, which soon led to the publication of a "Group of Letters from Women of the Warring Nations." In Britain, the new Union of Democratic Control, an anti-war group that included such luminaries as Norman Angell and the philosopher Bertrand Russell, was particularly sympathetic.

The Woman's Peace Party also devised a number of more innovative protests. That spring it sponsored—and the Carnegie Endowment financed—a lavish production of *The Trojan Women*, the classic anti-war play by Euripides, which toured big cities around the nation. In late February, female activists presented a two-mile-long peace petition signed by 350,000 children in forty-four states to Secretary of State Bryan, who was delighted to receive it. The young petitioners pledged "to work for schools instead of for battleships." On Mother's Day, the party sponsored a "Peace Day" in urban classrooms around the nation that featured songs and poems with anti-war lyrics and parades in which some children carried small flags of foreign nations, while others held banners adorned with doves and palms.[58]

"In the early months of 1915," Jane Addams remembered, "it was still comparatively easy to get people together in the name of Peace." From the nation's capital, Belle La Follette, wife of the anti-war senator, wrote to her best friend (and fellow suffragist), Elizabeth Glendower Evans, that the Woman's Peace Party was "*taking* like a prairie fire and I am like an imprisoned spirit set fire!!!"[59]

However, Belle La Follette, Jane Addams, and their fellow pacifists soon had to confront some disappointing realities. The movement

Wales evoked so confidently was still in the budding stage. Neither Hill-quit and his fellow Socialists nor congressional populists like Kitchin were ready to embrace her grand experiment in mediation. The former thought it evaded the imperial rivalries that had caused the war, while the latter trained their fire on the plutocrats of preparedness at home.

On February 8, Belle La Follette's equally passionate husband intro-duced a Senate resolution that authorized the president to organize a conference of neutrals that would promote "the early cessation of hos-tilities." "We can no longer avoid our responsibility," he told his col-leagues. "The balance of the world at peace waits on this Government. Neutral rights demand a clearer definition. Delay is filled with menace." But, despite some friendly comments in the press and supportive words from Secretary Bryan, the resolution failed to gain a hearing in the For-eign Relations Committee.[60]

The initiators of the Woman's Peace Party believed, or at least hoped, that determined women could rally American and world opinion to de-mand an end to this war—and perhaps to future wars. Powerful men had brought the cataclysm about and were doing nothing to stop it. But for the "Continuous Mediation Without Armistice" to become more than a well-meaning proposal, male politicians and diplomats would have to make the risky decision to endorse it. And that would take a good deal more pressure, continuously applied, than Addams's fledgling group could bring to bear.

Perhaps inevitably, the expansive turnout of individuals and groups at the party's debut in Washington soon dwindled into a smaller corps of dedicated activists. Carrie Chapman Catt and other suffrage leaders went back to campaigning for their preeminent issue. Most labor and temperance women returned to commitments they held more dearly and where partial victories could be won. During the Progressive Era, female reformers routinely supported one another's causes; they knew it would take more than a victory on an issue like suffrage or decent hous-ing for the poor to create "a kingdom of human kindness." Yet few were willing to transfer most of their energies to this new movement that faced particularly daunting odds. A year after its founding, the Woman's Peace Party reported a membership, on paper, of forty thousand. But peace was the priority of no more than a tenth of that number.[61]

At least Theodore Roosevelt considered the organization influential enough to try to blow it up with words. In April, the former president wrote a public letter damning the party as "absolutely futile" as well as "silly and base," "influenced by physical cowardice," and "vague and hysterical." What's more, he growled, it "subjects our people to measureless contempt." The Colonel compared the women's "peace at any price" attitude to that of the Copperheads during the Civil War.

Several well-known peace activists rebutted his charges. Most did so rather gracefully. Fanny Villard said his taunts insulted the only movement in both neutral and belligerent nations "which seeks to conserve human life"; while Belle La Follette declared that the party's program of "constructive statesmanship" was inspired by the example of Christ and was "based on the enlightened thought and experience of the world." But Catharine McCulloch, an attorney and suffrage leader in Illinois, snapped that Roosevelt's letter was "the cry of a barbarian out of his element." No one seems to have asked the Colonel why he bothered to attack a group he claimed was sure to fail.[62]

In contrast, Woodrow Wilson met frequently with leaders of the Woman's Peace Party and other peace groups until he decided to take the nation into war two years later. He always took care to praise their motives while turning aside their appeals that he volunteer to mediate a peace settlement. Still, the empathy Wilson voiced to these "progressive internationalists" was undoubtedly sincere. "I have unlimited faith in President Wilson," Addams told a reporter in the summer of 1915, and she was no fool. In fact, all the leading belligerents feared that Wilson's and Bryan's "do-good tendencies," as the German chancellor put it, would make it impossible to fight on to a decisive victory—if American statesmen ever decided the time for mediation was at hand.

Yet the president insisted that any effort he might make to end the Great War would occur only when he thought it had a chance to succeed. Only to Colonel Edward House, his sycophantic advisor and personal negotiator with European governments, did Wilson reveal his true thoughts about the matter. So the president and American peace advocates engaged in an extended, if wary, courtship. It would end badly, with accusations of bad faith on both sides.[63]

In mid-March, the president wrote to Addams that he would "welcome . . . with all my heart" any peace-minded messages she might send and would give the Wales pamphlet a careful reading. But he also doused any hope that he would take the plan seriously: "I think I do not exaggerate when I say that requests of a similar sort come from different quarters at least every week and I should have to draw distinctions which would become invidious before I got through with them, unless I granted interviews to all who applied for them in this matter. You will understand the delicacy this situation places me in."[64]

AT THE HAGUE, WITH HOPE

Perhaps a mass protest by distinguished women from nations at war as well as from ones that remained at peace would change his mind. As Wilson was brushing off Addams's plea, she and forty-six other Woman's Peace Party activists were preparing to cross the ocean to attend an International Congress of Women at The Hague. They would be returning the favor Rosika Schwimmer and Emmeline Pethick-Lawrence had done for the American peace movement the previous fall. They would also be assisting in a goal similar to but grander than feminists in one neutral, if large, nation could achieve on their own.

Delegates from twelve countries met at the end of April in the Dierentium, the largest hall in that symbolic capital of peaceful intentions. They wanted to demonstrate that women could "retain our solidarity" and "maintain a mutual friendship" across the same frontiers that men were slaughtering each other, in unprecedented numbers, to maintain. On the strength of that bond, the women at The Hague hoped to compel politicians to begin negotiations for a lasting peace, secured by the "democratic control of foreign policy" and "universal disarmament."[65]

As with the Woman's Peace Party, the impetus for this brave, if quixotic, undertaking came from European suffragists, whose numbers and confidence had been growing on the eve of war. Although only Finland and Norway had enacted universal suffrage laws by 1914, the movement was gaining strength among urban women from all classes and had the backing of Socialists and cosmopolitan liberals everywhere.

The mass bloodletting did drive a gash through their ranks. Most feminists in France, Britain, and Germany stood by their governments, hoping their support would earn them the vote. But for a sizable minority, the war only confirmed the evils of male power unrestrained by the pacific instincts of the opposite sex. The German feminist Lida Gustava Heymann cried out in February 1915: "The flesh and blood of men will fertilise the soil of the waving cornfields of the future. . . . Shall this war of extermination go on? Women of Europe, where is your voice? . . . Can these things not rouse you to blazing protest?"[66]

The conference at The Hague was planned jointly by American and European women who had long been partners in suffrage work and who shared an ideological affinity as strong as that of any group of transatlantic reformers. Dr. Aletta Jacobs, head of the Dutch suffrage society and a pioneering advocate of birth control, took the lead. With aid from Chrystal Macmillan, a Scottish lawyer, she invited pro-peace feminists from all over Europe and North America and asked Jane Addams to preside over the meeting itself.

Saint Jane immediately accepted the invitation and began trying to persuade her Woman's Peace Party sisters to sail with her. She admitted the "moral adventure" was terrifically ambitious; it could "easily fail—even do harm" to their larger mission. But how could American feminists turn down an opportunity to declare to all the world what they had already committed to working for at home?[67]

The women who did make the trip were taking a break from pursuing a variety of other good causes. Taken together, their politics veered more to the left than did those who had filled the hotel ballroom in Washington three months before. The American delegation to The Hague included such fellow Chicago reformers with national reputations as Dr. Alice Hamilton, an expert in industrial diseases; and Sophonisba Breckinridge, dean of the School of Civics and Philanthropy in that industrial metropolis. From New York City came Leonora O'Reilly, a working-class Socialist and the lead organizer of the Women's Trade Union League; and the journalist Angela Morgan, whose pacifist poem "The Battle Cry of Mothers" had, thanks to a handsome subsidy from Louise Carnegie, been distributed all over the United States. Julia Wales insured that "continuous mediation" would gain overseas renown, if not acceptance.

But Addams's failure to persuade the two major suffrage leaders in the United States to join her portended a split that would eventually weaken the peace movement's claim to speak for the majority of American feminists. Carrie Chapman Catt, who had been so keen on organizing the Woman's Peace Party, now backed away when she learned that most of her counterparts in Europe favored peace only after their nations' armies had destroyed their enemies. Anna Howard Shaw, who had looked forward to making a pact with her German "sisters," now wrote to Aletta Jacobs, "I feel that my first duty is here . . . the best thing I can do for peace and a thousand other things is to get votes for women."[68] So Addams and her pacifist comrades embarked on their voyage fearing that the grand alliance of women forged in January was already beginning to unravel.

Their two-week-long journey was fraught with a different sort of peril. Although the women booked passage on a neutral ship transporting wheat—the *Noordam*, under Dutch registry—they were crossing an active war zone. Allied ships with stores of munitions as well as food scanned the waters for U-boats seeking to destroy them. When the *Noordam* neared the English coast, a Royal Navy vessel aimed a machine gun at it, and sailors arrested two German stowaways. One yelled *"Hoch der Kaiser, Deutschland über Alles"* as he was taken away. When the ship entered the Channel, British authorities confined it there for four frustrating days. Local newspapers accused the "Peacettes" of undermining the morale of the troops. Finally, with no help from U.S. ambassador Page, the Americans were finally allowed to sail to their destination. They arrived at the congress on April 28, just minutes before it began. "This was no invitation to a clubwomen's pink tea," one historian remarked about the ordeal.[69]

What was most impressive about the gathering of some two thousand women at The Hague was that it occurred at all. As expected, most of the participants came from the Netherlands; the modest American delegation composed the second largest one. But what Jane Addams called the "sobriety and friendliness" of women from belligerent nations made headlines in major newspapers on two continents. Twenty-eight Germans, nine Hungarians, and six Austrians spoke and listened alongside three delegates from the United Kingdom, two from Canada, and five from Belgium. Another 180 British women wanted to come as well, but the government of Prime Minister Herbert Asquith forbade them to cross the North Sea. Whether from loyalty to their nations or pressure from their governments, not a single French or Russian woman appeared.[70]

Notwithstanding its international character, the three-day congress looked and sounded much like the inaugural gathering of the Woman's Peace Party. Most of those who attended, reported the American journalist Mary Heaton Vorse, were "well-to-do women of the middle class. . . . It was an everyday audience, plain people, just folks, the kind you see walking out to church any Sunday morning." But although their discourse and demeanor were utterly respectable, nearly every speech—carefully translated into one of the three official languages (English, French, and German)—brimmed with a quiet passion for both suffrage and peace. Helene Lecher, an Austrian delegate who had been working in military hospitals, asked "what was the use of healing wounds if they were to be torn open again." Resolutions, circulated in advance, called for an end to the manufacture of munitions for profit, against the transfer of disputed territories unless their inhabitants agreed, for democratic control of foreign policies, and for a league of nations. Delegates also endorsed the Wales plan for a conference of neutrals, signaling both the influence of the Americans who presented it and the lack of any other "practical" way to end this war without putting aside their hopes for a better world.[71]

The only moment of real discord occurred on the second day of the meeting. A German delegate, Anita Augspurg, invited her Belgian counterparts to join her on stage. Just two of the women from that occupied nation accepted, and they refused to shake hands with their sister pacifist. One of the Belgians, Eugénie Hamer, then asked to speak. "I am a Belgian before everything," she asserted, "and I cannot think as you do. There can be no peace without justice. The war must continue until the Belgians' wrongs have been righted." The audience applauded, and an American delegate quickly drew up a motion to insert the word "justice" into the resolution describing the lasting peace the delegates pledged themselves to attain. Most participants seemed to think that was a fitting, if temporary, way to resolve a bitter conflict they had done nothing to start. Jane Addams, tactful as ever, sat Augsburg on one side of her and Hamer on the other.[72]

On May 1, as the meeting was drawing to a close, Rosika Schwimmer brought up a novel idea for action. With characteristic boldness, she argued that only direct diplomacy by women could challenge male rulers to appreciate what the congress had done. The women should, she insisted, appoint delegates to visit the capitals of Europe and thrust their fine resolutions into their rulers' hands. Alice Hamilton and her

American compatriots considered the idea "hopelessly melodramatic and absurd." They were certain Jane Addams "would never consent to go from court to court" in this manner. But Schwimmer had skillfully lobbied the delegates from other neutral countries, and they strongly favored it.[73]

In the end, the Hungarian's arresting oratory carried the day. Schwimmer questioned the power of rational persuasion alone and dared her pacifist sisters to take a leap of faith for the sake of their sons: "If brains have brought us to what we are in now, I think it is time to allow also our hearts to speak. When our sons are killed by millions, let us, mothers, only try to do good by going to kings and emperors, without any other danger than a refusal!" Once the proposal passed, Addams agreed to appoint envoys for this daunting enterprise, one of whom, inevitably, would be herself. Despite her misgivings, Hamilton signed on too. To refuse Saint Jane was out of the question.[74]

Back in the United States, journalistic reaction to the International Congress of Women illustrated how quickly initial applause for the ardent neutrality of mothers had changed into a fierce debate about the motives and utility of their actions. Several newspapers in the urban East and Midwest echoed Theodore Roosevelt's attack. The *Detroit Free Press* jibed that the Americans had indulged in an "excursion of the innocents," while the *Washington Star* and *Pittsburgh Gazette-Times* agreed the women had wasted their time in a futile gesture. Most papers highlighted the statement by the Belgian Eugénie Hamer as proof that "the racial sympathies of the various delegations" could not be held in check, as the *New York Times* put it. Yet others were more sanguine about what the congress had achieved, at least rhetorically. "As a historic incident," observed the *Springfield Republican*, "it promises to be memorable because it boldly proclaims a pioneering principle with a future, to wit, the inherent antagonism to war of an entire sex."[75]

That feminist principle had brought two thousand women together, some through an embattled ocean and others across borders contested with blood. Emily Balch, a Wellesley professor of economics and sociology who, along with Addams, often spoke for the American delegation, responded to both the defenders and critics of the congress with praise for the simple power of words: "Futile as talk seems, the way it is dreaded shows that it does have its effect. Ideas seem so unreal, so powerless, before the vast physical force of the military masses to-day; it is easy to forget that it is only ideas that created that force and that keep it in action. Let war once be disbelieved in, and that force melts into nothing." For Balch, the decision to travel to The Hague was "a turning point in my life." She devoted the rest of it to trying to stop and prevent war, as a leader of the Woman's Peace Party and its successor groups. In 1946, Balch was awarded the Nobel Peace Prize, just after the most destructive conflict in history had ended.[76]

But the failure of her work, as heroic as it was, underlines a weakness of the approach she and her sister pacifists adopted. Evoking the sentiments of *all* women could not persuade many female workers or housewives inside or outside the Socialist parties of Europe and North America to feel comfortable in a movement dominated by the well educated and the well spoken. One radical American delegate complained that, in contrast to the gatherings of working people she attended back home, the Hague congress seemed sentimental and, at times, rather cold. "Why I've heard a little East Side striker rouse a meeting to a pitch of enthusiasm that was never touched by those clubwomen and suffrage leaders."[77]

A month earlier, the German Socialist Clara Zetkin—creator of International Women's Day—had convened a smaller gathering in Bern, Switzerland, of female radicals from several European nations, Rosa Luxemburg among them. Like Morris Hillquit, they declared that to prevent war one had to squarely condemn the imperial greed and conquest that caused it—and do the hard and dangerous work of releasing the grip of these evil forces on the world. Spinning grand designs for a mediated peace, they claimed, was a colossal waste of time.

Scant notice of the radical meeting appeared in the oft-censored European press, and the women at The Hague, who hosted dozens of reporters, did not mention it. Even if they had made an overture, an alliance probably would have been difficult to forge. Zetkin, who refused to call herself a "feminist," preferred to mobilize "proletarian" women to claim an equal place in the ranks of anti-war radicals of both genders than to join a movement of "bourgeois" suffragists whom she believed would never stay the course.[78]

Both at home and on their sojourn overseas, the leaders of the Woman's Peace Party tried to pursue two aims simultaneously. They yearned to stay above the battle, spiritually as well as literally, while exerting pressure on politicians who were ordering men into the fray or, like Roosevelt and Gardner, hoping to do so soon. But it was exceedingly difficult to combine the propagation of a womanly utopia with the polite, but firm, promotion of a mediation plan that would offend nobody.

On occasion, the spirit of nonresistance gave way to a cry of righteous fury. The words of Angela Morgan's popular poem clashed with the gentle, pleading tones of Fanny Villard, Jane Addams, and Emily Balch. Morgan opposed the militant toughness of the war-makers with a verbal militarism of her own:

> Warriors! Counsellors! Men at arms!
> You who have gloried in war's alarms,
> When the great rebellion comes
> You shall hear the beat
> Of our marching feet
> And the sound of our million drums.
> You shall hear that the world is at last awake—
> You shall hear the cry that the mothers make—
> *You shall yield—for the mothers' sake!*[79]

When Morgan read her poem to the women gathered at the Dierentium, they applauded with gusto.

For all its good and rational intentions, the conference at The Hague
revealed that an effective peace movement would not be built by a
motherly alternative alone. Women had been cajoling, fretting, arguing,
and organizing against the idiocy and destructiveness of man-made
war since ancient times—even, perhaps, since the dawn of the species.
But they could not, by themselves, convince leaders to make peace, and
their attempts to do so appeared increasingly quixotic. Male politicians
were not about to listen to women—however articulate, reasonable, and
well informed—who asked them to relinquish their absolute control
over the arms and machinery of state. A plea premised on the injustice
of women deprived of the vote was not going to change the minds of
men who either supported that deprivation or felt no urgency to end it.

Woodrow Wilson did tell reporters he "sympathized" with what
Addams and her fellow delegates had accomplished at The Hague.
When she returned home, he invited her to the White House, where he
politely listened to her advocate for the Wales plan. The president even
praised the conference resolutions as "by far the best formulation which
up to the moment has been put out by any body." Meanwhile, he was
drawing up his own plan to expand the military and sending Colonel
House back to Europe to hold secret negotiations with the prime minister of Great Britain. The mutual wooing of pacifists and president would
continue, never to be consummated.[80]

The International Congress of Women adjourned on May 1, exactly
nine months after Imperial Germany had declared war on the Russian
empire. In that short span of time, at least 2.5 million men had been
killed or maimed on the Western Front alone. Poison gas was deployed
on a massive scale for the first time in history. U-boats sank dozens of
merchant ships on the Atlantic, some sailing under neutral flags, including that of the United States.

The Kaiser's admirals knew the risk of angering Americans was great, but they saw no other strategy besides submarine attacks that might effectively counter the British blockade of their homeland, which was beginning to cause widespread malnutrition and death. Ambassador von Bernstorff did take the trouble of sending a notice to Americans who might be planning a trip across the ocean: "Travelers intending to embark on the Atlantic voyage," it read, "are reminded that a state of war exists" between Germany and Great Britain. "The zone of war includes the waters adjacent to the British Isles," and thus "vessels flying the flag of Great Britain, or any of her allies, are liable to destruction in those waters." The notice added, superfluously, that "travelers sailing in the war zone on ships of Great Britain or her allies do so at their own risk." Several newspapers in New York and other cities published the text on May 1. When the warning was read to Charles P. Sumner, the local agent for the British-owned Cunard Line, he thought it might be a hoax. At any rate, he assured a reporter, his ships were under the protection of the mighty Royal Navy. And, "as for submarines, I have no fear of them whatever."[81]

At ten o'clock that same morning, the *Lusitania*, a Cunard liner that was the fastest and most luxurious ship in the world, left New York harbor for Liverpool. It carried nearly two thousand crew and passengers, 197 of whom were Americans, and a hold stuffed with a variety of cargo including food, machinery, dry goods—and 4.2 million rounds of ammunition.[82]

TWO

CRY PEACE AND FIGHT PREPAREDNESS

May 1915 to May 1916

"To my mind, the word 'murderer' should be embroidered in red letters across the breast of every soldier."

—Henry Ford, April 1915[1]

"To an Oklahoman that has been living the free and easy life, without a lock on the door or a weapon in the house, and to whom a soldier is a curiosity, there is a long step from our condition to the plan laid down by the president, which I believe to be nothing but militaryism."

—W.C. Jarboe, real estate agent, Altus,
Oklahoma, January 1916[2]

"Once we were a fearless people. Are we to become a contemptible, fearful people?"

—Rabbi Stephen S. Wise, April 1916[3]

PIRACY AND PRIDE

The German torpedo that sank the *Lusitania* off the coast of Ireland on May 7, 1915, put an end to any real chance that most Americans would remain impartial in the Great War. Of the nearly 1,200 people who died, more than a hundred and twenty were U.S. citizens. For weeks, newspapers devoted their front pages to such heart-breaking details as the corpses of drowned mothers with babies clinging to their breasts. "Nothing in the annals of piracy can, in wanton and cruel ferocity, equal the destruction of the *Lusitania*," editorialized the *Louisville Courier-Journal*, the leading Democratic paper in its region. The *Nation*, whose publisher was Oswald Garrison Villard, Fanny's son, compared the perpetrators to "wild beasts, against whom society has to defend itself at all hazards." The *Literary Digest* curtly summarized the reaction of the American press: "Condemnation of the act seems to be limited only by the restrictions of the English language."[4]

It did not matter that the German government had warned Americans against booking passage on ships that flew the British flag. It did not matter that many of the doomed travelers could have sailed on a U.S. vessel—one departed from New York on the same day as the Cunard liner. It did not matter that U-boats were the only weapon the Germans had to prevent the British and their allies from resupplying themselves with war matériel at will, while tightening the North Sea noose on their enemy. Nor did it matter that the *Lusitania* carried a large store of munitions, a fact the British government denied but many observers assumed. All that mattered was that one of the Kaiser's submarines had, without warning, sunk what was perhaps the best known liner in the world and then made no attempt to rescue the survivors, as international law and the traditions of naval warfare obliged it to do. For the rest of their lives, millions of Americans would remember where and when they heard the shocking news—an experience future generations would repeat when Pearl Harbor was attacked, John F. Kennedy was assassinated, and the World Trade Center and nearly everyone trapped inside it crumbled into ash.[5]

The dreadful event on the Irish Sea presented Woodrow Wilson with an acute dilemma. For months, the president and several of his top advisors had been negotiating with German officials to prevent such a calamity from occurring. They made clear that the Kaiser's government would be held to a standard of "strict accountability" if U-boats killed Americans or targeted ships they owned. On March 28, Leon Thrasher, an American mining engineer, had died in a submarine attack on a small British vessel, the *Falaba*, soon after it left Liverpool en route to West Africa. But the flurry of outrage in Congress and the press soon subsided, allowing administration officials to delay making a formal protest.[6]

After the *Lusitania* went down, Wilson knew he had to confront Germany in the strongest possible terms, perhaps even break off diplomatic relations with Berlin. Yet he also realized that some Americans were going to continue to risk their lives by traveling on belligerent ships, and he would never surrender their right to do so.

The president did have some room to maneuver. Although the fury of the press undoubtedly reflected what most of the public was thinking, most citizens seemed no more eager to take up arms against the "Huns" than they had been before May 7. For three days following the tragedy, only a handful of editorials in the vast nation of journalistic opinion called for a declaration of war. Wilson remarked to the journalist Frederick Palmer that only citizens who lived east of the Allegheny Mountains favored a belligerent stand. While more Americans might now be rooting for the Allies, most still saw no reason to help them win the war—aside, that is, from selling them weapons and loaning them money.[7]

On May 10, Woodrow Wilson addressed the crisis for the first time, though indirectly. His impromptu comments came near the end of a short speech in which he mentioned neither the *Lusitania* nor the war in Europe. Four thousand newly naturalized citizens had gathered in Philadelphia's Convention Hall, where the president praised them for "leaving all other countries behind" and counseled them to heed what he called the nation's unique ability "to get rid of the things that divide and to make sure of the things that unite." Then he took the idea of American exceptionalism a big step further:

> The example of America must be the example not merely of peace because it will not fight, but of peace because peace is the healing and elevating influence of the world and strife is not. There is such a thing as a man being too proud to fight. There is such a thing as a nation being so right that it does not need to convince others by force that it is right.[8]

Despite Wilson's oblique reference to the foes of peace, everyone who read those sentences, which were featured in the next day's papers, knew whom he meant. Leading Republicans who rooted hard for the Allies were particularly livid. Henry Cabot Lodge thought the president could have persuaded Congress to declare war, although neither the Senate nor the House was then in session. At least, sputtered Lodge, he should have broken relations with Germany and seized its ships in U.S. harbors. The speech confirmed Theodore Roosevelt's opinion that Wilson was "a coward and a weakling" who catered to "all the hyphenated Americans" and "the solid flubdub and pacifist vote." General Leonard Wood, who had been army chief of staff during the Taft administration, snarled into his diary: "Rotten spirit in the *Lusitania* matter. Yellow spirit everywhere in spots." What Wilson called pride, his critics scoffed, was nothing but the fear to do what was necessary to confront a wicked enemy before he could strike again. They neglected the fact that the price of industrial stocks increased by almost 4 percent the day after the president spoke. Wall Street investors, according to the *New York Times*, "extracted much comfort" from learning that the nation was not rushing toward war. These heartening responses allowed anti-militarists to believe that Wilson shared their views, even if he did not think the time was right to become an active mediator for peace.[9]

Yet the sinking of the *Lusitania* also forced anti-warriors to confront an opposition that had grown larger and more determined to persuade Americans to join the Allies. The May attack, wrote the historian Arthur Link, "marked a dividing line between the time when there was no organized and vocal sentiment for American participation and the time when that sentiment existed in substantial measure." Peace activists who had been urging their neutral government to help mediate a settlement in the war now faced a struggle to keep their nation from joining the fray.[10]

"Preparedness" would no longer be just the cry of ferociously partisan figures like Augustus Gardner and his august father-in-law, Henry Cabot Lodge. Fueled with an avenging moralism, the movement for a giant military, led by such elite figures as Roosevelt and Wood, grew in boldness as well as size. Support for the National Security League and the Navy League soared; the latter gained eleven thousand new members by the end of the summer. In June, the NSL sponsored its first major conference; some three hundred delegates flocked to a fancy New York City hotel, "whose lobby had been decorated for the occasion with a torpedo and fourteen-inch shells." By year's end, the league boasted close to seven thousand donors. The American Rights Committee was created in May to sponsor a *Lusitania* memorial meeting; Ivy League professors, heads of several major publishing houses, the novelist Booth Tarkington, and other self-described "real Americans" soon filled its ranks.[11]

All these groups had the same explicit purpose: to create an army and navy equal to any in the world. Most agreed a permanent force of half a million soldiers—five times the current number—would be a good start. They also shared the belief, whether they expressed it openly or not, that an augmented military should soon be mobilized to help defeat Imperial

Germany. The very ubiquity of the term "preparedness" threw its critics on the defensive. Who could oppose the idea that the nation ought to be ready to confront whatever dangers might come its way?

In response to its emboldened adversaries, anti-war activists quickly organized a broad coalition of their own. Up to now, the cause of peace had animated a movement of men and women who saw no need to coordinate their actions, which were, in any case, largely rhetorical. The Woman's Peace Party was the only new body the movement had spawned. But the sinking of the *Lusitania* made it urgent to mount a larger and more ambitious effort. From then into the early months of 1917, social workers and feminists, left-wing unionists and Socialists, pacifists and nonpacifists, and a vocal contingent of senators and congressmen from both major parties (led by Robert La Follette and Claude Kitchin) worked together to stall or reverse the drive for a larger and more aggressive military. They could count on the eloquent assistance of William Jennings Bryan, who had resigned as secretary of state in June in protest against the president's refusal to criticize Britain's embargo as well as Germany's attacks on neutral vessels. The following spring, thousands of liberal Protestant ministers declared their support for the cause, as did Irish-Americans incensed at Britain's speedy execution of nationalist rebels who had seized the post office in Dublin.

When elected insiders cooperated with zealous outsiders, they managed to keep the forces they described as "militarists" at bay and made it more difficult for Woodrow Wilson to drift to that other shore. In reciprocal fashion, each section of the peace coalition assisted the other. The outsiders' sophisticated campaign to gain and mobilize popular support lent muscle to legislative initiatives by friends and challenges to bills authored by foes. Sympathetic federal lawmakers made their allies outside Washington, D.C., feel that they were not only respected in the halls of power but had a decent chance to succeed.

The anti-militarists made two different but complementary arguments against preparedness, a word they often confined within quotation marks. One argument was quite radical; it gestured toward a future world of democratic nations that would have neither a cause nor the will to take up arms again. As Crystal Eastman put it in November 1915, "The national genius cannot be directed to war preparation and genuine peace at the same time. If we are to fill the public mind with the kind of enthusiasm which will be necessary to make us a world union, we cannot at the same time rouse it with pictures of Germans bombarding New York and of Japanese invading California." Arming America, they feared, would extinguish the passion for global amity on which the only true hope of abolishing war depended.[12]

The second argument was largely defensive. It sought to preserve the supposed virtues of the prewar republic against the malignant growth of a state equipped to fight endless foreign wars. Evoking the traditional populist mistrust of concentrated power, such figures as Claude Kitchin hoped to rally ordinary Americans to reject a future in which they would be forced to pay higher taxes to satisfy the hunger of political and economic elites for world domination. They accused the National Security League, munitions manufacturers, and their political allies of hoodwinking Americans into believing in a nonexistent threat to the security of their beloved homeland.

After the war ended, the people who made such arguments would peel off in opposite directions—either toward utopian ventures for peace and, for some, proletarian revolution or against any ideology, whether Socialist or Wilsonian, that aspired to perfect the world. But for the time being, anti-militarists were united in their urgent desire to stop the country from repeating the fateful mistake made by Europeans who believed they could avoid war if only they were strong enough to fight one.

On the question of actually going to war, peace activists were justifiably convinced that most Americans were still on their side. Preparedness had become a clear and present danger; actual belligerence remained unpopular. Secretary of State Robert Lansing privately favored U.S. intervention. But he realized the country was not yet with him. As he wrote in his memoirs, "The majority of my callers during the summer and autumn of 1915, and for many months after that time, senators, representatives, and men high in financial and business circles, frankly said they were against war, or else stated that, though they favored it, the bulk of the people with whom they came in contact were opposed to it." It was going to take "a gradual process of education and enlightenment" before the people would come around.[13]

THE ADVENTURES ABROAD OF SAINT JANE AND HENRY FORD

In the wake of the Lusitania tragedy, most peace activists understood that, if they hoped to halt the slide toward a martial order, they would have to adopt a narrower, more single-minded strategy. They would, of course, never stop talking about the need for a more harmonious and democratic world. But to win the battle over preparedness, they would have to count votes in Congress and talk more about political changes they abhorred than about the grand transformation of society they ultimately desired.

Most also relegated the unwinnable demand for a blanket embargo on the sale of munitions to the back of a long wish list or dropped it altogether. Robert La Follette continued to point out that it was "hardly consistent that we should pray for peace and at the same time supply the ammunition to continue the war." But the time for organizing mass rallies and lobbying Congress to put a stop to that duplicity had passed.[14]

However, many pacifists were reluctant to give up the possibility that a fresh and thoughtful effort at citizen mediation might persuade the warring nations to lay down their arms. Before 1914, nearly every peace organizer had put great faith in the idea that thoroughly rational means—studies and manifestos, conferences and treaties—could put an end to profoundly irrational conflicts. The Woman's Peace Party and the delegates to the Hague conference certainly shared that belief, even as they questioned whether men in high positions had the will or talent to fulfill the task by themselves.

The attack on the *Lusitania* did nothing to shake that conviction. If anything, the war scare in the United States made promoting Julia Wales's Wisconsin Plan seem more urgent than ever. Later that month, Wales told the American minister to Denmark that mediation would not be as difficult as he and other diplomats feared. "I said that to the ordinary mind it seemed foolish that the world should destroy itself without any collective effort at systematic thinking."[15]

Just two days after the *Lusitania* went down, Jane Addams and her sister feminists embarked on a seven-week-long peace tour of European belligerent capitals. They began in London, then traveled to Berlin, Vienna, and Budapest. After passing through Switzerland, that citadel of neutralism, they ended their trip in Rome and Paris. In each country, they met either with the prime minister, the minister of foreign affairs, or both. At the Vatican, they had an audience with Pope Benedict XV, who "offered himself as a peace mediator if the occasion came for him to act"—which it did not until two years later. They also spoke to a variety of peace activists and visited wounded soldiers in military hospitals.[16]

Upon hearing their plea for a neutral conference, every official praised their motivations. Yet nowhere did they receive any encouragement to pursue their plan for continuous mediation. Edward Grey, the British foreign secretary, asked the pacifists to suggest terms for peace but insisted that his nation must fight on until victory. In Berlin, they met with Chancellor Theobald von Bethmann-Hollweg, who was mourning his own son's death in battle. He blasted England for vowing to "crush" German militarism. When Addams insisted that was not the same as threatening the survival of the German nation, the chancellor retorted that it was "a distinction but not a difference." Only in Vienna did a top official depart from diplomatic convention to vent his frustration at a war that appeared to have no end. "You are the only sane people who have been in this room for ten months!" exclaimed Karl von Stürgkh, the Austrian prime minister. He banged his fist on the table when he said it. In late June, as Addams and her compatriots prepared to sail back across the Atlantic, she summarized the results of their meetings to a reporter from the *Washington Post*. The interview bore the unwelcome headline: "Her Peace Trip Futile."[17]

But Addams was too dogged a crusader to leave it at that. A few days after returning to the United States, she delivered the featured address at a packed rally in Carnegie Hall, organized by an array of anti-war and progressive groups ranging from the sizable Woman's Peace Party and Women's Trade Union League to a tiny group with the puckish name the College League of Common Sense. Oswald Garrison Villard and Meyer London, the New York Jew who was the only Socialist member of Congress, warmed up the crowd.

Knowing she was among friends and admirers, Addams decided to speak without notes. Until the end of her forty-five-minute speech, she stuck to an informative and cautious tone. She described the gathering at The Hague and the subsequent conversations she and her sister delegates had held with Europeans—high and low. She displayed her maternalist convictions: "Women, who have nurtured these soldiers from the time they were little things," felt a particular agony to "see them destroyed." She also acknowledged that most women she had met on the tour were as zealously nationalistic as the men.

Then, toward the close of her remarks, Addams made the mistake of revealing the depth of her outrage at the waste of so many young lives. "This war was an old man's war," she claimed. In every nation, she visited soldiers, many badly mangled, who told her they would halt the fighting if they could. Some also told her they could only muster the courage to run sharp steel through the bodies of their enemies when they were drunk. "We heard in all countries similar statements in regard to the necessity for the use of stimulants before men would engage in bayonet charges. . . . In Germany they have a regular formula for it. In England they use rum and the French resort to absinthe."

This grim revelation actually gave her hope. If men would not engage in hand-to-hand combat unless they are "doped," then "in the end human nature must reassert itself. The old elements of human understanding and human kindliness must come to the fore." Loud applause swept through the hall as she stepped down from the stage.[18]

But the two sentences about liquid "stimulants" drowned out everything else she said that evening. Richard Harding Davis, a renowned war correspondent and Theodore Roosevelt's good friend, began the assault in a letter to the *New York Times*. Addams, he wrote, "strips [the soldier] of honor and courage. She tells his children, 'Your father did not die for France, or for England, or for you; he died because he was drunk.'" Only "a complacent and self-satisfied woman" would make such an ignorant charge. Dozens of male journalists rushed to echo his condemnation of a fifty-five-year-old woman who evidently neither knew nor cared to know about the heroic sacrifices of young men in combat.[19]

No reporter, it seemed, thought to question the combatants themselves. If they had, they may have discovered that Addams was at least partially correct. Before an attack, British soldiers received much larger doses of rum than their usual two tablespoons a day. According to the literary historian Paul Fussell, "One medical officer deposed after the war was over, 'Had it not been for the rum ration I do not think we should have won the war.'"[20]

The controversy deprived Addams of her image of utter respectability and aura of righteous calm. She insisted to reporters that she had meant to praise the soldiers' humanity, not to demean them. But she soon "gave up in despair," writing later: "At moments I found myself filled with a conviction that the next revolution against tyranny would have to be a revolution against the unscrupulous power of the press."[21] In the wake of the *Lusitania* outrage, the six-month-long effort by

American feminists to nudge the war makers toward a mediated peace, so zestfully begun at the New Willard Hotel back in January, seemed to be expiring in a hail of hostile columns written and edited an ocean away from the trenches.

Addams did help inspire a spectacularly ambitious attempt led by another prominent American to spur a negotiated end to the war. In April, just before she left for The Hague, she had dined at Henry Ford's 1,300-acre estate in Dearborn, Michigan. Sometime between the appetizer and coffee, Addams horrified the automaker and his wife, Clara, by telling them that some twenty thousand men were dying in Europe every day for little or no territorial gain and no worthy purpose.

At the time, the fifty-one-year-old industrialist was one of the most celebrated men in America. Ford had introduced the assembly line; in 1914, he started to pay most of his male employees the unheard-of wage of five dollars a day. A year later, his company dominated the worldwide automobile market with the Model T—the first mechanically reliable vehicle a middle-class family or a decently paid factory worker could afford. Boastful about all his creations, he surmised that people would be as eager to consume his political views as they were to buy his cars.

Before he met Addams, Ford had no contact with the peace movement, nor had he publicly disclosed what he thought about the great bloodletting overseas. But he had long harbored the populist notion that war was simply "a device of big financiers, the biggest cowards in the world." These cosmopolitan "interests," Ford charged, were plotting to destroy the allegedly harmonious, agrarian society he cherished—even while his own mechanical creations were helping to extinguish it in reality. The self-made tycoon from Michigan also espied a conspiracy that was regional in nature. "New York wants war," he told a journalist that June, "but the United States doesn't. The people west of New York are too sensible for war." Gotham activists like Crystal Eastman and Morris Hillquit would have strongly disagreed.[22]

By August, Ford had decided, as he told a Detroit reporter, to "do everything in my power to prevent murderous, wasteful war in America and in the whole world; I will devote my life to fight this spirit of militarism."[23]

"Everything" turned out to be reserving most of the berths on a ship, the *Oscar II*, that belonged to the Scandinavian American Line, and seeking to fill it with other well-known Americans eager to do what Addams and her sister feminists had failed to accomplish that spring: persuade the neutral nations of Europe to mediate an end to the war. "We are going to try to get the boys out of their trenches and back to their homes on Christmas Day," Ford rashly promised on November 24.

The idea to rent a large vessel came from the inimitable Rosika Schwimmer and Louis Lochner, a twenty-eight-year-old peace activist from Chicago, who had been ghostwriting most of Jane Addams's articles for newspapers. They teamed up to convince Henry and Clara that their wealth and fame could enable the movement to surmount the obstacles that had defeated the earlier attempt at citizen mediation. But it turned out to be the last effort of its kind, a lavishly hyped detour from the campaign to halt preparedness that drew comparisons to Don Quixote and worse.[24]

The major flaw in the plan was not so much in its ambition as in its execution. Ford, like many powerful men, confused his own commitment to a big idea with his ability to persuade others of its value. Fond of surprises, he announced just eleven days after he hired the *Oscar II* that the ship would sail to Norway from the port of Hoboken, New Jersey. With Lochner's aid, the auto tycoon rushed off telegrams to his famous friends and a bevy of other notable public figures urging them to come along. But John Dewey, William Dean Howells, Louis Brandeis, Rabbi Stephen Wise, Robert La Follette, Amos Pinchot, Thomas Edison, Luther Burbank, and the department store magnate John Wanamaker all refused—as did Colonel House.

So, a bit more surprisingly, did such veteran peace activists as

Crystal Eastman, Hamilton Holt, Emily Balch, and David Starr Jordan, an ichthyologist who had recently retired as president of Stanford University. Morris Hillquit received an invitation too, although the idea that a prominent Socialist would join a venture conceived and run by one of the major capitalists in the land revealed, as did the invitation to Colonel House, Ford's naïveté about the politics of the cause in which he had recently enlisted. The expedition, Jordan later wrote, "if successful would have been a world service of incomparable value." But, at the time, he doubted the industrialist and his "shipload of amateurs" could pull off something so grand, and so quickly.[25]

What happened during the days before sailing must have confirmed his suspicions. Ford engaged a suite of rooms at the luxurious Biltmore Hotel in midtown Manhattan, which became a magnet for anyone who wanted to assist, exploit, or chronicle the extraordinary adventure. "From early morning till long after midnight," Lochner recalled, "there appeared a continuous stream of callers, men and women leaders in the pacifist movement, reporters, photographers, agents of various sorts, and also, as was inevitable, scores of cranks." A number of actors and singers also offered "to keep the ship's company in good humour during the voyage."[26]

Deciding who would accompany Ford on the *Oscar II* added to tensions during the "eleven days of Inferno," as Lochner called them. Lochner and Addams had drawn up a list of pacifists they thought should be invited as delegates to a future conference of neutrals. But Rosika Schwimmer rejected anyone, according to Lochner, "with whom she had had unpleasant experiences in the past"—that is, anyone who had objected to her capricious, if occasionally shrewd, style of activism. For those who did pass muster, Ford's hastily assembled staff had to secure passports, hire interpreters, arrange for baggage, and supply the ship with all the materials a floating embassy of idealistic citizens might require.[27]

In the end, those who did make the trip were divided about equally

between peace activists and curious young people who came along
for what they hoped would be a dramatic, if not necessarily a history-
altering, adventure. Among the more notable "delegates" were Julia
Grace Wales; Samuel S. McClure, former editor of the pioneer muckraking magazine that still bore his name; Louis B. Hanna, the Republican governor of North Dakota who had few previous ties with pacifist
groups; and the feminist Inez Milholland Boissevain, renowned for
leading the 1913 suffrage parade in Washington, D.C., on a large white
horse, dressed in a long cape and crown. Also on board, at Ford's personal invitation, were some twenty-five college students of both sexes
whom the tycoon described as "fellows with sand." Only one of the students belonged to a peace society. Some forty journalists booked cabins
too. Most wrote or photographed for newspapers and magazines published in New York and other big cities.[28]

Before the ship left port, Ford's wildly optimistic promise to end the
war by Christmas, coupled with the comic disorganization at the Biltmore, made it easy for reporters to have their fun with the celebrated
pacifist and his entourage. Mark Sullivan, the influential editor of *Collier's*, wrote that Ford was "a fine earnest man whose impulses are not
sufficiently corrected by education nor by experience outside of me-
chanics." The *New Republic* headlined its editorial about the expedition
"A Little Child Shall Lead Them." Dispatches from the Biltmore were
liberally sprinkled with terms like "quixotic" and "innocents abroad."
One Broadway comedian quipped that Ford's factories were closing
down because "Henry is sending all the nuts to Europe."[29]

The miserable coverage did not stop some noted anti-warriors from
praising the intentions of the "Peace Ship" and its entrepreneur. Despite
her misgivings about the "eccentrics" gathered around Ford, Jane Addams would have joined them, if she had not been hospitalized with a
serious kidney infection. William Jennings Bryan saw the party off from
the dock at Hoboken and said he hoped to rendezvous with them in Europe. Oswald Villard wrote warmly about the expedition. According to

Louis Lochner, several leaders of neutral nations promised to cooperate as well.[30]

Still, rooting for the success of the enterprise was hardly the same as participating in it. The leading American peace organizations kept their distance. The Reverend Anna Garlin Spencer, the gifted orator who was vice president of the Woman's Peace Party, had planned to sail on the *Oscar II*. But when she failed to persuade Ford, Lochner, and Schwimmer to select a small group of trained mediators before taking off, she decided to stay home. So did Clara Ford, who declined to accompany her husband, in part because she feared a U-boat would torpedo the ship.[31]

For her part, Crystal Eastman melded her sense of the possible with her dream of the desirable. The day before the Peace Ship sailed, she wrote to Addams: "I think we are all glad that the Woman's Peace Party is not officially connected with it in any way. It is not deliberate and planned enough to be the undertaking of an organization." Still, she added, "when one reads the list with quite unprejudiced eyes, there are quite a number of real people aboard to furnish balance, and I am glad that Mr. Ford kept to his vision in spite of all the ridicule. Some altogether unexpected good result may come out of it. Anyhow, I think the enterprise will go down in history with honor as John Brown's Raid and Coxey's Army did. . . . I think it is rather inspiring after all."[32]

Across the nation, that sentiment seems to have been shared by Americans who saw no harm in a man they admired making a desperate attempt to end a demonic conflict. With the death toll growing daily and the president refusing to propose a mediation plan of his own, at least the inventor of the Model T was showing that *someone* was willing to act in an innovative, albeit impulsive, way. "If Henry Ford's a fool," wrote a liberal Baptist minister from Grand Rapids, Michigan, then so was Christ. Unlike the voyagers on the *Oscar II*, he lamented, "we are moral cowards. We run with the herd. We are afraid to stand up alone in defense of a gospel we profess to believe." The poet Edgar

Guest—whose simple, sentimental verses were syndicated in hundreds of daily papers—articulated the ambivalence felt by many:

> It may be folly, it may be wrong, as all the critics say,
> And to end the strife and slaughter grim this may not be the way . . .
> But just the same when your ship sets out,
> I'll cheer for your splendid pluck
> And wave my hand in a fond farewell and wish you the best of luck.[33]

Just before leaving his suite at the Biltmore, Ford granted a final interview to the swarm of journalists who, for almost two weeks, had been buzzing around and stinging him. "Have you any last word to say?'" asked one reporter. "Yes. Tell the people to cry peace and fight preparedness." What if his expedition failed? "If this expedition fails, I'll start another." And off he drove to the pier, where a crowd of up to fifteen thousand awaited him.[34]

The transatlantic voyagers endured the same mixture of earnest idealism and organizational chaos that had marked the planning. Three times a day, with reporters present, the delegates and college students debated how they should advance the cause of peace once they landed in Europe. They agreed, in principle, to advance the Wales proposal for continuous mediation; for Schwimmer and Lochner, that was the raison d'être of the mission. But Ford's insistence that everyone sign a statement condemning preparedness—which now meant opposing President Wilson—did not fare so well. In a letter to the delegates, the automaker asked: "What could be more absurd and inconsistent than for us to ask Europe to stop adding to her own military burdens, while supporting either actively or passively a proposed increase of them in our own country." But when Samuel McClure, Governor Hanna, and several others objected, Ford withdrew to his cabin and seldom emerged for the rest of the trip.[35]

Rosika Schwimmer damaged the enterprise in other ways. She was convinced, as Louis Lochner wrote afterward, that she had "as unique an opportunity for securing an exalted place in history as ever came to a member of her sex." Schwimmer asserted that her fluency in four European languages and her long experience in the peace movement on two continents made her the obvious choice to run the prospective conference of neutrals. She curtly dismissed objections that, as the citizen of a belligerent nation, she might not be the best person to assume that role.[36]

Meanwhile, the imperious Hungarian took to roaming around the ship carrying a large black bag, which she said held "secret" documents no one but she was allowed to see. This "air of mystery," wrote Lochner, "not only gave rise to rumours—that she was a foreign agent—but . . . alienated much sympathy from the Neutral Conference plan." In fact, he already knew and reporters soon learned that the documents were nothing more than bland statements of support for the idea of mediation from diplomats and heads of state that Schwimmer and the other women in the Addams delegation had gathered the previous spring during their fruitless tour of European capitals. "Her black bag," reflected one historian, "came to symbolize false hopes and empty promises."[37]

The hopes of the pacifists did rise, briefly, after the *Oscar II* landed in the capital of Norway, then known as Christiania. Although most Norwegians sided with Britain in the war, a variety of citizens' groups held serious meetings with the American delegates and students; Lutheran ministers and the Labor Party, led by Socialists, were particularly welcoming—although none formally endorsed the mediation plan. But Henry Ford's quicksilver mood had darkened. Just four days after arriving in Christiania, dissension among the delegates, a bad cold, and his wife's pleas to face reality all persuaded him to return home. Before leaving, he assured Lochner that he would continue to bankroll the venture. "You've got this thing started and can get along without me."[38]

In late February, a modest semblance of that "thing"—the long-desired neutral conference—did get organized in Stockholm, where

the Swedish government was amenable to pacifist experiments. Six
unaligned nations each selected a handful of delegates, most of whom
were professors or politicians; a third were women. They formed committees and drafted high-minded resolutions. At first, Schwimmer tried
to dominate the proceedings, but Ford made it known he would no
longer finance the conference if she were in charge, and she unhappily
resigned. Lochner took over as the main channeler of the automaker's
desires and largesse. But the conference stalled at the embryonic stage.
By the summer of 1916, as Ford kept tinkering with it via international
cables and unsympathetic personal aides on the ground, it slowly expired. The American press paid little notice to its passing.

The idea of citizen diplomacy, however, did not entirely die with it.
A year later, Morris Hillquit and two of his Socialist comrades would
attempt to travel to Stockholm to attend a gathering of fellow radicals
to stop the war, which, by then, the United States had entered. But the
failure of the Peace Ship ensured that the vision of well-informed, well-
meaning pacifists going over the heads of governments to make peace
with their counterparts—an idea suggested before the Great War by
both Andrew Carnegie and Jane Addams—would never again play a
significant role in the movement. Resisting the arming of America now
required their full attention and resources.

Ironically, months before, Henry Ford had suggested that his expedition might just be a sideshow to the main event. During the fall of
1915, he spent tens of thousands of dollars on ads opposing a military
build-up that ran in major newspapers and magazines. Amid the frenzy
before sailing to Norway, he told Lochner not to invite any anti-war
congressmen or senators to come along: "I want those fellows to stay
right there in Washington and fight 'preparedness.' They are more necessary there than on our Peace Ship."[39]

PACIFISTS WITH A PROGRAM

"The immediate function of the pacifist in America to-day is to fight
the agitation for increased armament as a step in the wrong direction,
as a long backward step away from the achievement of his ideals."

—Crystal Eastman, July 1915[40]

During the final months of 1915, Woodrow Wilson finally got around to
stating the kind of preparedness he favored, without going nearly as far as
the National Security League and its allies demanded. He proposed creating a Continental Army, a reserve force of up to four hundred thousand
"citizen soldiers," as well as building "incomparably the greatest navy in
the world." Yet, at the same time, he assured Americans that an expanded
military would be used "not for war, but only for defense" and that his
administration would continue its "record of genuine neutrality." Herbert
Croly, the editor of the *New Republic*, who sided with the Allies, spoke for
many on all sides of the debate when he complained that the president's
statements "leave us in the dark" and "will leave other nations in the dark"
about his true intentions. For Wilson, however, a decisive resolve would
have been neither wise as policy nor intelligent as politics. Better to seem
confused than to take a course sure to anger one side or the other.[41]

Peace activists were more disappointed than angered by Wilson's
proposal, but it also clarified their mission. They had now become the
only certain refuge for Americans who wanted to reject the siren song
of "militarism." Whether one held out hope that the president's indeci-
siveness betrayed his continuing discomfort with preparing for war or
thought Wilson was just another "jingoist" eager for America to join
the fray, the peace movement provided a variety of ways to both pressure and condemn him—as well as to pursue an alternative agenda of
reforms that excessive military spending imperiled.

Any effective protest campaign requires leaders as skillful at managing an organization as they are at articulating a stirring message. In the

anti-preparedness effort, only Crystal Eastman possessed both these talents and was willing to devote them completely to the cause. Born in 1881, she was "a natural leader," recalled Roger Baldwin, the future founder of the ACLU. As the agnostic daughter of progressive ministers from Elmira, New York, she felt a calling to cleanse the world of social evils.[42]

Until the outbreak of World War I, Eastman had devoted herself to the twin causes of labor and feminism. "The steady march of injury and death means suffering, grief, bitterness, thwarted hopes incalculable. These things cannot be reckoned, they must be felt," she wrote in a pioneering 1910 book about the thousand serious accidents that wage earners in the Pittsburgh area suffered during a single year.[43] Eastman's work in Pittsburgh, which the conservative New York Times praised for its "scientific method and judicial spirit," won her an appointment from Governor Charles Evans Hughes to New York's commission on employer liability, where she drafted the state's first workmen's compensation law.[44]

At the same time, she was busy in the growing feminist movement—writing and speaking for the right to vote and for women's right to be physically active and to wear clothing in public that allowed them to move freely. In 1912, after marrying a handsome insurance agent named Wallace Benedict and moving to his hometown of Milwaukee, she managed Wisconsin's first referendum campaign for woman suffrage.

Crystal's piercing dark eyes, high cheekbones, and tall, athletic physique drew attention to whatever she had to say. On meeting her in 1918, the radical black (and gay) poet Claude McKay, who became a pillar of the Harlem Renaissance, thought she was "the most beautiful white woman I ever knew." Crystal had "a magnificent presence," McKay wrote. "Her form was something after the pattern of a splendid draft horse, and she had a way of holding her head like a large bird poised in a listening attitude." She also had a knowing wit. "When you are in need of financial help, go out and ask for it," Crystal advised young suffragists in 1912. "Either they will help you because they are interested in the cause, or they will give you something to get rid of you, or they will hand you something because they like your looks." Many men, including her younger brother Max, were at least a little bit in love with her.[45]

Crystal faced down Socialists who questioned whether she were "sufficiently radical," dressed up as a western plow girl for a suffrage pageant on the Broadway stage, and galloped into Washington, D.C., on a horse to herald the coming of a big suffrage parade. She and her mother, Annis, both sought help from Abraham A. Brill, the first psychoanalyst to practice in the United States. Evidently, Crystal was anxious that her desire to have sex with her future husband was overwhelming her doubts about his lack of political ardor. The couple divorced in 1915.[46]

On the eve of World War I, Crystal Eastman was back in New York, separated from her spouse and thriving at the confluence of several rising streams of left-wing activism. She was close to the social work leaders Paul Kellogg and Lillian Wald and worked easily with both mainstream suffragists and radical feminists. She was one of the Village militant moderns who in the pages of the *Masses*, edited by brother Max, made class warfare seem both thrilling and amusing.

At first, she did not expect to devote her full and formidable energies to the cause of peace. From the summer of 1914 until the spring of 1915, Crystal did little for it besides invite Emmeline Pethick-Lawrence to speak in New York during the Englishwoman's tour of the United States. Otherwise, Eastman was busy promoting suffrage and launching a novel initiative, in partnership with the Maxwell Motor Company, to hire women to sell cars to other women—and to receive the same salaries and commissions as did men on New York's "Automobile Row."[47]

But by June, the *Lusitania* crisis had compelled her to make a change. From then until the end of the war, Eastman was the key figure in the two most influential peace groups in the nation: the American Union Against Militarism (AUAM) and the New York branch of the Woman's Peace Party. Nearly every day, she walked the half-mile from her apartment near Washington Square to an office near Union Square, where she took on a formidable array of tasks for both organizations.

She delivered speeches, orchestrated publicity campaigns, raised funds, chaired meetings, organized lecture tours and classes on the history of wars and how to stop them, set up a lobbying office in Washington, planned strategy with politicians, edited an anti-war magazine, and staged an innovative protest exhibit that drew tens of thousands of visitors. Crystal also found time to fall in love with Walter Fuller, a British artist and writer, who, unlike her first husband, fully shared her political passions. They married, in secret, sometime in 1916.[48]

Eastman balanced a pragmatic style of activism with a more confrontational one. "It is high time," she announced in mid-November, "that we pacifists had a program." Their "remote plans for world federation" must be put aside, at least temporarily, in order to defeat Wilson's "great program of military and naval expansion," which Congress would consider in its new session, to begin a month later. [49]

She was sanguine about their chances. That month, Eastman wrote up a "platform of real preparedness" designed to appeal to the widest possible audience. It began with a demand that Congress investigate "the state of our defenses" to see whether tax dollars were being efficiently spent. She also argued that the government should produce the weapons of war, not to nudge America toward socialism but simply "to clear the air of suspicion" that preparedness was driven merely by a hunger for profits.

To smooth the way, Eastman defined her fellow advocates of world peace as a bevy of concerned moderates. What she called "the real organic groups . . . —capital, labor, science, religion, finance, etc.," should join in the effort, even if they "are opposed on almost every other issue." We are not, she wrote, like the "few serene non-resistants" who respond to "every conceivable national emergency by laying down our arms." Instead, we belong to "a steadily growing body of thoughtful citizens" who recognize that the only real danger to the nation's security comes from those who, at a time of collective frenzy, would "tip the scales for war." It was rhetoric fit for a coalition that would exclude nobody.[50]

Unsurprisingly, not all "thoughtful" Americans were willing to restrain their sense of alarm. A day before Eastman's cautious platform was published, she presided over a debate at Cooper Union in lower Manhattan that threatened to erupt into a riot. Inside the Great Hall where, in 1860, Abraham Lincoln gave the "right makes might" speech that vaulted him to the Republican nomination, a mostly female crowd of pacifists and Socialists hooted and yelled at Henry A. Wise Wood, an engineer and consultant to the Navy Department, who was a prominent champion of turning the United States into the mightiest nation it could be. When Wood declared that a patriot had to be willing to sacrifice his life, he was booed and heard shouts that no "capitalists" were found in the trenches. When he claimed "this country is seething with spies," many yelled at him to "shut up." His debate opponent, the Socialist Allan Benson, added to the din by accusing Wood of being an apologist for J.P. Morgan. According to the *Times*, Crystal Eastman had to plead "for fair play" and only "silenced the rowdyism with much trouble." It was, observed the reporter, "one of the most remarkable meetings which has been staged in Cooper Union for a long time."[51]

Yet Eastman herself was not always content to heed her own moderate counsel. She was one of the more gifted of the Village radicals, the joyful modernists who insisted that a rebellion of style must accompany a revolt against capitalism and war. The *Masses*, the magazine edited by her beloved brother, had declared in its first issue "a sense of humor and no respect for the respectable" and described itself as "frank; arrogant; impertinent; searching for true causes; a magazine directed against rigidity and dogma wherever it is found." Under Crystal's leadership, the Woman's Peace Party of Greater New York—whose leading members were radical feminists—staged a lively repertoire of protest, with occasional aid from the AUAM. From the late fall of 1915 through the following spring, they put on an "anti-militarist" play with speeches in both English and Yiddish, protested against a state bill requiring schoolchildren in the state to drill like soldiers, and organized a parade of automobiles down Fifth Avenue to protest rearmament.[52]

Most impressive—and controversial—was their "War Against War" exhibit. Chiefly designed by Walter Fuller, it featured savagely witty cartoons, captivating speakers, and a number of imaginative displays meant to dramatize the foolishness of preparing for war in order to preserve peace. A metallic dragon represented the bellicose denizens of Wall Street who "are at all times willing to give their country's service the last full measure of conversation." A life-size, papier-mâché model of a stegosaurus symbolized the peril of having "all armour plate and no brains." There were two contrasting statues of Uncle Sam. One depicted him in military uniform, a bayonet clenched in his teeth and his arms full of little cannons and a saber—"as the Jingoes would have him; All Dressed Up—No Place to Go." The other showed him dressed in his customary garb, "as the Pacifists would have him—The World's Greatest Mediator."

"War Against War" opened in downtown Brooklyn in mid-April and moved to lower Manhattan a few weeks later. In both venues, it attracted an astonishing five to ten thousand visitors a day. That summer, it moved on to Philadelphia, where the reception was just as warm, and then to nine other cities around the country. By fall, for eight dollars, one could purchase thirty large, multicolored posters depicting the highlights of the exhibit. The AUAM recommended the display "especially" for labor unions, granges, clubs and churches, and "Village Improvement Associations."[53]

But "War Against War" also provoked citizens who regarded such flamboyant protests as close to sedition. They were particularly angered by the portrayals of Uncle Sam. At least one New York schoolteacher registered her shock at the bloodthirsty image of the American icon. A "justly indignant" Brooklyn grand jury tried unsuccessfully to find some legal basis for indicting the exhibit's creators for undermining America's "respect among nations." As one frustrated member of the jury put it, "Its doctrines are false, its influence insidious, and its purpose questionable, if not treasonable."[54]

War Against War Exhibit

"Seeing is believing."

5,000 to 10,000 people a day came to see the War Against War Exhibit in New York last May. This Exhibit set forth graphically and pictorially the stupidity and futility of the whole war system. Those who saw it never forgot it. It was so simple a child could understand it, so comprehensive it made the idea of world organization seem a practicable reality.

The original War Against War Exhibit which cost several thousand dollars to produce has now been reproduced in poster form and can be secured complete for $8.00 (transportation included).

SPECIMEN PANELS.

The Exhibit consists of 23 panels (3 by 5 ft.) and seven cartoons (2 by 3 ft.) printed in one, two and three colors on bill poster paper, suitable for indoor or outdoor use. The posters can be pasted on muslin or cardboard or simply tacked up for temporary use. (The large panels are each printed in two sections.) They are effective when displayed singly but are especially designed to be hung as an exhibit and thus form a complete graphic indictment of war.

The Exhibit is shipped in a large paste-board tube, is light, compact, and easily transported.

We especially recommend it for the immediate use of

Peace Organizations	Social Settlements
Anti-Militarist Societies	Civic Centers
Labor Unions	Village Improvement Associations
Granges	Clubs and Churches
Schools and Colleges	Chautauquas
	and

All Individuals who want to do their part toward winning the battle of democracy against militarism.

A special letter will be furnished on request, giving suggestions and directions for additional features, publicity schemes, literature, speakers and all the points which make an exhibit draw a big crowd.

WAR AGAINST WAR EXHIBIT, $8.00

produced by

THE AMERICAN UNION AGAINST MILITARISM

Munsey Building, Washington, D. C.

An advertisement for a portable version of the 1916 War Against War exhibit.

That Eastman could pursue the two modes of protest simultaneously was due, in part, to the different nature of the organizations she led. The AUAM was the more respectable of the two. It grew out of meetings held during the fall of 1914 at Lillian Wald's Henry Street Settlement House on the Lower East Side. Wald, a German Jew whose dedication to social uplift equaled that of Jane Addams, gathered around her a like-minded group of prominent reformers who worried that the more Americans got sucked into the growing war, the less desire they would have to advance programs that benefited workers, immigrants, and children.

The original band that met on Henry Street included such progressive luminaries as Oswald Garrison Villard, editor of the *New York Post* as well as publisher of the *Nation*; Rabbi Stephen Wise, the dean of Reform Judaism in the United States; John Haynes Holmes, a pillar of the Unitarian Church; Hamilton Holt, editor of the *Independent*, an influential weekly magazine; Florence Kelley, head of the National Consumers League, and William Hull, the veteran Quaker author and academic. Nearly all had graduated from an eminent college (Crystal went to Vassar) and came from a comfortable, if not a wealthy, background. Paul Kellogg, editor of the *Survey*, immodestly described the group he helped bring together as composed of the "first men and women of the United States."[55]

Crystal Eastman took over as executive secretary during the fall of 1915. She quickly turned this band of well-connected friends into a sophisticated organization with some political clout. She raised funds to hire a full-time lobbyist in Washington, Charles T. Hallinan, a former publicist for woman suffrage, and set up small but active chapters in twenty-one other cities. She published literature that featured speeches and statements by prominent foes of war in Congress like Claude Kitchin. She secured mailing lists as well as favorable coverage in some of the most widely read progressive periodicals—and not just those edited by founders of her group. Bryan's *Commoner* and *La Follette's Magazine* each reached tens of thousands of readers west of the Mississippi and had an impact on politicians from that vast region, few of whose rural and small-town constituents read magazines published in the concrete canyons of Gotham. She also encouraged radicals such as James Maurer, the Socialist who headed the Pennsylvania Federation of Labor, to take part. But the AUAM remained primarily a New York City operation, with six salaried staff members by the spring of 1916. The primary aim of Eastman's little dynamo of publicity and strategy was to counter the paladins of preparedness.[56]

To that end, the AUAM was careful not to break off its relationship with Woodrow Wilson, the one American whose views on war and peace mattered more than any other, even as they worked to defeat the president's plan to expand the military. Key members of the union had ardently supported Wilson's candidacy in 1912; Stephen Wise had even considered him a "philosopher king." William Hull, as a graduate student at Johns Hopkins, had heard him lecture. It is not true that "the anti-militarists trusted Wilson and regarded him as their leader," as one historian put it. In fact, the AUAM frequently criticized the president for betraying his peaceful rhetoric and urged its allies in Congress to vote against his plans for rearmament. Still, through the end of 1916, they continued to believe that goodwill and gentle pressure could keep the president from forsaking the neutral path. By meeting with AUAM leaders, individually or as a group, he encouraged them to believe that.[57]

But in Eastman's other position, at the helm of the largest local branch of the Woman's Peace Party, she felt freer to express the radical pacifism that truly inspired her. The aim of the national party, printed on its membership card, was "to arouse the nations to respect the sacredness of human life and to devise means other than war for settling international disputes." But its constitution allowed every branch to advance that end in its own way. Chapters in more conservative places like New England and California mainly distributed literature produced by the party's national headquarters in Chicago and lobbied their local representatives in Congress not to spend any funds on "war preparation."

While Eastman's branch offered free lectures on "America's Future Foreign Policy" by such prominent liberals as Norman Angell and Hamilton

Holt, she and her fellow modernist rebels were not content with such peda-
gogical fare. They organized protests at the New York state legislature when
it voted to require boys aged sixteen to nineteen to undergo several weeks
of military training. The Woman's Peace Party also advised parents not to
allow their sons to join the Boy Scouts, alleging that its fondness for discipline and uniforms groomed children for war. Local party members also
designed a leaflet featuring an inflammatory cartoon from the Socialist
New York Call; it showed a mother nurturing her baby while a line of older
male children, muskets in hand, ran "Forward to mutilation and death!"[58]

Socialists played as integral a role in the growing anti-preparedness
campaign as did Eastman and her fellow pacifists. From Morris Hillquit's debate with Augustus Gardner in April 1915 to the declaration
of war two years later, few Marxist writers and orators left any doubt
that they would stand firmly by the same principles most of their European comrades had betrayed. That December, Helen Keller, whose fierce
class-consciousness is now largely forgotten, told a cheering Manhattan
crowd of five thousand, "Let no workingman join the army that is to be
organized by order of Congress! . . . No conqueror will take his poverty
from him. No conqueror will beat down his wages or wreck his unions
more ruthlessly than his own fellow citizens of the capitalist class."[59] For
Keller and her comrades, patriotism preached on high was little more
than a smokescreen to hide baser motives of arrogance and greed.

The infamous U-boat attack on May 7 did not shake their convictions at all. "Fellow Citizens," began the Socialist Party's official statement, "the destruction of the *Lusitania* and the killing of hundreds of
non-combatants . . . bring more closely home to us the fiendish savagery
of warfare and should inspire us with stronger determination than ever
to maintain peace and civilization at any cost." The working class "who
pays the awful cost of warfare, without receiving any of its rewards,"
must take the lead in a cause that had suddenly become quite urgent.[60]

Morris Hillquit wrote those words, as he did nearly all the SPA's proclamations on the war, from the outbreak of hostilities in 1914 until the Armistice more than four years later. Why the party so often chose him for these critical tasks is not entirely clear. Weeks after the fighting began, Hillquit had taken the initiative not just to condemn the bloodshed but to sketch out a program of radical democracy and national self-determination on which a just peace could be made. As international secretary, he stayed in touch with Socialists in Europe who had vowed to build a new world together—until they started tearing the existing one apart. His correspondence from those years is sprinkled with letters in German, Russian, and French—all of which he spoke fluently. On occasion, Hillquit's comradely empathy got him into trouble. Before the war, he had been close to several leaders of the Social-Democrats in Germany. His statement that their initial decision to support the Kaiser's government had to be "understood" as a nationalist "impulse," rather than "scolded or praised," was blasted, predictably, by some on the SPA Left as a surrender to "craven chauvinism."[61]

But Hillquit was respected as a judicious spokesman even by those who occasionally disagreed with his views. Before the war, he had positioned himself at the ideological center of the party—between revolutionaries like Big Bill Haywood, who thought mass strikes would bring down the system; and evolutionaries like Victor Berger, who clung to the faith that Socialists would eventually triumph by getting elected to run cities and unions and running them well. Hillquit was able to balance his horror at the continuing war with a conviction that socialism would emerge from the ashes stronger than ever. In the fall of 1915, he predicted that the Russian people, led by radicals, would soon topple the tsarist regime and set up a constitutional government. Perhaps the simple fact that Hillquit was so good at summing up what nearly everyone in his party believed made him the logical choice to do that over and over again.[62]

In January, his stature also gained him a meeting in the White House. Hillquit had composed his party's latest resolution on the war and was chosen, along with Socialist congressman Meyer London and the labor leader James Maurer, to present it to Woodrow Wilson. To make common cause with liberal pacifists, the Socialists had also endorsed Julia Wales's Wisconsin Plan for neutral mediation.

At first, Hillquit recalled, the president "looked preoccupied and tired," but "as we proceeded with our argument he became interested and animated." The four men spoke for about an hour, and Wilson's apparent warmth toward their ideas stunned his guests. He "hinted," wrote Hillquit, that he might take the lead in making "a direct offer of mediation" and made clear that his "sympathies were entirely with us." As the meeting was breaking up, Maurer told Wilson that, whatever his promises, he would probably "succumb" to the influence of those "interests who want the war to continue." Wilson clapped the union leader on the shoulder and smiled. "If the truth be known," he said, "I am more often accused of being influenced by radical and pacifist elements than by the capitalist and militarist interest."[63]

Samuel Gompers was not so amiable toward his fellow champions of the American working class. By the end of 1915, the titular leader of organized labor who had once threatened to organize a general strike against war had become a vigorous champion of both preparedness and an Allied victory. The latter sympathy was due, in part, to his affection for the England where he had spent his childhood; the former stemmed largely from his assumption that labor would benefit, in jobs and political goodwill, from helping the nation rearm instead of opposing it.

Having made his choice, Gompers was determined to repel attempts by Socialists and other leftists to get the AFL to stick to its anti-militarist tradition. This put him at odds with two of the AFL's largest affiliates, the United Mine Workers (UMW) and the International Ladies' Garment Workers' Union (ILGWU), as well as with a number of municipal labor councils whose politically active leaders sought to represent the thinking of wage earners in their cities. European immigrants and their children made up a large proportion of the membership of both the UMW and ILGWU; so the notion that they should be ready to fight and die for their new homeland met with a good deal of skepticism.

In January 1916, the *United Mine Workers Journal* ran a cartoon in its Italian-language edition portraying a laborer, pick resting on his shoulder, pointing out to Uncle Sam a cemetery filled with the bodies of the thousands of workers who had died *"per la patria"* in mining disasters.[64]

That same month, Gompers claimed, in a lengthy Washington, D.C., address, that most American workers did support building a larger army and navy—as long as those forces were "democratically organized, democratically officered, and under the control of heads who are responsible to the citizens of the land." Such popular control, Gompers believed, would ensure that preparedness would be "something very different from militarism or navalism." He chided American Socialists for letting the "more violent pacifists" among them call the party's tune.

The AFL president made these remarks to the National Civic Federation, a group he knew every good Socialist abhorred. Founded by such industrialists as Mark Hanna and Andrew Carnegie, the NCF viewed collective bargaining with "pure-and-simple" unions as the best way to stifle the Marxist left. Its director, Ralph Easley, was both a staunch Republican and a booster of preparedness.[65]

Gompers had no illusions about how sharply his stand on this issue had divided his federation. The previous November, delegates to the AFL's annual convention in San Francisco had quarreled bitterly over a tough resolution introduced by Adolph Germer, a prominent Socialist active in the Illinois UMW. It "call[ed] upon all workers to desist from affiliating with any branch of the military forces" and condemned the distribution of "military propaganda" in public schools. The convention chairman, a Gompers ally, tried to squelch the resolution without a discussion. But Germer demanded the floor and, "amid frequent applause," inveighed against rich munitions makers and the notion that children should be taught "to snuff out human life." The debate continued, with what one reporter called "considerable oratorical fireworks" on both sides.[66]

Finally, Gompers decided he had to join the fray. "I am a pacifist," he declared, disingenuously. But since that faith "has been shot to pieces" in

Europe, there was no point in espousing it now. After Gompers finished speaking, Germer's resolution was defeated "by a considerable majority." That didn't stop several large AFL affiliates and the labor councils of Seattle, Minneapolis, Cleveland, Chicago, Milwaukee, and other places where Socialists were strong from continuing to resist a pro-war campaign they viewed as the project of a "few millionaires who arm the country." [67]

Yet internal opponents of the AFL leader made little effort to convert their discontent into a robust challenge to his authority. To do that would have sapped energy and resources they needed for the fight against stingy, anti-union employers; it risked blowing up the one institution that, despite its flaws, was doing more to improve the lives of wage-earning men and women than any other. So, apart from the Socialist Party, no national body committed to anti-preparedness would spring from working Americans themselves, no labor equivalent of the AUAM and the Woman's Peace Party. Still, the discontent of many unionists about the nation's course was palpable; even many who endorsed Gompers's position wanted the debate over arming America to continue. [68]

BATTLING MILITARISM ON CAPITOL HILL

In February 1916, the AUAM—then known as the Anti-"Preparedness" Committee—published a thick pamphlet featuring recent statements by seven congressmen who firmly opposed any plan to expand the American military, whether proposed by the president or his Republican rivals. On the cover appeared a cartoon of the Statue of Liberty, wearing a sash proclaiming "NO MILITARISM HERE." The lawmakers, all but one of whom was a Democrat, represented states from Wyoming to Texas to Pennsylvania, both rural districts and urban ones. But they all agreed with the opinion suggested by the image of the lady in green copper who stands watch over New York harbor: the clamor for "preparedness" was endangering the republic they cherished—and the nation could be defended quite easily without it.

Isaac Sherwood, an eighty-year-old Democrat from Toledo who had been a general in the Union Army, asked "why we should squander any more hard-earned tax money . . . to increase idle armies or top-heavy navies." Martin Dies, a representative from east Texas, and Clyde Tavenner, from western Illinois, blamed the war scare on what Dies called "the munitions makers" who "are reaping a harvest of gold out of manufacturing the instruments of death. They know their business is likely to play out when the European war is over, and they are fertilizing American soil with a view to another harvest." To buttress that view, the editors included a cartoon depicting a gathering of wealthy, portly men at an exclusive urban club. Its caption read "The Humble Origin of the Navy League."[69]

The pamphlet began, appropriately, with a statement by Claude Kitchin. The new majority leader of the House was the most prominent opponent of preparedness in Congress—and the only Democratic leader willing to defy the president of his own party on the paramount issue the country faced. That December, he called Wilson's proposal for a Continental Army "the biggest outrage that has ever been proposed to the Congress . . . in this generation and it is fraught with more danger to the republic and its institutions." The congressman had done a careful study of military expenditures in the United States and Europe and could present a case more based on "Facts and Figures" than on rhetoric about "jingoes and war traffickers." It was a short excerpt from a lengthy statement, half-brief and half-manifesto, which he released to the press the previous November, just before the Forty-sixth Congress opened for business.[70]

Most of what Kitchin said echoed Morris Hillquit's arguments in his debate with Augustus Gardner at Carnegie Hall seven months before. The majority leader established that the U.S. Navy—derided by militarists as "a little, puny, eggshell"—was actually larger than that of Germany and was nearing the size of Britain's mighty Royal Navy. The army, while certainly smaller than its European counterparts, was, Kitchin maintained, big enough to resist an invasion, in the quite unlikely event any transoceanic force would attempt one. The congressman also claimed that a bloated military would lead other powers to think the United States was preparing "wars of conquest." Then he departed from the views of the Socialist leader. Unlike Hillquit, Kitchin was concerned about increasing the federal budget and who would pay for it. A big boost in military spending, he feared, would put the federal government deeper into debt or force Congress to pass "an enormous increase of revenue"—at least $200 million, more than one-quarter of the current budget. For a faithful southern Democrat, neither alternative was acceptable.[71]

That Kitchin headlined a pamphlet issued by one of Eastman's organizations signaled how determined both were to block the slow but steady march toward war. The congressman from Scotland Neck and the left-wing feminist from Greenwich Village disagreed about nearly every other burning issue of the day. Kitchin opposed woman suffrage, endorsed prohibition, and, of course, bridled at any talk of weakening Jim Crow laws or restoring the franchise to African Americans in his district or anywhere else in the South. The congressman was a mild supporter of labor unions, but only if they remained lily-white and didn't raise costs for local industries.[72]

But on this overriding issue of arming for war, the Dixie Democrat and the Gotham radical needed one another. With access to major antiwar newspapers and magazines, the AUAM and the Woman's Peace Party could mobilize urban liberals and leftists to press their concerns on Wilson and his cabinet. Kitchin, for his part, was indispensable to gathering and grooming a like-minded bloc of representatives from the president's own party, whose rural and small-town constituents Eastman and her crowd could never reach. "It is true that you will get plenty of ridicule as will all of us who take a common sense stand on this matter," she wrote to Kitchin that fall after he sent her a copy of his statement, "but I feel quite sure that we are going to win."[73]

During the winter of 1916, Eastman had good reason to be confident—although much of the big-city press scorned her movement for favoring "peace at any price." The committees on military affairs in both the House and Senate held extensive hearings about preparedness in January and early February. Pacifists like Addams and Lillian Wald condemned the proposal for a Continental Army, but so did National Guard officials who wanted to preserve a mode of defense they felt had always served the republic well—and that paid their salaries. When Secretary of War Lindley Garrison suggested that the Continental Army would require a draft to fill its ranks, something only Theodore Roosevelt and his circle supported, the idea of the new force became even more unpopular. Just ten days after the hearings began, Joseph Tumulty, the president's secretary and one of his closest advisors, told his boss, "I get it from all sources that there is no enthusiasm on the 'hill' for preparedness, and that the country itself is indifferent because of the apparent inability of the country to grasp the importance of this question." He added, portentously, "Our all is staked upon a successful issue in this matter."[74]

On January 27, to alter public opinion, Wilson embarked on a weeklong speaking tour of thirteen cities in the middle of the Midwest. The president brought along his new wife, Edith, both for companionship and to slake the public's curiosity about the woman he had married just two months before. Everywhere, he spoke passionately, if rather abstractly, about his commitment both to keeping the peace and to preserving the nation's strength and honor at a time when "the world is on fire and there is tinder everywhere . . . and somewhere there may be material which we cannot prevent from bursting into flame." Everywhere, even in the German-American strongholds of Milwaukee and St. Louis, huge crowds turned out to greet the eloquent chief executive they had neither seen nor heard since the 1912 campaign, if then. But it is doubtful that he changed many minds, whether in the crowds or back in Congress. A few days after Wilson returned to the White House, he abandoned the plan for a Continental Army and gladly accepted Garrison's resignation. He appointed as his replacement Newton D. Baker, the progressive mayor of Cleveland. A year before, Baker had belonged to the League to Limit Armaments, precursor of the AUAM; he had recently called war "an anachronism" and soldiers "leftovers from the barbaric past."[75]

Democratic opposition in the House of Representatives was largely responsible for Wilson's retreat. A group of at least thirty congressmen stood firmly behind Kitchin; nearly all hailed from either the South or the Midwest. While they made up only about a seventh of the party's delegation in the House, no Democratic faction had yet emerged to oppose their consistent stand. The influence of the anti-preparedness caucus was also enhanced by the fact that several of its members sat on the Military Affairs Committee. What's more, it included many of the leading proponents in Congress of such measures as agricultural subsidies, stricter anti-trust laws, and a more progressive income tax—all of which the president favored. Thus Democrats who endorsed a stronger military had to explain why they were siding with a cause popularly identified with J.P. Morgan and other symbols of the "big money" whom, during election campaigns, they roundly condemned.

Kitchin's group also enjoyed the robust backing of the only Democrat with a national following that came close to rivaling the president's. William Jennings Bryan may have abandoned his hopes for the presidency, but he still enjoyed the esteem of millions of Americans who had three times voted to put him in the White House and still trusted him to take a moral, Christian stand on any vital issue of politics or religion. Since resigning from the cabinet in June 1915, Bryan had spoken all over the country against taking any steps that could embroil his nation in the "causeless" conflict destroying Europe. "The world has gone mad," Bryan told a throng of one hundred thousand at the San Francisco World's Fair that summer. "They need a flag that speaks the sentiment of the human heart, a flag that looks toward better things than war."[76]

In this new campaign, the man his followers dubbed the Great Commoner became Kitchin's most valuable, if informal, aide. They corresponded frequently during the late fall and winter of 1915–1916, sharing their mutual admiration and their growing dismay that Wilson might be pushing for "a bigger army and navy in order that he may go into this war." They also co-authored a pamphlet, "Do You Advocate Peace or

War: What the Preparedness Program Means." Bryan told Crystal Eastman's Anti-"Preparedness" Committee how "very much pleased" he was
with their efforts. At least one fan of both men urged Kitchin to challenge
Wilson for the 1916 presidential nomination. "With Bryan's personal
support, the pacifists and Socialists . . . and the German-Americans,"
wrote a college student from Seattle, "you can put up a great fight."[77]

Kitchin's partnership with Bryan insured that a sizable number of
Democrats in Congress would hesitate before deciding to oppose the
former leader of their party, one still respected by many of their constituents, as well as the man they had recently elected to command their
shrunken House majority. Kitchin was no doubt exaggerating when he
told a correspondent in November that "four-fifths" of his party's caucus "are at heart opposed" to the build-up Wilson proposed. But their
agonized ambivalence was real.

Most Republican politicians had little regard for Bryan himself, but a vocal
cohort in the GOP led by Robert La Follette did share his hostility to both
big business and war. La Follette, who was born in 1855, held no leadership position among the forty Republican senators in the Sixty-fourth
Congress. But on preparedness, a cohort of fellow Midwesterners and a
few lawmakers from the Pacific Coast nearly always followed his rhetorical cues. When Senator William Kenyon of Iowa said he could hear the
"jingle of the bloody dollar" whenever militarists spoke, he sounded much
like his friend and colleague from Wisconsin, who accused "a world-wide
organization" he didn't name for "stimulating and fomenting discord in
order that it may make profit out of the furnishing of munitions of war."
Republicans from North Dakota, Nebraska, Oregon, and several other
trans-Mississippi states echoed that invective too. These anti-preparedness
Republicans were not "isolationists." Before 1917, no group of senators,
wrote one historian "were as consistent in the call for American entry into
a postwar international organization as the Middle Border progressives."[78]

La Follette, their unofficial leader, viewed politics as an occasion to wage combat with words. He stood at just five feet and five inches tall. But to compensate for his size, he practically strutted when he walked, his thick hair brushed upward and his chest puffed out. More than modest height caused La Follette's insecurity. His father, who built the crude log house in central Wisconsin where he was born, died when Bob was barely eight months old, leaving no image of himself behind. A strict stepfather failed to take the emotional place of the unknown but cherished patriarch.

Unlike Claude Kitchin, La Follette made a name for himself by defying the leaders of his own party. As governor of Wisconsin from 1901 to 1906, "Fighting Bob" had forced the GOP establishment and state businesses alike to swallow a number of reforms, including a direct primary, a ban on child labor, and firm restrictions on lobbying. Then, as a U.S. senator, he earned the enmity of conservative Republicans and of President Roosevelt by filibustering a major currency bill and voting as much with the Democratic minority as with the ruling GOP. Two years later, he began campaigning for the presidency against both the incumbent, William Howard Taft, and Roosevelt, who hungered after his old job.

To those who denounced La Follette as a radical, he responded, "I have always believed that anything that was worth fighting for involved a principle, and I insist on *going far enough to establish that principle* and to give it a fair trial. I believe in going forward a step at a time, but it must be a *full step.*" In service to conviction and to his own ego, he became one of the most celebrated orators of his day, performing as often as possible inside the Senate chamber and in halls and on Chautauqua platforms all over the land. La Follette peppered his lengthy speeches with statistics, literary metaphors, vivid portraits of men both good and evil, and a surfeit of melodramatic, if sometimes eloquent, phrases.[79]

The issues on which he stepped forward, always pugnaciously, included several that few of his counterparts in either major party were ready to endorse. La Follette, whose father had been an abolitionist, opposed all Jim Crow laws and practices, in the North as well as the South. He also campaigned for woman suffrage years before either major party took that stand and believed so strongly in organized labor that he called a federal ban on unions for postal workers a violation of their constitutional rights. Lincoln Steffens, the muckraking journalist, admired La Follette and helped build his national renown. But he knew that the politician was only comfortable when he was living up to his combative image. "He made an issue," wrote Steffens about one fight in his subject's career; "LaFollette always has an issue."[80]

Belle Case La Follette was moved by the same political passions as her husband and could be an equally aggressive advocate for them. On her wedding day in 1881, she insisted that the word "obey" be scrubbed from her marriage vows. Although hampered by shyness, she developed into an effective orator and became the co-editor in all but name of *La Follette's Magazine*, the family's popular monthly, while privately criticizing her husband for lavishing so much of their income on the unprofitable enterprise. Belle was also active in the peace movement, before Bob himself had committed to the cause. "Except John Adams with his Abigail, no man in public life was to have so equal a mate," remarked Belle's son-in-law.[81]

Since opinion polling did not yet exist, it is impossible to know how many Americans agreed that preparedness to keep the country at peace really meant equipping it for war. The *Literary Digest's* surveys of editorial opinion were the only gauges of national thinking available. In mid-March 1916, the periodical asked five hundred editors drawn from every state to share their views on how large the army and navy should be and "whether there is reason to fear the peril of militarism" if both branches grew substantially.

Although the *Digest* referred to a "babel of opinions about preparedness" being "heard in the land," the published results confirmed the peace movement's charge that the press was not on its side. While only newspapers on the Atlantic Coast favored a regular army close to the size of those in the larger European countries, a majority of the editors endorsed a navy "as large as any in the world." Most feared an unprepared nation more than one armed and ready for war. "As the greatest nation the world has ever produced," declared the *Biloxi Herald*, "we prefer going down as a Republic in the hands of American militarists than being wiped off the globe by overseas culture."[82]

Such cynical militancy repelled most of the Americans who wrote to Claude Kitchin about the war. As Congress debated preparedness legislation at the end of 1915 and the first half of 1916, thousands of citizens, in and out of political office, wrote to inform its best-known opponent in the House of their sorrow and anger at Wilson's stance and their admiration for what one Texas attorney called Kitchin's "great leadership in this world crisis." Some letters included petitions filled with names of fellow townspeople, church members, and co-workers; others reported that nearly everyone they knew or met agreed with what the congressman was saying and doing. From the tiny town of Bristol, West Virginia, F.E. Davis wrote that he had learned, during a "trip of eighteen hundred miles and return among the Farmers of five states," that Kitchin "was by far the most poplar [sic] man in America to day."[83]

The bulk of the supportive letters to Kitchin echoed, often in colorful ways, the same criticism of munitions producers voiced under the Capitol dome and anywhere in the country where the peace movement was active. H.Q. Alexander, president of the North Carolina division of the National Farmers Union, blamed "the sordidly selfish" industries and their pet politicians who would "add millions of unrighteous wealth to the already bursting coffers of the few rich men who rule over us." Wilson's support for those "big criminal parasites who manufacture murder machines," wrote D.G. Gibson of Muskogee, Oklahoma, was "perfectly outrageous, absolutely uncalled for and unreasonable." These denizens of white, agrarian America may not have shared the pacifist ideals of Jane Addams and Crystal Eastman or believed Henry Ford's quixotic venture could somehow stop the war. But their shared mistrust of "the interests" had clearly weakened whatever faith they may have had in the institution of the U.S. military which that "parasitic" elite hoped to swell.[84]

Kitchin also received a good many supportive messages from Americans who were quite unlike his own rural constituents. William Dodd, a noted southern historian at the University of Chicago (and a future U.S. ambassador to Hitler's Germany), wrote about his efforts to stop his students from having to undergo military training. A letter penned by one of Kitchin's rare "colored" correspondents hailed "your manhood in taking the solid stand you have." An anonymous wit, referring to what was both the letter writer's and the president's alma mater, sent a postcard that read simply: "Princeton '79 has gone crazy. Stop him. Princeton '85." A smattering of Democratic correspondents did object to Kitchin's stance, often warning him not to divide his party and betray its leader. "If we don't get thru a sane, moderate program under Wilson," worried an employee of the Labor Department, "the party goes on the rocks and we'll get an insane program under some brass-tin-potting Republican."[85]

Whether critics or admirers, most people who wrote to Kitchin were comfortably articulate, used correct grammar and spelling, and identified themselves as either a professional, a businessman, a government employee, or the female relative of a man with such a career. But on occasion, a note arrived at his office from the other America—the poorly educated, manual-laboring majority. "More than 90% of the peopl [sic] uphold your view," wrote H.A. Davis from the Appalachian hamlet of Sands, North Carolina, "hoping you will never yield your point." He added a postscript: "I hope you will excuse my pencil, as 76 years hard farm labor has made my hands too unsteady to use pen."[86]

The anti-preparedness cause also enjoyed a good deal of support from the kind of men whom millions of Americans routinely turned to for spiritual and moral guidance. "We, Ministers of the Churches in the

United States," began a petition to Congress and the president circulated by the ecumenical Federal Council of Churches in February and March of 1916, "view with painful solicitude the organized and determined efforts to stampede the nation . . . into increased and extravagant expenditures for ships and guns, and desire to place upon record our earnest objection to the committing our nation to a policy of so-called preparedness for which Europe is paying an awful price."

Ten thousand Protestant clergymen and a much smaller number of rabbis received a postcard printed with the text of the anguished statement; at least thirty-six hundred signed it. Most who did pastored a congregation somewhere along the urban industrial corridor that stretched from Boston to Chicago, the most theologically liberal region in the country. That demography contrasted markedly with the largely rural constituencies of Kitchin's anti-war faction in Congress, underscoring the breadth of the resistance to arming America.[87]

That so many added their names to the federation's petition was not surprising. Its language sprang from the Social Gospel, the worldly creed espoused by preachers from nearly all the major Protestant denominations, as well as notable laypersons like Addams and Bryan. Serving Christ, they all believed, meant applying his gospel of compassion to the secular evils of poverty, the exploitation of labor, and war. As four New Jerseyans told Kitchin, to prepare to kill one's potential enemies betrayed "good Christian principles." If politicians aspired to be blessed, they should become peacemakers and work with other governments to construct what the petition called "a plan of international organization which shall render the recurrence of the present world tragedy impossible."[88]

Of course, in Protestant pulpits, pacifism was far from a universal faith. The sinking of the Lusitania had driven many a minister who sympathized with Britain to view Imperial Germany as a Moloch slaughtering innocents in its mad lust to dominate the globe. "If it were in my power, I would place a gun in the hands of every man, woman and child" in the Allied countries, the Episcopal archdeacon of Arkansas told Walter Rauschenbusch, a Baptist pastor and leading theologian of the Social Gospel, in September 1915. Then "Germany might be taught the lesson that she cannot defy and ignore the Christian sentiment of the world." In New York, critics of "peace at any price" circulated their own petitions among local ministers and reported that most either advocated expanding the military or believed they should devote themselves to "earnest prayer and spiritual counsel . . . abstaining from profitless addresses to the government." They also took heart in knowing that the president was an earnestly pious man who routinely invoked the Almighty when speaking about the role the United States ought to play in the world.[89]

None of these dueling petitioners seem to have solicited the backing of clerics from the nation's largest Christian denomination. Even the most theologically liberal Protestants were not yet ecumenical enough to make common cause with bishops and priests from the Roman Catholic Church.

In fact, American Catholics were engaged in their own fierce disputes about the war. These conflicts, like the sharpest divisions within the U.S. Church itself, were fought out largely along ethnic lines. Polish Catholics prayed that vanquishing the Kaiser's army would make possible, for the first time since 1795, an independent homeland for their embattled compatriots. Most German Catholics naturally sympathized with those fighting and dying for their erstwhile fatherland. But hardly any individuals from these groups participated in national organizations like the AUAM and National Security League that either opposed or favored a big increase in U.S. forces. One suspects their identity as doubly "hyphenated Americans"—whether they embraced or rejected it—proved too great a barrier to overcome.

In addition, most Irish Catholics were too preoccupied with their own internal quarrel to have time to devote to more inclusive campaigns. Nationalists who burned to liberate the Ould Sod from British rule aggressively campaigned to recruit other Hibernian-Americans to their cause. A minority of these activists openly sympathized with Germany and Austria-Hungary; nearly all condemned preparedness as a conspiracy to aid Great Britain. But other Irish-Americans dominated the hierarchy of the Church and edited nearly all its widely circulated diocesan newspapers; as clerics, they were reluctant to take a stand that Catholics from other ethnic backgrounds would surely resent and that might antagonize both the president and the many pro-British lawmakers in Congress.[90]

In early March 1916, an Irish Race Convention held at the George M. Cohan Theatre in Times Square brought this disunity to a head. Nearly two thousand delegates from various nationalist societies cheered speech after speech damning England as a "citadel of tyranny" and calling on the United States to stop aiding it by either word or deed. A few speakers openly advocated a German victory; every Irish-American, announced Jeremiah O'Leary, head of the American Truth Society, should stand up when "The Watch on the Rhine," Germany's patriotic anthem, was played. The conventioneers founded a new umbrella group, Friends of Irish Freedom. By 1920, at the height of the war for independence, it would boast a membership of more than one hundred thousand.[91]

But not a single Catholic bishop or prominent Irish-American politician attended the two-day meeting in 1916, and most official Church periodicals ignored it. Before the war, John Ireland, the archbishop of Saint Paul, Minnesota, and a leader of those who wanted to modernize the teachings of the American Church, had written that "next to God is country, and next to religion is patriotism. . . . I would have Catholics be the first patriots of the land." Early that May, like nearly every Irishman and -woman in the United States, he was infuriated when the British tried and executed sixteen leaders of the Easter Rising, the romantic disaster which "was the foundation of Irish freedom." But that infamous act of imperial vengeance persuaded neither the archbishop nor his fellow hierarchs to risk losing the political influence they had gained in both major parties and among Anglophiles like Theodore Roosevelt and the president himself.[92]

WILSON IN COMMAND?

As Congress wrangled over the merits of preparedness, the issue that had inflamed that debate in the first place had never been resolved. After a brief period of restraint, U-boats were once again planning to sink merchant ships flying the flags of enemy nations without giving any warning or making an attempt to rescue their passengers and crew. The Kaiser's government pointed out that most of these vessels were equipped with cannons powerful enough to sink a submarine. Thus, under the rules of naval warfare, a U-boat commander had a right to protect himself and his men by shooting first. Having done nothing since the *Lusitania* went down but dispatch stern notes of protest to Germany, Woodrow Wilson had kept his administration ensnared in the same dilemma: how to maintain neutrality while allowing U.S. citizens to sail across the perilous Atlantic on British ships.

In January, Secretary of State Robert Lansing came up with what seemed a clever solution to the problem. He drafted a modus vivendi under which the Germans would cease attacking enemy merchant vessels if Allied commanders removed all weaponry from their ships. At first, the president hailed the idea. Not only would it quiet lawmakers who, led by figures like Kitchin and La Follette, feared the United States would stumble into the war if another ship went down with a large number of Americans abroad. The plan might even, Wilson told Colonel House, work to Britain's advantage: "Germany is seeking to find an excuse to throw off all restraints in under-sea warfare. . . . If the English will disarm their merchant ships she will be without excuse and the English will have made a capital stroke against her."[93]

But on February 15, after conferring with Wilson, Lansing abruptly withdrew his proposal. Sensible or not, amid the deep mistrust endemic to total war, neither side was willing to accept it. A few days earlier, the Kaiser's government had announced that "enemy merchantmen carrying guns" would be "regarded as warships." At the same time, the British made clear to House, who was then in London negotiating with Foreign Secretary Edward Grey, that the modus vivendi would endanger their supremacy on the Atlantic. If the American president wanted to keep alive his dream of mediating an end to the Great War, he would have to abandon a scheme that pleased none of the belligerent powers.

Lansing then announced a new U.S. position in a statement that was a classic of tortured ambiguity. The secretary explained that, in the fog of naval warfare, it was quite difficult to tell whether a merchant ship was using its arms for offensive or defensive purposes. Therefore, the United States would not necessarily lodge a protest if a U-boat sank an armed vessel. It would depend on the facts in each case. Meanwhile, the administration would refuse to warn U.S. citizens not to travel on armed ships. "In other words," Arthur Link summed up Wilson's true intent, "the American government would do its best to avoid controversy with either side."[94]

That did not, however, succeed in calming the large peace contingent in Congress. "The President is anxious for war with Germany—his sympathies are so strong with the Allies," Claude Kitchin wrote to an advisor. Bryan made the same charge in a letter to his good friend Josephus Daniels, the secretary of the navy. For the moment at least, the administration's confusing turnaround on the question of armed merchant ships had put the majority leader and the Great Commoner in sync with most lawmakers in both chambers and from both parties. They rushed to act before another U-boat sank another British liner with large numbers of Americans aboard.[95]

The House and Senate quickly rallied behind resolutions designed to make such a calamity unlikely, if not impossible. On February 17, Representative Jefferson McLemore, a freshman Democrat from Texas who had once been a cowboy and a gold miner, introduced a measure asking the president to warn citizens not to travel on armed vessels. In the upper chamber, Thomas P. Gore, a blind former Populist from Oklahoma, gathered support for a stronger bill that would have denied a passport to any American who wanted to book passage on a belligerent nation's ship or on *any* vessel, including a U.S. ship, that carried munitions. Both men were keen admirers of Bryan and close allies of Kitchin.

In a clear sign of how most members of Congress were thinking, William Stone, the chairman of the Senate Foreign Relations Committee who had always followed the president's lead before, endorsed Gore's bill. Citizens "who ventured forth on belligerent ships into war zones," Stone declared, "are committing a crime against the government whose protection they seek."[96]

Woodrow Wilson acted just as swiftly to block this attempt to force his diplomatic hand. On February 21, he invited Stone and other Democratic leaders to the White House to demand that they scuttle the Gore and McLemore bills. Kitchin, unaccountably, was not there. Wilson made his policy clear: The British could keep arming their ships, and the Germans should be careful not to torpedo them. "Mr. President," Stone shot back, "would you draw a shutter over my eyes and my intellect? You have no right to ask me to follow such a course." Early in the morning of February 25, Kitchin did show up at the Executive Mansion, along with Speaker Champ Clark and the chair of the House Foreign Affairs Committee. Clark told Wilson that, if a vote were held on the McLemore resolution, it would pass by a margin of at least two to one. The president refused to back down. If a U-boat sank a merchant ship with Americans on board, "I believe we should sever diplomatic relations," he said—even if that led to war.[97]

Wilson was betting that the leaders of his party would, in the end, shrink from defying his authority over a decision of such consequence. He won that bet. The president had Lansing tell the press that Americans should travel only on merchant ships armed for defense; he did promise to keep talking to the Germans about the issue and reassured Senator Stone that "I shall do everything in my power to keep the United States out of war." Sensing that the mood of Congress was shifting, Wilson asked for a vote to table both the McLemore and the Gore resolutions. During the first week of March, they agreed, by overwhelming margins.[98]

Yet the surrender to the president's will changed few minds about his policy. Most Democrats clearly voted to table the bills to avoid embarrassing and undermining their leader. Lawmakers from the other major party felt freer to vote their consciences—or fears. After seven hours of heated debate in the House, a majority of Republicans, the bulk from the Midwest, voted against tabling the McLemore resolution. One of them was the minority leader, James R. Mann of Illinois, who snapped that Americans should "never be put to the test of having to fight because some fool has involved us by entering upon a joy ride."[99]

Robert La Follette decided this turn of events called for a strong and principled protest. Although the fight for the Gore resolution in the upper chamber was lost, he could still express the discomfort of many progressives in both parties at what they viewed as the White House's high-handed behavior. On March 10, a packed Senate gallery heard La Follette denounce the president for "demanding that Congress keep silent in all that pertains to foreign affairs." Wilson's refusal to even consider a travel ban, La Follette pointed out, contradicted his administration's earlier policy: In the fall of 1914, the State Department had refused to issue passports to Americans who wanted to visit belligerent nations "merely for pleasure." Because the Constitution "gave the war power exclusively to Congress," La Follette asserted that he and his fellow lawmakers had both a legal duty and a public trust to press their views on any decision that could jeopardize neutrality. Sadly, he concluded, "Congress betrayed its trust when it dodged the issue raised by the President. It will be forced to meet the issue ultimately." He never uttered a more prophetic remark.[100]

Other prominent opponents of Wilson's policy did not share La Follette's gloomy outlook. Claude Kitchin told Crystal Eastman that "nothing on earth could coerce Congress" to go to war over the issue of armed merchant ships, despite its reluctance to defy the White House's wishes. Bryan remained "confident that the jingoes can not drive us into war." Johann von Bernstorff, Germany's politically shrewd ambassador to the United States, cabled his superiors in Berlin that Wilson had scored only a "Pyrrhic victory." "There is no doubt," he wrote, "that the majority in both Houses is, even today, of the opinion that Americans should be kept off armed merchant ships." The president had prevailed only by promising "he would do all that he possibly could to avoid a war with Germany."[101]

Two weeks after Congress obeyed his wishes, Wilson was given an excellent opportunity to fulfill that promise. On March 24, a German submarine launched a torpedo into the hull of the *Sussex*, an unarmed Franco-British passenger ship, as it crossed the English Channel. The vessel did not sink, but the blast injured four Americans on board and killed eighty other passengers. The U-boat commander had ordered the attack because he believed the *Sussex* was laying mines. As soon as he saw "the bridge [was] covered with people," he knew he had made an awful mistake.[102]

The president decided to use this fatal error to force the Germans to abandon their new policy of sinking merchant ships without warning. Although he rebuffed the advice of House and Lansing to immediately sever diplomatic relations with Berlin, Wilson came close to threatening war. If the Germans did not stop killing civilians on the high seas, the somber president told a joint session of Congress on April 19, open conflict might be the only moral option. Convinced as ever of his righteousness, he intoned: "We cannot forget that we are . . . by the force of circumstances the responsible spokesmen of the rights of humanity, and that we cannot remain silent while those rights seem in process of being swept utterly away by the maelstrom of this terrible war."[103] Inspired by his words and incensed by the attack on a humble Channel steamer, most members of Congress and nearly every major newspaper echoed Wilson's resolve.

Some anti-militarists, both elected and unelected, directed their outrage more at the president and his supporters than at the Germans.

William Kenyon, the Iowa Republican, proposed that anyone who wanted to travel on an armed belligerent ship should first enlist in the military. Bryan wailed that joining the Allies would be a "crime against civilization." Hillquit charged that Wilson was exploiting the attack on the *Sussex* to aid his chances for reelection. But no lawmakers or activist group mounted a concerted campaign of opposition. The anti-militarists may have feared their campaign against preparedness would be endangered if they appeared to be undermining the president at the zenith of international tension. Or perhaps they thought Wilson was bluffing when he suggested that war was imminent.[104]

In the end, the Germans backed down. On May 4, after a bitter internal dispute between civilian and military leaders, Foreign Secretary Gottlieb von Jagow released a note pledging that U-boats would henceforth be careful to warn unarmed civilian ships before attacking them and would make every effort, as required under international law, to rescue the crew and passengers. In effect, Lansing had secured one side's agreement to his modus vivendi without compelling the British and French to reciprocate.

In truth, the Germans had little choice. In northern France, half the Kaiser's men thrown into the months-long battle of Verdun were killed or wounded. And his navy did not have enough submarines to attack most of the transatlantic commerce that kept flowing to the Allies. "We really have enough enemies," acknowledged a semi-official German paper from Cologne. "We must, therefore, avoid difficulties which might bring about war with America and leave responsibility for such a catastrophe to President Wilson, if he wants it."[105] Thus, one full year after the sinking of the *Lusitania* had awakened Americans to the possibility that they might be forced into history's biggest war, the chances of that occurring had suddenly diminished. The anti-war coalition had, with Wilson's help, won a temporary victory.

On May 8, a rather extraordinary meeting took place inside the Oval Office. A dozen leaders of the American Union Against Militarism came to probe exactly how the president felt about preparing the nation for war and to convince him to turn decisively toward peace. Lillian Wald led the delegation, which included Crystal Eastman and her brother Max, Paul Kellogg, Rabbi Stephen Wise, the Social Gospel minister A.A. Berle., and Amos Pinchot—the wealthy progressive who had, until recently, been one of Wilson's most fervent supporters. John Aldus McSparran, master of the Pennsylvania State Grange who had recently retired from a farming life, came along to show that the resistance movement stretched beyond the world of the urban Left.[106]

During the previous month, while Wilson was embroiled with the *Sussex* crisis, the AUAM had been holding large and boisterous meetings around the nation to disseminate "the truth about preparedness" and the need to counter militarism with pacifist democracy. From Manhattan to Buffalo and then to ten cities in the Midwest, several of which Wilson had visited on his own tour that winter, big crowds representing "all factors of the population" came to hear congressmen and left-wing ministers, labor leaders and settlement house workers warn against emulating the bloody nations of Europe and stand up for "the things essential to a world of love and order and law," as Lillian Wald put it.[107]

The president began the White House meeting by asking his visitors to tell him what they had said and learned on their tour. Soon they were engaged in an emotional discussion about the meaning of "preparedness" and whether an America ready to fight could preserve the "moral power" they all agreed was its most precious asset. Wald insisted the United States could not help make peace in Europe if "we" didn't go into it "with our hands clean, with our hands undefiled." Wilson countered that he had "never dreamed for a moment that America . . . had got any military enthusiasm or any militaristic spirit." "Reasonable preparation," he stressed, was not the same as militarism. He pointed to the Second Amendment as clear evidence that "it is not inconsistent with American traditions that everybody should know how to shoot and take care of himself."[108]

Wilson gave a masterful performance. Repeatedly, the president hinted he was exasperated with real militarists like those in the Navy League, who had always been the AUAM's primary target. Would he acknowledge, asked Wald, that "there is obviously an attempt to stampede the country" to make the U.S. military second to none? "Yes," replied the president, "but it is not working." He also declared his desire to "check" what Amos Pinchot called the "tremendously aggressive spirit" fostered by big corporations with an "international arrangement" to secure the peace.[109]

No one in the delegation doubted Wilson's good intentions, even though he refused to back away either from his desire for a larger military or even from the possibility that he might, in the future, endorse "universal compulsory training" for young men. Most AUAM leaders came away feeling that the man in the White House might yet be won over to their point of view. Crystal Eastman neither spoke at the meeting nor recorded her impressions of it. But her brother's report in the *Masses* glowed with a sympathy for the president sharply at odds with his magazine's usual disgust for the leaders of the plutocratic state. "We all liked him," wrote Max Eastman, "and we all sincerely believed that he sincerely believes he is anti-militarist."[110]

So at the end of a year of impressive feats of organizing and intense conflicts over policy, the anti-warriors were more hopeful than they had been at its start. "All the world is seeing red," Wilson told his visitors from the AUAM. "No standard we have ever had obtains any longer." Still, the anti-militarists were confident that most Americans wanted to keep their heads as millions of Europeans were losing theirs, figuratively and literally. Aided by a determined caucus of lawmakers, they had managed to stop Congress from expanding the armed forces as either Theodore Roosevelt or his adversary in the White House desired. And they had put together an agitational campaign whose arguments— both practical and visionary—seemed convincing to a cross section of Americans who had no yearning to join the Allied cause.

The escalating combat in the Great War proved a splendid argument for caution. In 1916, the belligerents fought two long and epic battles on the Western Front whose names—Verdun and the Somme—remain symbols of tactical stalemate and useless slaughter a century later. One of the casualties at the Somme was Corporal Adolf Hitler of the Sixteenth Bavarian Reserve Infantry Regiment, wounded in the leg by an artillery shell. During his convalescence near Berlin, Hitler was appalled by striking munitions workers he regarded as "cowards and traitors."[111]

That spring, for the first time in its history, Great Britain began conscription; it was the last of the warring nations in Europe to acknowledge that patriotism alone could not persuade enough men to replace those who had fallen. In Verdun, the fighting that cost more than seventy thousand casualties per month was reducing the landscape in that once sylvan countryside of northern France to a netherworld of mud, corpses, and splintered wood. "Humanity is mad," a French lieutenant scrawled in his diary that May. "It must be mad to do what it is doing. What a massacre! What scenes of horror and carnage! I cannot find words to translate my impressions. Hell cannot be so terrible. Men are mad!"[112]

The Americans who shared his dismay believed they could keep their government from hurling the nation into that inferno. Over the next year, they even hoped they might be able to nudge their ideal of a cooperative and peaceful world order a bit closer to reality. That winter, Max Eastman wrote, "Let men but understand themselves, and the mechanism of their emotions by which they are brought into this perennial catastrophe, and they will be ready enough in the sober intervals to take gigantic measures to prevent it."[113]

THREE

KEEP US OUT

June 1916 to January 1917

"We commend to the American people the splendid diplomatic victories of our great President, who has preserved the vital interests of our Government and its citizens, and kept us out of war."

—Platform of the Democratic Party, June 1916[1]

"We should face the new year, not so much in the mood of defeated reformers doggedly pressing on, as in the mood of fighters who have held their ground and even made a little headway against increasing odds."

—Crystal Eastman to the members of the American Union Against Militarism, October 1916[2]

"It is in your power to bring the war to an end by a just peace. . . . It is not too late to save European civilization from destruction; but it may be too late if the war is allowed to continue for the further two or three years with which our militarists threaten us."

—Bertrand Russell to Woodrow Wilson, December 1916[3]

A SEASON OF HOPE AND FRUSTRATION

The 1916 Democratic National Convention in St. Louis could almost have been mistaken for an enthusiastic gathering of anti-war activists, albeit one held in a hall decorated entirely in patriotic bunting. On the morning of June 14, Martin H. Glynn, a former governor of New York, delivered the keynote address. It was, he declared, a "self-evident truth" that the United States should aid neither the Allies nor the Central Powers: "The policy of neutrality is as truly American as the American flag." The throng of fifteen thousand roared as Glynn recited the multiple occasions when presidents from Jefferson to Lincoln to Wilson had resolved disputes with foreign nations through patient diplomacy instead of by rashly taking up arms against them. After each example, the crowd chanted spontaneously, "What did we do? What did we do?" And Glynn responded, "We didn't go to war." William Jennings Bryan, attending the convention as a journalist, wept as he listened.

The next morning, delegates and spectators were eager for a repeat of the performance. This time it was Senator Ollie James of Kentucky, chairman of the convention, who brought them to their feet, yelling in approval when he praised Woodrow Wilson for asserting the nation's will against Germany "without orphaning a single American child . . . without firing a single gun, without the shedding of a single drop of blood." Who, James asked, "would have our President exchange places with the blood-spattered monarchs of the Old World?"

At the start of the evening session, the delegates clamored for Bryan to speak, although the three-time nominee who had resigned from the cabinet in protest just a year before did not appear on the official schedule. But the Great Commoner had no trouble delivering the kind of sweeping, prophetic oration drenched in biblical references that had made him famous: "Today Christ and Pilate stand again face to face, and Force and Love are again striving for mastery and dominance." The Golden Rule, "the moral code that governs individuals," should, he sermonized, also guide America's policy abroad. Forty times, his short speech was interrupted with applause. When Bryan finished, every delegate stood in line to shake his hand.[4]

Yet, at almost the same hour that the Democrats in St. Louis were cheering Martin Glynn's praise of Wilson the peacemaker, the president himself was marching down Pennsylvania Avenue in a huge preparedness parade, carrying a large American flag made of silk. He fell in step with the other sixty thousand marchers, among whom were hundreds of veterans from either the Spanish-American or Civil War. Similar parades were taking place in several other cities on what Wilson had proclaimed the first official celebration of Flag Day.

The occasion, he hoped, would fan the embers of patriotism in a nation rent by ethnic and ideological discord. Wilson and Theodore Roosevelt detested one another. But they agreed that, in a world on fire, only an unadulterated Americanism would do. That evening, in a speech at the Washington Monument, the president lashed out at the "disloyalty" of those immigrants who were committing "political blackmail" by threatening to vote against candidates who refused to obey their particular "foreign sentiment[s]." Wilson mentioned no names of what the *Washington Post* called "alien-born plotters." But it was common knowledge that leading German-American and Irish-American nationalist groups opposed his reelection.[5]

On the question of preparing for war, the president clearly wanted to have it both ways. He had asked Glynn to keynote the convention and took care to approve the speech in advance, although he did not anticipate how passionately Democrats inside the hall felt about staying out of the conflict devastating Europe. But Wilson was also determined to see that his proposals for beefing up the military would make it through Congress. He hoped that flag-waving attacks on "hyphenated Americans"—immigrants who remained loyal to their old countries— might convince enough vacillating lawmakers to do their patriotic duty. They were sure to please most big-city newspaper editors and perhaps even help woo progressive Republicans who had bolted their party to back Roosevelt's Bull Moose candidacy in 1912.

These two faces of executive power snared peace activists, both inside and outside Congress, in an election-year dilemma. Although they had helped persuade most Democrats to oppose taking any step that might bring intervention closer, the president still wanted to expand the military. But the anti-warriors had far less faith in Charles Evans Hughes—the stern, uncharismatic Supreme Court justice and former New York governor whom Republicans had just nominated to run against Wilson. Any opinions Hughes held about diplomacy and war were known only to his friends and political intimates. Henry Cabot Lodge wrote the section about "Protection of the Country" in that year's Republican platform, and TR, after failing to win his party's nod, quickly rallied to Hughes, as did such fellow champions of the Allies as Augustus Gardner and General Leonard Wood. All this suggested that whatever the GOP nominee might say on the campaign trail, if elected, he would favor going to war.

That summer, Wilson gratified peace activists by bolstering his reputation as a social progressive. He signed landmark bills banning child labor and offering federal loans to farmers. To the delight of organized labor, he signed the Adamson Act, granting an eight-hour day to railroad workers, who had threatened a nationwide strike. Amid furious controversy, the Senate also confirmed Louis Brandeis, the pioneering legal reformer, as the first Jew to sit on the Supreme Court. All these moves convinced Robert La Follette—Brandeis's close friend—to refrain from endorsing Hughes and helped Wilson court GOP progressives who had never voted for a Democrat before.

The political mood at the Democratic convention also provided leaders of the anti-war coalition with an opportunity to alter their defensive image. With the president running as a foe of intervention and Hughes muddling his own views, Crystal Eastman, Morris Hillquit, and their allies in the House and Senate could make a strong case that they were saying what the majority of Americans wanted to hear. Continued peace seemed more popular than at any time since the *Lusitania* went down. Perhaps they could win the war against war after all.

That optimism was buttressed by a series of events that began a few miles south of the Texas border, just days after the Democrats nominated Wilson for a second term. On June 21, in the tiny pueblo of Carrizal, two regiments of the U.S. Cavalry fought a brief but bloody engagement with Mexican troops. Fourteen American soldiers, blacks and whites, lost their lives. Since 1910, when a revolution had broken out in that country, awash in U.S. investments, Washington policymakers had struggled to reconcile their desire for stability with their preference for a democratic regime. That March, several thousand U.S. troops, commanded by General John J. Pershing, had begun an unsuccessful campaign to find Pancho Villa and his band of rebels and punish them for attacking a New Mexico border town. Now Wilson, informed that U.S. cavalrymen had been gunned down in an ambush, prepared to ask Congress to send the "armed forces to clear the border area of bandit gangs." Suddenly, the unfriendly neighbors were on the brink of full-scale war.[6]

AUAM leaders decided to do whatever they could to stop it. A U.S. officer in Carrizal, Captain Lewis S. Morey, reported that the Mexicans had attacked his men only after the Americans insisted on invading their town. Lillian Wald and Amos Pinchot quickly raised enough money to print newspaper ads that highlighted quotes from Morey's letter. The AUAM also held a mass meeting at New York's Cooper Union to petition Wilson to withdraw U.S. troops and allow third parties to mediate the dispute. Around the nation, newspapers lauded the pacifists for seeking the truth about what had occurred in the border hamlet. Soon the White House was wading through thousands of frantic anti-war telegrams. At the end of June, Wilson prudently backed away from a conflict he had little appetite for waging. He would not be "the servant of those who wish to enhance the value of their Mexican investments" but would heed the "great many letters" from Americans who were praying for peace.[7]

The rapid victory renewed the pacifists' confidence in their ability to mobilize the democratic instincts of their fellow citizens. "We must make it known to everybody," announced Crystal Eastman, "that the *people* acting directly—not through their governments or diplomats or armies—stopped that war and can stop all wars if enough of them will act together and act quickly."[8]

But voting for or against a larger military establishment was the prerogative of Congress, not "the people." And the most the anti-preparedness camp could expect from Capitol Hill on that issue was a frustrating compromise. On June 3, Wilson signed the National Defense Act, a complex piece of legislation that essentially fulfilled his desire for a force capable of defending the homeland against any invader but not for waging combat overseas. The bill almost doubled the size of the regular peacetime army to 175,000 men and, for the first time, gave the president the power to federalize the National Guard. It also created the Reserve Officers' Training Corps, or ROTC. Near the end of the legislative grind, Representative Carl Hayden, a Democrat from Arizona, slipped into the bill an amendment that authorized the White House, during a future war, to begin drafting men if not enough volunteers signed up.

Only twenty-five House members voted against the final act. Claude Kitchin was not among them. A shrewd strategist, he realized that the Democratic Congress would not simply decline to support the larger army requested by a Democratic president. He must have smiled to hear Augustus Gardner damn the bill as one "that will please every pacifist throughout the country" and Theodore Roosevelt scorn it as "foolish and unpatriotic . . . [a] bit of flintlock legislation." The National Security League even urged a presidential veto. Of course, the AUAM denounced what it called the "Hayden joker" and urged Wilson to demand its repeal. But not enough of the group's friends in Congress were alarmed by the *potential* of a draft to mount what would have been a fruitless campaign against it.[9]

Kitchin and his sturdy faction of anti-preparedness Democrats were more troubled by Wilson's ambition to create a navy to match any in the world. In the House, they were able to limit naval appropriations to $244 million, which included no battleships, and managed to include an idealistic rider, written by Representative Walter Hensley from Missouri, that pledged $200,000 for a postwar conference on world disarmament—an idea Wilson had yet to embrace. In the upper chamber, La Follette backed Kitchin's position and offered an amendment to bar any U.S. Navy ship from acting on behalf of "any private citizen, copartnership, or corporation." Yet, the seven-hour speech he gave did not stop his fellow senators from voting to fund ten new battleships and sixty-seven submarines—or for getting their way in the conference committee with the House.[10] The only solace for peace advocates was that Hensley's rider made it into the final bill.

Kitchin condemned the final legislation as "criminal extravagance"; echoing La Follette, he charged it would put American taxpayers "permanently at [the] mercy" of the corporations that produced the ships and their deadly cargo. But opinion makers who had sided with him on expanding the army deserted him now. The ongoing conflict on the North Atlantic was a powerful argument for naval might. A cartoonist for the *San Francisco Examiner*, a Hearst paper often cool toward preparedness in the past, portrayed Kitchin's dark, disembodied head as a mine floating directly in the path of an American warship. The artist exaggerated the majority leader's sway over his colleagues. Kitchin was among just fifty-one House members who voted against the final bill that the president signed. The "outrageous" measure, the North Carolinian wrote to a pacifist in Massachusetts, "will be a fresh menace to the peace and humanity of the world." It would render "as hypocrisy and mockery" any future U.S. attempt to arbitrate international conflicts.[11]

As chairman of the Ways and Means Committee, Kitchin could

exact a kind of revenge against well-heeled champions of a more militarized state—and strike a modest blow against economic inequality as well. If the industrial and financial "interests" of the Northeast wanted preparedness, he insisted, they should have to pay for it. So should manufacturers whose exports, mostly to the Allied powers, had increased in value by a remarkable 700 percent since 1913. As James Maurer—the labor leader, Socialist, and AUAM stalwart—had told the Senate Military Affairs Committee earlier that year, "We are sick and tired of being turned into fodder for cannons and then have to pay for 'preparedness.' If it's right to take a poor man's life, it's right to take the rich man's fortune."[12]

In an era when most Americans believed the rich had grabbed too large a share of the nation's wealth and big corporations too much market power, it was difficult for self-described "progressive" lawmakers from either party to defy that simple logic. So during the summer of 1916, Kitchin steered a landmark Revenue Act through Congress and saw it pass by lopsided margins that convinced the president to sign it. The bill boosted the maximum income tax rate from 7 to 15 percent, established a special levy on munitions makers, and instituted the nation's first permanent estate tax. Americans who made more than $20,000 a year would now be expected to supply over 95 percent of federal tax revenues. Privately, Kitchin expressed the hope that the economic elite would hesitate before supporting additional military spending. At any rate, when Congress adjourned in early September after a long nine-month session, he returned to Scotland Neck, satisfied that he had spearheaded enactment of the most "just and equitable tax" in U.S. history.[13]

FIGHTING FROM BEHIND

After a momentous summer marked by both victory and defeat, antiwar activists were uncertain about what strategy to pursue for the remainder of 1916 and beyond. On the one hand, the votes in Congress left them worried that the champions of preparedness were winning. "Militaristic legislation has made great headway . . . during the last year," wrote Rabbi Stephen Wise in a fund-raising appeal for the AUAM. "It is obvious that military enthusiasts are strong in both the leading parties and that only continual vigilance will prevent further steps being taken." That July, two horrific terrorist bombings—of a munitions depot in Jersey City and a preparedness parade in San Francisco—made it more difficult to argue that Germany posed no threat to the U.S. homeland, although no one was ever indicted for the sabotage in the East and two non-Teutonic radicals were convicted (falsely, as it turned out) for the blast in the West.[14]

Yet, peace enthusiasts did have some cause for hope. In their lightning operation during the crisis with Mexico, they had played a crucial role in preventing further violence. That spring, Henry Ford had won presidential primaries in Nebraska and Michigan, although he made no effort in either state and announced he had no desire to run for the office. The reluctance of both Woodrow Wilson and Charles Evans Hughes to strike a belligerent posture in the fall campaign also suggested that the AUAM and other peace groups still had a decent chance to halt preparedness short of war.

It fell to Crystal Eastman to try to chart a sensible path between despair and optimism. In early October, she drew up a memorandum, "Suggestions for 1916–1917," for AUAM members around the country. To change the minds of the president and Congress, she maintained, only a vigorous strategy would do. First, turn the Hensley rider into a wedge to undermine "the whole preposterous naval program" by compelling Wilson to call an arbitration conference *before* any new ships could be built. Second, call public hearings and mount a lobbying campaign to alert Americans to the perils of conscription and military training in schools. Third, "make the most of our Mexican experience" by preparing a much larger "mobilization of people for the prevention of any future war that might threaten this country." Eastman acknowledged that all of this would require a sizable infusion of revenue, more organizers, and "all the literature we need, and a genius to design it." Coordination with peace activists abroad—particularly in those "countries expected to be our enemies"—was vital too. "It will," she promised, "be a glorious fight."[15]

Eastman's relish for peaceful combat was a great asset to her movement. But she knew the odds for its success were growing longer. One reason was a dearth of resources. The AUAM had only a thousand "contributing" or seriously engaged members, with a mailing list sixty times as large. The Woman's Peace Party boasted a paper membership of forty thousand. But neither organization mustered more than a handful of active chapters, concentrated in a few big cities in the East and Midwest. Their finances were inadequate to the immense tasks before them. Every branch of the Woman's Peace Party raised its own funds, which were always meager. The AUAM spent $34,000 from January to October 1916—equal to about $800,000 today—and planned to spend even less in the year to come. That fall, its coffers were so bare that Eastman had to ask Charles Hallinan, the skillful veteran publicist who doubled as the AUAM's Washington lobbyist, to take a pay cut of 20 percent. Not surprisingly, he balked and suggested that, at the new rate, he would only be able to work part time. In the New York office, only Eastman received a full-time salary.[16]

In contrast, the directors of the National Security League were able to mount the best campaign for preparedness that corporate money could buy. The top officers in their New York City headquarters alone earned close to the entire annual budget of the AUAM; by 1918, they supervised a paid staff of forty. Retired oil baron John D. Rockefeller wrote a personal check of $25,000 for the cause; other businessmen of his stature contributed lavishly as well.

A sizable share of that largesse flowed to local leagues. In the spring of 1916, the Pittsburgh NSL spent $1,500 on a single public meeting.

It announced the occasion with big newspaper ads, sent thousands of invitations to prominent citizens, and handed out an elegant brochure with a small, silk American flag to everyone who attended. None of this ensured a successful evening. According to the AUAM's report, dripping with schadenfreude, "there was not a full house," and the speeches were so dull that the league chairman "rushed to the front of the stage" and "implored the people" to remain in their seats or be branded "disloyal to their country." In contrast, an earlier anti-militarist rally in the same city, organized entirely by volunteers, had filled a downtown hall with an audience that "stayed and cheered till the rafters shook."[17]

Yet, by itself, the greater grass-roots passion of anti-warriors could not alter political reality. Once Congress had voted to bulk up the military and forced the wealthy to pay a large share of the cost, the process of contracting and taxing took on a life of its own. And the logic of a close presidential campaign required anti-preparedness Democrats like Kitchin to close ranks behind Wilson or be accused of aiding the triumph of war lovers like Roosevelt and Lodge.

Peace lovers also may have diluted their strength by working on a number of worthy projects that did little to stall the arming of America, at least not directly. In New York City, the AUAM and kindred groups promoted *Civilization*, a big-budget anti-war film whose producer and director, Thomas Ince, offered to donate a share of the gate during a special Peace Week in October. Quakers and parishioners of other liberal churches threw themselves into relief efforts for civilian victims of the war in Europe. Some activists in the Woman's Peace Party renewed their protests against the military training of teenagers. Others followed Jane Addams in lobbying Woodrow Wilson to pull American troops out of Haiti, which they had occupied in 1915, and to refrain from building a transoceanic canal across Nicaragua. Fervent apostles of neutral mediation and a cooperative postwar order continued to write manifestos and seek allies overseas. At the end of October, leaders of all the major peace groups got together in Manhattan to see if their "extremely divergent types of temperament and policy" could be reconciled. But all they could agree on was to meet again and, in the meantime, to fill out a questionnaire about what they were doing and why.[18]

As progressives, whether of the reform or radical cast, these men and women had never been willing to restrict themselves to a single issue or method of social change. They all believed, as the historian Richard Hofstadter once put it, "that everyone was in some very serious sense responsible for everything." While running the AUAM and the New York branch of the Woman's Peace Party, Crystal Eastman somehow still found time to speak at suffrage gatherings. Other key figures in the peace movement like Paul Kellogg and Jane Addams kept pushing for better housing, sanitation, and ethnic tolerance, while Morris Hillquit did not stop being a union lawyer.[19]

Perhaps these consummate altruists could only restrain their grand ambitions for healing the world as long as they believed they had a serious chance of persuading Congress not to expand the military. Yet none could ignore the importance of the November election. They all knew the road to war or to strict neutrality and a mediated peace might depend on its outcome.

FOUR PEACE CANDIDATES AND
ONE BEARDED ICEBERG

The electoral past weighed heavily on Woodrow Wilson and his party in 1916. Not since Andrew Jackson, in 1832, had a Democratic president won consecutive terms; no Democrat since Franklin Pierce in 1852 had received a majority of the popular vote. What's more, after the debacle of the 1914 midterm election, the party's control of the House was clearly at risk, even if Wilson did manage to win reelection. No political observer would have been surprised if the Republicans were swept back into the White House that fall and took charge on Capitol Hill. Since the Civil War, nearly everywhere outside the famously Solid

South, the Democrats had been the minority party. In addition, many businessmen still thought Wilson's party was too fond of Bryan's agrarian populism, while urban reformers like Jane Addams battled corrupt Democratic machines in Chicago, New York, and other cities. And the GOP, as the friend of eastern capital, could always outraise and outspend the opposition.

So Wilson's decision to run as the "peace" candidate in 1916 was dictated as much by necessity as desire. Roosevelt had declined to accept the nomination of the Progressive Party, knowing that to do so would assure the reelection of a man he accused of having "done more damage to the future of our national character than any President we have ever had." The reunited Republican party was now heavily favored to win nearly every state in the Northeast and the industrial Midwest, which, between them, accounted for 45 percent of the electoral vote. Only if Wilson could sweep the trans-Mississippi West, where, according to his campaign manager, voters wanted to stay out of the war in both Europe and Mexico "almost at any price," would he be able to emulate Old Hickory, the former general whose ardor for combat, ironically, rivaled that of TR.[20]

Few peace activists were ambivalent about the choice before them that fall. Whether as the lesser evil or a decent alternative, a second term for Wilson seemed the only way to prevent Roosevelt, Lodge, Gardner, and their ilk from grabbing the reins of foreign policy. In a lengthy analysis of political platforms, Paul Kellogg saluted the Democrats as the only party that sincerely vowed to maintain U.S. neutrality and that, due to its pledge to grant independence to the Philippines, "blazes the way for what might be called a new friendliness for weaker peoples." He endorsed Wilson, as did nearly every national leader of the AUAM or Woman's Peace Party—including Crystal Eastman, Jane Addams, Stephen Wise, Lillian Wald, and Amos Pinchot. The only holdout was *Nation* publisher Oswald Garrison Villard, who accused the incumbent he had praised during the *Lusitania* crisis of betraying his trust by backing preparedness. Wilson, snapped Villard, "has not a principle on earth that he would not bargain away." But, just a few days before the election, with "great reluctance," the grandson of William Lloyd Garrison and his magazine came out for the president as well.[21]

More remarkably, several prominent Socialists took the unprecedented step of endorsing the nominee of a "capitalist" party. For Max Eastman, the president who had impressed him when they met in the White House that spring had, by late summer, grown into a statesman who "has attacked the problem of eliminating war" and "has not succumbed to the epidemic of militarism in its extremist forms." To Mary Harris "Mother" Jones, the octogenarian labor and Socialist icon, Wilson was, thanks to the Adamson Act, the first president to "demand that the toilers be given an even break in the world." Jack London, Upton Sinclair, and Helen Keller announced they would vote for the president too.[22]

Most of these radicals were heeding their political brains, not losing their hearts. Everyone expected the 1916 election, unlike the previous four presidential contests, to be extremely close. Nearly every vote won by Allan Benson, the anti-war journalist who was the SPA's nominee, would be one that otherwise would have gone to Wilson. A leading left-wing magazine even scolded Victor Berger, the former Socialist congressman and leader of the party in Wisconsin, for his refusal to stop criticizing Wilson's support for a larger army. "To howl of militarism against a president who has kept the working class of America out of war," declared the International Socialist Review "is a species of treachery to the working class that does no good." Samuel Gompers and three-quarters of union members agreed, although most would not have phrased their support in such blistering terms. Thus, by September, when Wilson left the White House for the campaign trail, he enjoyed the support of the most left-wing, class-conscious coalition ever to unite behind a sitting president.[23]

Most of the politicians who had never wavered from the anti-war gospel were also up for reelection that fall. In the Northeast and urban Midwest, where preparedness sentiment was strong, lawmakers who had followed La Follette's lead in the Senate and Kitchin's in the House tried to avoid sounding like renegades from the standard-bearers of their parties. They understood that, in a hard-fought presidential race, Americans tended to vote their partisan loyalties all the way down the ticket.

In the second district of North Carolina, however, the only contest Claude Kitchin had to worry about was the Democratic primary. The demise of populism and the disfranchisement of black voters had turned most of the South into a one-party region. The majority leader's defiance of Woodrow Wilson's wishes on military matters had angered a cluster of local businessmen, so they went looking for a candidate who would, at least, scare Kitchin back into line. The only Democrat who stepped forward was a banker with the Dixie-fied name of Clingman W. Mitchell. As expected, he began attacking Kitchin for placing the nation's security at risk.

The congressman swatted away the challenge with superior resources and a deftly crafted message. The Tobacco Merchants Association mailed their endorsement of him to all their local members; his campaign spread thirty-three thousand copies of his speeches around the district; and friends and allies in county offices set up Kitchin Clubs to make sure his voters turned up at the polls. The incumbent's literature shrewdly downplayed his differences with Wilson and played up his sponsorship of the new revenue bill. "NO MAN IS PERFECT, AND IF YOUR CONGRESSMAN MUST HAVE A FAULT, WHAT BETTER FAULT COULD IT BE THAN TO FAVOR TOO LOW TAXES?" read a leaflet addressed to "Mr. Tax Payer!" It scorned "an army as big as Roosevelt wants" while lauding the revenue measure that "our President and the 299 Democrats in Congress" supported. Kitchin, who was embroiled in the fight over the navy bill, did not bother traveling back to the district to campaign for himself. Few local Democrats seemed to mind. When they went to the polls on June 3, Kitchin beat Mitchell by more than seven thousand votes. He would never face a primary opponent again.[24]

Halfway across the nation, in Wisconsin, Robert La Follette was running for a third term in the Senate. He would have rather been campaigning for the White House, but the party of Roosevelt, Lodge, and J.P. Morgan was not about to nominate a leading foe of preparedness who repeatedly scourged multimillionaires and the "Big Burglars" in the Republican Party for "sacrific[ing] human life for private gain." So, at sixty-one, La Follette, the most prominent anti-militarist voice in the GOP, embarked on a vigorous reelection campaign that would deliver a verdict on his contentious views.[25]

La Follette never considered whether, like Kitchin, he should tone down his rhetoric on matters of war and peace. In late April, the senator introduced a measure intended to give every adult American a say in deciding whether the nation should embark on an armed intervention. His bill authorized holding a public referendum whenever the United States broke off diplomatic relations with a potential enemy. Just 1 percent of voters in at least twenty-five states would have to initiate the process. A referendum, La Follette claimed, would show the world that Congress had faith in the "Jeffersonian principle of the intelligent electorate." He was confident that, if such a plebiscite took place, the antiwar side would win. William Stone and a few other senators warmed to his idea, as did William Randolph Hearst, the Woman's Peace Party, and William Jennings Bryan. Allan Benson, the Socialist candidate for president, thought the bill was too cautious; he wanted to amend the Constitution to *require* consulting the people before going to war.[26]

But La Follette was not surprised when his proposal failed to get out of committee. Popular referenda were just beginning to be employed in a few western states to pass or defeat legislation on local issues like taxation. But the making of foreign policy had nearly always been the bailiwick of a seasoned cosmopolitan elite. As Jane Addams and Henry

Ford had discovered, the press was quick to ridicule citizens who dared to question that assumption and engage in diplomacy on their own. "Wisconsin should get rid of this noisy 'reformer' . . . this miscellaneous agitator" who "has ceased to be even amusing," wrote the *New York Times* about La Follette. He would have to be content with introducing the idea that anyone expected to fight and/or finance a war should also help decide whether to wage it.[27]

Back in Wisconsin, La Follette attracted far more applause than jeers. In a lightly attended Republican primary, he easily vanquished an old conservative rival who had become an advocate of preparedness. The general election against William Wolfe, a German-American Democrat, appeared, at first, to be a more competitive race. Teutonic voters made up as much as a third of the state's electorate, and Wolfe spoke to them fluently in their own tongue. But he also favored a larger military and criticized La Follette for differing with Wilson on keeping the country strong.

Fighting Bob was campaigning not merely to keep his seat but to prove that "the people" appreciated his work for social reform and against a policy of arms. The aging senator delivered up to eight talks a day, traveling all over Wisconsin for the first time since he had served as governor. From other states, friends and notables like Justice Brandeis, Andrew Furuseth, head of the International Seamen's Union, and Nebraska senator George Norris came to praise him and warn voters that his defeat would be what Norris called the "severest blow that could ever be dealt the progressive movement throughout the country." Ordinary admirers from all over the country seconded that view. "You have never acquiesced in the excesses of the militarists . . . and have been no man's man but your own," said one fan from Los Angeles. La Follette's re-election would show that "in the state of Wisconsin, the wave of frothy reaction which came on the heels of the European war has begun to pass." On Election Day, La Follette crushed Wolfe by a margin of nearly two to one, scoring the largest plurality of any statewide candidate to that point in Wisconsin history. German voters, torn between their ethnic sympathies and their political ones, split their votes about evenly. By a narrower margin, Woodrow Wilson lost the state to Hughes.[28]

Many Socialists cheered La Follette's triumph, but they had little hope of emulating it. Since the party's founding in 1901, the SPA had managed to win several thousand local offices in cities as large as Milwaukee and towns as small as Antlers, Oklahoma. But most of the party's campaigns for Congress were undertaken primarily to educate the public about the evils of capitalism and the virtues of a future "cooperative commonwealth." Socialists gauged success by the size of their crowds and their steadily growing minority of the vote, not by the number of seats they won. In 1916, only one Socialist sat in the House of Representatives: Meyer London, a Yiddish-speaking union attorney from the heavily Jewish Lower East Side of New York.

Morris Hillquit aspired to be the second. He had run strong races for Congress twice before, in 1906 and 1908, while devoting the bulk of his time to speaking, writing, and lawyering. This time, he thought, could be different. Gotham Socialists had retained their strength in the garment trades and among a variety of intellectuals, from the philosopher John Dewey to the editors of the *Masses*. In a city full of first- and second-generation immigrants from Ireland and Germany, and Jews from the tsarist empire, the SPA was the only party that adamantly pledged never to join the Allies or to support a military prepared to do so. And Hillquit was running in the Twentieth District, centered in Harlem, where a majority of voters belonged to that same trio of ethnic groups. Against the nominees of the two major parties, both of whom were Jewish, he could win the seat with as little as 35 percent of the vote.

Hillquit's campaign certainly surpassed its competitors in the enthusiasm of its supporters. His headquarters in Harlem was packed with volunteers, day and night, and the largest local unions endorsed him and urged their members to canvass their neighbors and friends. Infused with sanguine zeal, Hillquit spoke more aggressively than he had since the Great War began. He charged that Democratic and Republican politicians "have joined in a conspiracy to build up in this country a system of militarism as stupendous and crushing as those of the most militaristic European monarchies." He accused them of fanning "race hatred and national prejudice" with their disdain for "hyphenated" Americans. He insisted that only the coming of socialism would bring "peace among nations and the brotherhood of all men of all races, creeds and nationalities."[29]

Hillquit, who seldom uttered a truly controversial remark, made news in mid-October when he put teeth into his dislike of the armed forces. If elected, he vowed not to appoint any young residents of his district to the service academies at West Point and Annapolis: "Instead of making officers of the young men who apply to me, I'll train them to be class conscious workers."[30]

His opponents and the newspapers that endorsed them shot back in kind. Hillquit "knows that an army and navy are necessary to the existence of a civilized state," observed the GOP-friendly *New York Sun*. Thus "to denounce the graduates of the military and naval academies is to invite the rudeness of saying that he talks like a fool, which nobody believes him to be." The *Times*, which usually endorsed Democrats but reserved its greatest scorn for radicals of any stripe, flatly accused Hillquit of detesting his adopted country. The "followers" of his "cult," the paper asserted, were "uneducated, highly emotional foreigners, most of them, who have much to learn before they can be regarded as worthy American citizens." In rebuttal, the Socialist nominee quoted the line in the Declaration of Independence about the "right of the people to alter or to abolish" oppressive governments. The heat of the rhetoric on both sides demonstrated, if nothing else, that the radical from Riga had an excellent chance to win.[31]

Indeed, soon after the polls closed on November 7, it appeared that

Hillquit had won. It was a glorious day to be a Socialist in Harlem. Following an election eve rally of up to three thousand people, canvassers fanned out all over the district. At the head of a tough brigade of Hillquit poll watchers was Benny Leonard, the twenty-year-old Jewish boxer who had already fought two close, but losing, bouts for the lightweight championship of the world. At midnight, unofficial returns showed that the Socialist was leading the Republican incumbent, Isaac Siegel, by about five hundred votes out of roughly fourteen thousand cast. Just two precincts had yet to report, and, according to Hillquit, they "were known to be favorable to us, and victory thus seemed assured."[32]

By the evening of the following day, joy had turned to ashes. Siegel surged ahead by 413 votes and was declared the winner. Socialists alleged that GOP and Democratic bosses, who ran the Board of Elections, had conspired to fix the results. Hillquit and his supporters "stormed" the officials in question, who "sat there impassively and cynically." They complained to a city magistrate and appealed to the New York Supreme Court. But the result was upheld, and Siegel returned to Congress. Hillquit sighed into the pages of his memoir: "For days [after] there was a spirit of general mourning in the district. . . .No crimes are treated in our republic more indulgently, even humorously, than crimes against the elective franchise."[33]

The most prominent peace candidate running nationwide in 1916 did not have to worry about being "counted out" of a narrow victory. But on Labor Day, when the presidential campaign began in earnest, every veteran politico agreed that Woodrow Wilson was running behind. States like New Hampshire, Minnesota, and California, which nearly always backed the winning candidate, were tilting toward Hughes. Irish-Catholics, the most critical bloc of Democrats outside the South, appeared disgusted with the president some viewed as no better than an "Ulster Orangeman." There was little fervor in the Hibernian and Catholic diocesan press for Hughes. But, as the New York Gaelic

American wrote, "He surely cannot be as bad as Wilson, for he is at least a man of honor."[34]

However, for the Republican to be confident of winning, he would have to run a clever campaign. Hughes had to avoid parroting either Roosevelt's views on war or taking swipes at labor and farmer groups that could lose him votes in the West and Midwest. Yet he could not support Wilson's domestic record, despite his own background as the progressive governor who had hired Crystal Eastman to write New York's workmen's compensation law. Hughes had to offer a sharp, appealing contrast with the embattled incumbent, who counted as many admirers as he did critics. Alas, as an orator, the Republican standard-bearer had always come off as sincere, if rather cold; the relentlessly passionate TR mocked him, in private, as a "bearded iceberg." With the press chronicling his every move and statement, Hughes did not have to thrill undecided voters; he did have to assure them he could live up to his reputation as a paragon of honesty and principle.[35]

It was a difficult balancing act, and Hughes performed it with all the grace of a man who would rather have been reading quietly in a judge's chamber than driving through the tempest of a tight presidential campaign. He condemned the Adamson Act as a cowardly "surrender" to railroad workers, thus alienating organized labor. His speeches about the war strained to please all sides with vague calls for a "firm and efficient foreign policy" and the "maintenance of American rights." But Roosevelt drew larger and far more enthusiastic crowds as he flailed Wilson for letting Germany get away with murder. Hughes assured the press he was in "complete accord" with TR's remarks, which kept his party united but stirred misgivings from the Irish and German groups that had endorsed him.[36]

In retrospect, the Republican nominee made his most fateful mistakes when he toured California that August. A majority of Golden State Republicans were strongly progressive; organized labor was powerful in the populous Bay Area, and most Californians regarded the

Southern Pacific Railroad, a standby of the pro-corporate faction in the GOP, as a corrupt monopoly. Hiram Johnson, the popular sitting governor, had been TR's running mate on the Bull Moose ticket, which carried the state in 1912, and he was running for the Senate in 1916. But Hughes—on the bad advice of his campaign manager, an old friend but political neophyte—neglected to pay tribute to Johnson and then failed to meet with him to repair the breach. In June, just before the Republican National Convention, William Barnes, a party stalwart from New York, wrote prophetically to a friend, "We're going to be strongest on nomination day and weakest on Election Day."[37]

Wilson and his managers adeptly capitalized on their opponent's flaws. They countered Hughes's equivocal statements on foreign policy with a forceful message of their own. Again and again, the president swore his commitment to neutrality and insisted, more explicitly than ever before, that, once the war ended, America should take the lead in forming a league of nations to keep the world at peace. He also made a pointed appeal to the more than 4 million Americans who had voted for Roosevelt in 1912: "We have in four years come very near to carrying out the platform of the Progressive Party as well as our own; for we also are progressives." Bryan, buoyed by the acclaim of his fellow partisans at the St. Louis convention, spent six weeks stumping in mostly western states, where huge crowds came to hear him flay the GOP as the party of militarism and reaction.[38]

In the end, Wilson's shift to the left probably decided the race, which he won by just twenty-three electoral votes. Allan Benson, the diligent but little-known Socialist nominee, received only two-thirds of the popular votes that Eugene Debs, the party's beloved standard-bearer, had drawn in 1912. Radicals who switched to Wilson almost surely put him over the top in Washington, North Dakota, and New Hampshire. His reelection was not confirmed until two days after the polls closed when California, with its critical thirteen electoral votes, was added to his column. He bested Hughes there by just 3,773 ballots. Four years earlier, Debs had won almost 12 percent of the California vote; but in 1916, over thirty thousand of his followers chose instead the Democrat "who kept us out of war."

California was also one of a dozen states where women could vote, and Wilson carried ten of them. In Montana, Jeannette Rankin, an anti-war Republican, became the first woman ever elected to the House of Representatives. It was assumed the sentiment expressed in "I Didn't Raise My Boy to Be a Soldier" and Wilson's domestic reforms were largely responsible for those results. Elsewhere, Hughes, as expected, captured nearly every state in the northeast quarter of the nation, while Wilson swept the South and most of the West—which helped Democrats retain their Senate majority.

For Republicans, the only consolation was that they took one more seat in the House of Representatives than did their rivals. Among the northern Democrats who lost were Clyde Tavenner and Warren Bailey, staunch foes of preparedness and close Kitchin allies. Due to a handful of seats won by third-party candidates, the GOP still fell short of a majority. No one could say which major party would control the lower chamber when the new Congress opened for business. One of the closest, most bitter campaigns in American history thus ended with Americans as politically divided as they had been when the contest began.

PEACE WITHOUT VICTORY

"The President thinks he is President of the whole world."
—Senator Francis Warren (R-Wyo.), January 1917[39]

Wilson's narrow triumph encouraged peace activists to think boldly again. The AUAM crowed that the incumbent's victory was "due primarily to the fighting pacifist sentiment in the United States." The campaign's "real issue," even if neither candidate had dared to admit it, was the contest "between jingoism and internationalism." La Follette's easy reelection and victories by several other candidates who echoed his views were, according to Crystal Eastman and her comrades, "pretty clear evidence" that the next Congress "will not yield as much ground" as the last one "on the issue of democracy versus militarism." Unsurprisingly, the combative senator from Wisconsin agreed. The president, warned La Follette, "must accept the outcome of this election as a clear mandate from the American people to hold steadfastly to his course against war."[40]

Other sprouts of peaceful resistance were growing as well. At its annual convention in late November, the American Federation of Labor passed a robust resolution, introduced by the Painters Union, that condemned all forms of military training in public schools. This reversed the stand the AFL had taken the year before. "President Gompers tried to stem the tide," wrote a reporter for the *Baltimore Sun*, "but for once his influence was apparently of little weight." In New York, a No-Conscription League, headed by Norman Thomas, a young Presbyterian minister in East Harlem, and backed by some of the most prominent liberal clergymen in the city and state, began to mobilize for the same purpose. America's volunteer army might be poised to grow, but that was no reason to persuade young civilians to regard themselves as soldiers-to-be. As Crystal Eastman wrote in the *Survey*, "We must make this great American democracy know, as we know, that military training is bad for the bodies and minds and souls of boys; that free minds, and souls, undrilled to obedience, are vital to the life of a democracy."[41]

All this activity obviously pleased the German ambassador, who had long been convinced that his nation would be crushed if the United States entered the war. In early December, from his legation's seventy-room mansion near downtown Washington, Johann von Bernstorff reported to Berlin that the American papers were full of "reports of the sessions of many and various peace societies." What's more, "everything bearing upon the question of peace which is to be found in news transmitted from overseas is printed in the most conspicuous places and made the subject of adequate comment in leading articles.'"[42]

Clearly, Wilson's victory had raised hope that the United States would not only keep out of the Great War but might finally take decisive steps to end it. For more than two years, citizen activists had pursued that vision—whether patiently, like Jane Addams and Julia Wales, or impulsively, like Henry Ford. After Congress passed Wilson's prepared-ness bills, the AUAM and other anti-war organizations clung to the Hensley amendment as a base, however weak, from which to build sup-port first for a negotiated peace and then for a world body dedicated to disarmament and the abolition of empires. In mid-December, pacifists sponsored a "Conference of Oppressed or Dependent Nationalities" in Washington, D.C., where immigrants from seventeen different "con-quered races"—from Albanians to Letts to Syrians—argued that self-government for their peoples must be the cornerstone of any postwar order.[43]

So fervent was the longing for a mediated solution that a new group, the American Neutral Conference Committee, even welcomed pre-paredness advocates as members and eschewed anti-militarist rhetoric (although Morris Hillquit did join its otherwise ultra-respectable "Gen-eral Committee"). The ANCC was, claimed Hamilton Holt, the liberal journalist who chaired it, "the only organization in the United States which aims to do what can be done by the American people to help bring the war to a just and permanent close." It was an erroneous claim, as well as an immodest one. But no one could accuse Holt of thinking small.[44]

Of course, none of these aims could advance beyond the wishful stage unless the reelected leader of the world's leading neutral nation agreed to promote them. Since the war began, Woodrow Wilson had re-peatedly told anti-war activists and the public at large that he would be willing to mediate the conflict if and when the belligerents allowed that to happen. In the 1916 campaign, he seemed to voice pacifist sentiments with more conviction than ever before. Two weeks after the votes were counted, he warned, in a private memo, that "victory for either side would inevitably lead to another war of revenge."[45]

Finally, in December, the president began to live up to his promises. On December 18, after weeks of consultation with his advisors, Wilson sent foreign embassies a note asking the warring powers to announce their respective terms for peace. To demonstrate he was unbiased, he stated that both the Allies and the Central Powers had "virtually the same" purposes—to preserve "the rights and privileges" of "weak peoples and small states" and "to be made secure in the future . . . against the recurrence of wars like this and against aggression or selfish interference of any kind." After millions had died and with no victory in sight, now was the time for each camp to make its objectives clear to the world. "Every part of the great family of mankind," Wilson reminded the belligerents, "has felt the burden and terror of this unprecedented contest of arms."[46]

Anti-war Americans greeted his note as an early Christmas gift, one particularly cherished since they had never quite expected to receive it. Bryan, who had urged such a move when he was secretary of state, gushed that Wilson had "rendered an invaluable service to a war-stricken world." Senator William Stone, chair of the Foreign Relations Committee, believed the offer heralded "the beginning of the end" of the awful conflict. To build momentum behind Wilson's initiative, the ANCC planned a series of mass meetings to begin in February in the nation's twelve largest cities; Bryan would headline the first one in Madison Square Garden. "Now that the President has taken his far-reaching step," asserted Rebecca Shelly, the group's secretary, "the least the American people can do is to support him."[47]

Since the election, like-minded figures from Britain had been anxiously urging Wilson to lead the world away from war. Charles Trevelyan, a Liberal member of the House of Commons and a leader of the anti-war Union of Democratic Control (UDC), predicted that the president's neutralist rigor and plans for a league of nations would "shorten" the war. The philosopher Bertrand Russell, whose speeches against conscription and for a negotiated peace had cost him his Cambridge lectureship, wrote an "Open Letter" to Wilson that eloquently described the mounting toll of corpses and spoke of the "Fear [that] has invaded man's inmost being, and with fear has come the ferocity that always attends it." He concluded, "In the name of Europe I appeal to you to bring us peace."[48]

However, most Republicans in Congress were in a partisan mood rather than a pacific one. Wilson issued his peace note two weeks after the House and Senate had begun their lame-duck sessions (mandated by the Constitution before the Twentieth Amendment was ratified in 1933). Few members of the opposition party, having gained seats in November and convinced that a more adroit nominee than Hughes would have captured the White House, were inclined to approve the president's plan. Henry Cabot Lodge was actively seeking to undermine it. "I sincerely trust the Allies will not be deluded into accepting [Wilson] as mediator or peacemaker," he wrote on December 21 to James Bryce, the former British ambassador to the United States; "it would be a fatal mistake."[49]

That same day, Senator Gilbert Hitchcock, a Nebraska Democrat who had once been close to Bryan, introduced a resolution to approve Wilson's note. Naïvely, Hitchcock thought it would pass quickly, with minimal debate. Didn't nearly every lawmaker agree that the president should at least try to persuade the warring powers to start negotiating? But Lodge, backed by most of the GOP caucus, managed to put off considering the measure until he had been able to strip away a clause that committed the United States to join a future league of nations. On January 5, the milder, revised resolution passed by a vote of 48 to 17. Despite the margin, it was not a solid endorsement of Wilson's initiative. Just ten of the forty Republicans voted aye; only one Democrat opposed it. A whopping thirty-one lawmakers abstained. From the snows of Wisconsin where he was on holiday, La Follette offered his support.

Over in the House, dozens of Republicans railed against their own minority leader, James R. Mann of Illinois, who had committed the sin of praising Wilson's objectives. Augustus Gardner accused Mann of abetting the president's "interference in European affairs" and of having "given encouragement to the Kaiser's wicked cause." Amid the strife in the opposition party, Kitchin and his fellow Democratic leaders decided not to put the resolution up for a vote, lest it jeopardize their chances of retaining control of the new House, which would convene in March.[50]

Aid to Wilson's critics also came from an unlikely source: his own secretary of state. Since succeeding Bryan eighteen months before, Robert Lansing had done his best to conceal his keen desire for an Allied victory, while advising the president against doing anything that might benefit the Central Powers. But on December 21, he called a hasty press conference at which he brazenly attempted to sabotage Wilson's landmark initiative. The note that appeared to be an opening for peace talks, the chief diplomat explained, was really just a prelude to U.S. intervention: "I mean that we are drawing nearer the verge of war ourselves, and therefore we are entitled to know exactly what each belligerent seeks, in order that we may regulate our conduct in the future." The president was furious, but he evidently thought that asking Lansing to resign would distract the administration from its new mission.[51]

Leaders of the major belligerent powers were no more smitten with Wilson's grand gesture than were Lansing and Lodge. The Germans, knowing how emotionally attached Wilson was to Britain and how dependent the U.S. economy was on trade with the Allies, did not trust the president to be a fair broker for peace. On December 26, the Kaiser's government thanked Wilson for his "noble initiative" but replied that it would agree to direct negotiations only with its adversaries. After the war, its ambassador to the United States admitted: "We did not want any intermeddling . . . in territorial questions." In London, Prime Minister

David Lloyd George and his cabinet thought it outrageous that Wilson considered the motivations of their enemies to be as moral as theirs. But, since the Germans had declined to submit their terms for peace, the British had an opportunity to please both the president and American public opinion by dispatching their own—which they dutifully did on January 10. Nearly everything they proposed—in particular, the independence of every land currently being occupied by one of the Central Powers—would require an Allied victory to achieve. Thus, less than a month after Wilson had belatedly launched his craft of neutral ambition, it was already underwater.[52]

American peace activists were not discouraged. At least, they reasoned, Wilson had begun a process that, if the stalemate in the war continued, would have to end in a negotiated settlement. Despite their differences over preparedness, anti-militarists and the man in the White House agreed about the need to abandon the selfish, balance-of-power diplomacy that had failed to prevent the Great War. American newspapers were full of reports about strikes, hunger, and rampant demoralization on the home front in Russia and France, as well as in Germany and Austria. A fresh proposal grounded in democratic principles rather than the self-interest of great powers might inspire ordinary citizens of those nations, after thirty months of death and destruction, to force their rulers to make a peace that would last. In mid-January, Jane Addams sent an appeal to female pacifists on both sides of the Atlantic to organize a "Women's International Congress" to occur alongside any future peace conference. At the same time, American Socialists called for representatives of all parties affiliated with the Socialist International to meet in The Hague in June to show that "loyal comrades . . . can do more to bring about a just, conclusive and enduring peace than all the world's diplomats and statesmen combined."[53]

Woodrow Wilson had always aspired to be a statesman of a more exalted kind. "I have a strong instinct of leadership. . . . I have a passion for interpreting great thoughts to the world," he told his first wife, Ellen,

LAUNCHING A MOVEMENT

Andrew Carnegie, industrialist turned anti-war philanthropist, praises President William Howard Taft, proponent of arbitrating disputes between nations, as "the peace dove," c. 1911.

The Women's Peace Parade in New York City, August 29, 1914.

3

Frances (Fanny) Garrison Villard, suffragist, leader of the Women's Peace Parade and of the Woman's Peace Party, at the International Woman Suffrage Conference in Budapest, 1913.

The most popular anti-war song of 1915. The sheet music sold about 700,000 copies.

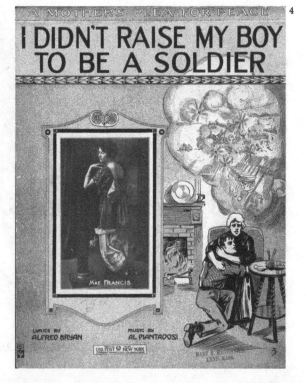

5

Crystal Eastman, suffragist and anti-war organizer, in 1913, when she was thirty-two.

6

Morris Hillquit, leading Socialist and union lawyer, who wrote most of his party's official statements on World War I. This photo was taken c. 1910, when he was forty-one.

7

Claude Kitchin, Democratic congressman from North Carolina, 1901–1923, and majority leader and chair of the Ways and Means Committee, 1915–1919. This photo was taken in 1905, when he was thirty-six.

8

Robert La Follette, Republican senator from Wisconsin, 1905–1925. This photo was taken in 1915, when he was sixty.

9

Jane Addams: feminist, pacifist, settlement house pioneer, and gifted speaker and author.

10

Delegates en route from the United States to the Woman's Peace Conference at the Hague in April 1915. Emmeline Pethick-Lawrence holds the banner on the far left; Jane Addams stands beside her. In the center, carrying an umbrella, is Anna Molloy, president of the Boston Telephone Operators Union.

MOBILIZING FOR THE CAUSE

11

The Ford Peace Ship approaches the hell of the European War, December 1915.

12

An anti-war skit by the Woman's Peace Party of New York, c. 1916.

13

A demonstration by the Woman's Peace Party against compulsory military drill in public schools passes down Broadway in Manhattan, c. 1916.

ANTI-WAR CARTOONS FROM THE *MASSES*, 1916

14

"Looking for Peace"
by Art Young.

15

"At Last, a Perfect Soldier"
by Robert Minor.

16

"Progress"
by Art Young.

17

Ridiculing pacifist demonstrators in Washington on George Washington's Birthday, February 22, 1917.

18

Jeannette Rankin, Republican congresswoman from Montana, speaking at the Washington office of the nation's main suffrage organization on April 2, 1917. The only woman in Congress, Rankin was one of fifty representatives who voted against declaring war.

decades before he began his political career. The rigor of his Calvin-
ist faith and the warmth of his romantic Americanism shone through
his rhetoric and had helped lift him into the White House. But since
August 1914, his desire to stay above the Old World's battles had kept
him from translating his "great thoughts" into a strategy for ending the
Great War.[54]

His postelection resolve to stop the war liberated his mind and loos-
ened his tongue. In early January, Wilson began composing an address
that would lay before the world the only true "conditions" for a moral
peace. On the afternoon of January 22, he gave that speech to a hastily
assembled U.S. Senate and a gallery packed with spectators, including
his wife and one of his daughters. "The present war must first be ended;
but . . . it makes a great deal of difference in what way and upon what
terms it is ended," Wilson instructed, in a voice that grew stronger as he
spoke. For this devout Presbyterian, "a peace that will win the approval
of mankind" had to be sealed by "a universal covenant . . . of cooperative peace."

The terms of that covenant closely resembled ones the peace movement had been advocating since Fanny Villard's black-garbed sister-
hood marched down Fifth Avenue thirty months before. Every nation
had the right to govern itself and enjoy the freedom of commerce on
the seas. Armies and navies should be only as large as needed to preserve order, not big enough to be "an instrument of aggression or of
selfish violence." Countries should join a League of Peace dedicated to
enforcing these principles. What he was advocating, Wilson said, really
just extended the Monroe Doctrine and George Washington's advice
to "avoid entangling alliances" that bred "competitions of power . . . in-
trigue and selfish rivalry." They were "American principles, American
policies." But the patriotic tribute did not hide the fact that the president of the United States was demanding an end to the empires that,
among them, ruled close to half the people in the world.

Tucked into the middle of the 2,600-word speech was the phrase by which it has always been known: "a peace without victory." In their responses to Wilson's note of December 18, both belligerent camps had denied they wanted to destroy one another. If that were true, they should end the conflict before additional savagery changed their minds. The alternative only invited perpetual war. Victory for one side "would leave a sting, a resentment, a bitter memory upon which terms of peace would rest, not permanently but only as upon quicksand." Nothing could be clearer than that: "Only a peace between equals can last."

It was a stunning act of oratory. "Not since the foundation of the republic," observed the *Washington Post*, "has a President of the United States, in public statement, declared the right of this nation to be heard in the terms which will settle a war in which the country has no active part." Although Wilson had secretly sent a draft of his talk to foreign capitals a few days earlier, envoys from belligerent and neutral countries alike still expressed their "amazement" at his daunting agenda but refrained from commenting any further. This was, they understood, a direct challenge to their imperial authority. "The real people I was speaking to was neither the Senate nor foreign governments," Wilson told a friendly journalist, "but the *people* of the countries now at war."[55]

Overseas, people who had been fruitlessly agitating for peace responded as if the American chief executive had suddenly thrown in his lot with them. In Britain, the UDC rejoiced that their program was now the president's as well. At the annual convention of the Labour Party, after the entire speech was read out loud, "the delegates stood and cheered Wilson's name for five minutes." Every Socialist member of the French Chamber of Deputies called on the belligerent nations to embrace his proposals. In Germany, anti-war Socialists were in the throes of organizing a new party of their own, which became the USPD, or Independent Social-Democrats; they too hailed Wilson's brave intentions.[56]

The reception from anti-warriors at home was equally ecstatic.

Buoyed by favorable press opinion, they allowed themselves to believe a corner toward a mediated peace had finally been turned. The AUAM praised Wilson for rendering "a service to humanity which it is impossible to exaggerate" and compared his speech to the Gettysburg Address. In the *Masses*, Max Eastman claimed that the defender of the Monroe Doctrine had magically transformed himself into the "one hope" of radicals everywhere for "preserving that struggle for a new civilization which we call Socialism, or Syndicalism, or the Social Revolution, or the Labor Struggle." Jane Addams exclaimed to Louis Lochner: "Isn't it fine and isn't the cause moving along?" From Chicago, her Woman's Peace Party pointed out how closely the particulars of Wilson's plan resembled the resolutions adopted in the spring of 1915 by the lamented International Congress of Women at The Hague. With "renewed courage and inspiration," the Woman's Party urged pacifists to lobby their state legislatures to reject compulsory military training in the schools.[57]

But in Congress, Wilson's speech largely reinforced the chasm between the two parties. Democrats predictably hailed it as an eloquent boon to peace, although many remained silent about the idea of joining a world federation. Most Republicans dismissed it as an exercise in fanciful, utopian thinking. Senator Lawrence Sherman of Illinois compared the speech to "a future Hague conference up in a balloon" that "would make Don Quixote jealous." Reed Smoot of Utah wondered why Wilson thought "the time has come for us to dictate to Europe," while others in his party considered the notion of a "peace without victory" simply impossible. No lawmaker went as far as Theodore Roosevelt, who, in a fit of historical pique, compared the president to the Tories of 1776 and the Copperheads of 1864. The erstwhile Rough Rider was, in effect, accusing Wilson of abetting treason at a time of war. Outside of a small coterie of midwesterners, no member of the GOP caucus seconded La Follette's admiration for a chief executive who had, in his view, delivered "the greatest message of a century."[58]

Alas, the brave new terms for peace could not change the calculus of war. The peoples of Europe might be exhausted; a growing number were ready to rebel against the leaders who had urged them to sacrifice so much to gain so little. But the idea of ending the war without gaining anything for all their sacrifices was inconceivable, particularly to the leaders themselves. "Peace without victory," wrote the novelist Anatole France, would be "stumbling and becrutched . . . a deformed peace squatting on its haunches, a disgusting peace, fetid, ignominious, obscene, fistulous, hemorrhoidal."[59]

No Allied government issued an official response to what was, unlike Wilson's December note, not a diplomatic message. But French, British, and Italian leaders all bridled at the president's attack on empires and vowed to make peace only after the "Huns" were defeated. In Germany, the liberal press lauded Wilson's evenhanded, humanitarian vision. One influential journalist, Maximilian Harden, hoped that "even in this fight for the German nation's right to live" his government could "maintain a worthy friendship with the progressive people of the United States and their highest representative."[60]

All the commentary—admiring, derisive, or doubtful—was largely moot. On January 9, Kaiser Wilhelm had issued a fateful order to his imperial navy: "I command that unlimited submarine warfare begin on February 1 with all possible vigor. You will please take all necessary measures immediately but in such a way that our intention does not become apparent to the enemy and to neutrals in advance." The Germans were abandoning the "*Sussex* pledge" they had made to the United States the previous May, which had quieted fears that another *Lusitania*-like incident could push the two nations into war.[61]

The Kaiser had arrived at this decision only after months of bitter arguments among his top advisors, the military ones pitted against the civilians. The generals and admirals worried that their forces could not withstand another Allied offensive like that of the Somme; given the dwindling morale at home, even a continued stalemate could spell "disaster for us." Naval officials confidently predicted that, if unrestrained, their U-boats could cripple British commerce as well as prevent American soldiers from swarming onto European soil. On the other side, Chancellor Theobald von Bethmann-Hollweg, his top deputy, and Germany's ambassador in Washington—whose wife was American-born—pointed to the industrial might and huge population of the United States. If we loose the seadogs of war, warned Vice-Chancellor Karl Helfferich, it will insure an Allied triumph; "then we are lost for centuries."[62]

Late in the afternoon of January 31, Ambassador Johann von Bernstorff walked into the office of the secretary of state, housed in the mammoth baroque building adjacent to the White House. He handed Lansing a copy of a document announcing that unrestricted submarine warfare would begin in just a few hours. "I am sorry to have to bring about this situation," said von Bernstorff, "but my government could do nothing else." Lansing told him it was an "unfriendly and indefensible act." As the Prussian nobleman turned to leave, his eyes were wet with tears.[63]

FOUR

DO THE PEOPLE
WANT WAR?

February 1917 to April 1917

"Congress has the constitutional power to declare war, but if war comes it will not be Congress that will do the fighting. . . . In death, in suffering, in sorrow, and in taxes to the third and fourth generations, the people who fight will pay. . . . Therefore, we say that the people themselves should speak before Congress is permitted to declare war."

—Advertisement signed by Max Eastman
and others, March 3, 1917[1]

"Just because we fight without rancour and without selfish object, seeking nothing for ourselves but what we shall wish to share with all free peoples, we shall, I feel confident, conduct our operations as belligerents without passion and ourselves observe with proud punctilio the principles of right and of fair play we profess to be fighting for."

—Woodrow Wilson, Address to Congress, April 2, 1917

"I won't vote for this war because if we go into it, we will never again have the same old Republic."

—Senator William J. Stone (D-Mo.), April 4, 1917[2]

"I think no unhappier lot of men ever assembled under this roof than the Members of this House."

—Representative James Slayden (D-Tex.), April 5, 1917[3]

BALLOTS BEFORE BULLETS

The unleashing of the U-boats did not make it inevitable that the United States would go to war. On February 3, Wilson severed diplomatic relations with the Kaiser's regime. But when informing Congress about his decision, he promised restraint: "We are the sincere friends of the German people and earnestly desire to remain at peace with the Government which speaks for them. We shall not believe they are hostile to us unless and until we are obliged to believe it." The president had not given up hope for a "peace without victory"; to him, the decision by the Germans revealed how desperate they were to gain an advantage over the Allies before exhaustion and revolt back in the Fatherland would make that impossible. Wilson also knew it would take more than just the threat of attacks on U.S. ships and passengers to convince most Americans that the moment for intervention had come. "Whether we will really go to war or not, Heaven only knows, and certainly Mr. Wilson doesn't," Theodore Roosevelt wrote privately on February 17. For once, TR's scornful remarks about his successor had the ring of accuracy.[4]

Uncertainty thus filled the two months from the break with Germany to the declaration of war on April 6 with constant tension. Peace activists clashed with interventionists, each claiming a mandate from "the people" for the most important decision of state since the Civil War. As the reelected head of the majority party, Wilson had an excellent chance of persuading Congress to do his bidding. Having proclaimed, however belatedly, his unselfish plan for peace, he could now argue that German aggression had dashed any possibility of realizing it.

Yet the American opponents of belligerence remained vigorous, although increasingly on the defensive. Most respected the president's motivations, but they were determined to show that most of their fellow citizens still wished to remain at peace. Toward that end, they concentrated most of their energies on a single tactic: the demand for a popular referendum on whether the United States should go to war.

These two months may have been the most consequential period in the history of America's relationship with the outside world since the nation's founding. Intervention could ensure a victory for the Allies and might give the United States the principal role in shaping the postwar order. But belligerence would also end a century of rapid economic and demographic expansion during which few Americans had felt the need to arm themselves against enemies from abroad. Since the British occupied and burned Washington, D.C., in 1814, "national security" had not been a problem. That would never be the case again.

The dire news about the expansion of U-boat warfare did not cause leading figures in the peace coalition to doubt their convictions. While supporting the diplomatic break with Germany, they urged Wilson to redouble his efforts at a mediated settlement. On February 1, twenty-six prominent members of the AUAM and/or the Woman's Peace Party signed an open telegram to the president that occupied half a page in the next day's *New York Times*. "We recognize the perplexity of the problem before you, and we wish to express our confidence in your wisdom and your power of leadership," began the group headed by the Eastman siblings, Paul Kellogg, Emily Balch, and Oswald Garrison Villard. They urged Wilson to make "a final and personal offer of mediation" to the belligerent powers, urging them, once again, to state their terms of peace and then agree to negotiate. "The men and women who elected you," they promised Wilson, "will back you in the most extreme measures for keeping the country clear of any ignominious eleventh-hour participation in a struggle for mastery which is not their own."[5]

Clearly, these influential foes of war and the man they had helped reelect still had a good deal in common. Both believed the United States could and should lead the belligerents away from further carnage and toward a world federation committed to democracy and open diplomacy. Both saw Theodore Roosevelt and his ilk, in and out of government, as militarists who posed the main obstacle to achieving those ends. But unlike the peace activists, the president tempered his internationalist convictions with a desire to advance the nation's power and status. That required preserving its "honor" from the insult of U-boat attacks on American vessels that were helping to fuel the Allied war effort. As the crisis with Germany intensified, the idealism of the head of state inevitably clashed with that of citizens whose desire that America be right always mattered far more than any wish that it be mighty.

For several weeks, however, anti-war organizers allowed themselves to imagine that a fresh surge of agitation could stay Wilson's hand. On February 2, several veterans of the moribund campaign for neutral mediation—including Fanny Garrison Villard, Louis Lochner, and Emily Balch—launched a new umbrella group called the Emergency Peace Federation. At the top, the new body just reassembled individuals who had worked together before—including some Socialists and labor officials; Fanny Villard was its chairman. But its name signified an obvious urgency, and branches quickly sprouted in Boston, Louisville, Washington, D.C., and several other cities.

The federation put together several events that drew more press coverage than established groups like the AUAM had garnered since the previous summer, when Congress's modest expansion of the military had cooled the fierce debate about preparedness. On February 2, William Jennings Bryan rushed up to New York City to deliver an impassioned version of his standard call for arbitration to resolve every serious dispute between nations. "I have faith, not only in the President's desire to keep us out of war," he assured the audience of five thousand in Madison Square Garden, "but in his ability to do so." Ten days later, on Lincoln's birthday, Fanny Villard led a delegation to Washington of hundreds of female and male activists from a variety of cities. They lobbied individual lawmakers and held a mass meeting. On a frigid, windy day, they then marched down Pennsylvania Avenue to the White House to present a petition to Woodrow Wilson. The president did not appear, but the activists left a large banner reading "Peace or War?" for him in the Oval Office. That week, thousands packed mass rallies in Minneapolis and Chicago.[6]

Such spirited actions could not obscure the deep anxiety of peace organizers. They had always believed American intervention would destroy the possibility of creating a democratic and nonviolent global order. They had rallied to Wilson during the 1916 campaign and his brief peace offensive that followed because they believed he thought so too. In the immediate wake of the U-boat decision, Wilson still hoped to stay neutral, but a single German torpedo that killed a large number of Americans would probably compel him to call for war.

On February 17, the *Survey* published a revealing personal statement by Paul Kellogg, its longtime editor and a founding member of the AUAM, which expressed that anxiety and signaled what belligerency would mean. Since the war began, his influential magazine had run frequent, always sympathetic reports on the peace movement's actions and thinking. But Kellogg himself had refrained from taking a position on military or diplomatic issues, for fear of alienating social reformers who cared more about woman suffrage, decent housing, and safe working conditions at home than about the war overseas. Now, in the wake of what he called "the ruthless extension of the U-boat campaign and the break with Germany," he decided to speak out. The result, titled "The Fighting Issues," was as eloquent—and prophetic—a document as the anti-war movement had ever produced.[7]

New submarine attacks, Kellogg asserted, could not alter the moral stakes of the terrible conflict. "I should want the United States to go into the war," he conceded, ". . . if it were a clear case of struggle between democracy and Prussianism." But "the root of Prussianism" was "an isolated nationalism which holds that force is the only method for maintaining its nation's rights"—and that "psychology" was as present in the United States as it was in Germany.[8]

Nor was Kellogg persuaded that, by entering the war, Americans could secure a peace that would make future resorts to arms less likely. Why would "the people of Europe . . . torn by the hates and heart burnings of thirty months of war" accept a just settlement imposed by an outside force? The progressive journalist pointed out that "the most active groups here in America" calling for intervention were usually on the side of "privilege" when it "lock[ed] horns" with democracy "in municipality, state capital, or Congress." A "war to end all wars" was thus a foolish delusion.[9]

So was the notion that citizens would be free in a belligerent America to oppose the actions of government. When Kellogg's piece came out, Congress was already debating bills to initiate a military draft and censor "disloyal" opinion. "The day war is declared," he predicted, "that day we are invaded—our liberties, our reason, our power to choose for ourselves."[10]

Even at the eleventh hour, the *Survey* editor did not shy away from proposing ways his nation might avoid going to war. Kellogg urged Congress and the president to "distinguish strongly" between the right of Americans on U.S. ships to sail across the ocean without military cargo and those who decided to sail on "a foreign ship, carrying munitions and armed with a naval gun on deck." He called on citizens to refuse to travel on belligerent vessels, voluntarily acting as the Gore and McLemore resolutions would have required. But these ideas differed only slightly from the ones Wilson and federal lawmakers had already rejected.[11]

Kellogg did endorse one proposal that was rapidly capturing the imagination of his fellow anti-warriors: holding a national referendum before

Congress could declare war. "The stake of all the people for all time, in the measure and burden and meaning of life," he wrote, "is too real and engrossing for anything less."[12]

It was not a novel idea. In 1899, Carl Schurz, a stalwart anti-imperialist and former cabinet member, had advocated holding a popular vote on whether the United States should colonize the Philippines. In 1914, Congressman Richard Bartholdt, a Republican from St. Louis, had called for amending the Constitution to require a referendum prior to a congressional vote authorizing war. By the end of 1916, the Woman's Peace Party, the Socialist Party, and both La Follette and Bryan had endorsed some kind of advisory plebiscite too. But movement organizers absorbed with battling preparedness and preaching mediation had little time for what seemed a worthy but impractical proposal.[13]

The break with Germany made that judgment obsolete. In February, most American peace activists and associations embraced a popular referendum as the best and, perhaps, last chance to halt the march to war. Bryan asked the crowd at Madison Square Garden to urge it on their congressmen and senators. The Woman's Peace Party and Emergency Peace Federation promoted it with public appeals and rallies. So did the Friends of Irish Freedom and the German-American Alliance, anxious as ever to show Wilson "that the vast majority of your countrymen and women want peace and abhor war." Two new groups, the Committee for Democratic Control and the Keep Out of War Committee, the latter led by union officials and Socialists, formed almost solely to lobby for the referendum. In Chicago, ingenious pacifists paid five local theater owners to run the slogan "Let the People Decide" across their screens and then asked moviegoers if they favored going to war.[14]

Most ambitiously, the AUAM staged a rehearsal for a nationwide vote. With the guidance of his wife, Crystal Eastman, Walter Fuller organized a mailing of a hundred thousand postcards to individuals supplied to him by peace groups and supporters in five congressional districts scattered around the country. The cards asked: "Do you believe

that the people should be consulted by referendum—in any event—
short of invasion—before Congress declares war?" To no one's surprise,
the "yes" vote was overwhelming. The AUAM suggested that postmas-
ters could carry out such an exercise all over America in a mere twenty-
five days.[15]

The movement's allies on Capitol Hill rushed to cobble together
legislation to make something like that happen. From February 9 to
February 23, nine different congressmen—seven of whom were Democrats from the South or Midwest—introduced referendum bills. One of
the anti-war Republicans was Charles A. Lindbergh from Minnesota,
father of the future aviator, who accused the "greedy speculators" of
"the Money Trust" of conspiring to force the United States into war.
Petitions of support flooded in from a variety of states. Bryan traveled
to Washington to make the case for adopting the idea. In an off-kilter
attempt to calm tensions, he compared the German U-boat decision to
a drunk driver who strikes a man on a sidewalk. The latter would be
"fully within his rights" to attack the driver, he said, but "I would prefer
to step aside and settle with him when he is sober."[16]

Claude Kitchin neither supported nor resisted these efforts; a savvy
legislator, he must have realized that the existence of so many bills dedicated to the same purpose would prevent the House from taking any of
them seriously. Indeed, the Foreign Affairs Committee debated just one
of the proposals, for only forty-five minutes. None of the bills made it to
the floor. And no senator, not even La Follette, volunteered to promote
the idea in the upper chamber. That didn't stop pro-war Republicans
from condemning it. "I will resign my office before I will vote for such
a proposition," snarled Senator (and future President) Warren G. Harding of Ohio.[17]

Still, the referendum had a potential appeal that was missing from
other major pieces in the movement's strategic repertoire. It asked only
for a simple statement of the popular will, avoiding the delays and funding problems that had plagued the attempt to set up a conference of

neutral nations. Neither did it require opposition to a larger military, and so it could have gained backing from Americans who wanted to be ready for a future war but did not want to intervene in this one.

The demand for a popular vote also drew on a critique that progressives, whether pacifist or not, had been making and the policies they had been enacting for the past two decades. Monopolies in business, city halls, and Congress benefited only venal elites, they argued. Direct democracy defied all the nasty backroom schemes. In Wisconsin and a growing number of other states, voters were already using referenda and initiatives to bypass legislatures. Why not use the same instrument to help decide the most profound question any nation could face?

Populist antipathy coursed through the language of the reformers and radicals who called for a referendum. If war comes, the Committee for Democratic Control pointed out, "The editors and ex-Presidents will not do the fighting; nor will our bellicose lawyers, bankers, stockbrokers and other prominent citizens, who mess at Delmonico's, bivouac in club windows, and are at all times willing to give to their country's service the last full measure of conversation." In early March, an editorial in the *Wall Street Digest* crowed that stock prices had been steadily increasing since Wilson broke relations with Germany; financiers, claimed the *Digest*, believed the United States was "now definitely committed" to an Allied victory. Peace groups quickly reprinted it. Perhaps, they hoped, a national referendum would rip the smiles from a lot of smug, well-fed faces.[18]

Demanding that the people have an opportunity to vote for or against war also rebutted the charge that pacifists were consciously or unwittingly "playing directly into Germany's hands." Many newspapers reported, erroneously, that the Kaiser's henchmen were funding several peace groups, including the AUAM. In New York City, the pro-Wilson *World* ran a cartoon depicting a German officer and an anti-war activist running into each other's arms, yelling "Kamerad!" But in calling for a plebiscite, anti-warriors were claiming that they had the support of their fellow citizens. Let the "jingoists" accuse millions of American voters of being German agents![19]

Despite such advantages, no referendum managed to advance beyond the agitational stage. In a single state, it was increasingly possible to secure a voice in passing or vetoing a law. But the AUAM and its allies never explained why Congress would voluntarily give up or weaken its constitutional authority to declare war.

To be credible, even a purely advisory nationwide referendum would have had to be administered by a public body, probably with the president's approval. On February 28, Paul Kellogg and Lillian Wald led a small delegation to the White House, where they presented Woodrow Wilson with the landslide results of their postcard poll. A separate group, led by Jane Addams, had just met with him for much the same purpose. This time, in contrast to their earlier encounters, the president showed no sympathy at all for their cause. War, he said, had become all but "inevitable"; victory would enable him to sit at "the Peace Table" to ensure a just and lasting settlement. As she departed, Addams "hotly and no doubt unfairly asked myself whether any man had the right to rate his moral leadership so high that he could consider the sacrifice of the lives of thousands of his young countrymen a necessity."[20]

TROTSKY AND TROUBLE

The increasing likelihood of war forced American Socialists to make some wrenching choices of their own. A few, like their European comrades in 1914, saw no alternative but to go along with their government, hoping the president would stick to his design of a postwar world even if he abandoned all efforts to keep the peace. In March, Charles Edward Russell, a celebrated muckraker and the SPA's last nominee for mayor of New York, organized a small group of radicals, most of them journalists, to issue a statement brimming with Wilsonian optimism. "The proper aim of Socialist world-politics at the present time," it asserted, "is an alliance of the politically advanced nations for the defense of the democratic principle." The new recruits to the interventionist cause took some solace in knowing that governments in many of the warring nations had taken over the ownership and operation of major industries, thus fulfilling a key aim of every Socialist platform.[21]

For most American Marxists, however, the prospect of fighting in an "imperialist" conflict remained as repellent as ever. On February 2, the Socialist Party of America called for an embargo on shipments to every belligerent. "It would be preposterous," declared the SPA, "for this country to go to war for the right to permit its selfish rich to still further enrich themselves by acting as accessories to murder." But Socialists had been making the same demand since the carnage in Europe had begun; repeating it now made the party sound pro-German, since only the Allies depended on American supplies. It also avoided the challenge of figuring out a serious strategy to resist the rush to war.[22]

Hillquit, as he had on numerous occasions since 1914, sought to craft a better response. He helped plan an emergency party convention for early April and sat down for interviews with the New York Times and other papers. He was quite aware that a growing number of party members had lost all faith in the American political system and wanted the party, in the event of war, to steel itself for insurrection against employers and the capitalist state. That view was held most strongly by immigrants from the crumbling tsarist empire who had recently joined the SPA. Some had taken part in the abortive Russian revolution in 1905 or had been active in the powerful Socialist movement in Finland, where a civil war between "Reds" and "Whites" would break out early in 1918. A compromiser by nature, Hillquit sought a middle ground between the pro-Wilsonians in his party and the swelling faction of militants on his left.

Thus, he predicted most Socialists would "refuse to enlist" in the military but would continue to "work for the earliest possible peace." At the same time, he warned against any attempt to wage a general strike to stop preparations for war; that, he feared, would alienate more Americans than it would persuade. Intent on preserving the SPA's alliance with pacifist reformers like Addams, Hillquit condemned war as "the brute method of settling things" and argued that Americans should cling to Wilson's ideal of "peace without victory" instead of "joining in the madness." Such moderation, he hoped, would allow Socialists to weather the tempests of war better than brazen calls for revolution from American comrades who, emulating Vladimir Lenin, longed to transform the present imperialist war into a civil war.[23]

Hillquit's stance enraged one prominent Socialist sojourning from abroad who would soon be helping to lead a revolution of his own. In the middle of January, Leon Trotsky landed in New York City from Barcelona. For two years, the charismatic organizer and intellectual with the dagger-shaped goatee had been agitating against the war in various European cities while narrowly avoiding deportation. After he and his family settled into an apartment in the Bronx, he began writing for *Novy Mir* (the "New World"), a Russian-language paper edited by Nikolai Bukharin and other exiles, and lecturing to radical immigrants up and down the eastern seaboard. Trotsky's English was poor, so he spoke either in German or his native tongue.

In every language, Trotsky made clear he detested any leftist who counseled compromise. A Ukrainian-born member of the SPA who often heard him speak in New York remembered: "Of all the species of political fauna, none was lower, none more contemptible, none more dangerous to the interests of Trotsky's working class than the Socialist who defended his country in time of war. . . . He loathed men like Hillquit . . . with more intense hatred than he felt toward J.P. Morgan or the Czar."[24]

In early March, at an SPA meeting in midtown Manhattan, Trotsky argued for an unrelenting, admittedly dangerous, struggle against Wilson's policies. He urged Socialists, in the event of war, to organize mass strikes and encourage young men to resist a draft, even if that provoked a bloody confrontation with the state. Hillquit firmly disagreed: "We should be asses to tell members . . . they must risk death and imprisonment rather than join the army." Following angry exchanges—and several fistfights—his moderate position carried the day. Later that month, after militant demonstrators in Petrograd forced Tsar Nicholas II to abdicate his throne, Trotsky sailed back home to hasten the triumph of the Russian proletariat.[25]

Despite his future travails, Trotsky would never soften his animosity toward Hillquit. In his memoir, published in 1930 after Stalin had expelled him from the Communist Party and exiled him from the USSR, Trotsky described his erstwhile American adversary in prose toxic with disdain. Hillquit, he alleged, was the epitome of the comfortable, automobile-owning Socialist officials who betrayed their radical ideals. They were chasing after "business connections" instead of liberating the working class. The champion of "permanent revolution" blasted Hillquit, memorably, as "the ideal Socialist leader for successful dentists." His ilk, concluded Trotsky, "seemed the rottenest part of that world with which I was and still am at war."[26]

The stinging accusations demonstrated something beyond the Russian radical's neglect or ignorance of Hillquit's long career spent defending his party and its causes before juries and the public. It revealed the political myopia of the mostly immigrant Socialists who, in 1917, had determined, like Trotsky, that a turn toward revolution was the only way forward for authentic opponents of the Great War. Quite soon, like other foes of American intervention, they would have to confront the question not of whether to mount a general strike but of whether they could freely voice any discontent about the war at all.

For Crystal Eastman, the two months after Wilson's break with Germany were probably the tensest and busiest of her life. On March 19, she gave birth to her first child, Jeffrey Fuller. Through the final weeks of a difficult pregnancy, Crystal kept working sixteen hours a day, promoting the referendum and other emergency measures. Lillian Wald and fellow co-workers urged her to take a vacation, but two days before she went into labor, Eastman was busy planning a national "Truth about Preparedness" campaign to begin in April.[27]

She also had to devote some of her attention to a troubling division among feminists. Since European guns began blazing in August 1914, nearly every ardent campaigner for women's rights had insisted that America stay neutral. The marriage of feminism and peace seemed unbreakable. In February, however, the executive committee of the NAWSA, the premier suffrage organization, pledged, in the event of war, to do whatever President Wilson thought necessary to aid and protect the nation.

The turnabout stunned many activists in the Woman's Peace Party, which Carrie Chapman Catt, the NAWSA's president, had helped initiate two years before. Anna Garlin Spencer, the minister whose grand oration had opened the WPP's inaugural meeting in 1915, warned Catt that to "commandeer" suffragists for war duty "would split the body from stem to stern." Margaret Lane—a leader, along with Eastman, of the party's New York branch—remarked, "I will not make a bandage until war is declared. What I might do then I don't know, but for the present I shall endeavor to keep the shreds of peace together as well as I can." The WPP stripped Catt of her honorary position as vice-chairman. The suffrage leader abruptly resigned from the group and yoked her group more firmly to Wilson's policies.[28]

The dispute stirred Eastman, Lane, and the other young activists who steered the New York contingent to reassert, in aggressive prose, the principles on which the Woman's Peace Party had been founded. "To our thinking," they announced, "the dragooning of this country into war with any of the bleeding nations of Europe, however grave be the provocation, would be the true forfeit of our national pride, an intolerable insult to our humanity." They printed the statement on the masthead of *Four Lights*, a provocative new magazine published every fortnight by the New York branch.[29]

Given her pressing tasks and swelling uterus, Crystal Eastman was unable to contribute to the early issues of *Four Lights*. Still, the little magazine brimmed with the witty, irreverent spirit present in all her writing, as well as in the "War Against War" exhibit of the previous spring and in the pages of her brother's *Masses*. There were tongue-in-cheek "Definitionaries to the Heathen," such as "Patriot—One who is ashamed of America because it is not imitating Europe." There were anecdotes about the hypocrisy of a Congress that refused to authorize a tiny amount of money for the Children's Bureau but could find tens of millions for armaments: "A hundred and eighty thousand dollars was not to be spent on trifling matters like this. Thrift, thrift, Horatio!"[30]

Four Lights also highlighted news and commentary that affirmed its slogan, "An Adventure in Internationalism." From reporting on the rise of anti-war sentiment in Canada and Germany to quoting equally bloodthirsty remarks made by Kaiser Wilhelm and Theodore Roosevelt, the magazine's editors affirmed their solidarity with the forces, feminist and otherwise, who might soon end the war, whether their rulers wanted to or not. Their message echoed Jane Addams, Paul Kellogg, and other progressives who had always favored citizen pressure on warmaking states. But their heated, explicitly "uncompromising" tone also aligned *Four Lights* with the position of left-wing Socialists—although they employed the vivid vernacular of an American tabloid instead of the catchphrases of Marxist dogma. More conservative members in Boston and other cities shuddered. Lucia Ames Mead, leader of the Massachusetts branch, said that reading *Four Lights* "distressed" her, and she warned Eastman and her sisters to speak patriotically if they wanted to avoid a split in the organization. The rebellious stance taken by the largest branch of what was still the largest anti-war organization in the land was sure to make trouble in the months ahead.[31]

ARMED SHIPS AND WILLFUL MEN

For most of February, Congress was in less turmoil than the coalition that was frantically trying to keep the nation at peace. Although the Democrats had won fewer seats in the House than the GOP, they managed to retain control with the support of several congressmen from minority parties—including the lone socialist in the chamber. American shipping companies left nearly all their oceangoing vessels in port, which reduced U-boat attacks to a minimum. Despite the diplomatic break with Germany, the president had not begun to mobilize the armed forces and said nothing in public to hint he might favor—or oppose— belligerency. Ambassador von Bernstorff, who lingered in the United States until Valentine's Day, wrote to Berlin that "the war feeling has greatly diminished"; hostilities might be postponed "for quite a while yet if we do not actually attack" the United States.[32]

In Congress, most Democrats agreed about how to finance the military, although Kitchin and his faction still resisted expanding its size. On the first of February, the House enacted another progressive revenue bill written by the majority leader and endorsed by the Wilson administration. It boosted the inheritance tax by a whopping 50 percent and enacted a new tax on any corporate profits that exceeded 8 percent. Business executives protested that these "exorbitant" levies might bankrupt their firms, but Kitchin's familiar argument that those who championed preparedness should pay for it appealed to most members of his party. The largest manufacturing firms in the nation, they knew, had increased their profits by from two to fifteen times since the war began. The new tax measure passed easily in the House. Later that month, the Senate affirmed it with a simple voice vote.[33]

Debate about the war did not cease, of course. Lawmakers from both parties delivered passionate speeches for and against taking new, aggressive actions to punish Germany. Interventionist newspapers like the *New York Times* predicted a swift economic decline if transatlantic shipping did not resume soon. Unless the president changed his mind, the anxious status quo might last—as the departing German ambassador hoped.

Yet, by mid-February, Wilson had privately arrived at a decision he knew carried the risk of war: The United States would place guns powerful enough to sink a submarine on merchant vessels bound for Europe. For the president, armed neutrality was a middle course—between letting the Germans have their way on the high seas and joining the Allies. It would also, he hoped, appease shipping companies who were seeing their profits rotting away on domestic wharves. Before announcing it, he told the members of his cabinet he wanted to seek the approval of Congress, although his advisors assured him he had the legal power to act without it.

Ironically, an article written earlier that month by a distinguished anti-interventionist helped persuade Wilson to take that step. In the *Survey*, Carleton J.H. Hayes, a history professor at Columbia, called for the United States to assemble a "league of neutral nations" from Europe and Latin America to arm their vessels as they traversed the Atlantic. Convoys led by U.S. warships, Hayes argued, would lessen "the menace of submarine warfare" and might even persuade the Allies to relax their boycott on the North Sea. For the first time since the Great War began, an American peace advocate was willing to use arms against Germany, albeit with the ironic aim of making a declaration of war unnecessary.[34]

On February 26, Wilson unveiled the idea before a joint session of Congress. He shrewdly appealed both to national self-interest and to the strong desire of most Americans to avoid war. Armed neutrality, he promised, would relieve "the very serious congestion of our commerce . . . which is growing rapidly more and more serious every day." He acknowledged that no U-boat had yet torpedoed an American ship of any size. Thus, "the overt act which I have ventured to hope the German commanders would in fact avoid has not occurred." But as long as the Kaiser's order remained in effect, the respite could not last.

The president reiterated his neutral convictions. "I am anxious," he said, "that the people of the nations at war also should understand and not mistrust us." During "nearly three years of anxious patience," he had proved "that I am the friend of peace and mean to preserve it for America so long as I am able." Even now, Wilson was not "proposing or contemplating war or any steps that need lead to it." In asking Congress to authorize funds for arming merchant ships, he referred vaguely to "other instrumentalities or methods" that might be needed "to protect our ships and our people in their legitimate and peaceful pursuits on the seas."[35]

No previous speech Wilson had delivered about the Great War was greeted so favorably—and by such disparate voices. Newspapers loyal to both parties and supporting either intervention or peace all praised his "wisdom," his "logical and reasonable appeal," and his "honor and courage." Even one of the few critical editorials, from the Illinois *Springfield State Journal*, acknowledged that Wilson "enjoys the confidence of the people," even as it warned him not to exercise "unlimited authority in a matter of this sort." Most Democrats, even those from Kitchin's faction, joined in the applause. Republicans, both conservative and progressive, argued that the president already had the authority to arm merchant ships; few opposed him doing so. Some did grumble that those "other instrumentalities or methods" might become a backhanded way of declaring war.[36]

Wilson's plan, however, divided the peace coalition, which was already fighting off false charges that it was financed by Germany. Crystal Eastman was dismayed that the president had tacitly rejected the idea of a league of neutrals in favor of a purely American effort. The Emergency Peace Federation urged Congress to deny Wilson's request to arm U.S. vessels. No single man, "however able and conscientious," it protested, had the constitutional power to make a decision that could embroil the nation in this, or any, war. All "injuries inflicted upon us" by Germany, Fanny Villard and her colleagues insisted, should be settled in court. Such faith in legal remedies echoed the punchless manifestos that Andrew Carnegie and other elite internationalists had issued in the halcyon days before the Great War.[37]

But most prominent peace workers refused to fault Wilson's plan. Lillian Wald predicted that armed neutrality was "a substitute for war that will not lead to war." Frederick Lynch, secretary of the venerable Church Peace Union, agreed, as did Paul Kellogg. What Hayes had written in the *Survey* convinced them that the United States, with or without other nations, had to do *something* dramatic to respond to the U-boat scourge. They were unwilling to give up confidence in a president who had "kept us out of war" and still "wishes to keep the peace." Henry Ford finally abandoned his hope for a neutral peace conference and asserted, with blunt irony, "sometimes the best thing a pacifist can do is to help get over a fight as quickly as possible." Either from conviction or fear, some leading German-American newspapers and spokesmen guardedly blessed the new tactic too. They added the plea, as if by rote, that Wilson "Be neutral; treat all nations the same and fairly."[38] Given the deep split in their ranks, anti-interventionists would have difficulty pressing Congress one way or the other.

Then, two days after Wilson's speech, banner headlines seemed to make it certain that lawmakers would grant his request. "Germany Seeks an Alliance Against US; Asks Japan and Mexico to Join Her; Full Text of Her Proposal Made Public," shouted the *New York Times*. "German Plot to Conquer U.S. With Aid of Japan and Mexico Revealed," exclaimed the *Washington Post*. Even most of those papers that, unlike the *Times* and *Post*, had consistently opposed belligerence now sadly agreed that war was probably inevitable.[39]

The cause of this alarm was the "Zimmermann Telegram," perhaps the worst conceived document in the annals of modern diplomatic history. On January 16, Arthur Zimmermann, the German foreign secretary, had sent a coded telegram to the government of Mexico. He proposed an alliance between the two nations if the United States declared war on Germany. In that event, the Kaiser's government would aid Mexico to recover "the lost territory in Texas, New Mexico, and Arizona" conquered by Americans in the 1840s. Mexico would then attack the colossus of the north. In the same message, Zimmermann urged Mexico to persuade Japan to desert the Allies and join the Central Powers. The diplomat, whose face was marked by a deep scar from his days as a student fencer, did not bother to explain how this switch would benefit the rising Asian power. Nor did he consider why Mexicans, who were still embroiled in a many-sided revolution, would be eager to attack their more populous and potent neighbor or how German troops pinned down in Europe would help them do it.[40]

The transmission of the telegram was bungled as badly as its conception. Zimmermann dispatched the encrypted document to his embassy in Washington via U.S. diplomatic cables. But since the Royal Navy had cut Germany's undersea cables early in the war, all such messages first passed through London—which the foreign secretary should have known. British intelligence agents quickly decoded the telegram and, after covering their tracks a bit, gleefully sent it to U.S. ambassador Walter Hines Page. An ardent Anglophile, Page was just as glad to pass it on to the president.

Zimmermann's remarkable blunder was not, however, quite the casus belli the British had hoped for. It did embolden the interventionist lobby in the United States, while hardening Wilson's position against making any compromise with the Kaiser's regime. His rebuff of the pacifist delegations who came to see him on February 28 indicated that much. However, absent a supportive response from Mexico, the telegram seems to have persuaded few Americans who opposed going to war to change their minds. At first, Crystal Eastman and her allies doubted that, as she put it, "with all her crudity Germany would scarcely do anything quite as crude and stupid as this." The telegram had to be a British forgery. Even after the German foreign secretary admitted, on March 3, that he written the document, every peace group in the United States affirmed its neutral stand. By the middle of the month, "coverage of Zimmermann's scheme had virtually disappeared from all American newspapers," according to its most thorough historian.[41]

If the infamous telegram did not make war inevitable, it did appear to ensure that American ships would soon be equipped to sink submarines. On the same day newspapers blared the news about the German plot, the House debated for seven hours before voting, by a margin of 403 to 13, to give Wilson the authority he requested. The lonely opposition included such unyielding anti-war figures as Isaac Sherwood, the Civil War veteran from Ohio; Charles Lindbergh; and Meyer London, the only Socialist in Congress. Except for London, all hailed from the Middle West, most from districts with large numbers of German-Americans or Scandinavian-Americans. One representative who voted no—Dorsey Shackleford, a Democrat from Missouri—pointed "an accusing finger at the press gallery" where, he charged, sat the men most responsible for driving the nation to war.[42]

This time, with misgivings, Claude Kitchin followed the leader of his party instead of his own conscience. In a brief speech, he reasoned that the president already had the power to place guns on American ships. Kitchin vowed he would "pray God daily" to give Wilson "the wisdom and the strength" to keep America from adding to "the increasing horrors of an almost universal war." Meyer London remarked, to general laughter, that "after the genial majority leader has announced that he will hereafter pray, I think that all opposition is about gone." Later that day, an amendment to stop armed vessels from carrying munitions to any country at war did gain 125 votes. Kitchin, for undisclosed reasons, was not among them.[43] He knew a majority in the upper house was prepared to back the president too.

But first they would have to deal with Robert La Follette and his band of brave, or foolhardy, senatorial allies. The twelve opponents of armed neutrality feared not just that a skirmish between U.S. ships and U-boats could escalate into war. They believed that giving Wilson the authority to employ "other instrumentalities and methods," as the House bill put it, would create a tyrannical presidency. Bypassing Congress, the man in the White House could decide to make war with Germany and perhaps even conscript young men to fight it. La Follette, employing the arguments of a Yale law professor who occasionally wrote for his eponymous magazine, even questioned whether it was legal for neutral ships to arm themselves for war. Wouldn't that, he asked, "place themselves outside the law and become, so to speak, pirates"?[44]

The anti-war lawmakers had time on their side. Under the Constitution, the term of the Sixty-fourth Congress would end precisely at noon on March 4, wiping all pending legislation off the books. Since the Senate only began debating the armed ship bill on Friday, March 2, preventing a vote for just forty-eight hours would frustrate the majority's will. La Follette was convinced, his daughter Fola wrote later, that delaying a vote until the new Congress could begin its work would allow "time for the anti-war sentiment . . . to register on Congress and defeat the measure." He also expected the furor over the Zimmermann Telegram to abate by then. Belle La Follette, who was still giving lectures for the Woman's Peace Party, urged her husband on.[45]

For the next two days, the U.S. Senate engaged in ferocious, if unarmed, combat. Fighting Bob exercised one parliamentary maneuver after another to prevent a vote on the measure. On March 2, he objected to bringing up the House bill, a step that would have forestalled a longer debate. Then he withdrew his objection in return for a recess until the next morning. "We've got them beaten," Senator George Norris of Nebraska told La Follette that evening as they traveled home together. "We've enough speakers to filibuster from tomorrow on." On March 3, the Senate gallery, which fit twelve hundred, was so packed with spectators and reporters that several lawmakers complained there were no seats left for their family members or those of the president.[46]

That morning, William Stone held the floor for over four hours, fielding hostile questions for much of the time. Up to this point, the seventy-eight-year-old Democrat who was chairman of the Foreign Relations Committee had nearly always echoed the president's views. He swore that Wilson "holds a high place in my esteem and a warm place in my affections." The senator declined to join the filibustering team La Follette and Norris had assembled; he did not mean to prevent a vote on the measure.[47]

Yet Stone believed as strongly as did his obstructionist colleagues that Wilson was about to commit "an unpardonable and perilous mistake." To arm civilian ships and let them sail off "loaded with war supplies" to a belligerent nation would make the United States "an ally of the government benefited. We would be in the war." Stone's aversion to the conflict inspired him to launch a bitter and extraordinarily vivid attack on the interventionist camp. The press and "jingoistic" Republicans like Lodge were seeking "to entice our people" into the "maelstrom of war" with "unadultered mendacity oozing like filth from vindictive inventions, supplemented by the most reckless and ferocious appeals to passion." He accused the executives of J.P. Morgan & Co. of scheming "to plunge this peaceful and happy Nation" into the great bloodletting in order to enhance their bottom line. When Stone concluded the harshest speech of his thirty-two-year tenure in Congress, he nearly collapsed on the floor and needed assistance to walk out of the chamber. He knew he had terminated his influence in national politics.[48]

But the Senate remained in session all through the night and into Sunday morning. Seventy-five lawmakers from both parties signed a petition, known as a "round robin," announcing their support for the bill and protesting the minority's attempt to thwart a vote. Still, several of them could not resist giving lengthy speeches to rebut the charges made by Stone and his allies. Ironically, the supporters of armed ships ended up declaiming for twice as long as their opponents. As Woodrow Wilson took the oath of office on the morning of March 4, confidence that the current Senate would give him the authority he requested was swiftly waning.

During the final hours, sharp differences erupted into bitter quarrels, a shocking occurrence in a body with a tradition of strict decorum. One of La Follette's closest allies—Asle Gronna, a Republican from North

Dakota—called the majority's petition an attempt to "bulldoze" the legislative process. John Sharp Williams, a Mississippi Democrat, snapped back that the minority was producing "one of the most humiliating spectacles in the course of American history." Speakers on both sides were frequently interrupted and repeatedly refused to yield the floor. Questions were shouted more often than asked. A reporter for the *Washington Post* tried to capture the scene: "The forensic struggle which ensued seldom if ever had been equaled in the history of the Senate. Voices were strained to shrieking, threatening fists were shaken at the presiding officer while the crowded floor and galleries looked on breathlessly."[49]

La Follette's temper rose to the breaking point. At about four o'clock that morning, he received an anonymous note, scrawled on an official Senate memo pad. It warned that "a scheme is hatching to have the Presiding officer ignore or refuse to recognize you when you rise to speak." Off the floor, a few of his adversaries hinted that if he attempted to prolong the debate, they would force him to remain silent. When he heard this, La Follette told his son Robert Jr., who served as an aide, to bring his small traveling suitcase and place it near his desk in the chamber. "I knew," recalled young Bob, "he had a gun in the bag," which his father kept for protection during long nights on the road. The son brought the bag but kept the revolver safely back in the senator's office.[50]

During its last hour, the Sixty-fourth Congress did almost expire in bloodshed. La Follette demanded he be allowed to make the speech that would close the debate, a characteristically theatrical gesture. Several hostile colleagues rushed toward him; one, the Kentucky Democrat Ollie James, carried a concealed revolver. Harry Lane, a Democrat from Oregon and a physician, gripped a small round "rat-tail" file he hid in his pocket. Later, he told La Follette he was ready to plunge the tool inside James's collarbone—where "on the left side you can reach his heart with one thrust and he will never move again." Fortunately, neither man drew his weapon. La Follette thundered, "I will continue on this floor until I complete my statement unless somebody carries me off, and I should like to see the man who will do it." A few minutes later, he picked up a spittoon and was about to hit the presiding officer, Senator Joseph Robinson, with it before George Norris calmed him down. Promptly at noon, the Senate adjourned without voting on the bill that had caused all the tumult.[51]

La Follette did not get to crown the filibuster with an oratorical flourish, but he had made his point. If arming ships was indeed an act of war, as even many supporters agreed it was, then any American alarmed at that prospect should cheer what the flamboyant senator from Wisconsin had done. Amid "the gravest international crisis in the nation's history," he had stood up for a peaceful way out.[52]

While the filibuster was in progress, La Follette received hundreds of supportive notes and telegrams. In the immediate aftermath came thousands more. "Workers Don't Want War Keep Up Brave Stand," wrote Nathan Arnold from Philadelphia. An anonymous "Irishman" from Ohio congratulated La Follette for his "manly stand against British dictation," while H.R. Adams from Minneapolis cheered him for pushing back against the press "clamoring . . . to create in Wilson an autocratic Czar with absolute power." With Marxian confidence, Eugene Debs predicted that "history will vindicate you." Walter Rauschenbusch, the renowned theologian of the Social Gospel, praised the "spiritual compulsion" behind the filibuster; it had, he believed, "stayed the rush of the nation in the direction of warlike action, and has given us a further chance to think." The Emergency Peace Federation telegrammed its gratitude to La Follette, Stone, and Norris for having "served the case of peace and democracy."[53]

Before the armed ship debate, most Americans had probably known La Follette more for what he done to regulate business and help labor than for how he thought the United States should behave in the world—although he had been vital to the anti-preparedness effort. In the aftermath, he would be universally regarded as the unofficial leader of anti-war stalwarts in Congress.

Of course, that made him a notorious figure as well. Just hours after the Senate adjourned, a furious Wilson typed up a statement for the press: "A little group of willful men, representing no opinion but their own, have rendered the great Government of the United States helpless and contemptible." From all over the nation, contempt rained down on the senator from Wisconsin. In words and editorial cartoons, he was depicted as a Benedict Arnold, a Judas, a German agent, a "pervert, lunatic, madman, and devil who humiliated the nation." Theodore Roosevelt stated simply, "He ought to be hung." Several state legislative bodies, including the Wisconsin senate, passed resolutions of censure against La Follette and his fellow filibusterers.[54]

But their defiance failed to prevent the action they dreaded. Anxious that any delay would embolden the Germans, Wilson acted on his own. On March 12, following the president's order, Secretary of the Navy Josephus Daniels gave American merchant ships the authority to attack any U-boat that approached close enough to threaten them. A few days before, in one of the first acts of the Sixty-fifth Congress, the Senate had met to grant another of Wilson's requests. They adopted a cloture rule allowing two-thirds of the members to cut off debate, once every senator had had the opportunity to speak on a given bill for just an hour. Willful or honorable, a "little group" of lawmakers would never again be able to have its way merely by talking a bill to death.

A FINAL STAND

On the same day that Congress adjourned, Woodrow Wilson delivered his second inaugural address. He sounded very much like a leader preparing his people for war: "We are provincials no longer. The tragic events of the thirty months of vital turmoil through we have just passed have made us citizens of the world. There can be no turning back. Our own fortunes as a nation are involved whether we would have it so or not." The president urged Americans to be "united in the conception of our duty and in the high resolve to perform it."

It would be another two weeks before he finally discarded the ambivalence that had dogged his policy since the sinking of the *Lusitania* two years before. Wilson never revealed why he changed his mind—and, as it turned out, the course of world history. But recent events across and beneath the ocean likely drove him to it. On March 15, massive street demonstrations in Petrograd and plummeting morale in the Russian military forced Tsar Nicholas II to abdicate his throne. The emergence of a new, if unstable, democratic regime in that vast empire meant a belligerent United States would not be chained to an alliance with a backward, absolutist regime. "With the cause of Russian freedom thrown into the scale," the *New York Post* commented, "there was an instant change of view. . . . .Men of reason know that with the uprising of the Russian people the moral issue for ourselves was clarified."[55]

At the same time, the new German offensive on the Atlantic was starting to bite hard. On Sunday March 18, newspapers announced that U-boats had sunk three American vessels, all of which were unarmed; fifteen seamen on one ship drowned before they could launch their lifeboats. Again, U.S. merchant firms shrank back from sending additional cargo into harm's way. At the same time, diplomats were reporting that the Kaiser and his key ministers had rejected the possibility of negotiating an end to the confrontation with the United States. U-boat attacks would continue into the indefinite future.[56]

The president, who had staked the nation's honor and prosperity on protecting "the freedom of the seas," now believed he had no choice but to go to war. He also thought a belligerent America could end the conflict more quickly and, perhaps, spur ordinary Germans to topple their leaders, emulating their revolutionary counterparts in Russia. Democratic nations, old and new, could then agree to the just and "cooperative" peace Wilson had called for back in January. By helping to win the war, the United States would succeed where neutrality had failed.[57]

But Wilson knew his choice, if ratified by Congress, was going to tear at the emotions of an already divided nation, and he understood what it would mean to enforce his will. "Once lead this people into war," he told Frank Cobb, editor of the *New York World* on March 19, "and they'll forget there was ever such a thing as tolerance. To fight you must be brutal and ruthless, and the spirit of ruthless brutality will enter into the very fibre of our national life, infecting congress, the courts, the policeman on the beat, the man in the street." To Cobb, one of his most loyal journalistic supporters, he wailed, "If there is any alternative, for God's sake, let's take it."[58]

On the afternoon of March 20, the cabinet met for two long, difficult hours. To ensure his administration would be united behind him, Wilson shrewdly asked each secretary to offer his advice about what Congress would do. All ten members agreed, as Robert Lansing put it, that "an actual state of war existed today between this country and Germany"; Congress should simply acknowledge that fact and then "enact the laws necessary to meet the exigencies of the case." But not everyone spoke with the same certainty as the secretary of state, who had long favored intervention. Albert Burleson, the postmaster general, a former congressman from Texas, where anti-war sentiment was strong, confessed there were "many personal reasons why I regret this step." Navy Secretary Josephus Daniels, who remained one of Bryan's closest friends, was reluctant to speak up at all. Yet, when Wilson asked his opinion, Daniels tearfully admitted "that do what we would [war] seemed bound to come." The next day, the president asked Congress to gather in special session on April 2 "to receive a communication concerning grave matters of national policy."[59]

Even as the navy was beginning to arm merchant ships, Wilson had effectively given up hope that the measure could avert war. Perhaps he had purposely misled the public, Congress, and his own appointees when he had so recently described armed neutrality as the last, best chance to preserve the peace. More likely, he had come to recognize—just as La Follette and his fellow protestors had claimed—that the United States might stumble into war following an unplanned battle on the Atlantic. Rather than take that risk, the president steeled himself to punish Germany's autocratic rulers for violating principles he believed every nation ought to honor. "The submarine issue had . . . become the symbol of Wilson's willingness to stand up for the rule of law, for international justice, and, as he termed it, for the rights of humanity," wrote historian Ernest May. "If he now retreated he would, in effect, prove America incapable of exercising influence compatible with her population, resources, and ideals." Ironically, not until April 1 did a U-boat destroy an American ship that was equipped to fire back. By that time, Woodrow Wilson had already chosen to forsake neutrality, whether armed or unarmed. The Kaiser's submarines did not force him to do it.[60]

The moment long feared by peace activists and their allies in Congress had come. Unless either the president or the Kaiser backed down, the United States would soon be at war. Faced with the nearly inevitable, opponents stuck to the predictable. They continued to speak and act much as they had at the end of 1916, when success seemed as probable as failure. They brushed off older ideas for protecting the rights of neutrals and mediating a peace settlement, sought to persuade leading reformers to condemn intervention, and planned a final spurt of protests in Washington, D.C. If nothing else, they hoped these desperate exertions might force Woodrow Wilson and the new Congress to realize how divided the nation was that they wanted to hurl into the bloodiest conflict in history.

Divided it surely was. After Congress failed to authorize a referendum, several anti-war congressmen conducted surveys in their own and neighboring districts, which recorded lopsided margins for peace. AFL president Samuel Gompers convinced most union presidents to pledge they would stand by a wartime government that advanced the fortunes of wage earners. Yet the central labor councils of St. Louis, Chicago, and

New York City passed resolutions demanding that Wilson "resist the selfish and sinister influences that would plunge our country into the world caldron of murder," as the officials from Gotham put it. Quietly, the heads of the Mine Workers and the Teamsters, among the largest affiliates in the AFL, also made their disagreement with the drift of policy clear. In Toledo, the large Machinists local threatened to lead a general strike in that industrial city, just fifty miles from Detroit.[61]

Most of the Americans who wrote to Claude Kitchin during the last two weeks of March vehemently protested the course the president was taking. The extremity of their language matched the extremity of their fears. From rural Minnesota, Franklin Calkins assured Kitchin that everyone he knew among "the private, stay-at-home folk" hated the idea of "going into this foreign haulocaust [sic]." From New York City, Frederick Kelsey, owner of a plant nursery, wrote, "It is easy enough to get into the world cataclysm. God only knows how or when we could ever get out." Nearly every correspondent from North Carolina, including local businessmen and pastors, urged Kitchin to keep resisting the rush to war. Five Protestant ministers from Littleton, a small town in his district, stated flatly, if awkwardly, that "war entered into until every effort that can be made to avert it is made is murder." By the end of the month, the congressman could spare only enough time to send most foes of intervention a brief, boilerplate replay: "I agree with you in many of the positions set out in your letter. I have been hoping, but it seems against hope, that we would be kept out of the European war. The situation confronting us now has been against my protest, efforts, and prayers."[62]

Pro-war Americans proclaimed their convictions just as ardently— and with a more aggressive and confident spirit. A flood of new members and contributions boosted the size and filled the coffers of the National Security League and the American Rights Committee. In the metropolitan East, as if to confirm Wilson's warning, pugnacious patriots abandoned the civic tolerance anti-war activists had hitherto taken for granted. In late March, the mayor of Rochester, New York, denied the local chapter of the AUAM permission to hold a rally in the largest hall in town; each of the city's three biggest churches shut its doors as well. "Any meeting of this sort now would interfere with the recruiting of the Army and the Navy," the mayor's secretary explained. At the same time, David Starr Jordan, as august a pacifist as Jane Addams, was making a lecture tour of Ivy League campuses and a few big cities for the Emergency Peace Federation. Crowds of student and faculty protestors heckled him at Princeton and Harvard. At Yale, a friendly professor introduced Jordan with the classic phrase: "We who are about to die, salute you." Then Jordan, the former college president, retreated before a hail of rotten eggs. In Baltimore, he had to flee a mob of nearly a thousand protestors, many belonging to "the most aristocratic families of the state," who invaded a meeting he was about to address, carrying flags and shouting curses.[63]

More quietly, the peace movement was also losing the support of prominent liberal intellectuals. The eminent Columbia philosopher John Dewey decided—as had Carrie Chapman Catt, Charles Edward Russell, and his band of pro-war Socialists—that the United States could not help create a more democratic world unless some of its citizens shed their blood in the struggle. "If we do nothing and [Germany] wins," Dewey, a renowned pragmatist, told Amos Pinchot, "we shall have to recognize that we were her accomplices. We cannot escape responsibility for consequences by *not* doing things." Dewey sought to assure Pinchot that the United States, unlike other warring nations, would never restrict the civil liberties of dissenters. "I should feel more apprehension," he wrote, "if the American people had not resisted so almost completely being swept away by emotionalism and sinister appeal. In my judgment the general attitude of our public mind is one of sober intent to make the best of a bad job, a job it would much prefer not to get involved in, but a job that has to be done." Such confidence, remarked one Dewey biographer, "was rooted less in pragmatic reason than in blind hope."[64]

Away from the cabinet room and the northeastern elite, the disunity Wilson had cautioned against in his inaugural address was undeniable. His two most distinguished biographers attest to that. "We can be confident," wrote Arthur Link, near the end of his epic five-volume study, "in making only one very crude generalization—that articulate Americans were profoundly divided up to the very end of American neutrality, and that organized peace activity and visible signs of peace sentiment were nearly as strong . . . as organized war activity and signs of war sentiment." John Milton Cooper Jr. agreed: In March, "there was no great rise in interventionist sentiment. . . . Most newspapers and magazines did not take a stand . . . and ordinary citizens did not seem to be in a belligerent mood. In Congress, several observers commented that more than half the members of the House would vote against war if there could be a secret ballot. Clearly, the president was not feeling a push for war from Congress or the public."[65] But, armed with his newfound resolution, Wilson was quite able to supply all the push that he needed.

The speech the president delivered on the evening of April 2 conveyed no new thoughts and expressed no original purposes. Wilson portrayed the choice that faced the nation the same way he had in the four other speeches about the war he had delivered at the Capitol since New Year's Day. Again, he argued that the submarines of the German empire had, since early February, already been engaging in belligerent acts against the United States. Again, he placed the blame for these acts on the Kaiser's government, not on the German people: "We have no feeling towards them but one of sympathy and friendship." As throughout his presidency, Wilson claimed that America's might would be used only to advance the goals of freedom and self-government. We will "fight," he vowed, "for the ultimate peace of the world and for the liberation of its peoples. . . . We have no selfish ends to serve. We desire no conquest, no dominion."

But his thirty-six-minute address thrilled nearly everyone packed into the chamber of the House, most of whom carried small American flags. As with many great political speeches, Wilson summed up a familiar case in arresting, often unfamiliar phrases. In what one witness called "solemn and burdened" tones, with "neither rhetorical artifice nor oratorical surge of personality," he made the case for war in a bracingly unwarlike way. The peroration—altruistic, self-sacrificing, unyielding—struck chords that stirred both longtime interventionists and idealistic waverers:

> It is a fearful thing to lead this great peaceful people into war, into the most terrible and disastrous of all wars, civilization itself seeming to be in the balance. But the right is more precious than peace, and we shall fight for the things which we have always carried nearest our hearts—for democracy, for the right of those who submit to authority to have a voice in their own governments, for the rights and liberties of small nations, for a universal dominion of right by such a concert of free peoples as shall bring peace and safety to all nations and make the world itself at last free. To such a task we can dedicate our lives and our fortunes, everything that we are and everything that we have, with the pride of those who know that the day has come when America is privileged to spend her blood and her might for the principles that gave her birth and happiness and the peace which she has treasured. God helping her, she can do no other.

Wilson was acclaimed with a fervor that transcended political differences. Midway through it, Edward D. White, the portly chief justice, who had been appointed by William Howard Taft, sprang to his feet. His eyes full of tears, White led his fellow jurists and lawmakers from both parties in "cheering at the top of their lungs." After the president declared "the world must be made safe for democracy," Senator John Sharp Williams from Mississippi applauded loudly enough to inspire a similar uproar. Such demonstrative zeal for popular rule by a leading politician from a state that barred nearly every black adult from voting did not, apparently, strike any white reporter as ironic. As Wilson left the chamber, Henry Cabot Lodge grasped the hand of the man he had always loathed: "Mr. President, you have expressed in the loftiest manner possible the sentiments of the American people." Almost alone, Robert La Follette was unmoved. After Wilson ended his speech, the senator from Wisconsin stood behind his desk, reported the *New York Times*, with "his arms folded tight and high on his chest, so that nobody could have an excuse for mistaking his attitude; and there he stood, chewing gum with a sardonic smile."[66]

The man La Follette disdained was still haunted by an abiding skepticism of his own. On returning to the White House, Wilson had a conversation in the cabinet room with Joseph Tumulty, the secretary who was one of his closest advisors. "My message today was a message of death for our young men," he blurted to Tumulty. "How strange it seems to applaud that."[67]

At noon the next day, the Senate met to consider the resolution that would thrust America into the Great War. One final time, La Follette was able to postpone the inevitable: He invoked a Senate rule requiring debate be put off for a day. But most of the hundreds of peace activists, led by David Starr Jordan, who had come to Washington to protest the president's speech, were already catching trains for home. The local police had barred them from staging a parade. On April 2, a frustrated would-be demonstrator from Boston, Alexander Bannwart, had exchanged insults and blows with Henry Cabot Lodge, who was many inches shorter than him and three decades older. Newspapers crowed that the pacifist had lost the fight. "I am glad that I hit him," Lodge told the press, adding: "The Senators all appeared to be perfectly delighted."[68]

But losers need not be failures. Although everyone knew what the result of the vote would be, minority voices in both chambers were determined to condemn it for as long as their colleagues would allow. Some opponents had their eyes set grimly on the judgment of the future. When you declare war, Senator William Stone scolded his colleagues, "you will commit the greatest blunder of history. I shall vote against this mistake, to prevent which, God helping me, I would gladly lay down my life." Others repeated at length, often eloquently, familiar arguments against viewing German torpedoes in the Atlantic any differently than the British mines that enforced the Royal Navy's blockade of the North Sea.

Nearly every protestor blamed Wall Street and the big-city press for bringing the nation to the brink of what Senator George Norris called a "great catastrophe," which will "take America into entanglements that . . . will live and bring their evil influences upon many generations yet unborn." The Nebraska Republican set forth the economic indictment in the harshest and most memorable terms: "We are going into war upon the command of gold. . . . We are about to put the dollar sign upon the American flag." Pro-war senators responded in kind. John Sharp Williams spoke for several of his colleagues when he charged that Norris "grazes the edge of treason." Williams added, "Wall Street and the money power of the capitalists did not sink the *Lusitania*." The heated tenor of the speeches and exchanges belied the certain outcome of the impending vote.[69]

The emotional persistence of the minority did not spring solely from a conviction that going to war would be an immoral and destructive act. While outnumbered at the Capitol, most of the senators and representatives who planned to vote no genuinely believed they still had the country on their side—or, at least, that a severely divided public should make Congress pause before following the president's lead.

La Follette and his allies filled several pages of the *Congressional Record* with a tiny sample of the many thousands of letters, telegrams, and petitions pleading for peace that flowed into their offices. Senator James Vardaman of Mississippi vowed that if Congress asked the "plain, honest people," particularly "the women and children," how they felt, the nation would remain neutral. Representative Isaac Sherwood, the Union Army veteran from Toledo, began his remarks by stating: "I cannot keep faith with my people by voting for this war resolution in its present form." He could only approve defensive acts by the U.S. Navy. Sherwood testified he had made that same pledge to Toledo voters in 1916, and they had elected him "by the largest majority of any Democrat running in a Republican district on that issue." Ernest Lundeen, a freshman Republican from Minneapolis, informed the House that, in a referendum, voters in his district had voted against war by a margin of ten to one. "The people have brains of their own;" he contended, "they are doing their own thinking, and they refuse to let a few warped and war-mad editors do their thinking for them."[70]

Remarkably, a few lawmakers on the other side also voiced doubts about whether their districts would back up their stand. Isaac Siegel, the Republican from New York City who had defeated Hillquit in the disputed race the previous fall, said he had been "threatened with retirement from public life" if he voted for war but swore, "I would be unworthy of American citizenship were I to be deterred from acting by such warnings." Several interventionists confessed what George Foss, a Republican from Chicago, called "the greatest reluctance and the deepest regret" that the United States was now "forced" by Germany's behavior "to enter this horrible and unnecessary war." Pro-war speakers dwelled on the ethical and strategic necessity of joining the Allies rather than on the public's desire to do so. The ever truculent Augustus Gardner thundered, "Too long have we suffered other nations to bear our burden in this war for liberty. Now we must descend from the seat of rest into the blood and dust." At a moment of unusually sincere congressional debate, it was the minority that demanded the will of the people be heard or, at least, consulted.[71]

La Follette and Kitchin, as the acknowledged leaders of the peace forces in their respective chambers, knew their colleagues and the press would pay particularly close attention to whatever they had to say. The senator from Wisconsin delivered one of his greatest, if also most lawyerlike, peformances. For close to four hours, La Follette sought to refute every major point of the case the president and his supporters in Congress had made for going to war. Since Wilson now admits he "was wrong when he proposed arming the ships," why should we believe his promises now? If Germany's attacks on commerce are "a warfare against all nations," why is no other neutral government following to join America's lead? If the United States has "no quarrel with the German people," why will our military soon be cooperating "with England and her allies in starving to death the old men and women, the children, the sick and the maimed" in that country? If we are to go to war "for democracy," why is Wilson proposing to fight alongside an empire that rules over tens of millions of Irish, Indians, and Egyptians? What's more, plans afoot to start conscripting young Americans show that "those responsible for this war fear it has no popular support." His eyes rimmed with tears, La Follette concluded his talk with a defense of strict neutrality, as respected legal authorities and Thomas Jefferson had defined it. If we had been faithful to their principles, "we would not now face war." To Amos Pinchot, who sat in the gallery, Fighting Bob resembled "a person who had failed to keep his child from doing itself irreparable harm." But the next speaker, Senator John Sharp Williams, mocked La Follette as someone who always longed to "pose as the last, if not the chief actor" in every legislative "drama." Williams then cursed him as "a pusillanimous, degenerate coward." In this nasty personal and political conflict, there would be no cease-fire.[72]

That same day, the Senate voted for war by an overwhelming margin of 82 to 6. Besides La Follette, the only dissenters were two fellow progressive Republicans from the upper Midwest—George Norris and Asle Gronna—and three Democrats—William Stone, James Vardaman, and Harry Lane. Each belonged to the band of principled, if "willful," men who had stalled armed neutrality a month before. It was, if nothing else, a bipartisan coalition.

On April 5, when the House took up the question of declaring war, Kitchin announced his objections with a mournfulness that contrasted with La Follette's angry, prosecutorial manner. The majority leader testified to "the depth of my sorrow, the intensity of my distress." He invoked his religion and his patriotism: "This nation is the last hope of peace on earth, good will toward men. I am unwilling for my country to . . . extinguish during the long night of a world-wide war the only remaining star of hope for Christendom." Finally, Kitchin waxed prophetic: "All the demons of humanity will be let loose for a rampage throughout the world. . . . I shall always believe that we could and ought to have kept out of this war." Unlike La Follette, Kitchin did not vow to keep up the fight. Once war was declared, he pledged to obey the wishes of the commander in chief.[73]

But Kitchin's decision to speak out may have convinced some wavering Democrats to vote against war as well. If he could buck the demand of fellow party leaders to "stand by the president" and risk being "denounced from one end of the country to the other," then perhaps they could too.[74]

Yet, in the end, their numbers were far too small to make a difference: 373 House members voted for the resolution, while only 50 voted against it. The opponents included thirty-four Republicans, fourteen Democrats, one Prohibitionist (Charles Randall, who represented the more pious neighborhoods of Los Angeles), and Meyer London, the lone Socialist in Congress. Also voting in the negative was Jeannette Rankin, an active suffragist and member of the Woman's Peace Party whose election in 1916 made her the first woman to serve in the federal legislature. "I want to stand by my country—but I cannot vote for war," declared Rankin, who had received thousands of messages from fellow suffragists on both sides of the question. The thirty-six-year-old Republican from Montana anxiously symbolized both the continued presence and waning influence of the feminists who had organized the first anti-war protests back in the summer of 1914.[75]

That nearly two-thirds of the opponents—63 percent, to be exact—hailed from the Midwest came as no surprise. Many representatives from that region, home to large numbers of German- and Scandinavian-Americans and where labor and farmer mistrust of "Wall Street" was strong, had always been dubious about intervention. The pattern of the vote did not, however, bear out the conventional notion that rural districts were more prone to "isolationism" than urban ones. Just as many legislators who opposed the war represented such big cities as Toledo, Minneapolis, Chicago, and Milwaukee as districts populated mainly by farmers. Neither did a lawmaker's ethnic background determine how he—or she—voted. Most in the anti-war camp came, as the phrase went, from "English stock." As the indefatigable scholar of this subject put it, "The majority of congressmen who opposed the resolution . . . acted because of their ideas about the causes of the war."[76]

If so many Americans wanted to stay out of the conflict, why did so few of their elected representatives heed their wishes? The opinions of newspaper publishers and corporate leaders certainly helped sway the vote; that spring, even longtime elite doubters about intervention, like William Randolph Hearst and Henry Ford, had fallen into line. The auto mogul vowed that anything his factories turned out for the war would make not "one cent of profit." For many in Congress, the shock of the Zimmermann Telegram, followed by the German silence about armed neutrality, ended all hope that the Kaiser's "arrogant autocracy" might be willing to restrain its submarines to prevent the United States from becoming its enemy. The president still seemed open to negotiating, but in Berlin there was no talk of retreat. It appeared that the time for diplomacy had passed, even as millions of Americans still dreaded the thought of going to war.[77]

For two years, Woodrow Wilson had endured the attacks of

Republicans like Lodge and Roosevelt who called him a coward unwilling to perform his moral duty. Once the president had finally decided the United States had no choice but to intervene to preserve democracy, it was difficult for those politicians—particularly the Democrats among them—who had shared his ambivalence to vote no. Still, even after Congress backed Wilson by a large margin, some of those who voted in the affirmative believed the outcome could have been different. Without the president's "forceful and persuasive message," recalled Fiorello La Guardia, then a pro-war Republican House member, "I am not sure that a majority could have been obtained for the declaration."[78]

Would a President Charles Evans Hughes have done as well? If the dour jurist had eked out a win in California and moved into the White House with just 46 percent of the popular vote, the opposition in Congress may have been more implacable and a good deal larger. La Follette and Kitchin might not have been lonely outcasts but confident leaders of the opposition, one swelled by dozens of Democrats freed from the obligation to support a president of their own party and by progressive Republicans who had long clashed with the pro-war chieftains of the GOP. Indeed, a President Hughes would have found it difficult to persuade the many disciples of Bryan and allies of Kitchin in the House and Senate to give up objections they had voiced consistently since the summer of 1914. Representative George Huddleston—who represented Birmingham, Alabama—had lambasted support for the war "as a racket foisted upon the country by eastern bankers, industrialists, publishers, armchair jingoes from the Yale and Harvard clubs . . . the natural enemies of democracy." He opposed every preparedness bill. But on April 5, as a loyal Democrat, Huddleston sided with the majority.[79]

With Hughes in the White House, Crystal Eastman and other leaders of the peace movement who had worked so hard to reelect Wilson could have mobilized their followers to come to Washington in big numbers to influence the vote. Even if Congress did, more narrowly, approve a declaration of war, President Hughes may have struggled to govern a bitterly partisan nation—one in which resistance to conscription and to higher taxes to pay for a much larger military might have overwhelmed him. Thus, ironically, the defeat of Wilson, the peace candidate, in 1916 may have made it less likely that the United States would go to war in 1917.

But Wilson did win a second term and then led the nation into an armed conflict in Europe for the first time in its history. Early in the afternoon of April 6, the president signed the declaration of war on Imperial Germany. The United States remained at peace with Austria-Hungary and Turkey, the other Central Powers, which had neither injured America's citizens, its interests, nor its honor. It was Good Friday. Millions had already suffered and died in the Great War. But the twentieth century's time on the cross had just begun.

FIVE

THE WAR—OR AMERICAN PROMISE: ONE MUST CHOOSE

April 1917 to November 1917

"There never was a war for which conscription would be crueler because there never was a war in which so many men so passionately disbelieved."

—Charles T. Hallinan, AUAM, April 1917[1]

"The government of a modern organized plutocracy does not have to ask whether the people want to fight or understand what they are fighting for, but only whether they will tolerate fighting."

—Randolph Bourne, September 1917[2]

"In traveling about your country . . . it does not seem to me that you have a surplus of democracy here—certainly not enough to warrant exporting any of it."

—A British member of the Woman's Peace Party, September 1917[3]

"Jined de army fur to get free clothes,
What we're fightin' 'bout, nobody knows."

—from a song popular among African-
American soldiers, 1917[4]

A CONSERVATIVE RESISTANCE

At the onset of nearly every war the United States has fought, the overwhelming majority of Americans have quickly rallied to the cause.
That was true even at the start of conflicts that soon became far more
contentious—against Mexico in the 1840s, the Vietnamese revolution
in the 1960s, and Iraq in 2003. But, during the spring of 1917, anti-war
sentiment endured.

Certainly, after Congress took its fateful vote, millions of citizens
and recent immigrants fell into line, many enthusiastically. Businesses,
unions, and churches invested in Liberty Bonds; most young men registered for the draft in an orderly fashion; vigilante groups, egged on by
pro-war politicians who enacted the Espionage and Sedition Acts, os-
tracized, harassed, and sometimes violently attacked those whom they
charged with refusing to show respect for the flag, the military, and/or
the mission to save democracy. At the same time, the Committee on
Public Information (CPI), created by the president just one week after
war was declared, recruited seventy-five thousand speakers, published
millions of pamphlets and a daily newspaper, and made several feature
films—all to "drive home the absolute justice of America's cause, the
absolute selflessness of America's aims," as its chairman, George Creel,
later boasted.[5]

To the Americans whose zealous efforts to keep the peace had
failed, the contradiction was glaring. In no previous war had there been
so much repression, legal and otherwise. Not since 1798 had Congress

passed a law to punish seditious speech, and that one soon expired, taking down the presidency of John Adams along with it. Never before had the federal government created a propaganda agency whose sole aim was to make an altruistic, near messianic case both to its citizens and to the wider world. Both new functions of the federal machinery were operating at full power more than half a year before U.S. troops engaged in any serious combat on the Western Front.

As peace organizers suspected, both the carrot of the CPI and the stick of severe new laws and civic aggression sprang largely from fear that agitation for peace would persist and, if unchecked, grow stronger. Only ten of the fifteen hundred Americans arrested under the Espionage Act were actually accused of being German agents. Woodrow Wilson, his executive appointees, and their allies in Congress and the judiciary believed that critics of the war had to stay silent or suffer for their dissent. The alternative might be disobedience large enough to prevent the nation from sending enough troops to Europe to achieve victory.[6]

The battle between the pro- and anti-war camps was fought on the ideological terrain of Americanism itself. In a nation riven by ethnic differences and clashing conceptions of how a citizen should express his or her love of country, it could hardly have been otherwise. On the one hand, Wilson's government enticed the loyalty of immigrant workers, many of whom came from lands that had been at war since 1914, with the promise of achieving "industrial democracy" and the idea that, in America as opposed to Germany, "the People ARE the Government." Theodore Roosevelt, leading advocate of "the melting pot"—enforced coercively, if necessary—thundered, "There can be no fifty-fifty Americanism in this country. There is room here for only 100 percent Americanism, only for those who are Americans and nothing else."[7]

On the other side, Jane Addams continued to insist that true patriots should reach beyond U.S. borders to engage in "a strenuous endeavor to lead all nations of the earth into an organized international life worthy of civilized men." Rebutting TR, the eloquent young critic Randolph Bourne hailed the ethnic pluralism that had the potential to turn the United States into a "transnational" republic that could become an exemplar of tolerance to the world. Nearly every war opponent challenged the patriotic intentions of an administration that sent young Americans across the Atlantic to slay German dragons, while it all but banned serious debate about that decision back home.[8]

On June 14, Flag Day, the president left no doubt about his views or future intentions. Standing near the Washington Monument during a driving rainstorm, he repudiated his prior sympathy for the advocates of peace. Bluntly, he all but equated opposition to the war with treason. The Kaiser has many "agents and dupes" in this country, Wilson alleged. They claim there is no threat to our "lands or her institutions" and prattle on about the alleged sins of the British Empire. But "it is only friends and partisans of the German Government . . . who utter these thinly disguised disloyalties"—and they should receive no quarter. "Woe be to the man or group of men that seeks to stand in our way in this day of high resolution when every principle we hold dearest is to be vindicated and made secure for the salvation of the nations." The Olympian statesman who five months before had vowed to achieved a "peace without victory" now snarled as an avenging commander in chief. The next day, he signed the Espionage Act into law.[9]

But none of the men (or women) Wilson accused had any fondness for the rulers of Imperial Germany. In fact, anti-militarists labeled the new onslaught against them a domestic form of "Prussianism"—employing the might of the state to crush the liberties of its citizens. As Max Eastman put it in an August speech, "There is no use making the world safe for democracy if there is no democracy left in the world. There is no use waging a war for liberty if every liberty we have must be abolished in order to wage war." He and his fellow activists had begun to resist both the war and efforts to squelch any serious criticism of it.

Some organized new groups to demand an early and just peace settlement; others struggled to exempt pacifists from conscription; while others defended their First Amendment rights in every venue still available to them. For the first time since 1914, numerous African Americans also protested against what had become "Mr. Wilson's war."[10]

With their periodicals routinely banned from the mails and their speakers hounded by federal agents, peace activists continued to tell their truths but learned to tell them slant. When Morris Hillquit waged a strong campaign for mayor of New York City in 1917, he "opposed the killing of our manhood and the draining of our resources in a bewildering pursuit of an incomprehensible 'democracy.'" But he was careful not to disparage the draft. Crystal Eastman insisted the AUAM stood for "democracy first" and had no intention of obstructing the war effort, while she and her sisters in the New York Woman's Peace Party kept speaking up, wittily, for global pacifism to a reduced, if still appreciative, audience.

For his part, Claude Kitchin grimly acknowledged the United States now had to win a war he had never believed it should fight. During the next year, the congressman devoted nearly all his energy to advancing bills that would force corporations and individuals earning super-profits from military contracts to pay nearly all the costs of belligerence. He declined to follow the lead of Robert La Follette, whose persistent vilification of the war and conscription made him a pariah in the Senate.[11]

What each of the four figures had in common was a conviction that "the people"—or, at least, a sizable minority of them—regretted the stand the president and a majority of Congress had taken and the punitive fashion in which they were prosecuting the war at home. Hillquit and Eastman based that belief on an abiding optimism about the common sense and innate idealism of ordinary, mostly working-class people. Both activists spent the war years in Manhattan, surrounded by like-minded leftists in a city whose residents were ambivalent at best about Mr. Wilson's war. But thousands of Americans away from the metropolitan East wrote to La Follette and Kitchin, pleading with them to do *something* to reverse the nation's course. "You have the unbounded sympathy of millions of people whose sons you tried to save from war," an admirer from Nampa, Idaho, wrote to the senator from Wisconsin. "I would rather walk with you 'barefoot and alone' than be the President of my country with the responsibility of war upon my soul." "THIS IS A RICH MAN'S WAR. Make them pay for it!" a tobacco manufacturer from Winston-Salem wrote to the congressman from his own state who was attempting to do just that. Correspondents routinely told both La Follette and Kitchin that if the question had been put to a popular vote, the nation would still be at peace.[12]

Such assurances, voiced so frequently during the years of neutrality, could not slow the rapid mobilization and expanded federal powers undertaken in the name of waging a great, if not quite a total, conflict. The war was indeed "the health of the state," as Randolph Bourne famously wrote just before his death from influenza in 1918. The apparatus of repressing "disloyalty" was merely one tentacle of the newly potent Leviathan. Wilson's government created a War Industries Board and a War Labor Board, public corporations to finance shipbuilding and construct barracks, and a new bureau to regulate the production and consumption of food. It nationalized the railroads for the duration of the conflict and turned such private organizations as the Red Cross and the YMCA into virtual appendages of the military. Taken together, all these changes fostered a new kind of political obligation, not to one's community or local government but to the national state, whose power radiated out to the world from the growing city of four hundred thousand, located at the confluence of the Potomac and Anacostia Rivers.[13]

To resist these changes was indeed a conservative act, in the literal sense of the word. It meant standing athwart the transformation of one's country and yelling "Stop!"—to paraphrase how William F. Buckley Jr. would later summarize his own traditionalist credo. In the fall of 1917,

Randolph Bourne recognized that "war determines its own end—victory, and government crushes out automatically all forces that deflect, or threaten to deflect, energy from the path of organization to that end."

The women and men who composed those forces retained their conviction in what Bourne called the "American promise"; they clung to the braided ideals of individual liberty, global comity, and mass democracy that had inspired the peace coalition in the first place. That promise had always been their moral equivalent of combat, and they could not abandon it now that the nation had, in the name of Americanism, plunged into the greatest war in history. But most of the anti-warriors understood that, as long as the conflict continued, resisting it would probably yield them more hardships than victories.[14]

THE COALITION DIVIDES

One of their most painful adversities was self-inflicted. After April 6, every peace activist had to choose whether to defy, explicitly or subtly, the demands of the wartime state or to support them in hope of advancing toward the future of self-rule the president kept promising, even as he damned foes of war who shared that vision. Paul Kellogg set the tone for many progressives who took the safer path. He abandoned his pacifism and resigned from the executive committee of the AUAM, which he had helped to found. Yet the reforming editor still defended the right of anti-war stalwarts like Jane Addams to speak their minds, and he kept meeting with former comrades to build support for an early peace. The cover of the first issue of the *Survey* published after war was declared expressed how grudging was Kellogg's endorsement. It depicted Uncle Sam, dressed in work clothes, reluctantly reaching for an antique musket that hung on his wall. The caption read: "Gosh! I had so many other things to do!" For the remainder of the year, Kellogg's magazine focused on such "other things" as improving working conditions in munitions plants and addressing the health problems of potential draftees.[15]

The withdrawal from the AUAM of influential national figures like Kellogg and Lillian Wald, who also resigned from the board, left the organization in disarray. Crystal Eastman pleaded with them to remain in the fold, even claiming that, since "the war was a fact," the AUAM *did* want "America to win." But the editor of the *Survey* now thought the collective feeling bred by war could hasten the coming of a true welfare state; Wald feared, with reason, that the philanthropists who financed the Henry Street Settlement and her other good works would abandon her if she stuck by the AUAM, which one wealthy patron charged was "disloyal and bordering on treason." By August, postal authorities were delaying the delivery of mail from Eastman's office in New York, and her organization was seriously in debt; only a series of "emergency" meetings and personal appeals enabled it to survive. Whether the AUAM's main priority should be campaigning for a "peace without victory" or defending the rights of dissenters was left up in the air.[16]

The war became a similar test of endurance for leaders of the Woman's Peace Party. Jane Addams, who remained its president, lectured around the country for the Food Administration, headed by Herbert Hoover. Hoover, a devout Quaker, persuaded her that by urging Americans to conserve food, she would be serving a function unrelated to combat. One Chicago paper that had savaged her earlier pacifist statements now praised her as a "good sport." Yet her party's ranks were sharply divided between those members who wanted to avoid criticizing the government and those who believed the principles of global pacifism were more urgently needed than ever.

At the WPP's convention that fall, Addams pushed through a truce-seeking resolution: "Let those of opposed opinions be loyal to the highest that they know, and let each understand that the other may be equally patriotic." Such tolerant phrases had no effect on the Secret Service, which raided the party's headquarters in Chicago, searching for violations of the Espionage Act, or on the anonymous vandals who smeared excrement all over its incoming mail. The members of the WPP executive board were so fearful about meeting in public that they gathered at a home in the Philadelphia suburbs, masquerading "as guests at a house party in order that their hostess might not suffer from public opinion."[17]

But in New York City, the party's radical activists had patience with neither compromise nor caution. "Why have we American women declared war on German women?" the editors of *Four Lights* asked in July. Katharine Anthony, a public-school teacher, went on to mock the "deluge" of female "volunteers, amateurs, and underbidding competitors" who were doing, for free, the jobs of working-class women in garment factories who badly needed the pay. In the same issue, Anthony's lesbian partner, Elisabeth Irwin, lambasted the head of the Food Administration for lecturing housewives to economize while scolding women who protested high prices. "Mr. Hoover's admonitions are little short of satire," remarked Irwin. "A wise official should know that the housewives of the country are in no mood to be taunted." The New York party was committed not merely to "an emotional anti-war cause" but to a transformation of society. One member denounced their cautious adversaries in the Massachusetts branch as "women who are, always have been, and always will be reactionaries."[18]

Up in Boston, Lucia Ames Mead and her sister officials of the WPP's second largest branch had heard enough. They demanded that "rebuking the government" during wartime should cease and argued that peace would only be possible after Germany had been crushed. Early in 1918, realizing their internal critics would never surrender, Mead and her allies left the party of unreconstructed pacifists to its fate.[19]

Around the nation, the rending of the AUAM and the Woman's Peace Party was repeated among individuals who had, up to that spring, been the warmest of comrades. On the day war was declared, William Jennings Bryan told the president to "enroll me as a private whenever I am needed and assign me to any work that I can do until called to the colors." Since Congress had voted for war, the erstwhile secretary of state believed it was his duty as a Democrat and a patriot to comply. Wilson had no taste for seeing the fifty-seven-year-old outfitted in khaki and puttees, but he did appreciate Bryan scolding anti-war activists for "abusing free speech." In response, Max Eastman scoffed: "This Christian gentleman . . . boasts that he will devote his declining years to a cause which he considers wicked. Like Abraham who would slaughter his son at the bidding of God, Bryan is ready to do murder . . . for the sake of his country."[20]

The most significant falling-out, at least as judged by how many historians have written about it, occurred between John Dewey and Randolph Bourne, his former student at Columbia who had been a keen promoter of the philosopher's vision of education as a democratic activity. By 1917, Dewey had come to believe that an America at war, guided by his fellow liberal intellectual in the White House, could speed the coming of self-government throughout the world as well as weaken "the individualistic tradition" at home. United for so worthy a purpose, Americans would learn to welcome "the supremacy of public need over private possessions." Progressives had embraced this ideal before the war began; now a victorious military could help achieve it. In the *New Republic*, Woodrow Wilson's favorite magazine, such writers as Herbert Croly and Walter Lippmann echoed Dewey's confidence.[21]

Bourne retorted that Dewey and his esteemed colleagues were fooling themselves, with awful consequences for the world as well as for the credibility of their pragmatic worldview. "If the war is too strong for you to prevent," he asked, "how is it going to be weak enough for you to control and mould to your liberal purposes?" Dewey accused pacifists of weakening Wilson's world-saving undertaking and, in effect, giving comfort to the enemy. Bourne rebuked his former mentor for turning pragmatism into merely another excuse for repression. "A good many people still seem to believe in a peculiar kind of democratic and antiseptic war," he wrote in September. "The pacifists opposed the war because they knew this was an illusion, and because of the myriad hurts they knew war would do to the promise of democracy at home. For once the babes and sucklings seem to have been wiser than the children of light."[22]

THE UNWILLING

As Americans continued to fight about the war, no issue stirred up more emotion and dissent than whether young men should be compelled to be soldiers. Conscription had not been attempted since the Civil War, and no one wanted to repeat *that* particular experience. In the Northern states, for three hundred dollars, a gentleman of means could remain safely at home. Mobs of men from the poorer classes rebelled against the war and draft in what were among the most devastating riots in U.S. history. In July of 1863, thousands of mostly Irish Catholic, working-class New Yorkers, who dreaded the prospect of competing with freed slaves, burned and looted the homes of wealthy abolitionists and lynched black people on the streets of the city. In Boston, troops killed more than twenty rioters who tried to storm the National Guard Armory. In the South, the draft imposed by the Confederacy violated the gospel of states' rights; resistance to it mounted as defeat of the slave regime grew near.

No other English-speaking nation had a tradition of compulsory service—in sharp contrast to France and Germany, where a stint in the military helped bind able-bodied male citizens to the modern state. Great Britain initiated conscription only in 1916, after appalling losses on the Western Front made it doubtful whether the army could continue to fill its ranks with volunteers alone. Canada did not follow suit until the late summer of 1917; Australians, in popular referenda, *twice* voted down a draft for overseas service. In each of these settler outposts of the British Empire, most labor and left activists had rallied to the war but reviled conscription as an assault on their liberty. In England, the No-Conscription Fellowship, or NCF, drew mass support—as well as stern charges of disloyalty—and pressured the government to broaden its definition of conscientious objection. The philosopher Bertrand Russell, who often spoke at NCF meetings in 1916, celebrated the growing movement as "the most inspiring & happy thing I have known since the war began."[23]

In the United States, an energetic debate about reinstituting a draft began more than a year before Wilson made his decision for war. The controversy was one episode in the conflict over preparedness, with many of the same antagonists facing off along the same lines. Theodore Roosevelt, General Leonard Wood, and their apostles in the National Security League and Navy League argued strenuously that universal service would be a boon to society as well as the only efficient way to raise a force large enough to take on Germany or Japan. "I want to see each man put to work at what the country needs," asserted TR in 1915. That would mean sending "unmarried brother[s] to the front," while their married brothers with children stayed home to "work in the munition factory." The AUAM and other peace groups countered that it was "monstrous" to force men to learn how to kill. Max Eastman warned that a draft would "cultivate the instinct of submission," while William Green, secretary-treasurer of the United Mine Workers (and no radical), blasted conscription as "a menace to Labor and to our democratic institutions." Why, asked Green—a former coal miner and a loyal Democrat—would the nation even consider emulating an institution so beloved by Prussian militarists?[24]

Not every foe of the draft wanted the nation to remain at peace. Green echoed Samuel Gompers's support for intervention. And even as the crisis with Germany intensified during the winter of 1917, Woodrow Wilson seemed determined to expand the army solely on a volunteer basis. He knew most congressman and senators from the West and South had no desire to further provoke constituents already leery of throwing in their lot with the Allies.

Then, without warning, the president abruptly changed his mind.

At the end of March, he directed the secretary of war, Newton Baker, to quickly write a bill for a selective draft much like that which Roosevelt and his friends desired. On April 7, just one day after signing the declaration of war, the legislation was ready for Congress to debate. Wilson never explained his reasons for adopting an idea he had long rejected, one that would affect more Americans more profoundly than any other expansion of government power the war would bring.

His decision seems to have stemmed from two pressing political concerns. First, an all-volunteer force could leave most Americans disengaged from the military. It would sow the seeds of disunity at a time when the nation urgently needed to pull together in a great, democratic cause. The Selective Service Act was designed to be, in the words of one historian, "the centerpiece of wartime citizenship and its defining obligation."[25]

But Wilson was also determined to silence the growing call, voiced largely by Republicans, to grant Roosevelt his wish to dash once more into combat. At the age of fifty-eight, the old Rough Rider wanted to assemble his own volunteer division and depart for the trenches as soon as it could be organized and trained. Henry Cabot Lodge had already introduced a bill authorizing such a force. Ironically, TR ended up getting the draft he wanted, in part, because the president he loathed prevented him from fighting in a war he had long thought the nation should enter.

In opting for a draft, Wilson was *not* yet worried about having too few troops to carry the flag into battle. Along with his top advisors and most members of Congress, he assumed at first that the main burden of the war effort would fall on the navy, which would ship ample munitions and other supplies across the Atlantic, while sinking every U-boat it could find. The chief duty of the new conscript army would be to defend the nation and its allies in the Western Hemisphere—not to shed their blood on the killing fields of northern France and Belgium. Fiorello La Guardia recalled later that a majority of his fellow congressmen had "voted for war . . . in the belief and firm conviction that we would never have to send a single soldier to Europe."[26]

By late May, however, Wilson and his advisors realized that if the Allies were to win the war, they would require a good many American troops as well as American-made ships, food, and weapons. French and British diplomats who traveled around the country after Congress declared war stressed the need for reinforcements from the sole unbloodied belligerent. But to train and supply an expeditionary force of millions of men who had never considered joining the army was an unprecedented process, and an unavoidably slow one. Not until the spring of 1918 did enough "doughboys" arrive in France to help the British and French push back the largest German offensive of the war.

In Congress, Wilson's draft plan quickly ran into resistance from predictable sources. Many southern Democrats and midwestern Republicans bridled at the idea that men who were, at best, grudging supporters of the war might suddenly have to prepare to fight it. The AUAM reprinted a speech by Daniel Webster, given during the War of 1812. "If the administration has found that it cannot form an army without conscription," warned the great orator, "it will find. . . . that it cannot enforce conscription without an army." Military affairs committees in both chambers held two weeks of closed hearings on draft bills at which Jane Addams and other critics testified; floor debate on the measures began on April 21.[27]

In the meantime, thousands of Americans voiced their alarm at what they perceived as both an impractical step and a lamentable departure from national tradition. No issue in 1917, apart from the decision to go to war itself, drew more constituent mail—whether for or against. "A volunteer makes a hardier, more reliable and persistent soldier," a white missionary at a "colored" school and Civil War veteran wrote to Claude Kitchin. The president of Wake Forest, the congressman's alma mater, begged him to raise the age of eligibility (which was to start at twenty-one) so college men could complete their training "for important public services other than military." One could easily refresh a brief against belligerency into a case against conscription. "If this war was to protect the free institutions of America, our homes, our women and children," wrote the head of the North Carolina Farmers Union, "patriotic men would rally to the call of our country." But only coercion, in the European style, could make it possible to wage an unpopular conflict.[28]

The National Security League and Navy League were not about to let such skeptics defeat a measure they had long claimed was essential if America was to become a world power. They urged their tens of thousands of members, most of whom were men of standing and some wealth, to demand that Congress do its duty. A volunteer system would be "a hardship on the best element" and force an "unequal sacrifice of the educated classes," complained a banker from New York City who sat on the Federal Reserve Board. A prominent citizen from Eau Claire, Wisconsin, assured his congressman that all "the intelligent men of this section" believe that a draft was needed to "make good American citizens" of the "over two million Jews of military age and many millions of pacifics [sic]." Most big-city newspapers, including those from the Hearst chain that had been dubious about entering the war, also endorsed the president's bill.[29]

Buffeted by cross-cutting sentiments, several lawmakers rushed to propose alternatives that would compel the government to try recruiting large numbers of volunteers before drafting anyone for war. One bill, written by Representative Hubert Dent, chair of the House Military Affairs Committee, appeared to have the best chance of passing. Dent— a conservative Democrat from Montgomery, Alabama—wanted to establish conscription to defend the homeland but retain an all-volunteer army for combat elsewhere. His bill sailed through the committee with a bipartisan majority drawn largely from the West and the South. Over in the Senate, the members of Military Affairs narrowly voted down a similar measure, sponsored by Kenneth McKellar of Tennessee. Faced with opposition from the leaders of his own party, Woodrow Wilson had to ask the ranking House Republican, Julius Kahn from San Francisco, to manage his bill to victory.[30]

Once the debate shifted to the floors of both chambers, the pressure to support the president proved impossible to resist. Peace groups, still recovering from their inability to stop Congress from declaring war, had neither the time nor the resources to mount a serious campaign against conscription. Most of the senators and congressmen who agreed with them fell to reprising the same arguments that had been used during the waning days of neutrality. Young Americans, asserted Senator Thomas Hardwick of Georgia, should not have to risk their lives "for European squabbles" over "who shall have Alsace or Lorraine or Bosnia or Herzegovina, or some other outlandish country over there." La Follette thundered that Wilson's bill would "clothe one man with power, acting through agents appointed by him, to enter at will every home in our country." Again, he called for an advisory referendum and pointed out that "after almost three years of war Canada has not even considered" a draft. But as he talked, the nearly empty gallery testified to his impotence.

More attention was paid when Speaker of the House Champ Clark rose in opposition to the president. For two hours, Clark pleaded for the Dent bill with rhetoric drenched in nostalgia. He sang the virtues of the militia system, under which men from his own state of Missouri would "serve shoulder to shoulder, elbow to elbow, heart to heart, with their neighbors, friends, and kindred," rather than "be broken up into small squads and distributed among strangers from distant localities." But a single remark of Clark's, meant in jest, led press coverage the next day and undercut everything else he had said: "In the estimation of Missourians there is precious little difference between a conscript and a convict."[31]

By the time both chambers prepared to vote on April 28, the outcome was no longer in doubt. Just 109 House members backed Dent's proposal; in the Senate, McKellar's bill drew only eighteen supporters,

Claude Kitchin and Robert La Follette among them. But when Congress voted later that night to authorize conscription, neither the House majority leader nor Speaker Clark joined the 24 representatives who voted nay. They acquiesced to the will of the most powerful Democrat of all; in wartime, cooperation between the party's chieftains at both ends of Pennsylvania Avenue would be imperative. Who knew how long the great conflict would last? In defeat, a rump of populist-minded lawmakers did have one last card to play: "Persistent efforts were made," reported the *Washington Post*, to require "all members of Congress" to be eligible for the draft. But, predictably, "all of them failed." A conference committee was left to reconcile small differences between the House and Senate bills.[32]

In mid-May, when Woodrow Wilson signed the Selective Service Act, he understood that the overwhelming vote for it in Congress might not be an accurate gauge of its popularity in the nation at large. So he cleverly, if disingenuously, clothed the bill in the language of voluntarism: "The significance of this cannot be overstated. It is a new thing in our history and a landmark in our progress. It is a new manner of accepting and vitalizing our duty to give ourselves with thoughtful devotion to the common purpose of us all. It is in no sense a conscription of the unwilling. It is, rather, selection from a Nation which has volunteered in mass."[33]

Yet a great many Americans *were* profoundly unwilling. Some expressed their discontent through institutions—both secular and religious—that predated the draft. Some encouraged young men to register as conscientious objectors (a practice sanctioned in both legal and religious tradition) and helped them endure the harsh treatment the military meted out to those who did not qualify for that exemption. A few even took up arms in a futile attempt to force Congress to repeal the law they despised. Tens of thousands of individuals refused to obey the law but left no documentary trace of their reasons for doing so.

The only older peace group that made a major commitment to fight

the draft was Crystal's Eastman's struggling AUAM. Just before the conscription bill was enacted, the union published its "war-time program."
The first two items were opposition to "compulsory military training
and service" and providing "legal advice and aid" to conscientious objectors. After Congress acted, some local AUAM branches held protest
meetings, which proved dangerous for any young resisters brave enough
to attend. In early July, police raided a gathering of two thousand people
in the immigrant mill city of Paterson, New Jersey, who were demanding repeal of the conscription law. The lawmen took thirty-one "alleged
slackers" into custody—but only after their attempted escape touched
off a furious melee. It took a company of the National Guard with fixed
bayonets to quell the near riot. That June, a similar disturbance occurred in New York City, where, according to the *Times*, a crowd of ten
thousand was "gathered, hissing and cursing the soldiers" who "tried in
vain to stem the tide."[34]

The main speaker at the Paterson rally was Norman Thomas. Since
founding the No-Conscription League the previous fall, the thirty-two-
year-old Presbyterian clergyman had become the nation's chief organizer of anti-draft protests. He joined the AUAM's executive board and
headed its committee devoted to that burning issue. Thomas struck a
tall and handsome figure, whether giving powerful speeches to supportive crowds or lobbying tough-minded administration officials to
treat resisters humanely. Unlike Crystal Eastman, who broke with her
parents' religiosity, Thomas was a paragon of Christian pacifism. Most
other ministers who had once balked at preparedness were now gird-
ing their theology for combat. The president of the Federal Council of
Churches hailed America's "war for righteousness," and Catholic and
Protestant divines alike condemned Germany for substituting worship
of an authoritarian state for that of a loving God. But Thomas, in a May
lecture to a group of young Quakers, called "the oft-repeated comparison of the soldier's sacrifice with Calvary" a false reading of the Gospels.

"Christ indeed laid down his life," he said. "He did not first try to kill as many others as possible."[35]

For Thomas, as for several other leaders of the AUAM, the war terminated a warm relationship with Woodrow Wilson. A dozen years before, while Thomas was a Princeton undergraduate, he had studied with and become friends with the distinguished political scientist who was then president of his university. Both were the sons of Presbyterian ministers and shared a calling to Christian service. Thomas, who worked his way through college, was valedictorian of the Class of 1905. Wilson, according to one of his biographers, saw the younger man as "a later generation's embodiment of himself."[36]

In his work against conscription, Thomas had to tread carefully, lest he slip from advocate to victim. The Espionage Act, passed on June 15, made it a felony to "wilfully obstruct the recruiting or enlistment service of the United States." Thomas and his fellow AUAM activists urged young men to register for the draft and only then to seek every legal exemption available to them, including filing as conscientious objectors. They also set up information bureaus staffed by sympathetic attorneys to give advice to dissenters willing to take a step that might land them in prison. The most important of these new bodies was the National Civil Liberties Bureau; it was headed by Roger Baldwin, a thirty-three-year-old social worker from a wealthy Massachusetts family, who had recently joined the AUAM staff and begun a friendship with Thomas that would last a lifetime.

But any doubt they had about the legitimacy of the draft was dispelled in January 1918, when the Supreme Court unanimously rejected a constitutional challenge to the law, based largely on the Thirteenth Amendment's ban on involuntary servitude. The lead attorney for the plaintiffs was Harry Weinberger, a sometime lobbyist for the AUAM. "The very conception of a just government and its duty to the citizen," asserted Chief Justice Edward D. White, "includes the reciprocal obligation . . . to render military service in case of need and the right to compel it."[37]

Thomas did not have to wait for the Court's ruling to discover what it would mean to defy the Wilson administration on this vital issue. The previous July, Emma Goldman and Alexander Berkman, prominent anarchists and sometime lovers, had been sentenced to two years in jail for conspiring to "induce persons not to register" after they had organized several big anti-draft rallies in New York City. Upon their release, several months after the war ended, they were quickly rearrested under a new Anarchist Exclusion Act and deported to Russia.

Thomas and most other peace advocates did not launch a direct assault on the draft, but they did seek to undermine it with a more subtle, less confrontational strategy: speaking out for the rights of young men who, based on deep faith and/or moral principle, declined to obey the law. Activists met with the secretary of war on several occasions, circulated petitions, and vigorously maintained that an individual's decision not to violate his religious scruples was a patriotic act. Hadn't James Madison wanted to include a clause in the Second Amendment that would have guaranteed that right?[38]

In truth, the number of conscientious objectors (COs) who ran afoul of the new federal regulations was quite small. Officially, the government allowed any active member of a pacifist church to claim an exemption; most such men belonged either to the Society of Friends (the Quakers) or the Mennonites. A man who qualified on theological grounds did, however, have to wear a uniform, drill with weapons, and perform whatever alternative service the military commanded—all of which aided the war effort, albeit in a nonviolent way. Of the roughly sixty-five thousand Americans who registered as COs, fewer than four thousand refused orders once they were drafted. By the end of the war, a majority of that group had surrendered to the dictates of Mars, accepting such noncombatant tasks as hospital work or farming.[39]

Military officials subjected "absolutists"—those who continued to resist—to an arbitrary regimen of punishment that, at times, resembled torture. As Randolph Bourne predicted soon after the draft began, "Those who are conscripted will have been broken in on. If they do not want to be martyrs, they will have to be victims." Four members of the Hutterites, a small Anabaptist sect, who refused to wear uniforms spent several weeks manacled in rat-infested solitary cells deprived of bedding, light, or any nourishment besides bread and water. Two of them died in prison from easily treatable illnesses. Some absolutists—like Evan Thomas, Norman's younger brother—were forced to stand for nine hours a day, their wrists chained tightly to the bars. On occasion, guards compelled some of these men to stand so their toes just scraped the floor, "strung up like sides of beef, their blood draining down," as one historian describes it. Ironically, unlike his sibling, Evan Thomas never turned against the man who had taken the country into a war he detested. "My admiration for Pres. Wilson steadily increases," Evan wrote to his older brother, Norman. Just as Evan Thomas was following his conscience by going to prison, so he believed the head of state was carrying out what he considered to be his duty to the nation and the world. Wilson did not reciprocate the sentiment.[40]

On the plains of eastern Oklahoma, a band of tenant farmers set out to fight the draft in a different and quite literal fashion. During the summer of 1917, a secret, loosely structured group known as the Working Class Union built a membership as high as thirty-five thousand with angry denunciations of the war and conscription. Unlike most radical organizations at the time, the WCU included both black and Native American members. Along country roads, the radicals hung posters that kindled a hope for insurrection: "Now is the time to rebel against this war with Germany boys. Get together boys and don't go. Rich man's war. Poor man's fight. If you don't go J.P. Morgan Co. is lost. Speculation is the only cause of the war. Rebel now." They vowed to stop Woodrow

Wilson, whom they dubbed the "Big Slick," from sending them and their neighbors off to war.⁴¹

On August 3, several hundred members of the WCU, joined by unaffiliated militants, began to act on that threat. Night riders sliced through telegraph wires and torched railroad bridges. Other radicals took up swords and rifles and prepared to march all the way to Washington, D.C., expecting thousands of the discontented to join them along the way. Vowing to subsist on unharvested corn and barbecued beef, they became known as organizers of the Green Corn Rebellion.

The uprising ended before it really began. A large posse of local townsmen swooped down on a bluff of the South Canadian River in eastern Oklahoma and quickly dispersed as many as a thousand radicals who had gathered there. "Some of the men in the posse were neighbors of ours," recalled the frustrated militant Walter Strong, "and we couldn't shoot 'em down in cold blood. That's the way we felt 'bout the Germans too. . . . We didn't have no quarrel with them at all."⁴²

Millions of Americans shared Strong's disgust for the war, although not necessarily his left-wing politics. The War Department and the daily press hailed the first Draft Registration Day on June 5 as an unalloyed triumph. Indeed, 9.6 million men signed up at more than four thousand freshly established local boards; the new ritual of state was marred by relatively few protests. Members of the radical Industrial Workers of the World did pass out anti-draft leaflets in cities up and down the California coast, while other Wobblies led a march of two hundred proud resisters to the courthouse in Rockford, Illinois, where they asked the sheriff to arrest them and were promptly granted their wish. But the AUAM and Woman's Peace Party kept their silence.⁴³

However, by the end of the war seventeen months later, the ranks of noncooperators had grown to a stunningly large number. Roughly 3 million men never registered at all—nearly 15 percent of the 24 million who did. And some 338,000 who did register either failed to obey an induction notice or deserted after they had joined the ranks. Despite the government's zeal for enforcing the draft, the Justice Department was able to arrest only about ten thousand—less than 4 percent—of these flagrant lawbreakers. A large, if unknown, number of Mexican-Americans and men of other ethnicities slipped across the southern border, where prosecutors could not touch them. Many others claimed exemptions for ailments from which they did not actually suffer or for "essential" occupations like agriculture, which they did not perform. Taken together, a higher percentage of American men successfully resisted conscription during World War I than during the Vietnam War half a century later.[44]

In an effort to stem an epidemic of draft dodging in northern cities, the Bureau of Investigation, an arm of the Justice Department (and the forerunner of the FBI) resorted to deputizing private citizens. Short of trained agents, the Bureau had little choice. Members of the American Protective League (APL), formed early in 1917, volunteered en masse for the job. They began to hunt down and arrest suspected slackers in Minneapolis and Pittsburgh in March 1918. Nearly all of those detained were soon released by military authorities; their only "crime" had been neglecting to carry an identity card listing their draft status.

Yet, cloaked by legal legitimacy and cheered on by the press, the APL expanded its mission to cities from coast to coast. Its most ambitious—and most contentious—raids took place in New York City and its nearby suburbs from September 3 to 5. With the aid of police and off-duty soldiers and sailors, league volunteers stopped close to half a million men and brusquely demanded to see their draft cards. They raided firms on Wall Street, audiences at Broadway plays, and diners at restaurants all over town. In the end, after the APL vigilantes had brought ordinary life in the metropolis to a halt, just 199 of the men they detained were found to have purposely evaded the draft. Woodrow Wilson privately told one of his cabinet members that the raids had "put the fear of God in others." But many members of Congress were outraged at what Senator Hiram Johnson called a "Reign of Terror," and the American Protective League soon lost its federal authority and dissolved.[45]

Slacking may have been a problem in every region, but it was particularly common in the South. Over 80 percent of the eligible men in Dixie requested exemptions during the first draft call in June; in New York City, a hub of anti-war sentiment, 70 percent did so. Throughout the war, the percentage of nonregistrants and deserters remained higher in the South than in any other section of the country. Most of these slackers had little or no contact with peace activists; self-interest seems to have motivated them as much, if not more, than ideology. To grasp their reasons is to appreciate the range of discontent roiling America's poorest and most socially divided region. As Jeanette Keith, the only historian who has investigated this phenomenon in depth, explained:

> Some opposed the war itself. Steeped in years of anti-preparedness arguments, they believed that American troops were being sent overseas . . . to uphold the economic interests of monopolistic corporations and the financiers of Wall St. Some men deserted because they were religious pacifists. Others deserted because they had families to support and people to care for. Certainly, many Southern men must have been driven into war resistance by the combination of federal draft policies, which penalized the poor, and local draft boards which proved all too willing to exempt rich men's sons and [industrial] workers.[46]

It was easier to evade the draft in backwoods farming communities and tiny hamlets than in northern cities and factory towns thicker with native-born enforcers and scrupulous record keepers—who were less reluctant to arrest lawbreakers of a "foreign" race or ethnicity. Roughly three of every four southerners still lived on the land, and millions of them had neither a birth certificate, a bank account, nor a marriage license—and they had never paid either income or poll taxes. This was particularly true for African Americans, who had their own reasons to mistrust any white authority that demanded their obedience. The undermanned Justice Department, wrote Keith, "spent an inordinate amount of time in the rural South trying to find out how old black men were," and the authorities failed as often as they succeeded. They had little more success on Indian reservations, many of whose inhabitants believed, erroneously, that their special legal status made them exempt from conscription.[47]

If a small farmer or sharecropper could not confuse the Feds, there was, at least for white southerners, always a chance he could terrorize them into leaving him alone. The abortive insurrection in Oklahoma remains the best-known attempt at armed defiance of the draft. But most rural southerners owned guns, and some who resisted the command of the wartime state were willing to use them. Alleged slackers shot at officers of the law in multiple locations around the rural South; in four states, National Guard and regular army troops were called out to arrest deserters; nearly everywhere, they suffered casualties.

One of the largest efforts of this kind took place in Cherokee County, Georgia, in the early spring of 1918. Fifty U.S. soldiers, accompanied by federal officials, raided a farm where a dozen or so white deserters were said to be hiding. They sought to crush what they viewed as a nascent uprising as well as to capture a particularly brazen band of slackers. Some of the lawbreakers or their relatives were known as followers of the populist firebrand and noted bigot Tom Watson, who hated the war and the draft as vehemently as he did blacks, Jews, and Catholics. After the authorities had captured just two of the men they were seeking, their day ended in disaster. The troops got back into their heavy trucks and began crossing an old wooden bridge forty feet above the Etowah River that suddenly collapsed. Three soldiers died, and eight others suffered serious injuries. Just before the accident, nearby residents had gathered at the bridge, expecting something like this might happen: The beams supporting the structure had been sawed nearly all the way through. None of the other deserters the troops hunted for were ever captured.[48]

During the Vietnam War, fifty years later, young radicals who resisted the draft sometimes wore a button emblazoned with the words "Not With My Life, You Don't." If they heard about that slogan, a few elderly men from Cherokee County may have allowed themselves a smile.

THE AMERICAN SOVIET FOR PEACE

Although the pressure to support America's armed mission intimidated some erstwhile pacifists and gave others a good reason to change their minds, one group integral to the prewar coalition still articulated the ideals that had inspired the movement in the first place: the vision of a world in which the citizens of self-governing, socially progressive nations would have no reason to annihilate one another. That group was the Marxist Left.[49]

The day after Woodrow Wilson signed the declaration of war, two hundred delegates from the Socialist Party of America held an "emergency convention" in St. Louis. Scheduled in March as Congress was rushing to judgment, the gathering had a single task—to decide whether the largest body of American leftists would side with their "bourgeois" government as, in 1914, most European comrades had sided with theirs. In reality, the decision had already been made. The SPA's prowar faction, while it included such popular writers as Upton Sinclair and William English Walling, was small and isolated from the party's working-class, small-farmer, and increasingly immigrant base. At the St. Louis convention, a report written by the journalist John Spargo, who argued that by defeating "German militarism" the SPA could advance its own domestic aims, won a mere five votes.[50]

The choice of Morris Hillquit, with his moderate reputation, to deliver the keynote address confirmed that the Socialists gathered in St.

Louis were not going to allow thoughts of practical gain to turn them away from their radical principles. "We have been violently, needlessly, criminally drawn into this conflict," Hillquit charged. If the president cared so much about a world "made safe for democracy," why had he not asked the people, in a referendum, if they agreed? Hillquit struck a chord as patriotic as it was defiant. "We are the only force in America now with clear vision," he remarked, "and it remains for us to protect it against the butchery that has deluged Europe with blood." His official report swore "continuous, active, and public opposition" to both the war and the draft. Nearly 70 percent of the delegates in St. Louis agreed. The majority's position was submitted to the party's members around the country. As expected, nearly 90 percent endorsed it.[51]

But in describing the Socialists as intent on saving their beloved nation from ruin, Hillquit was out of step with sentiment at the emergency convention, if not in the party as a whole. Patriotism during wartime, many of his fellow leaders believed, was a trap to snare an unwitting populace. In 1914, love of country had helped convince the working-class parties of Europe to make their fateful choice—one they increasingly regretted as the body count grew ever higher. In St. Louis, the charismatic orator Kate Richards O'Hare announced, "I am a Socialist, a labor unionist and a believer in the Prince of Peace *first*, and an American second." The delegates named O'Hare, an idol of the evangelical Left, to head the party's new Committee on War and Militarism. Radical immigrants in New York and other big cities were no more inclined to vent their outrage in Americanist terms. Like Lenin and Trotsky, many hoped to turn the "imperialist" war into a revolutionary conflict of classes. They had no use for a patriotism that, wrote Max Eastman in the *Masses*, was "an almost animal craving" that made men "willing to be dead, if they can only be dead in a pile."[52]

But only the most deluded Socialists believed they could mount an effective resistance to the nation's bloody course all by themselves. For nearly three years, a coalition of radicals and reformers, stalwart feminists and tough-minded labor officials, the secular and the religious, had helped keep the United States out of war. Although some of these partners had now turned into foes, there were still plenty of men and women from such groups eager, despite the threat of repression, to call for a halt to the Great War and for making the kind of peace settlement that could bring about a world of equals. In May, they created the People's Council of America for Democracy and Peace.

The People's Council was a hybrid of liberal hopes and radical ambitions—and of individuals who personified those impulses. For staff, it hired three young pacifists—Louis Lochner, Lella Faye Secor, and Rebecca Shelly—all of whom had sailed on the Ford Peace Ship in 1915. Without Lochner's calm guidance, the auto mogul's venture would probably never have left the dock in Hoboken at all. He became the council's executive secretary. The trio had to inform, encourage, and harmonize the efforts of a socially diverse fifty-four-member "organizing committee." Joining its ranks were such movement veterans as Crystal Eastman and David Starr Jordan; unionists like James Maurer, who headed the Pennsylvania Federation of Labor, and Benjamin Schlesinger, who ran the powerful Ladies' Garment Workers; a handful of Protestant ministers and one distinguished rabbi; and Fola La Follette, a suffragist who was the Wisconsin lawmaker's eldest child. The committee even included a former Republican senator, John D. Works from California, who had just retired after serving a single term.[53]

But, unlike the ideological diversity of the prewar coalition, the People's Council (the PCA) tilted in a decidedly Socialist direction. That was not only because nearly half the members of its organizing committee either belonged to the SPA or strongly sympathized with its aims—and that it attracted relatively few activists from the AUAM and the Woman's Peace Party, which had been committed to maintaining as broad an anti-war alliance as possible. The very name of the People's Council was an homage to the revolutionary Soviet—or Council—of Workers and Soldiers in Petrograd, then the capital of Russia, whose compelling terms for peace were making headlines and gaining support across the globe.[54]

"Socialists of the allied countries," the Soviet proclaimed in mid-March, "you must force your Governments to proclaim resolutely the platform of peace without annexations or indemnities and the right of the people to settle their destinies." Just a month later, the left-wing Independent Social-Democratic Party in Germany endorsed the call, as did three hundred thousand strikers in Berlin and Leipzig. A growing number of Socialist deputies in France and Labour MPs in Britain did so too. If these forces had been able to bend all three governments to their will, the result would have been a "peace without victory" more radical than anything Woodrow Wilson had yet proposed. In his big January speech, the president had only extolled the virtues of democratic rule; he did not call for an end to empires or a complete ban on the spoils of war.[55]

In one sense, the People's Council was simply extending the tradition of American peace workers reaching across the ocean for empathetic partners. From the prewar meetings of elite lawyers and statesmen to the 1915 women's conference at The Hague, presided over by Jane Addams, to Ford's Peace Ship, the desire and need for transatlantic connections had always been taken for granted.

But the PCA was also explicitly following the lead of rebels who had just played a major part in toppling the tsar and were fast becoming a "dual power" in their vast and chaotic nation. Never before had a major U.S. peace organization declared its chief aim to be the promotion of the goals of a movement grounded firmly on foreign soil. And the Petrograd Soviet was a movement of revolutionaries, eager to transform their poor and brutal society where no one group was really in control. It was an open question whether the reformist leaders of the new Provisional Government, faced by growing demands from exhausted and hungry citizens in and out of uniform to stop the war, could withstand this militant challenge from below.

In mid-May, just before the PCA was born, Hillquit and two fellow Socialist leaders—Victor Berger and Algernon Lee—tried to join their European comrades in the flesh as well as spirit. They made plans to travel to Stockholm to attend a conference of Socialists from both neutral and belligerent nations, a gathering that was sure to echo the peace terms of the Petrograd Soviet. But Secretary of State Robert Lansing, citing a previously obscure 1799 law prohibiting private citizens from conducting diplomacy, refused to issue passports to the American trio. When the other Allied governments barred their Socialist citizens from attending as well, the summit meeting had to be scrapped. In New York, a radical poet composed a satirical quatrain about his government's action:

> Berger, Hillquit and Lee one night
> Planned a cruise across the sea;
> "Oh dear no," said Woodrow, "we're in this fight
> To make the oceans free."[56]

To be sure, most American peace activists had always espoused the same diplomatic principles now being trumpeted in Petrograd. Hillquit and La Follette, Kitchin and Crystal Eastman all loathed the imperial appetite for territory and treasure they believed had been largely responsible for the Great War. And in the spring of 1917, the Petrograd Soviet was still committed to democratic elections and hesitant to call for a separate peace with the Central Powers. But in hitching its new and untested wagon to an unstable dynamo in a peasant nation four thousand miles away, the People's Council had exposed itself to the charge of "disloyalty" being voiced at swelling volume everywhere from the White House to the street corner. Thus, at its hour of birth, the PCA all but guaranteed that its life would be short and perilous.

However, inside Madison Square Garden, where the council held its coming-out party at the end of May, not a fatalist word was spoken.

The crowd of more than fifteen thousand cheered orators who mingled familiar pacifist themes with a more combative tone emulating that of the rebels in Petrograd. Hillquit kicked off the meeting by asserting: "We cannot force democracy upon hostile countries by force of arms." Then he praised his comrades on Europe's eastern fringe who were fast replacing "dark and despotic Russia" with a "new, free, and democratic" order. Rebecca Shelly urged repeal of the conscription law and suggested it was time for Americans to establish "a lay Congress" on the Soviet model as an alternative to the war-loving, "undemocratic" body on Capitol Hill.[57]

But perhaps the most impressive speaker at the Garden avoided any hint of revolution. "We do not pretend to advise as to the conduct of the war—we have no talent for that," assured Rabbi Judah L. Magnes. "We do, however, think that we can be of aid in advising our Government and the people of America as to the necessity and the method of bringing about a speedy and universal and democratic peace." Magnes was a relative newcomer to the anti-war cause. Until that spring, the transplanted San Franciscan in his late thirties had devoted himself to nurturing the Kehillah—a communal body that attempted to unite the prosperous Reform Jews of New York City with the largely working-class and mostly Orthodox Jews who had immigrated more recently from Eastern Europe. Magnes preached: "Let all of Jewish life be represented by a circle of 360 degrees." He was also a fervent pacifist and had eagerly stepped in to take the place of Rabbi Stephen Wise, whose backing for the war had robbed the movement of its only prominent Jewish voice who was neither a secularist nor a Socialist.[58]

Magnes described the Petrograd principles as essentially a set of friendly amendments to the plan Woodrow Wilson had set forth when he had called for "Peace without Victory." After a detailed attack on the annexationist desires of all the major belligerents, the rabbi warned the president that his true allies were not to be found among the generals and heads of state who kept sending other men to kill and die. "The

plain peoples of the world will find it hard to forgive this riot of power
in the hands of a few overlords," Magnes predicted. The plain people of
Russia were simply offering a return to sanity. "The President's peace
aims can now be achieved without the killing of more millions," he concluded. "But the killing of more millions can never achieve those peace
aims."⁵⁹

To the big city's pro-war press, these passionately stated ideals mattered not at all. "New Police Arms Awe Socialists" beamed the *New
York Times*, headlining the account of what it called an "Anti-Draft
Meeting." For ten long paragraphs, the unnamed reporter gleefully described how four hundred and fifty of Gotham's blue-clad finest had
taken advantage of the "opportunity they had been looking for to demonstrate the effectiveness of their new war-time defensive organization."⁶⁰

To anyone attending the council's rally, the "defensive" must have
felt more like its opposite. The police arrested several people for hand-
ing out anti-conscription literature, shined powerful floodlights on
streets around the Garden to illuminate "every nook and corner where
a troublemaker might seek to hide," rode back and forth in automobiles
brandishing loaded rifles, and sent seventy-five stenographers into the
hall to record any subversive utterance. The scribes were bolstered by a
group of soldiers and sailors who waved an American flag and tried to
rattle the orators by applauding at inappropriate times. Only midway
through its story, deep on an inside page, did the *Times* quote any of the
speeches and note, in passing, that aside from the hecklers, "there was
little trouble."⁶¹

The response of the New York police was a portent of how the authorities would treat the People's Council in the months to come. As
its young staff busily organized dozens of branches around the country and its leaders sought to coax opponents of war, old and new, into
the fold, government officials—from the White House to city halls—
labeled the council a threat to the security of the nation and used every

legal weapon to stop it from operating. This was one of the aims of Wilson's Flag Day speech. The president, through his secretary, also refused to see a PCA delegation headed by Magnes that came to Washington soon afterward. That August, Wilson told his cabinet that the group was headed by "eminent crooks and others who have sense in normal times." Indeed, the council never signed up many members. But, as one historian has written, "they gave voice to the broad doubts about the war in the country at large. That was why the Wilson administration was determined to squash them."[62]

Critical to the squashing was a quarantine on ties between the anti-war Left and the bulk of the labor movement. Quietly, the president directed George Creel to help Samuel Gompers set up and finance a new organization explicitly intended to counter the PCA's appeal to any union members who felt uneasy about endorsing "a rich man's war." Formed that summer, the American Alliance for Labor and Democracy quickly gained the enthusiastic support of pro-war Socialists like John Spargo and William English Walling—as well as the official, if at times perfunctory, allegiance of most AFL unions. Because it could draw on the ample funds of Creel's Committee on Public Information, the alliance essentially became the government's "labor propaganda agency." In contrast, the People's Council always gasped for lack of funds. The Socialist Party badly wanted to keep a broad anti-war coalition alive. But depending as it did solely on fees and donations from its members, the party that was now at the core of the existing movement had no money to spare.[63]

Through June and July, peace activists struggled to establish a council that could last. They staged big rallies in Los Angeles, Philadelphia, and Chicago. The latter was supposed to take place at the Cubs' ballpark, before the team's owner had second thoughts. The organizing committee publicly urged the secretary of state to telegram its support for the Russian peace plan to the Reichstag in Berlin. This would, they assured Robert Lansing, "encourage the democratic forces of Germany in their advocacy of the same program." In Manhattan, the council's small staff pumped out a steady flow of leaflets, referenda, and pamphlets about the virtues of free speech and the evils of conscription, as well as its program for a just peace. They tried to avoid the rhetoric of radicalism; among its literature was a reprint of Wilson's "Peace without Victory" speech. Helpful advice on "How to Organize a Local People's Council" suited a campaign for better sewers more than the emulation of foreign revolutionaries: make a list including "trade unions, socialist locals, branches of the Consumers' League, single tax leagues, peace societies, church and civic clubs, parents and teachers' associations, etc."[64]

But local branches of the PCA, unlike local unions or chapters of the Socialist Party, could accomplish little or nothing on their own. To stop the war or even to resist the militarization of American society required a national presence and an inclusive reputation that might give pause to Wilson and the council's other powerful foes. So the leaders of the PCA devoted most of their time to planning a national convention for the first week of September, which they hoped would compel the press to floodlight its constructive aims and inspire thousands of new members and allies to join "a 'people's power' body in constant operation . . . a clearing-house for the democratic forces of the country."[65]

Yet, instead of saving the council, the struggle to hold the convention proved its undoing. The members of the organizing committee talked about moving the crucial gathering to New York City or Philadelphia, before deciding on Minneapolis. A venue in the upper Midwest, they reasoned, was more likely to attract sympathizers from a region that had long been a bulwark of anti-interventionist sentiment. Minneapolis, unlike any eastern metropolis, had also recently elected a Socialist mayor. Upon taking office, Thomas Van Lear, who was also the leader of the local machinists union, spoke out against the draft and named one of his SPA comrades as chief of police. "About two thousand delegates were expected," Hillquit remembered, "and accommodation was to be provided for no fewer than fifty thousand visitors. . . . Farmers were preparing to come by automobile 'from a radius of one hundred miles.'"[66]

The prospect that delighted Hillquit and his fellow council leaders alarmed their powerful critics, and the latter attacked with all the tools at their disposal. George Creel slammed the PCA as a haven for "traitors and fools" whom "we are fighting . . . to the death"; he confidentially advised "patriotic societies and civic organizations" in Minneapolis to damn it as "pro-German and disloyal." The local dailies echoed his charge and intimidated the city's businessmen into denying the council use of any large hall in the city. Three days before the convention was set to open, the pugnacious Republican governor of Minnesota, Joseph Burnquist, declared he would allow no "anti-American" meeting to take place in his state. Van Lear responded that the governor did not have the legal authority to carry out his wish. "I assume," the mayor told reporters, "that constitutional democracy is still the form of government in the United States and the people may, with all propriety, peaceably discuss subjects of vital importance to themselves." But the members of the People's Council could lease no building big enough to allow them to exercise that right. As a last resort, Louis Lochner spent five thousand dollars on tents to be pitched on a vacant lot. But, perhaps fearing ridicule, he and his fellow convention organizers decided to move on.[67]

What followed was a frantic quest for an alternative site, a search that turned into a dark comedy of frustration. Sympathetic politicians in North Dakota and Wisconsin invited the People's Council to meet in their states—before a series of hostile local officials quickly rescinded the (informal) invitations. Meanwhile, hundreds of delegates from the East were sitting on a slow-moving, chartered railroad car, awaiting instructions. "They were kept informed by wire of the kaleidoscopic changes," wrote Hillquit, "and finally made up their minds to stop in Chicago and try their luck." The mayor of that city, William Hale Thompson, did let the council hire a hall of modest size—before the governor of Illinois, Frank Lowden, vowed to send the state militia to break up the meeting. To prevent Lowden from carrying out his threat, the delegates who managed to get to Chicago quickly passed bylaws and resolutions that affirmed those passed earlier at Madison Square Garden—and dispersed. Then it was the governor's turn to taste frustration. According to Lochner: "By the time the special train conveying the militiamen arrived from Springfield [the state capital], our delegates had long concluded their business, and a Polish wedding festival was in full sway in the hall in which we had met. It was upon this innocuous conviviality that the determined soldiery descended."[68]

In the wake of the convention fiasco, the People's Council had neither the means nor the reputation to attract a sizable constituency. Judah Magnes and David Starr Jordan resigned from the organizing committee, and Crystal Eastman found other ways to continue the dangerous work of defending free speech and challenging the draft. The PCA managed to keep operating for the rest of the war, chaired by Scott Nearing, a radical economist whose heterodox, if eloquently rendered, opinions had gotten him fired from two different colleges. But by 1918, the People's Council had become little more than a cheerleader for the Bolsheviks, whom Nearing said "we must humbly follow," than a place where anti-warriors of different stripes could gather. The council's monthly budget had never been sufficient for its needs; by October, it had fallen to just over seven hundred dollars.[69]

In 1917, against rising pressure, the People's Council had tried to keep alive what Randolph Bourne called the American promise. Whatever their differences, its spokespeople considered themselves to be patriots who decried the spoils of empire and maintained that only a government that protected individual rights could help make the nation and world safe for democracy. But they also believed a thrillingly novel promise from Russia could galvanize the American one—although the Petrograd radicals had a radically different history, and the rise of the Bolsheviks made it easy for pro-war politicians and newspapers in the United States to brand them a violent menace instead of an apostle of peace. In 1920, a hostile investigation by a special committee of the New York State Senate reported that the People's Council had been "thoroughly in sympathy with the Socialist program of Russia" and was "preparing to join them [sic] in an effort to overthrow the so-called autocracies (our own Government included . . .) of the world." No former leader of the PCA mounted a rebuttal.[70]

EXCESS PROFITS AND A SHADOW HUN

During the summer and fall of 1917, as it became dangerous for ordinary Americans to utter a forthright dissent against the war, erstwhile protestors in Congress also held their tongues. Following passage of the conscription law and the Espionage Act, not a single member of the House or Senate, including the lone Socialist congressman and everyone else who had voted against the declaration of war, dared give a floor speech questioning whether the United States should have embarked on the vast, expensive, and unprecedented mobilization in the first place. Lawmakers did engage in furious debates about everything from favoritism in the awarding of military contracts to whether prohibition of "the liquor traffic" should be enacted to conserve grain supplies and stiffen the nation's moral spine. With the major parties at almost equal strength in both chambers, these legislative conflicts were often preparatory skirmishes for the 1918 midterm elections. Republicans demanded investigations of a variety of alleged administration misdeeds. "We cannot beat the Kaiser by standing silently by Wilson," Henry Cabot Lodge, the unofficial leader of the GOP minority, told a friend that December. "Sooner or later the exposure must come and just when to start it is the problem now confronting us."[71]

Back in the first week of April, a Philadelphia admirer of Claude Kitchin wrote to the congressman: "If only you and Senator La Follette will work now and keep working for us we have hopes we will save our country after all." Neither man ever repudiated his vote against going to war. But after his eldest son had enlisted in the army, Kitchin kept his doubts about the mission to himself. That summer, the two lawmakers did work together to enact a series of revenue measures that would have forced wealthy individuals and any corporations making "excess profits" thanks to the war to pay at least half of its cost; the remainder of the military budget would come from loans and expanding the money supply. Yet only the senator from Wisconsin continued to rail against the repression of free speech and to question, away from Washington, the rationale for fighting. Rescuing the nation from its descent into militarism—particularly in the face of hostile criticism—had always meant more to him than passing any single bill.[72]

As a leader of the House, Kitchin wielded more influence over legislation than did La Follette, whose views confined him to the left of his party. From his chairmanship of Ways and Means, the North Carolinian cajoled and maneuvered to see that every revenue bill be based on the principle that "the only possible way to levy a democratic tax is to base it strictly upon ability to pay." From all over the nation, he received a steady stream of correspondence backing up his stand. At first, William Gibbs McAdoo, the powerful secretary of the treasury and the president's son-in-law, seemed to agree. In late May, the House passed a bill, largely drafted by Kitchin, that included a sharply progressive levy on all corporate profits that exceeded 8 percent on invested capital. If made permanent, the "excess profits" tax would have shifted a much greater percentage of the burden for financing the government onto big manufacturers in the North and away from farm and textile firms based in the South.[73]

But when the Senate took up the measure, opposition grew fierce and implacable. Henry Cabot Lodge and other Republicans representing industrial states whose leading firms would have to pay a good deal more blasted Kitchin's bill as infected by sectional bias toward the agrarian South. It was also, they charged, a vindictive attempt to "cripple" businesses that had favored preparedness in the past and were now vital to the war effort.

On the Finance Committee, La Follette tried to rebut these arguments by pointing out that the excess profits tax in Great Britain was higher than any yet proposed in Congress. But his notorious views about intervention made it difficult for even former allies to stand with him. "La Follette is simply impossible," Senator Hiram Johnson wrote to a California newspaper publisher in mid-September. "His attitude upon the war and every question in connection with it has tainted him so that his leadership even in a just cause . . . will militate against that cause. I determined I would not get in that category, nor be part of any movement which he led." When McAdoo announced at the end of July that the government would need more than twice as much money as he had previously thought, a severe modification of the House's sweeping change became inevitable. A majority of senators would never agree to loading a massive tax bill onto the wealthiest corporations in the land.

As a result, the Revenue Act the president finally signed on October 3 raised "excess taxes" only slightly. The war would henceforth be financed primarily with bonds purchased by ordinary Americans and a torrent of new greenbacks. "The People Lost—Wealth Won," read the blunt headline in *La Follette's Magazine*.[74]

By the time Wilson signed the Revenue Act, Fighting Bob was facing a greater danger—to his career as well as his reputation. On September 20, he had traveled to Saint Paul to address the annual convention of the Nonpartisan League (the NPL). Founded in 1915 by former Socialists in North Dakota, the league grew rapidly across the Great Plains with a program of public cooperatives, the stringent regulation of railroads, and state-run banks with abundant rural branches. While the league had opposed both preparedness and intervention, its leaders were now careful to stay within the letter of the Espionage Act. "We are against this God-damned war," Nonpartisan founder Arthur Townley confided to an organizer, "but we can't afford to advertise it."[75]

But most in the crowd of fifteen thousand, largely farmers and wage earners, who filled the auditorium in Saint Paul were no more reconciled to the war than was La Follette—and they looked forward to cheering one of his typically uncompromising, dramatic performances. The senator had indeed prepared a lengthy address that lambasted the government for betraying the American tradition of protecting civil liberties during wartime. But he prudently showed the text in advance to two NPL leaders, who feared a spirited attack on repression would only bring the hammer of the state down on their organization. So, that evening, as La Follette stood at the podium, following a five-minute-long demonstration of acclaim, he intended to give only a few rather predictable remarks about how the war should be financed in an equitable way. "The very men who are shouting at the top of their voices about democracy today," he announced, "are the men who have been pillaging the hard-working sons of toil not only upon the farms, but in the factories of the country."[76]

Midway through his talk, however, he returned, almost in passing, to the decision to go to war. Yes, La Follette told the crowd, he had opposed that fateful step. "I don't mean to say that we hadn't suffered grievances," he quickly added, "we had—at the hands of Germany. Serious grievances!" But then, as if to soften the point, he mentioned the violation of "the right of American citizens to travel upon the high seas—on ships loaded with munitions for Great Britain." That right, he said, was a "small privilege" to enjoy at the great price of involving "this Government in the loss of millions and millions of lives." La Follette reminded his audience that the Lusitania had been secretly carrying millions of rounds of ammunition. He also claimed that Bryan, who was then secretary of state, had warned Wilson in advance that the Cunard liner had those munitions on board. So, "I say that the conditions that carried us into that war" should "be weighed carefully." A few minutes later, the senator stepped down, to a loud and seemingly unanimous ovation from his fellow dissidents. "Now, Belle, aren't you glad we stayed," he asked his wife, who had advised him not to appear if he couldn't deliver his original text.[77]

Their satisfaction soon turned to alarm. A local journalist working the convention for the Associated Press dispatched a report to the more than a thousand newspapers that carried the syndicate's feed. La Follette, he wrote, had flatly declared: "We had no grievance against Germany." The senator and his allies blamed the misquotation on the animus of the Saint Paul press toward the NPL and progressives more generally. But the famous orator's persistent misgivings about the decision to go to war may have also confused the reporter. After all, La Follette *had* implied that Americans should hold a "grievance" as much against President Wilson as against Kaiser Wilhelm.[78]

In any event, a whirlwind of public loathing blew away any ambiguity. "La Follette Defends *Lusitania* Sinking," headlined the *New York Times*. The *Wisconsin State Journal* accused him of "consciously or unconsciously . . . lending aid and comfort to the greatest and most cruel military despotism the world has ever known." Governor Burnquist of Minnesota, the bane of the People's Council, mused about whether the veteran lawmaker could be tried under the Espionage Act. Theodore Roosevelt called him "a shadow Hun," while the president of Columbia University jeered, "You might just as well put poison in the food of every American boy" who goes overseas "as to permit La Follette to talk as he does." His old friend William Jennings Bryan denied, quite sincerely, that he had known about the lethal contents in the *Lusitania*'s hold before it sailed. In self-defense, even the leaders of the Nonpartisan League, who had cheered La Follette's remarks in Saint Paul, now denounced him as "disloyal and seditious." Nooses began to arrive in his office mail at the capital; La Follette made a point of showing them off to visitors.[79]

Across the nation, pro-war newspapers and prominent citizens, including a majority of the Wisconsin senate and all but two faculty members at the state university in Madison, demanded a punishment that had not been levied since the start of the Civil War—against fourteen senators who had sworn allegiance to the Confederacy. They called for the U.S. Senate to expel Robert La Follette.

Characteristically, Fighting Bob refused either to surrender or apologize. On October 6, he took the Senate floor to deliver the same speech he had intended to give in Saint Paul, adding only some excerpts from recent attacks on him in the press—to illustrate the "lawless defamation" that had become common in the six months since the nation had gone to war. His message was simple: The "right of the people freely to discuss all matters pertaining to their Government" must always be protected because "the people are the rulers in war not less than in peace." For close to two hours, La Follette gave the Senate and the packed gallery a history lesson in the theory and practice of the First Amendment. Quoting at length from statements made during earlier wars by Henry Clay and Daniel Webster, Abraham Lincoln and Charles Sumner, he drove his point home. La Follette concluded with a plea for "a clear statement of our objects in this war" that any organizer for the People's Council could applaud. If the Wilson administration intended to support the Allies in their "dreams of conquest," he urged the president to let Americans know that now.[80]

La Follette's many enemies were in no mood to debate the past. Joseph Robinson, a Democrat from Arkansas, bizarrely suspected his colleague of hoping to run for the presidency on a pro-German platform. Then he snapped: "The kaiser and the senator from Wisconsin talk about no war for conquest and no indemnities. That may be free speech; a senator can say it, a fool can say it, but it isn't patriotic Americanism." The chairman of the Senate Committee on Privileges and Elections prepared to investigate whether La Follette's remarks in Saint Paul were outrageous enough to warrant expulsion. Although the contest between "loyalty" and "free speech" in wartime would shape the future behavior of American citizens, on this day it was also good theater. October 6 was the final meeting of the session of Congress that began on April 2 with Wilson's plea for war. "La Follette Thrills Congress at Closing," read the front-page headline in the *Washington Post*.[81]

The Senate's investigation turned into an extended anti-climax. After learning that La Follette had not uttered the exact words the AP had reported, the committee allowed his lawyers to raise countless objections to both the witnesses and the evidence against him. Then, both the ongoing war and a serious illness suffered by young Robert La Follette Jr. provided many good excuses for delays and postponements. So did the persistent popularity of the accused. In the fall of 1917, Fighting Bob received even more mail backing his stand than he had earlier that year, when he was desperately trying to halt the march toward war. He would remain in the Senate, a pariah to his colleagues but a hero to many citizens and immigrants whose disgust at America's intervention matched his own.[82]

STICK BY YOUR RACE

After Congress voted to declare war, one large and historically abused group of Americans who had stood apart from the peace coalition before finally began to make themselves heard. The previous absence of black voices had signified neither fondness for the Allies nor an eagerness to fight. In 1915, the black author and civil rights activist James Weldon Johnson, later a top official of the NAACP, condemned the "hollow hypocrisy" of preparedness zealots who wanted to avenge the sinking of the *Lusitania* but kept silent "when a citizen is taken from court and burned at the stake by a mob." African-American journalists, bitterly aware of the atrocities King Leopold and his emissaries had wrought in the Congo—a genocide that took as many as 10 million lives—rejected the popular view that the German invasion and "rape" of Belgium had been acts of unparalleled bestiality. "The Belgians are reaping what they sowed," asserted one black editor in March 1917. Two years earlier, Booker T. Washington's wife, Margaret, had joined the Woman's Peace Party, while the "Wizard of Tuskegee" endorsed its mission. In contrast, the National Security League made no attempt to appeal to African Americans.[83]

Still, black activists were too absorbed with the difficult fight against Jim Crow to devote much time or political capital to the cause of peace. At a White House meeting in November 1914, William Monroe Trotter, editor of Boston's black weekly, the *Guardian*, had an angry exchange with the president over the recent segregation of two cabinet departments. Trotter was also the leader of the National Equal Rights League— a small, all-black group that aspired to be a militant alternative to the NAACP, most of whose founders were white. But at no time during the period of U.S. neutrality did he or his organization criticize Wilson's policies toward the Great War. For their part, the major anti-militarist organizations operated in a nearly lily-white environment and relied on their partnership with such federal officeholders as Claude Kitchin, who, for reasons both personal and electoral, would have shunned any interracial alliance.[84]

But once the United States had intervened, both black leaders and the mass of African Americans had critical decisions to make. Most black spokespeople endorsed the war, either because they had no taste for martyrdom or because they calculated that, by battling for democracy abroad, their people could prove themselves worthy and able of enjoying the same right to self-government and civil respect at home. "As this nation goes forth to fight 'the natural foe of liberty,'" Trotter declared in Lincolnian phrases, "let Americans highly resolve that all shall have liberty within her borders." In July 1917, W.E.B. Du Bois, writing in the *Crisis*, the NAACP's journal, which he edited, told readers "they should never forget that this country belongs to us even more than to those who lynch, disfranchise, [and] segregate." A year later, he appeared to contradict himself when he urged African Americans to "close ranks" and, "while this war lasts, forget our special grievances." Both Trotter and Du Bois were Harvard graduates and felt keenly the irrationality, as well as the immorality, of a racial order that devalued their great talents.[85]

Few black Americans who did not belong to that tiny minority of well-educated activists seem to have felt such a balancing act was either necessary or relevant. Like whites in rural parts of the South, some African-American men evaded the draft by simply making it impossible for the authorities to find them. Others, both in Dixie and in the northern cities that were filling up with black migrants, grudgingly joined the segregated military, resigned to what was, for most, just menial labor done in uniform—although with small but steady wages, regular meals, and a chance at seeing something of the world, with a gun in hand. Fear of what black combat soldiers might demand in return for risking their lives for the country was one reason southern Democrats like James Vardaman vehemently opposed conscription. "One of the horrible problems that will grow out of this war," warned the Mississippi senator, ". . . is the training as a soldier that the Negro will receive." What alarmed a hardened racist like Vardaman filled many African Americans with a sense of pride and strength.[86]

But the clash of the old bigotry with the new hopes of a long-exploited race also resulted in the bloodiest internal rebellion in U.S. military history. In Houston, thousands of black infantrymen who had formerly been stationed in the North or in the Philippines seethed at having to ride on Jim Crow streetcars and endure abuse from white men with guns. They had also endured a series of humiliating police attacks on themselves and on their female relatives and sexual partners. On the night of August 23, amid the stifling heat of a Texas summer, 156 black soldiers marched out of Camp Logan in disciplined formation to avenge these injustices. Before a National Guard unit could assert control, the mutineers had killed twenty white residents, including several soldiers and policemen. "They shouted 'Stick by your race' as they started down the road to Houston for the largest—and last—battle of their lives," writes one historian. That fall, after a series of courts-martial, nineteen of the rebels were executed, and many others were sentenced to life in prison.[87]

Even before the Houston riot, the Wilson administration viewed mounting black rage, expressed violently or peacefully, as a potent threat to national unity. In April, a St. Louis daily had run an alarming story, "Germans in Plot to Stir up Negroes." It was one of several widely publicized reports that agents for the Kaiser, working out of schools in Lutheran churches, were allegedly inciting black people to sabotage the war effort. The Bureau of Investigation, an arm of the Justice Department, quickly began recruiting black informants to finger and follow anyone who might be considering putting such a plan into action. Yet, despite a massive sleuthing effort, no pro-German conspiracy among African Americans was ever discovered.

That did not mean, however, that black "disloyalty" existed only in the fevered minds of government officials and white journalists. As Joel Spingarn, a white army major and chair of the NAACP board, put it, "There are adequate reasons for the unrest and dissatisfaction which is at present manifest throughout twelve millions of Americans of Negro descent. . . . No assumption of a special propaganda on the part of pro-German sympathizers is necessary to explain this situation."[88]

Overt black resistance took a variety of forms. Several ministers and parishioners of African-American denominations with a pacifist creed—the largest of which was the Pentecostal Church of God in Christ—refused to support or register for the draft and were clapped into jail. In 1917, marchers took to the streets in several cities to protest a white mob's murder of as many as a hundred black residents of East St. Louis, Illinois. Some of the ten thousand demonstrators in New York City carried posters demanding that the president "Bring Democracy to America Before You Carry it to Europe." In Washington, D.C., Archibald and Francis Grimké, brothers prominent in the nascent civil rights movement, counseled other blacks not to volunteer for the army and, instead, to seek manufacturing jobs at home. Francis Grimké, longtime pastor of a Presbyterian church that catered to the District's black elite, rejected appeals to help sell Liberty Bonds for a war "to ensure white supremacy throughout the world." In the wake of the Houston riot, the reverend wrote in his journal: "Dying in the defense of democratic principles is just as honorable as dying on a foreign soil."[89]

The most forceful black dissenters, and the most skillful at publicizing their opinions, lived in Harlem. Swollen with tens of thousands of new residents from the rural South and the islands of the Caribbean, the neighborhood was well on its way to becoming the political and cultural "capital" of black America and a hub of activism for freeing Africa from colonialism as well. Anti-war radicals who demanded a world "made safe for Negroes" found an audience there more receptive to their message and less fearful of being punished for it than elsewhere in the country.[90]

Leading the way were Chandler Owen and Asa Philip Randolph, black Socialists in their late twenties. Arriving from the South just a few years earlier, they had studied Marxism together at the left-wing Rand School in downtown Manhattan and become convinced that only a proletarian alliance across the color line could liberate African Americans. Before that could happen, it was crucial to stop the war and agitate for a peace that would demolish empires. Of course, "the damages and ravages" that Belgium endured should be "repaired," they wrote that summer. But Belgians should also "prepare for peace by giving to the blood soaked and massacred Congo the freedom which you . . . ask for yourself."[91]

Such views pulled the pair into the orbit of the People's Council, which, despite its troubles, remained the only national organization actively opposing American intervention. That November, inside the front cover of their new magazine of politics and the arts—appropriately named the *Messenger*—Owen and Randolph ran a full-page advertisement offering "The Truth About the People's Council" and soliciting members and donations. Until the Armistice a year later, they continued to promote the council and its goals, while fearlessly mocking the notion that black Americans would be eager for war if the Kaiser's spies had not turned their heads: "The Negro may be choosing between being burnt by Tennessee, Georgia or Texas mobs or being shot by Germans in Belgium.... We don't know about pro-Germanism among Negroes. It may be only their anti-Americanism—meaning anti-lynching."[92]

THINK WHAT IT WILL MEAN FOR HUMANITY

"While we socialists are branded ... in increasingly strong language as unpatriotic, disloyal and un-American, the Socialist Party is the only political party, the only strong organized force, which today stands in defence of American Democracy, and the American Constitution."

—Morris Hillquit, October 1917[93]

During the fall of 1917, Randolph and Owen threw themselves into what became the most impressive organized challenge American leftists would ever mount to Mr. Wilson's war: Morris Hillquit's race for mayor of New York City. Despite the healthy number of Socialists in the metropolis of 5.5 million, the party had never made a serious run for the office—due, in part, to the patronage available even to local radicals who backed a winning candidate instead of one who merely shared their politics. No previous SPA nominee for mayor had drawn more than the 5 percent of the vote won by Charles Edward Russell in 1913.

But discontent about the war and a field of three rivals (a Tammany Hall Democrat, a Republican, and the incumbent, John Mitchel, an independent Democrat) made it reasonable to imagine what had always seemed impossible: that a foreign-born Jewish Marxist could be elected to govern the most populous city in the nation and, after London, the largest in the world. It was, recalled Hillquit, "the only great political contest in the United States" since the declaration of war. For once, the SPA's election propaganda was hopeful as well as hyperbolic: "A Socialist, elected mayor of the largest city in the world! THINK WHAT IT WILL MEAN TO HUMANITY at this crucial moment, when the people of the whole earth are longing for the war to end."[94]

However, for the Socialists to triumph, they would have to assemble a coalition stretching far beyond their own members. That effort began right after Hillquit was nominated in July. The forty-eight-year-old attorney's long involvement in the peace and labor movements had made him a good many friends and allies who admired his intelligence and trusted his moderate instincts. Crystal Eastman, Amos Pinchot, Roger Baldwin, and others in the shrunken core of the AUAM quickly announced their support—as, predictably, did the local leaders of the People's Council. The Irish nationalist press endorsed Hillquit too. More significantly, so did the officials of the two major garment workers unions (the ILGWU and the ACW), which had thousands of members in the city; and the *Forward*, the pro-Socialist daily read by most Yiddish-speaking New Yorkers. Norman Thomas gave numerous speeches to boost the SPA ticket and persuaded some of his fellow Social Gospel clerics to back it as well. Gilbert Roe, Robert La Follette's law partner and close friend, took up Hillquit's cause as part of his crusade for free speech. Randolph Bourne lent his eloquence and his contacts in literary circles.[95]

More surprisingly, the Socialist candidate won the endorsement of a close friend and advisor to the president himself. Dudley Field Malone, a respected attorney, had been a key figure in Woodrow Wilson's 1912 campaign. In gratitude, the new president had appointed him an assistant secretary of state and then collector of the Port of New York. Since whoever held the latter post was in charge of collecting tariffs on imported goods, it was perhaps the most coveted patronage job in the country. Malone shared neither Hillquit's unyielding opposition to

American intervention nor his view that capitalists and their minions had made it happen. But he did believe the president should be working hard to achieve a "peace without victory" before any American soldiers would have to shed their blood in Europe. Electing a Socialist mayor might pressure Wilson to act on his prewar convictions. Malone, who resigned his government job after making his endorsement, praised Hillquit for demanding "no separate peace for America, but the quickest possible peace that can be negotiated in the interests of the masses of all nations, with no annexations and no punitive indemnities. If this be Socialism, it is also sound Catholicism, Protestantism, Judaism and Americanism."[96]

Hillquit welcomed Malone's endorsement as evidence that "progressives of all parties" were flocking to his side. He was overstating the case. But newspapers both locally and around the nation agreed that "the most conspicuous Socialist in the United States" might actually win the race. For the anti-militarist movement, whose fortunes over the past three years had cycled from growth to decline, and from optimism to despair, that would be the next best thing to peace itself.[97]

But a powerful combination of individuals and forces was determined to turn Hillquit's campaign into the anti-warriors' last hurrah. Woodrow Wilson endorsed nobody in the race, while privately agreeing with the Justice Department's reluctance to investigate whether Hillquit was violating the Espionage Act. "In my judgment," Attorney General Thomas Gregory wrote to his boss, "any proceedings against him would enable him to pose as a martyr and would be likely to increase his voting strength." Still, the army's refusal to allow Hillquit to speak to the thousands of uniformed New Yorkers stationed at Camp Upton on Long Island made the administration's bias clear enough.[98]

On the first day of fall, the staunchly pro-Wilson *New York World* reported, "There is not a political leader of importance in this city at present who is not bothered about the Socialist vote at the election in November." Samuel Gompers, Theodore Roosevelt, and Charles Edward

Russell put aside their differences to brand Hillquit a German stooge. TR, with brutal panache, called him a coward "who cringes before the Hun within." Rabbi Stephen Wise, showing how far he had moved from his erstwhile pacifism, warned New Yorkers, at a Brooklyn rally, that if Mitchel were not reelected, their city would become "the American suburb of Berlin." Hoping to sway fellow Jews inclined to favor a member of their ethnic tribe, Wise swore he would not vote for Hillquit even "if he were an angel fallen from the heavens."[99]

The Tammany candidate, a little-known judge named John Hylan, took a different and craftier approach. With the help of a legion of precinct walkers and the Hearst press, he appealed to skeptics about the war by attacking businessmen who had lobbied for intervention. Mayor Mitchel was, charged Hylan, the captive of Wall Street and other "predatory interests." But the judge said nothing about the merits of the conflict itself. He was, wrote Hillquit, "an ideal candidate for a silent campaign." Meanwhile, the Business Men's League, an ostensibly nonpartisan group of industrialists and real estate brokers, endorsed Hylan as the only candidate who could prevent the "dangerous menace" of a Socialist victory. The local chamber of commerce advised its members to vote for anyone but Hillquit, whom it scorned as Senator La Follette's "unpatriotic and seditious" twin.[100]

As Election Day drew near, the "menace" tried to avoid alienating swing voters. Remembering how close he had come to winning a seat in Congress the year before, Hillquit often sounded more like a frustrated Wilsonian than a radical zealot. He stopped talking against conscription and rebuffed criticism that he was pro-German by asserting that he favored only a just peace that would allow no nation to annex territory belonging to another. Electing Hillquit would "strike" a "telling blow against the Kaiser's Government," declared an SPA leaflet handed out to soldiers at Camp Upton, because it would show that New Yorkers favored "destruction of the root causes of war." In the traditionally Democratic city, Hillquit trained his rhetorical fire on TR rather than on the president himself. "It is not socialism but Rooseveltism that is the true enemy without our gates," Hillquit told a big crowd in Brooklyn on October 30. "And it is against just this type of politics that the City of New York is now rising in moral and political revolt." When Crystal Eastman came to the platform to ask for donations and vowed that Wilson "may learn a lesson" if Hillquit won, the negative reaction prevented her from completing her remarks.[101]

But to strike a balance between asserting Socialist principles and reassuring the nonradical majority required the unlikely cooperation of a hostile press. On October 22, an enterprising, albeit anonymous, reporter asked each of the four major candidates for mayor whether he had purchased Liberty Bonds and, if so, at what amounts. Only Hillquit answered no. "I am not going to do anything to advance the war," he told the *Times*. "I would subscribe with all my heart to any fund whose efforts are for the advancement of peace." Although he continued to speak confidently to large rallies, his candid refusal to contribute to the "patriotic" mission dogged the Socialist's campaign during the final two weeks. The election, declared the *World*, "will determine whether New York is a traitor town, or a quasi-Copperhead town or an American town devoted to American ideas and pledged without reservation to the war policies of the United States government." On its front page, the *Herald* featured a cartoon of a fellow it named "Hillkowitz or Hillquitter" assuring the Kaiser that he wanted "Peace at any price." "All Turn Guns on Hillquit," announced one newspaper.[102]

The fire was too heavy to overcome. On November 6, John Hylan won an easy victory. He drew just over 314,000 votes, about 47 percent of the total. Hillquit came in third, with more than 145,000 ballots—or a bit less than 22 percent. The incumbent, John Mitchel, edged him by roughly ten thousand votes; the lackluster Republican finished way behind. Hillquit was most competitive in the Bronx, home to many factories and Jewish immigrants, where he finished second, with more than 31 percent. He also gained a quarter of the vote in Harlem, aided by Randolph and Owen, who gave numerous speeches on his behalf. "President is Relieved by Hillquit Defeat," announced the next morning's edition of the *New York Tribune*.[103]

Yet neither the losing candidate nor his comrades were particularly disappointed. New York voters had humiliated Mayor Mitchel, the only candidate who ran as a champion of the war. And the Socialist branded a traitor by the most popular English-language newspapers in town had surpassed his party's best prior citywide performance by over 400 percent. Counting the more than twenty thousand votes won by the nominee of the dogmatic Socialist Labor Party, the two anti-war radicals together actually outdrew the pro-war incumbent.

In districts where Hillquit ran best, more of his party's candidates for lesser offices came out on top than ever before. Voters elected ten Socialists to the state assembly, seven to the board of aldermen, and even put a Red judge on the municipal court. The SPA's expanded vote also helped pass an initiative giving women the vote in New York State, a reform Socialists had long favored. The triumph of female suffrage in the nation's biggest state made enactment of the Nineteenth Amendment all but inevitable.[104]

The party's performance in other urban elections that fall was just as encouraging. Socialists running for mayor on anti-war platforms took a third of the vote in Chicago and Buffalo; 44 percent in Dayton, Ohio; and 20 percent in Rochester, New York. Each total far exceeded what the party had achieved in earlier contests. Everywhere, Socialists did best in precincts full of laboring men, among immigrant and native-born wage earners alike. Perhaps, at least in the United States, the notion that the working class hated "capitalist" wars might yet prove correct. "Even convinced opponents of the Socialist party in this country," wrote the sympathetic *New York Post*, "must admit, if they are not blind, that since Tuesday it has added a cubit to its stature."[105]

Meanwhile, in Russia, the most radical and best organized foes of the Great War had just accomplished a feat whose consequences would

reshape the history of the present conflict—and the rest of the twentieth century. On November 7, as Morris Hillquit and his allies reflected
on the meaning of the election, Red Guards were seizing the Winter
Palace in Petrograd, the massive baroque structure that was the seat
of the weak Provisional Government and, until recently, had been the
official residence of the tsar. Without firing a shot, the Guards installed
Lenin, Trotsky, and the other leaders of the Bolshevik Party as the rulers of the largest nation on earth. In France, just five days earlier, the
first U.S. soldiers had died in a skirmish with German troops. The work
of American anti-warriors was about to become both more auspicious
and more perilous.

SIX

A STRANGE SET OF CRIMINALS

December 1917 to December 1918

"The spirit of heresy hunting and witch burning had come back to America in the year of our Lord 1918."

—Morris Hillquit[1]

"What we demand in this war . . . is that the world be made fit and safe to live in; and particularly that it be made safe for every peace-loving nation which, like our own, wishes to live its own life, determine its own institutions, be assured of justice and fair dealing by the other peoples of the world as against force and selfish aggression."

—Woodrow Wilson, address to Congress, January 1918

"At the very moment of [Wilson's] extremest trial our liberal forces are by his own act, scattered, silenced, disorganized, some in prison. If he loses his great fight for humanity, it will be because he was deliberately silent when freedom of speech and the right of conscience were struck down in America."

—Oswald Garrison Villard, November 2, 1918[2]

SEDITIOUS WEAKLINGS

Two days before Christmas in 1917, the *New York Times* published a gleeful quasi-obituary for the American peace movement. A coalition that earlier that year had stretched from anti-militarists in Congress and social workers in big cities to nearly every radical in the land had now "shriveled" into a husk dominated by what the reporter, George MacAdam, dubbed "the professional gasbag element." Its numbers were few, and its political clout was gone. The *Times* reporter crowed that such celebrated figures as Henry Ford, Upton Sinclair, and William Jennings Bryan had all abandoned their repugnance for war and rallied to the flag and the president. MacAdam interviewed Roger Baldwin and Louis Lochner, anti-warriors in their early thirties, who explained their modest reasons for soldiering on. "We're trying to make a fight to keep people's mouths open and printing presses running," insisted Baldwin. The man from the *Times* was not impressed. A few months ago, wrote MacAdam, "in our principal streets the gutters ran with seditious speeches." Now, fortunately, "the peace movement is dead, or in a state of suspended animation."[3]

His own opinion aside, MacAdam did have a point. Eight months after Congress had declared war, most liberals and some Socialists who had vehemently opposed that step were now resigned to making the best of it. Despite her distaste for conscription, Lillian Wald let a draft board operate in one of the houses owned by her Henry Street Settlement. Until the Armistice, Paul Kellogg spent much of his time in Europe—first as an advisor to the American Red Cross and then as an enthusiastic ally of the British labor movement. In his absence, the pages of the *Survey* were filled with reports about wartime housing and factory work and included almost nothing about the merits of the conflict itself.[4]

The departure of such influential progressive allies turned what remained of the peace coalition into a beleaguered citadel, guarded largely by a stalwart corps of radical pacifists and Socialists. They had no more than a handful of allies in Congress, and, as La Follette's plight demonstrated, they were compelled to defend themselves constantly against charges of disloyalty or outright treason. Until the war ended in mid-November, activists in the shrunken movement fought to reconcile their fear of and disgust at the government's repression with a hope that Wilson might still embrace a "peace without victory," even as masses of American troops made their way to France and into battle.

As the *Times* reported, the anti-war remnant was spending most of its time just keeping itself alive. The People's Council shrank to little more than an office in Greenwich Village where Scott Nearing, Lochner, and a few of their fellow radicals cheered on the Bolsheviks and pumped out denunciations of "profiteers, who grow sleek and fat while men who love their country bleed and die." Officially, the Woman's Peace Party retained twenty thousand members—half the number it had boasted in 1915. But most branches were devoting themselves to such uncontroversial tasks as conserving food and demanding better pay for soldiers. Jane Addams still gave speeches advocating a postwar federation of democratic nations in which women would play a major part. But she had grown estranged from close friends like John Dewey and Lillian Wald who viewed her pacifism, however muted, as thoroughly impractical, if not unpatriotic. "The war years," wrote one biographer, "were the loneliest of Addams's life."[5]

Crystal Eastman, leader of the New York branch of the Woman's Peace Party, was now devoting most of her formidable energies to two new enterprises on the anti-war left. First, she helped Baldwin create the National Civil Liberties Bureau, which split off from the AUAM in the fall of 1917 but set up shop in the same office building at 70 Fifth Avenue. Then, on Lincoln's birthday in 1918, Crystal joined her brother Max in launching the *Liberator*, a new radical monthly to replace the *Masses*—which the government had recently prohibited from the mails. Crystal's departure left the AUAM floundering to find a purpose safe

and inspiring enough to keep its small membership of about three thousand intact. "Is there anything which we can legitimately do to identify
ourselves with our country's plight a little more sympathetically than
we have thus far done?" asked Charles Hallinan, the group's longtime
lobbyist. He suggested raising funds to buy and equip an ambulance
"which will bear our name."[6]

The two men who had spearheaded the anti-war coalition in
Congress—Robert La Follette and Claude Kitchin—also refrained from
expressing any doubts, at least in public, about the nation's armed mission overseas. In February, La Follette, who was still in danger of being
expelled, pointed out that, since hostilities began with Germany, he had
voted for nearly every war measure that had come before the Senate
(he did pad the list with such innocuous bills as one that "encourage[d]
retired officers to reenter the army in the engineer corps"). Then the
Wisconsin firebrand left the Senate and did not return until the fall; he
spent most of the intervening months at the bedside of his son Bobbie,
who, at twenty-three, was suffering from a life-threatening streptococ-
cal infection. Bobbie recovered, and the unplanned absence proved to
be a political boon for his father. One senator recalled that La Follette's
"devotion to the boy he loved removed him from the worst of the storm
against him."[7]

For Kitchin, there would be no respite from legislative combat on
the financial front. In the spring of 1918, Woodrow Wilson asked Congress to raise at least $8 billion in new taxes to supplement the greater
amount in Liberty Bonds that millions of Americans were purchasing,
whether willingly or not. As chairman of Ways and Means, Kitchin
worked long hours through the humid Washington summer to produce
a bill that placed the main burden on corporations that had made "excess profits" from military contracts since the war began. He lambasted
his critics as people "who believe . . . that the flesh and blood and bones
of the boys who go to the front should be used by a few who remain
at home as a means to get rich." The House easily passed the bill in

September. But after newspapers in New York and New England blasted Kitchin as an anti-capitalist from Dixie who wanted to punish efficient northern businesses, the Senate put off the matter until after the midterm election. That fall, an exhausted Kitchin caught the Spanish flu then raging though the nation and spent three weeks in bed. Ironically, in order to make sure his own county in North Carolina would meet its quota of Liberty Bonds, he borrowed two thousand dollars to purchase the remainder himself.[8]

Of course, the plight of movement activists and their erstwhile political friends was inseparable from what government officials were doing to silence Americans from opposing the war, whether in print or conversation. In 1917, the hammer of state had come down mainly on the People's Council and other groups and individuals who were working diligently, if ineffectively, to stop the draft and end the war. But by the spring of 1918, it was getting hard to tell the difference between "seditious speech" and the sort of grievances Americans had normally voiced about public authorities without risking a felony indictment. To express one's displeasure with Mr. Wilson's war had become a perilous act—for avowed radicals and ordinary citizens alike.[9]

Two stories, among thousands, demonstrate the reckless fury of the wartime state. After William Powell of Lansing, Michigan, felt pressured to buy a Liberty Bond, he allegedly told a relative, "I hope the Government goes to hell so it will be of no value. . . . This is a rich man's war and the United States is simply fighting for money." He was sentenced to twenty years in prison. In Pomeroy, Ohio, Thomas E. Moore, while stewing in the county jail after a drunken brawl, griped to a sheriff that John D. Rockefeller had "started this war" and went on to accuse "the whole United States Army" of being "a God damned legalized murder machine." For such slurs, Moore received two and a half years in a federal penitentiary.[10]

Congress provided the legal basis for such draconian penalties. The Sedition Act, passed in May, went far beyond the Espionage Act of the previous year, which had at least required some evidence that an individual had attempted to aid the enemy by obstructing the draft or the military. Under the new statute, it was possible to indict people simply for uttering "disloyal, profane, scurrilous, or abusive language" about the government, the flag, or even the "uniform of the armed forces." Immigrants from one of the Central Powers were a particular target of the new law. In Covington, Kentucky, private detectives placed a primitive recording device in a shoe shop owned by C.B. Shoborg, a former city councilman who, as a child, had emigrated to the United States from Germany. He received a ten-year sentence after the machine picked up his conversation with two friends in which they supposedly complained about the Red Cross, cursed Theodore Roosevelt, and cheered a German victory on the battlefield.[11]

But federal officials determined to punish anti-war activists could find ample means in the Espionage Act as well. Postmaster General Albert Burleson had used that law to ban the *Masses* and dozens of other left-wing and/or pacifist publications from the mails. For fomenting strikes in mines and factories that produced military goods, more than a hundred officials of the radical Industrial Workers of the World (IWW) were convicted to long jail terms under the Espionage Act. For violating the same law, Eugene V. Debs, the Socialist icon, received a ten-year sentence for a speech he delivered on June 16 at a picnic for party members in Canton, Ohio. On that occasion, the four-time presidential candidate had neither railed against conscription nor specifically condemned the war Americans were currently fighting. In familiar Socialist tropes, he merely—if passionately—denounced the fact that "the working class have never yet had a voice in declaring war" but were taught it was their "patriotic duty . . . to have yourselves slaughtered at command." For the Justice Department, that was evidently too much.[12]

Debs's attorney was Seymour Stedman, a prominent Chicago Socialist, who was also representing Max Eastman and three of his fellow editors of the *Masses* against the charge that several of their articles and satirical illustrations in the irreverent periodical had conspired to obstruct the draft. At one point in the *Masses* trial, Stedman paused to comment on the irony that his clients had asked a federal judge to compel the post office to mail their magazine to its thousands of subscribers: "Do men who are committing a crime go into a Federal Court and face a District Attorney and ask the privilege of continuing it?" asked Stedman. "A strange set of burglars! A strange set of footpads! A strange set of smugglers! A strange set of criminals!"[13]

LEAPS OF FAITH

During the winter of 1918, most peace workers adopted an ironic posture of their own: They applauded the president who had signed the Espionage Act for being, at least rhetorically, once again on their side. On January 8, Woodrow Wilson stood before a joint session of Congress and announced the Fourteen Points—peace terms he hoped would bring to birth a just global order from the ashes of history's bloodiest conflict. "The moral climax of this, the culminating and final war for human liberty, has come," he declared. Wilson called for an end to secret treaties; told the Germans he did not wish to change their form of government; advocated "autonomy," not self-determination, for the nationalities ruled by the Ottomans or by the dual monarchy of Austria-Hungary; hailed the Bolsheviks (without naming them) for wanting to make peace with Germany "in the true spirit of modern democracy"; called for reducing "armaments to the lowest point consistent with domestic safety"; and concluded with a ringing proposal for "a general association of nations" that would secure "political independence and territorial integrity to great and small states alike."

The Fourteen Points address was hardly a statement of "uncompromising anti-imperialism," as one historian has claimed: Wilson kept silent about the vast and lucrative overseas colonies held by Great Britain and France. But for those Americans who blamed the president for reneging on his promise to win a "peace without victory," the big new speech sounded like something close to redemption.[14]

The warmth of their acclaim was rather startling. Jane Addams, speaking for the Woman's Peace Party, called Wilson's speech "the most profound and brilliant formulation as yet put forth by any responsible statesman." Debs, who was still a free man, hailed the speech as "thoroughly democratic" and deserving of "the unqualified approval of everyone believing in the rule of the people." Robert La Follette admired the Fourteen Points but did wonder why Wilson had not announced them "at the time of our entrance into the war, or at any time since, as now." Morris Hillquit called the address "an excellent statement of the ideals of internationalism and of democratic war aims" and noted that Wilson "agrees very largely" with the program of Socialists on both sides in the war—a sentiment both the British Labour Party and the French Socialists quickly echoed. Max Eastman applauded the president's proposal without reservation and quipped that Wilson might now be ready to "come round and join the Socialist Party. I should take the risk of accepting him as a member." Even Lenin praised the address as "a great step toward the peace of the world." The Bolsheviks printed millions of copies of the president's speech and, with help from American officials, circulated them in Russia's biggest cities and, by themselves, to the German soldiers then occupying the western parts of the defeated nation.[15]

Of course, Woodrow Wilson had not suddenly regretted taking his nation into war. The president, reflected Max Eastman, "always let times make the first move." As hundreds of thousands of American soldiers were completing their training and beginning to sail off to France, Wilson decided it was the right moment to make a forceful case for a peace without conquest, if not a peace without victory. Three weeks before, David Lloyd George, the British prime minister, had given a speech along similar lines; Lloyd George had even declared his support for the "self-determination" of national groups, a term the Petrograd Soviet had first made popular.[16]

Wilson also had more immediate, and more urgent, aims. He hoped to persuade the Bolsheviks not to conclude the separate peace with Germany they were negotiating in the town of Brest-Litovsk, near the current border between Poland and Belarus. He also wanted to give the exhausted, disillusioned soldiers of the Allied nations a good reason to keep on fighting. Perhaps most important, he hoped to nudge ordinary Germans to regard themselves as future partners instead of bitter adversaries. Wilson, the great idealist, was thus engaging in a breathtaking act of realpolitik; before more than a smattering of Americans had died in battle, he was seeking to win the war on his own terms and as rapidly as possible.[17]

In retrospect, the ardor with which Addams, Hillquit, and Eastman received the Fourteen Points speech may seem naïve, if not delusional. After all, the same man who waxed so eloquently about "human liberty" was also letting his postmaster drive left-wing newspapers out of business and allowing his Justice Department to prosecute peace activists—including Max Eastman and other editors of the *Masses*—for what George Orwell would later call "thought crimes."

But did anti-warriors have a realistic alternative? The president was setting forth a vision and a program that closely resembled ones peace groups had long championed; although he did not extend the right of "self-determination" to all peoples, he did imply it. To challenge Wilson for betraying liberty at home while vowing to spread it throughout the globe might have been a gratifying punch to throw. But, with every peace group dispirited and under attack, such a blow would barely have grazed the powerful. That Socialists all over Europe hailed the Fourteen Points while Theodore Roosevelt condemned them also made Wilson look better to American peace activists. Some repeated the rumor that the president was working privately to curb press censorship. And hadn't the secretary of war just agreed that a young man could be a conscientious objector even if he were not a member of a pacifist church?

Most radicals thus craved a measure of legitimacy by endorsing the president's speech. "Trotsky, Lenin, [Lloyd] George, and President Wilson are on our side and the People are ready to listen to us," declared Elisabeth Freeman of the People's Council. Woodrow Wilson had betrayed the faith of war critics in his good intentions before. But to warm up to him again seemed a lesser risk than to denounce him as a hypocrite and a fraud.[18]

Their renewed regard for Wilson did not prevent most members of what remained of the peace coalition from taking, at the very same time, an optimistic leap to the left. The labor movement was rising in numbers and power, and most anti-warriors hoped to rise with it. In the manufacturing centers of Europe, and in many American industrial workplaces too, wage earners were exercising a new militancy on behalf of demands both economic and political. In January 1918, some 4 million Germans, Hungarians, and Austrians went on strike to protest the war and the privations they were enduring; Italian and French workers with similar grievances would soon be occupying their factories too. In the United States, millions of war workers, emboldened by the government's desire to keep them reasonably content and on the job, called for "de-Kaisering" such industries as steel, coal, and textiles, all of which had a long history of treating workers as expendable drudges. American wage earners laid down their tools and engaged in close to six thousand wildcat strikes; some workers, embracing the slogan of "industrial democracy," even demanded the power to help run and eventually own the mines, warehouses, and factories in which they toiled. Federal and local authorities were crushing the life out of the IWW, whose leaders had vowed to keep waging the class struggle during a war they loathed. But many workers in AFL unions who kept any "treasonous" thoughts to themselves were engaging in militant actions on a scale that surpassed anything the unabashed revolutionaries of the IWW had ever conducted.[19]

"Workingmen everywhere are becoming aware that they are being exploited for the benefit of others, and that they cannot be truly free unless they own themselves and their labor," wrote Helen Keller that March. "The achievement of such economic freedom stands in prospect—and at no distant date—as the revolutionary climax of the age." That confident assertion by the celebrated deaf and blind author and speaker, who had joined the Socialist Party of America back in 1909, was published in the *Liberator*. It was rather typical fare in the monthly the Eastman siblings edited and owned. Crystal, confessed her brother, "really ran the magazine," while Max composed its lengthy editorials and seduced many of the talented writers and artists from the *Masses*, now defunct, to contribute to the new enterprise.[20]

The same inaugural issue of the magazine—named after the famous abolitionist organ edited by William Lloyd Garrison—adroitly straddled praise for both the liberal in the White House and the revolutionaries who had recently seized power in Petrograd. Max's enthusiasm for the Fourteen Points appeared alongside John Reed's lengthy reports that came "straight from Russia." Most of Reed's dispatches later appeared in *Ten Days That Shook the World*, his widely read and utterly sympathetic account of the Bolshevik triumph. "With the Russian people in the lead," Max editorialized, "the world is entering upon the experiment of industrial and real democracy. . . . The Liberator will endorse the war aims outlined by the Russian people and expounded by President Wilson."[21]

That thoughtful radicals like the Eastmans could cheer on both Lenin's violent revolution and Wilson's proposal for a lenient peace did not appear so surprising at the time. On March 3, the German high command forced the new Russian government to sign, at Brest-Litovsk, what Lenin admitted was "an incredibly oppressive and humiliating" treaty. To stop the Kaiser's army from marching into the heart of their country, the Bolsheviks ceded sovereignty over a vast portion of the territory they had inherited from the tsars—Ukraine, Belarus, and the Baltic lands. American Socialists who had refused to favor one side or the other in this ruinous clash of empires now began to fear the consequences of a German victory. Not only might the "Huns" threaten the survival of the pioneering workers' state—snuffing out what Debs called "the very breath of democracy, the quintessence of the dawning freedom" in Russia. They might also extinguish the fires of revolution burning throughout Central Europe. "It is now clearer than ever," Morris Hillquit told an assembly of his comrades, "that Prussian and Austrian junkerdom is the foe of liberty and peace." In New York, some Socialists began to recruit members of an American Red Guard that would rush to the aid of the Bolsheviks, guns in hand. Thus, for the moment at least, the leader of capitalist America seemed to be aiding the survival of the world's first Socialist nation.[22]

The *Liberator*'s tilt toward Wilson had a self-protective motive as well. The Eastmans took care to publish nothing that might provoke the authorities either to ban their new magazine from the mails or bring a repetition of the kind of trial that followed the demise of the *Masses*. As Hillquit later wrote, the *Liberator* "adjusted itself to the conditions of war and censorship with better grace than its rebellious predecessor." Neither the magazine's editors nor other radicals who hailed the Fourteen Points ceased denouncing the federal judges and cabinet secretaries who were closing down anti-war newspapers and prosecuting dissenters. Until he fell sick that summer with tuberculosis, Hillquit (whose popularity in New York City may have saved him from indictment) kept "exceedingly busy" representing "many of my less fortunate comrades." Still, he found time to praise the gains workers were making in the wartime United States and in the other belligerent nations. Hillquit even gave Wilson credit for trying to persuade Americans "that the world does not end with the United States, and that no nation can be free so long as a single nation anywhere in the world is enslaved." A German victory would endanger all these salutary changes.[23]

Not every prominent radical softened his or her opinion of Wilson. Debs remained a steadfast foe of American belligerency—as did Big Bill Haywood and the other 105 IWW officials confined to a Chicago jail.

From her own cell in a Missouri penitentiary, Emma Goldman blasted those leftists "who were serving as war drummers for the Government." She saw no reason to alter her conviction that only a proletarian revolution could establish a genuinely free and democratic society. Soon after returning from Russia, John Reed, who burned with a desire to emulate the insurrection he had just chronicled, resigned from the masthead of the *Liberator*; he could not abide sharing "responsibility for a magazine which exists upon the sufferance of Mr. Burleson." The Eastmans, Reed's old and close friends, were quite comfortable describing both Lenin and Wilson as two of the great "statesmen" of their era.[24]

RADICAL TO THE BONE

Roger Baldwin also understood that his new National Civil Liberties Bureau (NCLB) would have to avoid condemning the president if it were to give sustained aid to anti-war Americans in legal trouble. To that end, he convinced several pro-war attorneys who held fast to libertarian principles to take the cases of individual dissenters. To persuade the government to treat conscientious objectors humanely, Baldwin met and often corresponded with Frederick Keppel, an assistant secretary of war and the former dean of Columbia University, who agreed that the harsh measures ordered by prison officials should cease. The relationship between the two men was relaxed enough that Baldwin addressed some of his letters to "Dear Fred."[25]

The bureau's literature swore fidelity to American ideals. It existed to maintain "in war time the rights of free press, free speech, peaceful assembly, liberty of conscience, and freedom from unlawful search and seizure"—paraphrases of the First and Fourth Amendments. One of its pamphlets quoted Woodrow Wilson's own warnings against "mob spirit" to denounce prominent figures like the former ambassador to Germany, James W. Gerard, who growled: "We should 'hog-tie' every disloyal German-American, feed every pacifist raw meat and hang every traitor to a lamp-post." To win the war while betraying the First Amendment would be a hollow victory indeed.[26]

But the balance between principle and caution was not easy to sustain. In January, the bureau invited seventy "well-known" liberals, some of whom backed the war and some who did not, to endorse a New York rally to protest the repression of "constitutional rights throughout the country." But such pro-war leftists as Charles Edward Russell denounced the meeting as "anti-American and anti-democratic" and insisted it be canceled. In March, with Keppel's support, the NCLB managed to persuade Woodrow Wilson to allow local draft boards to grant CO status to men whose pacifism was rooted in secular convictions— as long as they were willing to perform alternative service. But the Harvard-educated Baldwin was a revolutionary at heart; he wanted to protect civil liberties so that people like him could freely organize to change the world.[27]

The spark of radicalism had been lit within him by the most eloquent anarchist in America. Before the war, Baldwin, then a handsome young settlement house worker in St. Louis, had met Emma Goldman and thrilled to her lectures about "the organized power of the exploited." She dismissed him as "a very pleasant person, though not very vital . . . a social lion surrounded by society girls." Despite Goldman's snub, Baldwin was committed from that point on to advancing "all struggles for emancipation from the arbitrary power of government or the rule of one set of men over others." Like all anarchists, he longed for "a world in which all men and women should be free of compulsions, and each free to join in a network of voluntary associations to satisfy human needs." Since most of the activists prosecuted during the war were fellow radicals, Baldwin's politics meshed comfortably with his organization's defense of them—and of the First Amendment.[28]

But an organization dedicated to keeping or getting members of the Socialist Party and the Industrial Workers of the World out of prison inevitably became a target of federal authorities itself. The post office banned from the mails a dozen NCLB pamphlets that defended the rights of draft resisters, including a particularly eloquent one—"War's Heretics," by Norman Thomas. "If this is indeed a people's war for freedom," wrote the radical reverend in August of 1917, "the people can be trusted to see it through, without any coercion of conscience. To deny this is either to distrust democracy or to doubt the validity of the war as its instrument."[29]

That December, Military Intelligence officials began a thorough investigation of the civil liberties group. Keppel warned Baldwin that he was suspected of engaging in "a direct conflict with the Government." Then, one night the following March, federal agents broke into the NCLB's office near Union Square. Six months later, a squad from the Justice Department's Bureau of Investigation (the future FBI) was polite enough to come by during working hours; this time, they seized all its records.

The federal sleuths discovered a number of incriminating documents. Some letters encouraged men to become conscientious objectors—a far cry from just defending those who already had declared themselves as such. Baldwin and his assistants wrote often to IWW leaders like Big Bill Haywood about their cases and were deemed guilty of having an "intimate" relationship with the strike-happy insurgents. In 1920, a committee of New York State legislators out to expose "revolutionary radicalism" reported that Baldwin, "to the naked eye a charming, well-bred liberal, of good American stock and traditions," was "in reality a radical to the very bone."[30]

Of course, the director of the Civil Liberties Bureau had no quarrel with that description. A few days after the September raid on his office, Baldwin refused to comply with an order from his New York draft board to undergo a physical examination—the first step toward induction. "The government," he explained, "required every man of military age to become a soldier or a convict, and the choice was inescapable." On October 30, in a courtroom packed "with my colleagues and friends," Baldwin was sentenced to a year in prison, the stiffest sentence the law allowed. Before being led away to the Tombs, the infamous prison in lower Manhattan, Baldwin cast off the restraint he had imposed on himself when he believed "Dear Fred" and a few of his government colleagues might still uphold the First Amendment. "I am opposed to this and all other wars," Baldwin declared. What's more, he proudly confessed that he had long "felt myself heart and soul" with the IWW and other "world-wide radical movements for industrial and political freedom—wherever and however expressed." After the judge announced his sentence, Scott Nearing, Norman Thomas, and Judah Magnes rushed up to shake their friend's hand. From her jail cell in Missouri, Emma Goldman praised his "unreserved repudiation of the right of the state to coerce the individual." She also apologized for being "unkind" to him in the past.[31]

This stark narrative of a conflict between a proud leftist and the repressive state was somewhat mitigated by Baldwin's good luck and, perhaps, the waning zeal of government officials for the war itself. He spent most of the days between his arrest and trial in the Manhattan offices of the Bureau of Investigation. The raid on the NCLB had made a complete mess of its voluminous files, and the federal agents needed Baldwin to put them back in order. They "treated me as a guest," he recalled, "and often took me out to dinner and the theater" before driving him back to prison every night. They even let the ardent pacifist invite friends to lunch and showed him how they had created dummy IWW locals, complete with phony membership forms and incendiary pamphlets. Baldwin was also fortunate that the U.S. marshal in charge of his case was "against the war and the draft but didn't have the guts to resist. He had sought the marshal's job to escape, and he hated himself for it. He atoned a bit by giving me every privilege within his limited power."[32]

That summer, A. Philip Randolph and Chandler Owen defied the prohibition on anti-war agitation in a fashion that seemed just as certain to land them in prison. Early in August, the editors of the *Messenger* traveled to Cleveland to get "the colored people interested in the Socialist Movement," as Randolph put it. They hawked copies of their paper, and Randolph made a speech to a large crowd gathered in a downtown auditorium. Just by showing up at the rally, he said, they were "doing their bit to make the world safe for democracy. And unsafe for hypocrisy." Then Randolph asked a rhetorical question he knew would make any federal agents in the audience see red. "How can we make the world safe while Americans are unsafe, especially Negroes, from lynching, while this great crusade is going on?" As soon as Randolph stopped speaking, two officials of the Justice Department arrested both him and Owen and confiscated every unsold copy of the *Messenger*. One of the same G-men had recently served Eugene Debs with the warrant charging him with violating the Espionage Act for the speech he delivered in nearby Canton.[33]

Unlike Debs and Baldwin, however, the two most prominent black Socialists in America appeared before a judge who dismissed the charges against them. The cause of their reprieve was not ideological sympathy but racist condescension. Aided by their counsel, the untiring Seymour Stedman, the activists hoped to mount what Randolph later called "a grand political defense, indicting the war and everything else." But the judge in Cleveland refused to take them seriously. To him, "we were nothing but boys." He admonished Owen and Randolph to stop "carrying on this agitation against the law"—which he assumed they were too ignorant to have initiated unless white Socialists had put them up to it. Then the judge released "these boys" into Stedman's custody. "I want you to see that they return to their parents' home," he told the attorney. Both "boys" were twenty-nine years old; Owen was a college graduate, and Randolph was a married man.[34]

Rarely did African Americans who questioned why they should fight for a government that did not protect their liberties get treated so leniently. Both the Bureau of Investigation and the Military Intelligence

branch of the War Department spent thousands of man-hours seeking to root out any German sympathizers who might be lurking on
the staffs of black newspapers and civil rights organizations. They also
hired informers in black neighborhoods to report on anyone uttering
or printing "treasonable" statements. Long-established weeklies like
the *Chicago Defender* and the interracial NAACP—neither of which
opposed the war—were as much a target of surveillance as were the
Messenger and black members of the Socialist Party and the IWW. An
editor or activist did not have to be "radical to the bone" like Randolph,
Owen, and their white counterparts to be suspected of disloyalty.

In 1918, federal investigators were particularly concerned that protests against the Jim Crow order might weaken support for the war
among the black population at large. In late June, a National Colored
Liberty Congress met for six days in a black church a mile north of
the White House. The delegates called on Congress to pass a sweeping
civil rights law and also make lynching a federal crime. Two months
later, Monroe Trotter's National Equal Rights League met in Chicago
and issued similar demands. "Colored Americans," the league declared,
should "exhaust every peaceable means to bring to pass the end of the
undemocratic condition in which they alone, of all citizens, live in the
country which is the moral leader and military savior of the Allied Nations."

Neither meeting drew more than a few hundred people, but many
who attended were ministers or journalists—leaders in their local communities. One of the most famous delegates in Chicago was Ida Bell
Wells-Barnett, who had spent years publicizing the "red record" of
lynchings of black men and women; Military Intelligence viewed her as
a "known race agitator." Press coverage of both meetings accomplished
what Trotter and his fellow organizers had hoped for: It signaled that
an untold number of black Americans was not about to "close ranks"
behind a presidential administration that did nothing to attack, or even

address, racial inequality. For their part, the federal authorities considered Trotter an "advanced radical" who could cause "some trouble" for
the war effort.[35]

It was not an irrational fear. The decision to go to war had quickened
the migration of black people out of the rural South to cities all over the
country, where better jobs, pay, housing, and a degree of dignity beck-
oned. Nearly everywhere, their raised expectations met stout resistance
from white residents and the officials who shared their alarm and their
bigotry. In 1917, the East St. Louis riot and the Houston massacre were
only the most horrifying examples of this larger clash. Its postbellum
consequences would include the militancy of "New Negroes" in cities
all over the country—and the growth of a reborn Ku Klux Klan.

Yet few African Americans who protested Jim Crow were willing
to speak out against the war itself. They realized how easily the government could silence them for doing so. Ben Fletcher, black leader of
an integrated IWW local of Philadelphia longshoremen, was sentenced
to a ten-year jail term for sedition, even though he had counseled the
members of his union to register for the draft. Fletcher's political beliefs
were his only crime. After the soldiers who took part in the Houston
riot were executed, Ida Wells-Barnett ordered a batch of buttons honoring them as "martyred Negro soldiers." She proudly had her photograph taken with one of the buttons pinned to her elegant silk dress and
faced down the Secret Service men who threatened to arrest her. But
she refrained from denouncing W.E.B. Du Bois or other black activists
who believed that helping beat Germany could aid their cause at home.
Late that spring, James Weldon Johnson, the author who was then an
NAACP field secretary, wrote in the *Liberator*: "America's participation in the war is based solely upon the determination to secure for the
peoples of the world a larger degree of democracy; so we feel that in
pressing the claim for a larger degree of democracy for the black people
within the borders of the United States, we are not only not hindering

but acting in the fullest harmony with its ultimate aims." To equate loyalty with the anti-racist ideal was the only safe posture for African Americans who wanted to be heard while staying out of prison.[36]

THE DIFFERENCE THE DOUGHBOYS MADE

Flawed though it was, Woodrow Wilson's vision of a better world had little chance of being realized if American troops did not play a decisive role in defeating the German military. During the exuberant days just after Congress voted for war, the entertainer George M. Cohan had penned the deathless lyric: "Over there, over there, / Send the word, send the word over there, / That the Yanks are coming, the Yanks are coming, / The drums rum-tumming everywhere." The British and French implored the president and General John J. Pershing, commander of the American Expeditionary Forces (the AEF), to dispatch legions of Yanks to reinforce and relieve their battered troops. Yet, by the end of 1917, fewer than two hundred thousand doughboys had made their way across the English Channel; nearly all were training far from the front, rehearsing for war while German attacks pushed the weary French and British troops to the breaking point. Not until the end of May 1918 did the AEF undertake a small offensive of its own. In that one-day battle, with the support of their Allies' tanks and planes, Americans captured the tiny village of Cantigny in northwestern France. Three hundred doughboys lost their lives. The war ended less than six months later.

The tardy arrival of Americans on the killing fields was, in part, an ironic tribute to the success of the peace coalition in the United States during the neutral years. Hundreds of thousands of Americans would probably have been fighting in France by the summer of 1917 if Theodore Roosevelt, Leonard Wood, and their colleagues in the National Security League and Congress had won the fight over preparedness in 1915 and 1916. These soldiers could have been skilled at firing artillery pieces and machine guns made in U.S. factories; American pilots could have logged hundreds of hours flying airplanes built in American plants. Most doughboys could have sailed to Europe on U.S. vessels. But the working alliance between radical pacifists like Crystal Eastman and progressive foes of the military like Robert La Follette severely limited what the advocates of a European-style force could achieve—before Woodrow Wilson shed his own ambivalence and resolved that Americans had to sacrifice to advance self-government abroad and preserve the nation's honor.

Yet, even before the men of the AEF could leave their mark and thousands of their bodies on the field of combat, their specter forced the Kaiser's generals to adopt a risky strategy they hoped would prevent the Americans from ever having the opportunity to play that role. On the first day of spring in 1918, forty-seven German divisions launched Operation Michael, the largest coordinated assault since the beginning of the war. It was conceived more in desperation than optimism. We must strike, General Erich Ludendorff told his fellow commanders, "before America can throw strong forces into the scale." Supported by a barrage of more than a million artillery shells, German forces surged through British lines and advanced over sixty-five kilometers, an extraordinary distance on a Western Front where, since the fall of 1914, territorial gains had usually been measured by the length between one's own trench and that of a captured enemy's as little as a hundred meters away. Soon, mammoth German howitzers were moved close enough to Paris to bombard it day and night; many residents fled the capital for safer regions in the south.[37]

But the massive offensive could be sustained only if it led to a rapid and decisive victory. Germany, according to the historian John Keegan, had "to win the war before the New World appeared to redress the balance of the Old . . . before German manhood was exhausted by the ordeal of a final attack." Although Ludendorff's infantrymen remained on the offensive into mid-July, the grim calculus of resources was turning inexorably against them. Even the million soldiers transferred from the Russian front after the Bolshevik surrender did not create a force as large as that of their enemies. What's more, the British and French together flew almost a thousand more planes and fired almost five thousand more artillery pieces. Their eight hundred tanks completely dominated the puny number the Germans had built. By late summer, most ominously for Reich commanders, almost 2 million fresh troops of Pershing's AEF were ready for either battle or to supply those at the front. If needed, a million more would soon be on their way.[38]

In the end, it was the ever-increasing number of American soldiers, as much as the intense combat they waged, that made the difference. The AEF clashed with the German Army in major battles for only about 110 days—nearly all of which took place during the final two months of the war, and 50,280 Americans lost their lives in combat. More than half—26,277—died in a single battle, the Meuse-Argonne, which began in late September and ended on Armistice Day nearly seven weeks later. It was, one historian has pointed out, "the deadliest battle in all of American history."[39]

Soon after the Armistice, General Paul von Hindenburg, who, with Ludendorff, had been in command of German forces, gave an interview to the American journalist George Seldes. In Hindenburg's view, the British food blockade of Germany and the million U.S. troops who fought in the Meuse-Argonne had decided the outcome. "The balance" between the two sides, Hindenburg asserted, "was broken by the American troops." Without them, "the war could have ended in a sort of stalemate."[40]

Yet the casualty toll in the Meuse-Argonne and in many of the other engagements the AEF fought was needlessly high. Pershing believed fiercely—and foolishly—in rifle and bayonet charges unsuited to a war in which a small number of experienced machine gunners could direct withering fire at hundreds of men advancing toward them over open ground. Officers in training camps instructed recruits to fight with an aggressive spirit that might cow the enemy and show that intrepid

Yanks were superior to their supposedly undaring counterparts from the United Kingdom and France. But the ethos of a Western gunslinger did not fit the mechanized war into which the AEF had plunged.[41]

In an autobiographical novel, the former French infantryman Gabriel Chevallier testified to the dangerous inexperience of a regiment of African Americans who briefly fought in his sector of the front during the final month of the conflict:

> They keep all their weapons ready to shoot. . . . If one gets dropped, it goes off. If someone gets killed, it is an inevitable accident of war, something of which they only have a vague notion. They came to France like they would set off to the lands of Alaska or Canada, to become gold prospectors or fur trappers. They go out on crazy, boisterous patrols in front of their lines, making a lot of racket, something which does not always turn to their advantage. They throw grenades like fireworks at a festival.

One could dismiss this as racist caricature, if other observers did not tell similar stories about doughboys from a variety of ethnic backgrounds. "[U.S.] Commanders claimed that they could not stop men who understood the desirability of aggressiveness from rushing straight into machine-gun fire," writes Jennifer Keene, an authority on the AEF.[42]

Such zeal for combat did not mean American soldiers echoed the war aims their president articulated so eloquently and so often. Most doughboys, in fact, did not seem inspired by any moral principle at all. In his novel *Three Soldiers*, John Dos Passos described the attitude of one draftee: "He had not had the courage to move a muscle for his freedom, but he had been fairly cheerful about risking his life as a soldier, in a cause he believed useless." A lieutenant wrote to his family back home: "I know that nine out of every ten of our enlisted men do not know what they are fighting for, the idea is simply to kill the Boche."[43]

Informed about this attitude by military censors (who read soldiers' outgoing mail), War Department officials scurried to change it. In May 1918, they set up a morale division that supplied training camps in the United States with films, lectures, pamphlets, and other forms of propaganda, similar to the fare civilians were getting from the ubiquitous literature and speakers of the Committee on Public Information. But Pershing had neither the time nor the desire to replicate these efforts for the troops in France.

In February, the AEF commander did endorse the launching of *Stars and Stripes*—an official weekly paper produced by doughboys themselves. It proved to be one of his shrewder decisions. Alongside war news and statements by the top brass, *Stars and Stripes* presented the opinions of and stories about ordinary soldiers, as edited and designed by a squad of gifted, as well as uniformed, journalists. The staff included Private Harold Ross, who later founded the *New Yorker*; and Sergeant Alexander Woollcott, soon to become a popular and influential drama critic. From an office down the street from the Paris Opera, they skillfully mixed humorous anecdotes and cartoons with sentimental tales about "war waifs adopted as mascots" by U.S. troops and pugnacious vows—often couched in baseball or boxing metaphors—about defeating the Huns. "World's Series Opened—Batter Up!" read the headline above a front-page photo of a doughboy hurling a grenade "toward a ducking Fritzy's bean." "The Army's Poets," a regular feature, included both gentle swipes at military cooking and bureaucratic folly and verses that sought to exorcise the enemy's evil soul: "Red is the flag of Germany. / Red for the blood she spilled; / White is the flag of Germany / White for the shame she willed; / Black is the flag of Germany / Black for the graves she filled!"

Stars and Stripes encouraged its readers to view themselves as members of an immensely strong, relaxed, and confident, even arrogant, team—Americans who loved to fight and were fighting for a virtuous cause. Yet defining the cause itself was usually relegated to the back pages, in dispatches that drew on the president's rhetoric.

The paper was an extraordinary success. By the end of the war, *Stars and Stripes* sold more than 340,000 copies a week, at the cost of fifty centimes apiece.[44]

Some doughboys did openly voice doubts about the value of their mission. In June 1917, news that enlisted men were taking part in peace demonstrations reached General James Franklin Bell, commander of the Eastern Department of the army. He immediately ordered his adjutant general, the chief legal officer, to court-martial any soldier who had attended a protest and to warn others not to follow their lead. Behind the front lines, as many as 150,000 doughboys "straggled" away from their units. Some were shell-shocked, others afraid, while others decided the cause was not worth the sacrifice of their lives. The problem was serious enough to cause the military police to place some stragglers in cages with big signs on their backs that listed their offense. One general, Preston Brown, ordered his police to hurl grenades into any dugout soldiers built, against orders, behind the lines.[45]

For their part, many black draftees echoed the kind of indignation that had led to the lethal riot in Houston. They were forced to live in separate and manifestly inferior barracks and were commanded by indifferent or hostile white officers. "To put it all in a nutshell," one black sergeant complained to W.E.B. Du Bois soon after the Armistice, "the American Negro soldier in France was treated" by his superiors "with the same contempt and undemocratic spirit as the American Negro citizen is treated in the United States." Perhaps for fear of losing their lives, no other mass protest—violent or nonviolent—occurred. Yet several black soldiers were prosecuted for setting down on paper thoughts similar to those others were likely whispering to one another. "We feel like we have nothing to Do with this war," wrote Private Sidney Wilson (under an assumed name) in a misspelled jolt of anger mailed to his local draft board in Tennessee. "So if you all Thinks it Just wait until uncle Sam puts a Gun in the niggers Hands and you all will be Sorry of it because we is Show goin to Come Back and fight and whip out the united States." Instead of being shipped off to France, Private Wilson was sentenced to ten years at hard labor.[46]

For soldiers of any race, the brevity of the AEF's combat experience probably kept such protests to a minimum. It was easier to keep morale high when most soldiers fought in just one or two battles. And the majority of American troops spent the war in supply or labor battalions, where they never had the opportunity to exchange fire with a German.

Ironically, the two doughboys, both white, whose exploits in the Meuse-Argonne brought them the greatest fame back home had both wanted the United States to stay out of the war. Alvin York, who belonged to a pacifist congregation in rural Tennessee, had registered for the draft as a conscientious objector. "I was worried clean through. I didn't want to go and kill. I believed in my Bible," he recalled. But at York's training camp in Georgia, an equally devout officer convinced him that America's cause was a righteous one. On the morning of October 8, the sharpshooter killed twenty-five Germans and took another 132 of them prisoner. York was awarded the Medal of Honor.

A few days earlier, Major Charles Whittlesey, a recent graduate of Harvard Law School, was commanding several hundred men on the offensive in the Argonne Forest. They unknowingly advanced too far into enemy-held territory and were surrounded by a much larger force of German troops. Despite low rations, no blankets, and a dwindling supply of ammunition, Whittlesey managed to keep his "Lost Battalion" from annihilation or capture until reinforcements rescued them on October 7. He too received a Medal of Honor and, like York, a storm of popular acclaim.

Few Americans knew that the patrician attorney had been a staunch anti-militarist who, as an undergraduate at Williams College, had roomed and become friends with Max Eastman. Whittlesey had voted for Eugene Debs in 1912 and then switched to Wilson in 1916 because of the president's vow to keep the nation at peace. In 1917, he enlisted because, according to one historian, "his sense of duty outweighed the personal morality that rejected war." William James would have understood.[47]

LOSING AN ELECTION, WINNING A WAR

The dreadful truth about the battle of the Meuse-Argonne was that tens of thousands of men died on both sides without knowing that Germany's leaders were already suing for peace. At the end of September, Reich military commanders told the Kaiser and the highest officials in his government that they had to find a way to end the war quickly before the army was destroyed—and the nation dissolved either into chaos or revolution. On October 4, with the military's support, the new chancellor, Prince Max of Baden, dispatched a note to Woodrow Wilson proposing a peace agreement based on the Fourteen Points. In effect, the rulers of the German empire were willing to accept that, after four years of total war, they would gain neither territory, nor wealth, nor even a guarantee of future security. Wilson demurred while he consulted with his Allies. Two weeks later, Ludendorff suddenly bridled against the humiliating offer and told Prince Max he was determined to win more favorable terms "by fighting for them."[48]

But it was much too late to kill—or bargain for—a peace with honor. In the North Sea ports of Kiel and Wilhelmshaven, German sailors mutinied when ordered to take on the British Royal Navy in what they knew would be a suicide mission. On October 21, the imperial admiralty had to call the U-boats back to their bases. Days later, both the Ottoman Turks and the Austro-Hungarians admitted defeat and signed armistice pacts that spelled the demise of their empires. On November 1, American troops crossed the Meuse River and surged toward Sedan, railroad hub for the enemy's forces on the Western Front. In nearby sectors, the British and French armies were advancing rapidly toward the German border. A week later, the Kaiser's generals told him his soldiers had lost the will to fight. All they wanted, said one officer, was "an armistice at the earliest possible moment." The next day, the bewildered monarch fled by rail to neutral Holland, where he formally abdicated his now worthless throne. At eleven o'clock on the morning of November 11, the Great War finally ended.[49]

The final month of the terrible conflict happened to coincide with the climax of another American election campaign. Everyone assumed the Armistice would be a turning point in world history; Woodrow Wilson firmly believed, despite his Allies' determination to punish the vanquished nations, that he could achieve a "healing peace" that would speed the advent of democratic government throughout the world. But he had overestimated his ability to persuade most Americans to follow his lead.

During the fall of 1918, the Democrats who ran Congress were engaged in a defensive struggle of their own. A variety of mounting resentments about what the federal government had recently done or failed to do made it difficult to focus the campaign, as they would have liked, on how Wilson's leadership had brought Germany to its knees. Farmers and ranchers enduring a savage drought in the West were furious that Congress had voted down a $20 million bill earmarked to help them. Agrarian producers everywhere chafed under price controls. Hundreds of thousands of workers, their real earnings slashed by inflated housing costs and their expectations lifted by talk of "industrial democracy," took part in short but effective strikes, which some lawmakers alleged gave comfort to the enemy. From Minnesota to Montana, Nonpartisan League candidates, running on a platform that blasted "big-bellied, red-necked" profiteers and called for state-owned banks and railroads, leached support away from progressive Democrats.[50]

Meanwhile, the White House was under assault on its right flank from a unified and well-financed Republican campaign. GOP chairman Will Hays, a wily conservative from Indiana, accused the White House of rushing to conclude the war before Election Day, even if an

THREE WHO VOTED AGAINST
DECLARING WAR IN APRIL 1917

On right, Senator George Norris,
progressive Republican
from Nebraska.

Senator James K. Vardaman,
white supremacist–populist
Democrat from Mississippi.

Representative Isaac Sherwood, pro-labor Democrat from
Toledo, Ohio. The former Union officer was the only Civil War
veteran to vote against going to war with Germany.

4

Emma Goldman, photographed
riding on a streetcar in
New York City in spring 1917.

5

Roger Nash Baldwin,
leader of the National Civil
Liberties Bureau, later
renamed the American
Civil Liberties Union.

ATTACKS ON ANTI-WAR STALWARTS AS TRAITORS

6   UNCONDITIONAL SURRENDER

Morris Hillquit as a stooge of the Kaiser during his 1917 race for mayor of New York City.

OUR CANDIDATE FOR MAYOR—OF BERLIN—
SAYS THIS IS THE ONLY ROAD TO PEACE.

7

Robert La Follette leads a band of senators who filibustered the Armed Ship Bill, March 1917. President Woodrow Wilson branded them "a little group of willful men," and they were accused, as in this cartoon, of having pro-German sympathies.

THE ONLY ADEQUATE REWARD.

AFRICAN-AMERICAN OPPONENTS
OF MR. WILSON'S WAR

Asa Philip Randolph, Socialist
editor and civil rights organizer,
photographed in 1911.

9

Ida Bell Wells-Barnett,
leading anti-lynching activist,
photographed in 1922.

CONTRASTING IMAGES
OF CONSCRIPTION

10

THIS man subjected himself to imprisonment and probably to being shot or hanged

THE prisoner used language tending to discourage men from enlisting in the United States Army

IT is proven and indeed admitted that among his incendiary statements were—

THOU shalt not kill

and

BLESSED are the peacemakers

This illustration, titled "Blessed Are the Peacemakers," shows the conscientious objector as Christ figure.

11

A Registration Day reminder.

12

Cover of the first issue of the *Liberator*,
successor to the *Masses*.

13

14

Max Eastman, editor of both the
Liberator and the *Masses*.

Crystal Eastman, managing editor
of the *Liberator*, in 1916.

OPPONENTS OF WAR REDEEMED

15

Eugene Debs on his release from federal prison in Atlanta, 1921.

16

Robert La Follette, campaigning for president in Chicago, 1924.

Norman Thomas, speaking at a peace rally in Washington, D.C., June 1940.

William James in 1907.

A poster against the Vietnam War, printed in 1971. The artist is satirizing the iconic, pro-war poster from 1917 by James Montgomery Flagg.

"inconclusive peace" would leave the enemy able to fight again. "No peace that satisfies Germany in any degree can ever satisfy us," declared Henry Cabot Lodge, "[We] must go to Berlin and there dictate peace." Theodore Roosevelt scoffed at the naïveté of the Fourteen Points: "I gravely doubt whether a more silly or more mischievous plan was ever seriously proposed by the ruler of a great nation." The National Security League joined the fray with a widely distributed chart listing how incumbents had voted on preparedness bills that Congress had debated before the United States entered the war. Far more Democrats than Republicans appeared on the "unpatriotic" side of its ledger.[51]

The hostile campaign by the opposition party infuriated Woodrow Wilson. With the Germans desperate to make peace, he could, at last, carry out his plan for how to end all wars. But the GOP leaders who had long belittled the president in public and despised him in private could now think only of undermining his authority and grabbing back the reins of government.

Just ten days before the election, Wilson unleashed a counterattack. He declared that the only appropriate response voters could make to Republicans who "have sought to take the choice of policy and the conduct of the war out of my hands and put it under instrumentalities of their choosing" was to keep Democrats in control of Congress. As in all his more important statements, Wilson was expressing a profound conviction that both the majority of Americans and the logic of history were on his side. He assumed, in the words of the interior secretary, Franklin K. Lane, that Democrats "would win because the President had made a personal appeal for a vote of confidence."[52]

This time, the president was mistaken. In late May, he had told a joint session of Congress that "politics is adjourned" for the duration of the war; victory in the midterm election, he predicted, "will go to those who think least of it." Wilson was quite aware that a spirit of nonpartisanship in wartime was likely to aid the fortunes of the party in power. But to repudiate his spring plea on the eve of the fall vote sounded anxious and hypocritical. "Mr. Wilson wants only rubber stamps, his rubber stamps in Congress," responded a confident Will Hays. "Republican congressmen must be defeated and Democratic congressmen must . . . yield in everything. That is . . . the idea of an autocrat calling himself the servant but bidding for the mastery of this great, free people."[53]

The president was also appealing to the public's sense of collective morality. The price of "a *secure* and *lasting* peace," he told a crowd that filled New York's Metropolitan Opera House in late September, was "impartial justice in every item of the settlement, no matter whose interest is crossed." To drive that argument home to voters, Wilson could have used the goodwill and organizing skills of his sometime champions on the left—the anti-militarist progressives and radicals who despised TR and Lodge as much as he did. Their rhetoric and votes had been essential to his narrow victory in 1916; after the Fourteen Points speech, they seemed open to helping him again.[54]

However, as the midterm election drew near, many of the prominent Americans who had opposed the war decided they would not be fooled again. For admirers of the Russian Revolution, Wilson had changed from a convenient friend into a confirmed enemy. In August, several thousand U.S. troops invaded Siberia in a confused effort to protect American property and help a Czech regiment stranded in the Far East. To Max Eastman and other pro-Bolsheviks, this limited intervention was a naked attempt to overthrow a popular government and "establish a monarchy or a business republic" in its place. The editor of the *Liberator*—who, just months before, had joked that Wilson was almost a Socialist—now coldly predicted that the League of Nations would become nothing more than "a Capitalist International." Americans who wanted to establish a genuine workers' international should, advised Eastman, be sure to vote for Socialist candidates. Morris Hillquit was again running for Congress, from the Twentieth District in northern Manhattan. Elsewhere in the country, his comrades expected to match, if not exceed, their good showing from the previous year.[55]

For liberals, the break with Wilson was more agonizing. They still believed a more harmonious world order could emerge from the ruins of the Great War, and that only a vigorous assertion of the Fourteen Points would prevent America's allies from imposing a brutal settlement on Germany. Yet the president's refusal to stop or even slow the repression of peaceful protest first baffled and then enraged them. "He puts his enemies in office and his friends in jail," snapped Amos Pinchot. At the *Nation*, Oswald Garrison Villard still hoped Wilson's party would triumph at the polls. But he devoted little time or energy to that purpose after the post office banned the September issue of his magazine from the mails because it included an editorial titled "Civil Liberty Dead." The government's decision drove even the *New York World*, Wilson's staunchest journalistic defender, to charge that the administration was "undertak[ing] the Prussianization of American public opinion."[56]

On November 5, enough American voters had reasons to be unhappy with the Democratic Party to give Republicans control of both chambers of Congress for the first time since 1910. It was not a landslide. The GOP gained six seats in the Senate and twenty-five in the House. If the Armistice had occurred just a week earlier, the result might well have been different. As it was, several key Republican victories over Wilsonian contenders were won by quite narrow margins. In Michigan, safely Republican since the Civil War, Truman Newberry, a businessman serving in the navy, defeated the Democratic nominee for Senate—who was none other than Henry Ford—by a few thousand votes. The state GOP far outspent its rival. The auto magnate, who had never run for office before, evidently thought his fame would be enough to carry the seat for the president's party. A year later, Newberry was indicted for accepting illegal campaign contributions from relatives and friends, and he spent much of his congressional term defending himself against the charges.[57]

Despite the rhetoric of Hays and Roosevelt, most voters in 1918 did not seem eager to punish politicians who had doubted the wisdom of

entering the great conflict. Nearly twice as many congressmen who had
voted against declaring war retained their seats as lost them. Long service in their districts certainly boosted some of these incumbents. Republican Gilbert Haugen had represented the farmers of northwestern
Iowa since 1898; his vote against the war could not shake their loyalty,
particularly since he was in line to chair the Agriculture Committee.
Neither were the Democrats in the Second District of North Carolina
in a mood to unseat Claude Kitchin, despite or perhaps because he frequently disagreed with the president's policies. If anything, northern
Republicans who blasted Kitchen's crusade to tax excess profits probably ensured that he would not face a primary opponent back home.[58]

For the one political party that had never wavered from its anti-
militarist stand, the results were frustratingly ambiguous. On the one
hand, Socialists did quite well in parts of the upper Midwest, as distaste for Mr. Wilson's war merged with the material discontents of small
farmers. In Wisconsin, Victor Berger won back the seat in Congress he
had lost in 1912, and the SPA elected twenty-two state legislators—a
gain of nine. Socialists took legislative seats in Minnesota as well and
won local offices in Michigan, South Dakota, and a few other states.

But in New York, the party lost most of the ground it had gained in
1917—before many U.S. soldiers had arrived in France and before the
government had begun its repressive assault in earnest. Morris Hillquit
was defeated again, as was every other SPA nominee for Congress in the
big city– including its lone incumbent, Meyer London, erstwhile idol of
the Yiddish-speaking Lower East Side. Only two of the party's ten state
assemblymen retained their seats. The SPA also did poorly in other cities where the Justice Department had repressed its newspapers and put
its leaders on trial. Local branches struggling just to survive rarely had
the time or resources to stage campaign rallies and get out the vote.[59]

Unlike in 1916 and 1917, Hillquit never really expected to win.
Still sick with TB, he spent the entire campaign convalescing by Saranac Lake in the Adirondack Mountains, three hundred miles north of

his district. His absence did not stop a charismatic Manhattan Republican, and future liberal mayor of the city, from branding him a traitor. "I charge Hillquit with being a tool and an ally of the Kaiser," charged Major—and Congressman—Fiorello La Guardia. "I say Hillquit is part of the German Army. I say Hillquit is an enemy of every man in uniform."[60]

These defeats did not trouble Crystal Eastman. In one of her rare articles in the *Liberator*, she pointed out that, in New York City and its suburbs, the Socialists had increased their vote by some 50 percent. Women, casting ballots for the first time in the state, boosted the party's numbers. If local Democrats and Republicans hadn't united on fusion tickets, more radicals would have won. "The steady growth of the Socialist vote is always remarkable," Crystal declared. "This year it is amazing." The party, she gushed, is more than a "political institution." It is "a deep-rooted faith and a thoroughly understood intellectual conception which must grow because it satisfies the vital desires of real human beings."[61]

As do victors at the end of nearly every war, the Allies in the Great War looked forward to a future order they expected to dominate. Although his party had just lost its majority in Congress, Woodrow Wilson still expected to lead the shaping of the peace treaty he would soon be negotiating with other heads of government in the Palace of Versailles, outside Paris. Surely, the Senate would not reject a pact that 116,000 young Americans had effectively lost their lives to achieve.

Stalwart figures in the frayed anti-war coalition were just as certain they were witnessing the dawn of a just and egalitarian epoch in world history. Believing the old European monarchies would soon be swept away, Robert La Follette predicted to a friend: "The next twenty five years ought to be big with events for masses of mankind. I would like to be permitted to have a part in it." The progressive from Wisconsin was, after all, still the member of the party that was about to take control of the U.S. Senate. Three days after the election, a multiracial audience of thousands gathered inside Harlem's New Star Casino to celebrate the first anniversary of the Bolshevik Revolution. A. Philip Randolph and Scott Nearing were among the speakers who dedicated their "hearts and lives to follow" the "noble example" of their "Russian comrades" and "establish in our country a free working class."[62]

On January 1, Morris Hillquit greeted his thousands of friends and political supporters. In a holiday letter from Saranac Lake, he wished a happy new year to "the hundred and fifty million proletarians of factory and field in all Russian territories, the pioneer-warriors for human rights and human dignity, for liberty and bread." He offered similar words of praise to the workers of Germany, Austria, Poland, Bohemia, Great Britain, France, Belgium, and Italy—and, finally, the United States—"the rearguard in the onward march of revolutionary international labor." "The coming year," Hillquit predicted, "will probably mark the turning point in human history. It will be a decisive year for international Socialism."

The veteran party leader could not entirely abandon his instinctive sense of caution: The year, he warned, "will bring us great triumphs and conquests, but also hard struggles and trials." Yet, Hillquit had little doubt that he and his comrades would soon be inhabiting "a happy new era, a happy new world."[63]

SEVEN

LEGACIES

"There isn't a story in the world that isn't in part, at least, addressed
to the past."

—Colum McCann[1]

A SPECIES OF REDEMPTION

Anti-war movements are not like other collective attempts to change society. In contrast to those who seek to win rights and a measure of power for
women or workers or people of color or gays and lesbians, peace organizers have no natural constituency. Neither can their movement grow slowly,
taking decades to convince ordinary people and elites to think differently
and enact laws to embody that new perspective. A massive effort to stop
one's country from going to war—or to stop a war it is already waging—
has to grow quickly or it will have little or no influence. What's more,
it has to lure talented activists away from other, more enduring political
commitments. Every new war also requires peace activists to create a new
movement and then to find partners for a coalition that might be capable
of pressuring the government to end it. There have always been pacifists
in the United States. But during periods of peace or brief conflicts, they
endure on the margins, unknown to most of their fellow citizens.

The Americans who fought a war against war from the summer of 1914 until the Armistice fifty-one months later managed to surmount all these obstacles. They were unable to convince the president and Congress to keep the nation at peace. But their legacy is not simply one of failure. By warning, credibly, about the consequences of American intervention, they were transformed from "traitors" into something akin to prophets. Senator William Stone was quite accurate when he predicted, in April 1917, that if the United States declared war, "we would never again have the same old republic." A few decades later, when the United States became the strongest military power in world history, many Americans continued to question how that force was being used and the assaults on civil liberties that often accompanied it. Consciously or not, they were echoing the same question posed by dissidents during the First World War: Can one preserve a peaceful and democratic society at home while venturing into the world to kill those whom our leaders designate, rationally or not, as our enemies?[2]

After the Great War ended, mass anger and global crises soon dashed the rosy visions of both peace activists and their opponents. After smashing left-wing uprisings, fascist regimes came to power in Germany and Italy. By the late 1920s, Joseph Stalin had consolidated his despotic control over the USSR. Then, during the 1930s, the mass fear and hunger caused by the Great Depression ripped open wounds of national hostility that had never healed. A quarter-century after Congress had declared war on Germany, Americans were once again fighting soldiers from that nation, as well as troops from the empire of Japan. "The Second World War was the continuation of the First," writes the historian John Keegan, "and indeed it is inexplicable except in terms of the rancours and instabilities left by the earlier conflict."[3]

The dark days had begun less than a year after the guns fell silent on the Western Front. Woodrow Wilson landed in France in December 1918 to a popular acclaim no American president—perhaps no statesman from *any* land—had ever received outside his nation before. The soaring idealism of the Fourteen Points, the dream of lasting self-rule and self-determination, had, in the words of H.G. Wells, "transfigured" Wilson "in the eyes of men. He ceased to be a common statesman; he became a Messiah." But at the Versailles peace conference the following spring, the leaders of Great Britain, France, and Italy forced the president to agree to a punitive settlement against their former enemies, while they insisted on retaining their own empires. The "Wilsonian moment" soon passed.[4]

The former Allies did establish the president's cherished League of Nations, with its headquarters in the ornate Palais Wilson, named in his honor, on the shore of Lake Geneva. But back home, a group of senators, led by Henry Cabot Lodge, adamantly opposed Article X in the organization's founding covenant because it obliged its members to protect from "external aggression the territorial integrity and existing political independence of all Members of the League." Enforcement, they feared, would actually imperil the independence of the *United States.* Article X, thundered Senator William Borah of Idaho, was "in conflict with the right of our people to govern themselves free from all restraint, legal or moral, of foreign powers." Wilson refused to compromise, and the treaty failed to gain the necessary two-thirds margin in the upper chamber. The absence from the Palais Wilson of delegates from Wilson's own rich and powerful nation became what one top British diplomat called, echoing *Macbeth,* "the ghost at all our feasts."[5]

Before the United States plunged into the Great War, peace advocates in the United States had warned against the sanguine expectations of those who favored that decision. Late in 1915, Crystal Eastman predicted that an "exhausted Europe" would reject the "world federation proposals" of a country that had surrendered to militarism itself. In the end, it was the United States that refused to join the League of Nations, which then failed to prevent the next global conflagration. On the eve of intervention in 1917, Claude Kitchin wailed that "all the demons of humanity will be let loose for a rampage throughout the world." He seemed prophetic when the victors in the Great War grabbed spoils to justify the sacrifices they had made, while the vanquished in Germany and elsewhere plotted their revenge.[6]

The lofty hopes of the American Left survived no longer than did Woodrow Wilson's. In 1919, the largest strike wave in the nation's history shut down industries from coast to coast. Some 365,000 steel workers walked off the job in plants from Pennsylvania to Illinois to demand recognition of their union. The Boston police, previously Irish-Catholic icons of order, refused to work unless they got a raise. In Seattle, wage earners united in a general strike that the city's mayor decried as "an attempted revolution."

Many Americans hoped, or feared, that the real thing might soon be at hand. That August, radicals who had failed to capture control of the Socialist Party formed two new Communist parties, each claiming to be the genuine outpost of Bolshevism in the benighted land. Together, they boasted seventy thousand members. Neither upstart group had the will or patience to continue the educational and electoral strategies that Morris Hillquit and his fellow leaders had pursued for decades. "The working class must organize and train itself for the capture of state power," declared the Communist Labor Party, led by John Reed. "The new working class government—the Dictatorship of the Proletariat—will . . . accomplish the transition from Capitalism to the Communist Commonwealth."[7]

But by 1920, that power-hungry "proletariat" was in retreat, if, indeed, it had ever existed at all. Unyielding opposition by local and corporate officials and splits among wage earners along lines of skill and ethnicity defeated every major strike. American unions were thrown on the defensive; most would remain there until the coming of the New Deal. A ferocious Red Scare, its flames fanned by Attorney General A. Mitchell Palmer, forced radicals to worry more, as during the war, about staying out of jail than about building a new world in the ashes of the old. When Jane Addams criticized "this suppression and spirit of intolerance" and gave speeches to raise funds to feed German children, she was roundly attacked as a traitor. In November, the Republicans, aided by a sharp recession and the collapse of Wilson's global dreams, captured the White House in a landslide and significantly expanded their majorities on Capitol Hill. Eugene V. Debs ran again for president on the Socialist ticket. But he had to do so from inside a cell in Atlanta's federal prison. This blizzard of calamities turned the American Left from a growing, buoyant movement into a divided and dispirited one.[8]

But soon, the erstwhile foes of the Great War began to experience a kind of redemption. The former Allies, claiming penury, refused to pay back their war loans to the United States. In 1922, Robert La Follette was reelected to the Senate by the largest majority in Wisconsin history. Led by Jane Addams and Emily Balch, the Women's International League for Peace and Freedom—the successor to the Woman's Peace Party—gained thousands of members during the 1920s both in the United States and abroad with a platform of unyielding pacifism and opposition to empire. In 1922, Addams asked: "Was not war in the interest of democracy for the salvation of civilization a contradiction in terms, whoever said it or however often it was repeated?" Most Americans probably would have responded in the affirmative.[9]

In 1931, Addams was awarded the Nobel Peace Prize. The committee in Norway saluted her for holding "fast to the ideal of peace even during the difficult hours when other considerations and interests obscured it from her compatriots and drove them into the conflict." The *New York Times*, which had once routinely disparaged Addams's pacifism, now hoped her "wartime prophecy" of "international cooperation" might be "coming true."[10]

Most Americans had come to look back at the Great War with the same retrospective regret, if not loathing. In the United States, the

number of war commemorations dwindled rapidly; construction of the
Tomb of the Unknown Soldier at Arlington National Cemetery was de-
layed for five years as officials argued about "whether it should symbolize war or peace." In 1929, with just a single dissenting vote, the Senate
approved a grand, if unenforceable, treaty to "outlaw war" drafted by
Secretary of State Frank Kellogg and Aristide Briand, his French coun-
terpart. Sixty nations signed the pact by year's end. In 1934, a special
Senate committee, chaired by Gerald Nye of North Dakota, began to
investigate the charge that munitions producers had dragged the nation into the Great War. No conspiracy was ever uncovered, but the
well-publicized hearings persuaded many that, as Nye put it, "war and
preparation for war is not a matter of national honor and national defense, but a matter of profit for the few."[11]

Popular histories published at the same time also took a sharply
negative view of U.S. intervention—although they did not fix blame on
the "merchants of death" whom Nye and his fellow lawmakers had fin-
gered. The appeal of these "revisionist" interpretations of the Great War
easily eclipsed accounts written by its defenders. In 1935, the journalist
Walter Millis, in Road to War, a best-selling narrative, downplayed the
role of big capital; instead, he depicted both Wilson and his supporters as naïve romantics who thought they could bend the world to their
wishes. On the April day when Congress took its fateful vote, wrote
Millis, "the war had mangled its usual number of human bodies, inflicted its usual hurts and tortures." The United States "was in the war,"
he concluded, but "none quite knew how it happened, nor why, nor
what precisely it might mean."[12]

A few perceptive novelists, veterans of the war, translated that
same judgment into indelible prose. Ernest Hemingway's A Farewell to
Arms and Erich Maria Remarque's All Quiet on the Western Front vividly described a conflict that Remarque, a former soldier of the Reich,
bluntly called a "crime." Both books sold well in the United States and
were adapted into successful films. As the critic Andrew Delbanco has

observed about the best literature of modern war: "It . . . shuts out concepts while delivering sensations—fear, relief, exhaustion, boredom, restlessness—on the premise that larger meanings are retrospective impositions, impertinent and inconceivable to men in chronic shock."[13]

Early in 1937, to no one's surprise, the Gallup Poll found that 70 percent of Americans believed it had been a mistake for the United States to fight in World War I. The peace coalition, it seemed, had been right after all. In each of the previous three years, Congress, by overwhelming majorities, had voted for neutrality acts that essentially took the same actions that anti-warriors had vainly demanded two decades before: an embargo on selling arms or loaning money to belligerents and a prohibition on Americans traveling on the ships of such nations. In 1937, lawmakers also slapped a ban on U.S. vessels carrying either people or matériel to nations at war. In opinion polls, large majorities supported a constitutional amendment that would require a national referendum before the United States could go to war. Only the vigorous opposition of Democratic leaders prevented such an amendment—drafted by Representative Louis Ludlow, a Democrat from Indiana—from gaining a full debate on the House floor.[14]

During the mid- to late 1930s, the press and newsreels were full of stories about tyrants on the march around the globe. But with joblessness so high and strikers battling for union recognition at some of the mightiest corporations in the land, most Americans had more immediate concerns than Germany's rapid remilitarization, Italy's conquest of Ethiopia, Japan's invasion of China, or the fierce civil war in Spain.

VINDICATION AND DECLINE

None of the four Americans who had played such a pivotal role in trying to keep the United States out of the Great War lived long enough to witness any of the events that presaged the outbreak of the second and far greater global conflict. La Follette, Kitchin, and Crystal Eastman all died in the 1920s; Hillquit lived on until 1933. But none renounced the stand they had taken. All would have seconded the lines La Follette wrote to his son-in-law as the First World War was ending: "I may not live to see my own vindication," he predicted, "but you will."[15]

As it happened, the flamboyant senator was the only member of the quartet who enjoyed a second political act of much consequence: In 1924, he finally got a chance to head a presidential ticket. The summer after his triumphant reelection to the Senate, La Follette embarked, with his wife, Belle, and son Robert Jr., on a three-month tour of Europe. Although suffering from heart disease, he met with top leaders in Germany, Italy, the Soviet Union, and five other nations. The war and its violent aftermath had bequeathed a legacy of disillusionment and economic hardship: "Between the upper and nether millstones of imperialistic and communistic dictatorships," he wrote in the Hearst press, ". . . the institutions of democracy are being ground to dust." "Instead of peace, I found new wars in the making."[16]

Back home, La Follette learned that a variety of activists on the left were eager to create a serious alternative to the major parties, both of which had drifted rightward since the war. In 1922, they formed a new organization, the Conference for Progressive Political Action (CPPA), and made plans to run an independent presidential campaign. La Follette declared: "The greatest contribution that America can make to Europe and the world is to restore and perfect her democratic institutions and traditions, so that they will stand as a beacon lighting the way to all the peoples." He had always hungered for the presidency, and the broad left had no more famous, consistent, or eloquent figure on its side. So La Follette easily won the CPPA's nomination to run as the candidate of the new Progressive Party. The group took the same name as the defunct party whose standard Theodore Roosevelt, his deceased nemesis, had borne twelve years earlier.[17]

For a candidate with only $200,000 to spend and virtually no

organization behind him, Fighting Bob did remarkably well. The Socialist Party, the AFL, the Railroad Brotherhoods, and what was left of
the Nonpartisan League endorsed him—as did Jane Addams, Helen
Keller, and W.E.B. Du Bois. As the only progressive in the race, he attracted big crowds throughout the Midwest and Northeast with attacks
on the "rule of oil and gold" and denunciations of courts that favored
the interests of the rich over those of ordinary Americans. Although La
Follette still favored measures to outlaw war and conscription, he seldom mentioned them. On Election Day, he won a sixth of the popular
vote, as President Calvin Coolidge triumphed in a landslide. Although
he won a plurality only in Wisconsin, La Follette outpolled the hapless
Democratic nominee, a Wall Street lawyer, in eleven other states, most
of which bordered the Great Lakes. He looked forward to renewing the
electoral combat. But the 1924 contest would be La Follette's last fight.
The following June, days after his seventieth birthday, his heart finally
gave out. Less than a decade later, Franklin D. Roosevelt would embark
on a New Deal that embraced several of the key proposals the Republican from Wisconsin had championed in his final campaign.[18]

Claude Kitchin effectively concluded his own lengthy career with an
equally dramatic, if less conspicuous, act. After the Republicans wrested
control of Congress in 1918, the North Carolina Democrat became the
minority leader of a party sharply divided over Wilson's campaign for
the League of Nations. In April 1920, Kitchin suffered a paralytic stroke
on the House floor just after completing what one newspaper called
a "spirited attack" on a resolution that ended any real chance that the
United States would sign the Treaty of Versailles. That same day, the bill
he had railed against passed easily. Twice more, Kitchin won reelection to Congress and to his leadership post, but he was never again a
healthy man. From his sickbed, he struggled to persuade colleagues on
both sides of the aisle to retain the excess profits tax he had labored to
enact during the war. But big business was once again in the saddle, and
Kitchin lost that battle too. He died in the spring of 1923.[19]

The *Washington Post*, a longtime critic, ended its brief obituary by allowing that while "none could doubt his sincerity . . . they might at times have doubted the soundness of his judgment, as in his dealing with the issues raised by the world war." Kitchin was one of the last prominent southern Democrats to combine a deep mistrust of corporate power with a principled opposition to military intervention abroad. In the 1930s, the left-wing writers and multiracial organizers who upheld both views made no attempt to restore the reputation of the congressman from Scotland Neck who had begun his career by terrorizing black voters and concluded it as the ailing remnant of an embattled progressive coalition.[20]

Crystal Eastman's vigorous involvement in postwar politics was similarly passionate, frustrating, and short. Between 1919 and the spring of 1921, she simultaneously edited the *Liberator*, helped start the Women's International League, organized large gatherings of American feminists, and helped write and campaign for the Equal Rights Amendment. She also debated with Jane Addams and several other longtime allies who opposed the ERA because it would eliminate protective laws for female workers.

Unfortunately, Eastman's health was not equal to her ardent desire to work relentlessly for a multitude of causes. In 1921, after giving birth to her second child (Annis, named after her mother), she began a long, gradual decline. It did not help that Walter Fuller left for England to find work, and Crystal and her children traveled back and forth across the ocean in an attempt to keep the marriage together and to pool the family's dwindling resources. Although Eastman had to relinquish her editorial duties on the *Liberator*, she was able to contribute regularly to magazines like *Equal Rights* in the United States and *Time & Tide* in Britain about such "women's issues" as housework, co-education, and the psychic benefits of married couples living apart. All these matters, she sensibly maintained, should matter just as much to men. In 1928, her kidneys failed her; she was just forty-seven years old. Many years earlier, Crystal had written to her brother Max: "To live greatly—that's the thing, and it means joy and sorrow both." Two decades later, her son Jeffrey Fuller began to work as an attorney for the ACLU, the most durable of the organizations dedicated to peace and human rights his mother had co-founded.[21]

If Crystal Eastman's final years were rather tragic, Morris Hillquit's were something of an anticlimax. The Socialist leader who had crafted his party's official denunciations of the world war, the politician who had fought off charges of treason to run a strong race for mayor of the largest city in the nation, and the attorney who had represented some of the leading critics of the war spent the 1920s and early 1930s preaching the gospel of a reformist Marxism to an aging and diminishing flock. But optimism never flagged. "It is a mistake to assume that because the Socialist movement in the United States has made no appreciable and visible progress in the last forty years," Hillquit told a party meeting in the summer of 1932, "it may not prove victorious in the course of the next twenty years."[22]

Not all his political judgments were so mistaken. At a time when many on the left were in thrall to the rulers of the USSR, Hillquit called the Soviet state "the greatest disaster and calamity that has occurred to the Socialist movement." Hillquit also hoped La Follette's presidential run in 1924 would lay the groundwork for a durable third electoral force in which liberals and radicals would find common ground. His own party had never realized that goal. In 1932, Hillquit did receive nearly a quarter-million votes as the SPA's nominee for mayor of New York City. But the metropolis had grown much larger since the war, and his total was about 10 percent less than he had won in 1917. No American Socialist would ever draw so many votes for any office again.[23]

All four of the erstwhile anti-warriors managed to pass away with their reputations intact. Kitchin's Democratic colleagues reelected him as minority leader, even after he was physically unable to perform the duties of the job. La Follette had regained the popularity and respect he had lost during the maelstrom of wartime attacks. Feminists and progressives of all stripes lamented Crystal Eastman's death: Freda Kirchwey, editor of the *Nation*, eulogized the life of a woman who had "a contagious belief in the coming triumph of freedom and decent human relations"; for "thousands of young women and young men," Eastman was, wrote Kirchwey, "a symbol of what the free woman might be." Twenty thousand mourners filed past Hillquit's body in lower Manhattan in October 1933 in appreciation of what he had done to uphold a vision of fundamental, yet peaceful, change. At the time, opposing World War I seemed the most prescient choice each member of the quartet had made in his or her public life. Of course, it was hardly the sole type of vindication any of them desired. Yet it has endured as well as any other.[24]

WHAT IS IT GOOD FOR?

Few scholars or politicians shared that judgment during the quarter-century of hot and cold war that followed the Japanese attack on Pearl Harbor in 1941. With millions of Americans again in combat or preparing for it, Great War revisionism fell out of fashion and even appeared unpatriotic. Franklin D. Roosevelt, who had served as assistant secretary of the navy during the Wilson years, echoed his Democratic forerunner in calling for the United States to take the lead in advancing self-government and ending military aggression all over the globe. Most commentators now viewed the successive conflicts against totalitarian regimes of the right and left as sequels to the same virtuous, necessary cause Americans had begun to defend in 1917. In the wake of the Holocaust and the defeat of the Nazi and Japanese empires, Jane Addams and her fellow anti-warriors seemed dangerously naïve: During the Second World War, the United States and its allies *did* rescue civilization and *did* destroy a mortal threat to democratic government.

One consequence of the turn away from World War I revisionism is that "isolationism" became a synonym for anyone blind to the danger of well-armed evils from abroad. With the backing of Congress, presidents from FDR to Lyndon Johnson created a military and intelligence apparatus bigger and more permanent than anything the United States had ever known. It would, agreed most politicians and much of the public, be cowardly and self-defeating not to use that machinery to make the world safe for democracy, American-style. In a popular postwar textbook published in 1962, two of the nation's leading historians compared the "terrible alternative" faced by Woodrow Wilson to that of Abraham Lincoln during the secession winter a century before. "President Wilson ... doubtless felt that the lesser evil was for America to join the conflict and try to direct the peace that must eventually come into channels that would justify the sacrifice," wrote Samuel Eliot Morison and Henry Steele Commager. "Few would doubt now that he was right."[25]

Then came the debacle in Vietnam. In justifying intervention against an enemy force led by Communists, President Johnson echoed his Democratic predecessor from half a century before. Our aim, LBJ declared in 1965, is a "peace without conquest." "We fight because we must fight," he explained, "if we are to live in a world where every country can shape its own destiny. And only in such a world will our own freedom be finally secure." But after 540,000 U.S. troops and millions of tons of bombs had failed to vanquish a peasant army fighting in its own land, those messianic phrases sounded increasingly hollow, if not ludicrous.[26]

In response, leftists and feminists who were building another large and powerful anti-war movement began to discover, or revive, the legacy of their anti-militarist forerunners. Christopher Lasch, Noam Chomsky, and other critics portrayed Randolph Bourne, almost forgotten since his death in 1918, as a prophet who warned about the dangers of clothing an imperial adventure in the language of civic virtue. Several prominent, now elderly men and women who had vigorously opposed U.S. intervention in the Great War were still around to reprise their youthful

performances. Norman Thomas and A. Philip Randolph delivered rous-
ing speeches against the bloodshed in Indochina; A.J. Muste organized
seminarians to burn their draft cards. At the age of eighty-seven, Jeannette Rankin led an eponymous brigade of about three thousand women
in a 1968 march to the capital, where they delivered a petition against
"the ruthless slaughter in Vietnam" to Speaker of the House John McCor-
mack, himself a veteran of World War I. In a 1970 soul record that briefly
rose to #1 on the *Billboard* chart, Edwin Starr posed the rhetorical question "War . . . What is it good for?" Crystal Eastman and other members
of the Woman's Peace Party would have applauded his answer: "It means
destruction of innocent lives / War means tears to thousands of mothers'
eyes / When their sons go off to fight and lose their lives. / War. What is
it good for? Absolutely nothing."[27]

Several years after Americans had left Vietnam in defeat, the journalist Philip Caputo was struggling to finish what became a popular
memoir about the wrenching year he had spent as a marine in that
country. He "fell under the spell of the great British memoirs from
World War I" by Siegfried Sassoon and other hardened veterans of that
earlier catastrophe. "The form somehow felt right," wrote Caputo, "and
it seemed to me that Vietnam, though a far less bloody and horrible
conflict, resembled the First World War in its pointlessness, in its ultimate disillusionment, and in the changes it wrought in cultural and
social values."[28]

One of the changes the U.S. defeat in Vietnam helped bring about
was a deep reluctance on the part of most Americans to hurl what remains the world's most potent military machine into world-saving wars.
Popular majorities did support the invasions of Afghanistan in 2001
and of Iraq in 2003. But most did so to revenge the terrorist atrocities
of September 11 and prevent new ones, not because President George
W. Bush assured U.S. troops that "the peace of a troubled world and the
hopes of an oppressed people now depend on you." Long before those
interventions stretched on into a second decade, the public had grown

cynical about the mission, while still honoring the men and women in uniform struggling to complete it.[29]

Amid persistent economic troubles and political stalemate at home, Americans increasingly adopted what the political philosopher Michael Walzer has called the "default position" of the Left on interventions abroad: "The best foreign policy is a good *domestic* policy." Without being aware of it, they were seconding the critique Randolph Bourne had lodged in the fall of 1917 against pro-war intellectuals like John Dewey:

> If America has lost its political isolation, it is all the more obligated to retain its spiritual integrity. This does not mean any smug retreat from the world, with a belief that the truth is in us and can only be contaminated by contact. It means that the promise of American life is not yet achieved, perhaps not even seen, and that, until it is, there is nothing for us but stern and intensive cultivation of our garden.[30]

As it was a century ago, that reluctance to go crusading abroad was not merely the province of liberals and radicals. Just as southern, small-government populists like Claude Kitchin and James Vardaman had railed against intervening in the Great War, so libertarian conservatives like Ron Paul and George Will balked at sending the U.S. military overseas to fight a seemingly endless "war on terrorism."

Contemporary historians on the right and left disagree about a great many things—from the virtues of capitalism, to the role and size of the federal government, to the primacy of racism in the past and present. But their verdicts about the United States in World War I are remarkably similar, and similarly negative. Compare these interpretations from two books published in 2012:

1. "The isolationists' charge that bankers were drawing the United States into war was not entirely wrong. . . . To a large degree,

Wilson actively forced Germany into a box from which there was no good strategy for escape . . . [and then was guilty] of egregious violations of civil rights."

2. "Economic interests clearly placed the United States in the Allied camp. . . . Congress passed some of the most repressive legislation in the country's history. . . . The agents hired to enforce this crackdown on dissent were part of a burgeoning federal bureaucracy."

The first quotation comes from *A Patriot's History of the Modern World*, whose authors are proud conservatives. The second is taken from *The Untold History of the United States*, by Peter Kuznick and the filmmaker Oliver Stone, equally steadfast members of the radical Left.[31] There's a certain irony in this convergence of views. The First World War, the event that touched off seven decades of brutal, sometimes genocidal conflict—international, regional, and civil—between armed representatives of the left and right generated something quite different in the United States: a loose alliance among people of contrasting ideologies during the conflict and then ambiguous and shifting loyalties in its aftermath.

REVIVING WILLIAM JAMES

Writing in 1910, William James could not have foreseen the horrors, unprecedented and nearly unspeakable, that the next century of wars would produce. He brilliantly examined how organized killing took on the allure of selfless service for one's fellow citizens, even for humanity as a whole. But James also thought it was growing more difficult for "civilized man" to justify it. "Pure loot and mastery seem no longer morally allowable motives," he wrote in "The Moral Equivalent of War," ". . . pretexts must be found for attributing them solely to the enemy." "No legitimate interest of any" European nation," he observed, "would seem to justify the tremendous destructions which a war to compass it would necessarily entail. . . . Common sense and reason ought to find a way to reach agreement in every conflict of honest interests."[32]

Sadly, what James considered "legitimate," "honest," and "rational" had little bearing on how nations in Europe or elsewhere, then or now, go to war or why their citizens take part in them. Most of the wars the United States has fought over the past two centuries have been no less optional than World War I. The conflict with Mexico in the 1840s, the war with Spain in 1898, the Korean "police action" during the early 1950s, the Vietnam ordeal of the 1960s and 1970s, and the recent invasions/occupations of Afghanistan and Iraq were all wars of choice— although, in the case of Korea, the decision to fight probably saved half that nation from a long nightmare of tyranny and hunger. Only the Second World War stands out as an unavoidable conflict in which Americans were arguably fighting for national survival instead of just exercising a strategic or moral option. The outsized place that World War II holds in our historical memory thus gives Americans, reflects the historian Jonathan Ebel, "a narrative of military triumph without a cautionary narrative to leaven it."[33]

James, the great pragmatist, would have appreciated that the idea of one "good war," particularly when it was the biggest and most destructive one in history, bestows a respect and honor on soldiering that no other occupation enjoys. By the time Barack Obama became president, most Americans thought it had been a mistake to wage war in Iraq and in Afghanistan. But they still automatically paid tribute to those on active duty as if they were defending us from imminent attack or struggling to defeat a tyrant bent on conquest. In 1910, James bemoaned the fact that the "militarily-patriotic and the romantic-minded everywhere, and especially the professional military class, refuse to admit for a moment that war may be a transitory phenomenon in social evolution." A century later, it is his hope that human beings might evolve their way toward peace that seems tinged with romantic longing.[34]

To reverse that course, we might learn from the Americans who fought so zealously and diligently against the Great War, knowing what a failure to halt it short of victory for one side might mean. Pacifists and Socialists, Democrats and Republicans, progressives and conservatives, feminists and racists and crusaders for black rights, none were under the illusion they could keep the United States at peace by staying aloof from the rest of the world. They made alliances, in practice and in sympathy, with their counterparts in Europe. They argued, passionately and consistently, that a durable settlement depended on the United States forging a tolerant, nonaggressive relationship with other nations—one based not on preparing for war but on avoiding it.

A moral equivalent of war may be more elusive than when James explained why it was both difficult and imperative. His grim judgment remains as true now as a century ago: "History is a bath of blood." Only by recognizing that fact and arming ourselves with alternatives, both pragmatic and visionary, may we be able, someday, to change it.

ACKNOWLEDGMENTS

Wars are one of the few inescapable facts of history; they affect nearly everyone and everything and have a decisive influence on what comes after. In my youth, I spent a good deal of time protesting the Vietnam War, and that experience started me wondering and writing about the fate of social movements. It also turned me into a skeptic about American military interventions abroad. But this is the first book I have written about either a war or its opponents. And World War I is an infinitely complex and morally ambiguous subject. In the words of the critic Michael Wood, "the catchphrase applied to the 1914–1918 conflict— 'the war to end all wars'—was one of those definitions that not only ask for trouble but also seem to contain the trouble they ask for."[1]

When I began research, I soon realized the depth of my ignorance about the subject. Fortunately, good friends and friendly scholars were willing to help. I received excellent criticism at talks I delivered at Columbia University, Princeton University, Cambridge University, and Georgetown. Thanks to Julian Zelizer, Casey Blake, Gary Gerstle, and Anna von der Goltz for inviting and challenging me at those schools. I am also grateful to Vartan Gregorian and Lewis Lapham for asking me to take part in a symposium about the Great War at the New York Public Library, and to Jackson Lears for helping me hone my ideas for an essay in *Raritan*, the fine magazine he edits.

I pestered several fine historians of World War I and/or the era in which it took place for sources and advice; each responded gracefully. Thanks to Christopher Capozzola, Jennifer Keene, Jeanette Keith, David Nasaw, Robin Archer, and John Milton Cooper Jr. John Cooper also read the entire manuscript and helped me avoid saying foolish things about Woodrow Wilson. My friend Gary Gerstle made it through the whole draft and made wise suggestions, as did Jennifer Ratner-Rosenhagen, Lynn Dumenil, and Amy Aronson. Lynn's forthcoming book on American women and the war and Amy's on the life of Crystal Eastman will be required reading for anyone who cares about this vital period of U.S. history. Eric Arnesen let me read some of his sources for and several draft chapters of what will be a landmark biography of A. Philip Randolph. At Georgetown, Carolyn Kahlenberg mined the Catholic and Irish-American press and discovered nuggets of opinion and insight. Kevin Magana did the same for press response to the *Lusitania* disaster. Benjamin Feldman corrected my endnotes with admirable precision.

I wrote a large chunk of this book while a fellow at the Advanced Research Collaborative, part of the Graduate Center of the City University of New York. Don Robotham, ARC's director, was as intellectually discerning and welcoming a host as exists in the sometimes chilly world of academia. And my colleagues at the Georgetown History Department are just as warm and supportive. It is a pleasure to work with and learn from them.

People at Simon & Schuster have taken great care of this book and its author. Priscilla Painton edited it with a keen eye for careless thinking and slipshod prose. Sophia Jimenez and Megan Hogan, her assistant editors, brilliantly steered me through a maze of requirements and deadlines. Bob Castillo was an exacting and historically astute copy editor. Thomas Colligan, with help from Alison Forner, conceived a strikingly original cover, and Ruth Lee-Mui designed the bracing interior. Phil Metcalf and Lisa Erwin made sure the book reached the finish line in style.

Sandy Dijkstra again proved herself to be an agent sublime. She helped shape my proposal and settle on a title and was always eager to unravel the mysteries of publishing. She and her expert staff seem to know everything about the book business; I am fortunate to be one of their authors.

During the years I spent writing *War Against War*, I have been coeditor of an essential magazine of the American left, thriving in its seventh decade of life.

My fellow editors at *Dissent*—Michael Walzer, David Marcus, Maxine Phillips, Sarah Leonard, Nick Serpe, Tim Barker, Kaavya Asoka, Colin Kinniburgh, Mark Levinson, Grace Goldfarb, and Natasha Lewis—have been wonderful comrades and teachers. To paraphrase what Daniel Webster once said about his college, "It is . . . a small magazine, yet there are those who love it."

When I completed my first book, my children were not yet born. Now, Danny is getting Democrats elected to Congress, and Maia is becoming a splendid actor. They are the kindest and funniest people I know. Beth Horowitz's beauty, intelligence, and moral sensibility fill me with pleasure and a bit of awe. We met forty years ago on the green fields of Stanford University. It was the luckiest day of my life.

KEY EVENTS INVOLVING THE UNITED STATES IN THE FIRST WORLD WAR AND THE AMERICANS WHO OPPOSED IT

12/10/1910: Carnegie Endowment for International Peace established.

6/28/14: Assassination in Sarajevo of Archduke Franz Ferdinand and his wife, Sophie, the duchess of Hohenberg.

7/27/14: Austria declares war on Serbia.

8/2/14: Germany declares war on Russia.

8/3/14: Germany declares war on France.

8/4/14: Germany invades Belgium; United Kingdom declares war on Germany. President Woodrow Wilson declares U.S. neutrality.

8/6/14: First Lady Ellen Wilson dies in the White House at age fifty-four.

8/15/14: Beginning of the British naval blockade of Germany.

8/29/14: Fifteen hundred women march in New York City against the war.

12/8/14: Woodrow Wilson, in his annual message to Congress, declares, "We shall never have a large standing army."

1/10/15: Three thousand delegates establish the Woman's Peace Party in Washington, D.C.

2/4/15: Germany proclaims a war zone around the British Isles, in which enemy merchant ships are subject to attack without warning.

2/9/15: Senator Robert La Follette (R-Wisc.) introduces a resolution calling for a conference of neutral nations to offer joint mediation to the belligerents. He also proposes a federation of neutral nations "to safeguard the peace of the world." The Foreign Relations Committee declines to consider it.

4/28-5/1/15: More than eleven hundred female peace activists from twelve different nations meet at The Hague; Jane Addams presides.

5/7/15: A German U-boat sinks the *Lusitania*; more than 120 U.S. citizens are killed.

5/10/15: Woodrow Wilson gives his "Too Proud to Fight" speech to four thousand new citizens in Philadelphia.

6/7/15: William Jennings Bryan resigns as secretary of state to protest what he perceives as Wilson's tilt toward the Allies.

6/17/15: League to Enforce Peace established in Philadelphia.

7/9/15: Jane Addams gives a controversial speech at Carnegie Hall after returning from her peace mission in Europe.

9/1/15: Germany makes the "*Arabic* pledge" not to attack unarmed passenger ships without warning.

9/27/15: The Henry Street group meets for the first time. Crystal Eastman and others vow to take a more aggressive, public stand to convince Woodrow Wilson to mediate the war. In 1916, the much expanded group is renamed the American Union Against Militarism (AUAM).

10/15/15: American bankers, organized under J.P. Morgan & Co., authorize a $500 million loan to the British and French governments.

11/4/15: President Wilson announces his intention to expand the military in a speech to the Manhattan Club.

11/12/15 and 11/23/15: Wilson meets with David Starr Jordan and Louis Lochner in the White House; he demurs on their idea of having neutral countries mediate a negotiated peace.

11/26/15: Wilson meets with peace activists Rosika Schwimmer and Ethel Snowden.

12/4/15: Ford's "peace ship," the *Oscar II*, sails from Hoboken, New Jersey, for Europe.

12/7/15: In his annual message, President Wilson proposes to expand the military.

1/25/16: Wilson meets in the White House with Socialist leaders Morris Hillquit, Meyer London, and James Maurer and appears to sympathize with their views.

3/3/16: U.S. Senate tables, by vote of 68–14, the Gore resolution to forbid Americans to travel on belligerent ships.

3/4/16: Irish Race Convention meets in New York City, organized primarily by the Clan-na-Gael. It calls for the United States to cut off all aid to Britain.

3/7/16: House of Representatives, by a vote of 276–142, tables the McLemore resolution to warn Americans not to travel on armed merchant vessels.

3/24/16: A U-boat sinks the *Sussex*, a French-British passenger ship, in the English Channel, killing eighty people, four of whom are Americans.

4/6/16: The newly organized AUAM holds a mass rally in Carnegie Hall to begin a national tour.

4/18/16: Wilson issues an ultimatum to Germany, warning of a break in diplomatic relations if U-boats don't stop attacks on merchant ships.

4/24/16: The Easter Rebellion begins in Dublin.

May–June, 1916: "War Against War" exhibit draws thousands in Brooklyn and Manhattan.

5/4/16: Germany issues the "Sussex Pledge": Following protests from Washington about unrestricted submarine attacks, the Kaiser's government promises not to sink any more merchant ships without prior warning and without time for passengers and crew to abandon ship.

5/8/16: An AUAM delegation meets with the president in the White House. He brings up the idea of a league of nations, including an international force to stop war.

5/27/16: Wilson speaks to the League to Enforce Peace and outlines what will become the Fourteen Points.

6/3/16: Congress passes the National Defense Act in response to deteriorating relations between Germany and the United States. The act modestly expands the standing army to 175,000 and the National Guard to 450,000. It also creates the Reserve Officers' Training Corps (ROTC).

6/14/16: President Wilson marches in a Preparedness Day parade in Washington, D.C., carrying a large American flag.

6/14-16/16: The Democratic National Convention meets in St. Louis and renominates Wilson on a platform that praises him for holding "scrupulously and successfully . . . to the old paths of neutrality and to the peaceful pursuit of the legitimate objects of our National life."

7/22/16: Bombing at Preparedness Day parade in San Francisco kills ten people. The radical unionists Tom Mooney and Tom Billings are convicted of the crime, based, it is later revealed, on false testimony.

11/7/16: Woodrow Wilson reelected president over Republican nominee Charles Evans Hughes. The electoral vote is 277–254; the popular vote, 49 percent to 46 percent.

12/12/16: Germany announces it is ready for peace negotiations.

12/18/16: Wilson requests statements of war aims from all warring nations.

1/22/17: Wilson's "Peace without Victory" speech to a joint session of Congress.

2/1/17: Germany resumes unrestricted U-boat attacks.

2/3/17: The United States severs diplomatic relations with Germany.

2/6/17: The initial meeting of the Emergency Peace Committee (soon Federation); William Jennings Bryan speaks.

2/12/17: Small anti-war marches in Washington, D.C., and other cities. Prominent anti-war activists meet in the capital.

2/26/17: The president asks Congress for the authority to arm merchant ships

2/28/17: Final meeting of AUAM leaders with Woodrow Wilson. He also meets with leaders of the Emergency Peace Federation.

3/1/17: Zimmermann Telegram published in the American press.

3/2-4/17: La Follette and Senator George Norris (R-Neb.) lead a filibuster of the Armed Ship Bill in the U.S. Senate.

3/8/17: Senate passes Rule 22, imposing cloture on debate for the first time in the history of that body.

3/12/17: Wilson announces arming of merchantmen by executive order after Congress fails to approve it.

3/15/17: Tsar Nicholas II abdicates; a provisional government takes power in Russia.

3/28/17: William Jennings Bryan makes a final anti-war plea to Congress.

4/2/17: Woodrow Wilson delivers a speech calling for war to a joint session of Congress.

4/4/17: Senate, by a vote of 82–6, enacts a declaration of war against Imperial Germany. Voting no are Democrats Lane (Ore.), Stone (Mo.), and Vardaman (Miss.) and Republicans Gronna (N.Dak.), La Follette (Wisc.), and Norris (Neb.).

4/6/17: Early in the morning, the House, by a vote of 373–50, passes the declaration of war. Voting no are sixteen Democrats, thirty-two Republicans, one Socialist, and one Prohibitionist. The president signs the document later in the day.

4/7/17: The Socialist Party of America, meeting in an emergency convention in St. Louis, opposes the declaration of war.

4/14/17: President Wilson issues an executive order creating the Committee on Public Information and appoints progressive Denver journalist George Creel to head it.

4/16/17: Vladimir Lenin arrives at the Finland Station in Petrograd and begins to plan for the Bolsheviks to take power in Russia.

4/24/17: President Wilson signs a bill instituting the first Liberty Loan drive, authorizing Secretary of the Treasury William G. McAdoo to sell $3 billion of debt at 3.5 percent interest to the public.

4/24/17: Emergency Peace Federation holds a mass meeting in Madison Square Garden.

4/28/17: The Senate and House pass different versions of the Conscription Act, 81–8 (La Follette against) and 397–24 (Kitchin for). Prior to that, both chambers defeat a bill that would have kept the volunteer system in place unless a draft were needed: 69–18 (La Follette for); 313–109 (Kitchin for).

5/18/17: After Congress passes a conference committee version of the Selective Service Act, President Wilson signs it.

5/30-31/17: The People's Council of America for Peace and Democracy is launched at a big rally in New York's Madison Square Garden, presided over by Rabbi Judah Magnes.

6/5/17: First Draft Registration Day.

6/15/17: Congress passes the Espionage Act.

6/26/17: The first U.S. troops arrive in France; large numbers do not arrive until the following spring.

7/28/17: Five thousand African Americans march down Fifth Avenue in New York City in silent protest against a race riot in East St. Louis, Illinois.

8/13/17: Pope Benedict XV appeals for peace on a status quo ante basis.

8/23/17: Enraged by racist treatment, 156 black soldiers march through Houston, killing some twenty white residents.

9/5/17: Federal agents stage raids against the Industrial Workers of the World in twenty-four cities, seizing literature and arresting top leaders, including William "Big Bill" Haywood.

9/20/17: Senator Robert La Follette delivers a controversial anti-war speech to the convention of the Nonpartisan League in Saint Paul, Minnesota.

10/6/17: In the Senate, La Follette defends himself with a long address, "Free Speech in Wartime."

11/3/17: The first engagement involving U.S. forces in Europe takes place near the Rhine-Marne Canal in France.

11/6/17: Morris Hillquit wins nearly 22 percent of the vote in a four-way race for mayor of New York City. Fellow Socialists win state and local office in numerous cities and towns across the country.

11/7/17: The Bolsheviks take power in Petrograd.

1/8/18: Woodrow Wilson gives his Fourteen Points speech to a joint session of Congress.

3/3/18: Russia and Germany sign the Treaty of Brest-Litovsk, ending hostilities between them and ceding large areas of Russia to the Kaiser's regime.

3/21/18: On the Western Front, the Germans begin the Michael Offensive—their final attempt to win the war before U.S. troops arrive in large numbers.

5/16/18: Congress passes the Sedition Act, far-reaching amendments to the Espionage Act.

5/28/18: U.S. victory in the Battle of Cantigny, the first major action by the AEF.

5/29/18: By executive order, President Wilson creates the War Industries Board.

6/6/18: U.S. Marines win victory at the battle of Belleau Wood.

6/30/18: Eugene V. Debs gives an anti-war speech in Canton, Ohio, for which he is soon arrested.

9/5/18: Second Draft Registration Day.

9/12/18: U.S. forces are victorious in the Saint-Mihiel salient.

9/12/18: Third Draft Registration Day (for men ages eighteen to twenty and thirty-one to forty-five.)

9/14/18: Debs is sentenced to a ten-year jail term for violating the Espionage Act.

9/26/18: Beginning of the Meuse-Argonne Offensive, the largest and bloodiest U.S. battle of the war.

10/3–4/18: Germany and Austria send notes to Wilson, requesting an armistice on the basis of the Fourteen Points.

10/21/18: Germany ceases unrestricted U-boat attacks.

11/5/18: Republicans win majorities in both houses of Congress—a two-seat majority in the Senate and a fifty-seat majority in the House.

11/9/18: Kaiser Wilhelm abdicates and flees to exile in the Netherlands.

11/11/18: Armistice Day.

ABBREVIATIONS USED IN NOTES

APP–Amos Pinchot Papers, Library of Congress

AUAMP–American Union Against Militarism Papers, Swarthmore College Peace Collection

CE–Crystal Eastman (also Crystal Eastman Benedict and Crystal Eastman Fuller)

CEP–Crystal Eastman Papers, Radcliffe Institute

CK–Claude Kitchin

CKP–Claude Kitchin Papers, University of North Carolina, Chapel Hill

CookDiss–Blanche Wiesen Cook, "Woodrow Wilson and the Antimilitarists, 1914–1917," PhD dissertation, Johns Hopkins University, 1970

CR–Congressional Record

LFFP–La Follette Family Papers, Library of Congress

LFM–*La Follette's Magazine*

LIB–*The Liberator*

MarchandAPM–C. Roland Marchand, *The American Peace Movement and Social Reform, 1898–1918* (Princeton, NJ: Princeton University Press, 1972)

MH–Morris Hillquit

MHP-T–Morris Hillquit Papers, Tamiment Institute, New York University

MHP-W–Morris Hillquit Papers, Wisconsin State Historical Society

NYT–*New York Times*

PCAP–People's Council of America for Democracy and Peace Papers, Swarthmore College Peace Collection

RLF–Robert M. La Follette

RML–Belle Case and Fola La Follette, *Robert M. La Follette, June 14, 1855–June 18, 1925*, 2 vols (New York, 1953)

WPPP–Woman's Peace Party Papers, 1915–1919, part one of the Women's International League for Peace and Freedom Records, Swarthmore College Peace Collection

WP–*Washington Post*

WWP–*Papers of Woodrow Wilson*, ed. Arthur S. Link, 69 vols. (Princeton, NJ: Princeton University Press, 1967–1994)

NOTES

INTRODUCTION: AGAINST A GREAT, FORGOTTEN WAR

1. Max Eastman, "What Shall We Do with Patriotism?," *Survey*, Jan. 1, 1916, 404.

2. "Our Fleet at Kiel," *London Sunday Times*, June 28, 1914. On the same page, there appeared a small item from Sarajevo, reporting that the army of Austria-Hungary had concluded successful maneuvers in Bosnia-Herzegovina.

3. On occasion, one member of the quartet would comment on their similarity of views. Kitchin thought La Follette "had no business" being a Republican, and Eastman advised her fellow suffragists that when women got the vote in Wisconsin they should "back up La Follette's [faction] in the State and the Socialist administration" that then governed Milwaukee. Alex Arnett, *Claude Kitchin and the Wilson War Policies* (Boston: Little Brown, 1937), 27; CE to Max Eastman, Jan. 17, 1911, CEP, Box 6.

4. The widespread use of "isolationism" and "isolationist" began only after World War I. See the graph in Google Books Ngram viewer: https://books.google.com/ngrams/graph?content=isolationism%2C+isolationist&year_start=1800&year_end=2000&corpus=15&smoothing=

3&share=&direct_url=t1%3B%2Cisolationism%3B%2Cc0%3B
.t1%3B%2Cisolationist%3B%2Cc0.

5. Bourne quoted in Casey Nelson Blake, "War and the Health of Randolph Bourne," *Raritan* XXXIV (Summer 2014), 86.

6. I have borrowed some phrases from an article I wrote for the *New Republic*: http://www.newrepublic.com/article/118435/world-war-i-debate -should-us-have-entered.

7. Niall Ferguson, *The Pity of War* (New York: Basic Books, 1999), xxiii. As of this writing, a competition has begun to design a small memorial to the veterans of World War I, one that, if completed, will be far more modest than those dedicated to those who fought in World War II and Vietnam. http://blogs.rollcall.com/hill-blotter/national-wwi-memorial-to-come -to-pershing-park/. For the secondary works on which I have relied the most, see "Good Reading."

8. A.G. Stock, *W.B. Yeats: His Poetry and Thought* (Cambridge, UK: Cambridge University Press, 1964), 165. On the British poets and novelists, see Paul Fussell's classic work *The Great War and Modern Memory* (New York: Oxford University Press, 1975). In contrast, American writers turned out work that was mostly banal and propagandistic. See Mark W. Van Wienen, *Partisans and Poets: The Political Work of American Poetry in the Great War* (New York: Cambridge University Press, 1997), a book whose title unintentionally conveys the functionalist content of its subject. In the 1930s, John Dos Passos became a great novelist. But his 1921 work on World War I—*Three Soldiers*—provides only a few passing, and quite forgettable, scenes of combat. His characters spend more time attempting to seduce French women, hanging out in cafes, and complaining about the boredom and rigidities of military service.

9. The historian Jonathan H. Ebel makes this point well: "There are certain memories that live at the heart of a culture and reveal truths imagined as essential. These memories—these myths—are difficult things from which to distance oneself while still identifying fully with a culture. In the United States, the Second World War is one such memory. The Civil War is another. The Great War is not. The Doughboys have not taken their place alongside the Minutemen, Union and Confederate soldiers, even the

Rough Riders." Ebel, *Faith in the Fight: Religion and the American Soldier in the Great War* (Princeton, NJ: Princeton University Press, 2010), 192.

PROLOGUE: A BETTER WORLD IN BIRTH?

1. James, "The Moral Equivalent of War," 1910, first line. Accessible on multiple websites.

2. Roosevelt quoted in Norman Angell, *The Great Illusion: A Study of the Relationship of Military Power to National Advantage*, fourth edition (New York: The Knickerbocker Press, 1913 [1910]), 165.

3. Jane Addams, *Newer Ideals of Peace* (New York: The Macmillan Company, 1915 [1907]), 24. On the establishment of the Carnegie Endowment, see David Nasaw, *Andrew Carnegie* (New York: Penguin Press, 2006), 742–745.

4. "The Moral Equivalent of War." On the dissemination of the essay, see Ralph Barton Perry, *The Thought and Character of William James* (Cambridge, MA: Harvard University Press, 1948), 229.

5. "Moral Equivalent," ibid.

6. William I. Hull, *The New Peace Movement* (Boston: The World Peace Foundation, 1912), v.

7. *Oxford English Dictionary* (Oxford: Oxford University Press, 1971), 4033.

8. Hull, *New Peace Movement*, iii.

9. Taft in December 1911, quoted in *The Eagle and the Dove: The American Peace Movement and United States Foreign Policy, 1900–1922*, ed. John Whiteclay Chambers II, second edition (Syracuse, NY: Syracuse University Press, 1991), 21. On Taft's treaties, see John E. Noyes, "William Howard Taft and the Taft Arbitration Treaties, "*Villanova Law Review* 56 (December 2011), 535–558, quotes at 549.

10. Merle Eugene Curti, *Peace or War: The American Struggle, 1636–1936* (New York: Garland Publishing, 1972 [1936]), 197.

11. Carnegie quoted in Nasaw, *Andrew Carnegie*, 743.

12. Clark was a leading figure in the development of pro-capitalist, marginalist economic theory. Quoted in MarchandAPM, 78.

13. Angell, *The Great Illusion*, 36–40, 179–180. The reviewer was Floyd Dell,

later a key figure in the cultural Left that thrived in Greenwich Village. Quoted in front matter, unpaginated.

14. Ibid., x, 385, 387. On Angell's background and popularity, see J.D.B. Miller, *Norman Angell and the Futility of War* (New York: St. Martin's Press, 1986), 1–24.

15. Stanton quoted in Harriet Hyman Alonso, *Peace as a Women's Issue: A History of the U.S. Movement for World Peace and Women's Rights* (Syracuse, NY: Syracuse University Press, 1993), 44–45.

16. Quoted in ibid., 49. Also see John M. Craig, "The Woman's Peace Party and Questions of Gender Separatism," *Peace & Change* 19 (Oct. 1994), 379–380.

17. Eliot, probably in 1912, quoted in MarchandAPM, 134.

18. Addams, *Newer Ideals*, 3, 18. In 1903, she gave a speech, "A Moral Substitute for War," that presaged James's more celebrated essay of seven years later.

19. Ibid., 3, 13, 19. During the 1912 campaign, Addams kept silent about her disagreements with TR's militarist stand.

20. Liebknecht, "Militarism and Anti-Militarism," https://www.marxists.org/archive/liebknecht-k/works/1907/militarism-antimilitarism/index.htm.

21. Quotes from http://www.marxists.org/history/international/social-democracy/1907/militarism.htm.

22. Simons quoted in Ira Kipnis, *The American Socialist Movement, 1897–1912* (New York: Columbia University Press, 1952), 244.

23. Debs, "Speech of Acceptance," in *Writings and Speeches of Eugene V. Debs* (New York: Hermitage Press, 1948), 365. For an account of American socialism in this period, see my *American Dreamers: How the Left Changed a Nation* (New York: Alfred A. Knopf, 2011), 109–154.

24. Gompers quoted in Simeon Larson, *Labor and Foreign Policy: Gompers, the AFL, and the First World War, 1914–1918* (Rutherford, NJ: Fairleigh Dickinson University Press, 1975), 18. On the AFL's support for peace initiatives, see Delber Lee McKee, "The American Federation of Labor and American Foreign Policy, 1886–1912," PhD dissertation, Stanford University, 1952, 111–112, 207–221.

25. Curti, *Peace or War*, 217; McKee, ibid., 221.

26. Quoted in McKee, ibid., 216.

27. Bryan quotes from Genevieve Forbes Herrick and John Origen Herrick, *The Life of William Jennings Bryan* (Chicago, Buxton Publishing House, 1925), 236; Robert David Johnson, *The Peace Progressives and American Foreign Relations* (Cambridge, MA: Harvard University Press, 1995), 32.

28. Curti, *Peace or War*, 220. Quotes from Johnson, *Peace Progressives*, 35, 37.

29. Quote from Johnson, *Peace Progressives*, 36; David Sarasohn, *The Party of Reform: Democrats in the Progressive Era* (Jackson: University Press of Mississippi, 1989), 21. For his part, Roosevelt thought the organized peace movement was an exercise in "sentimentalist" folly. In 1911, he wrote to his friend Sir Cecil Arthur Spring-Rice, soon to be named Britain's ambassador to the United States, that "if Andrew Carnegie had employed his fortune and his time in doing justice to the steelworkers who gave him his fortune, he would have accomplished a thousand times what he has accomplished or even can accomplish in connection with international peace." Quoted in Nasaw, *Andrew Carnegie*, 749–750.

30. Hull, *New Peace Movement*, vii–viii.

CHAPTER ONE: EVER WIDENING CIRCLES

1. http://www.firstworldwar.com/source/usneutrality.htm.

2. Quoted in Chambers, *Eagle and Dove*, 51.

3. Gardner, *Must We Arm?: Hillquit-Gardner Debate* (New York: The Rand School of Social Science, 1915), 26.

4. Hillquit in ibid., 41.

5. *New York World*, August 30, 1914, 10.

6. Fanny Villard quoted in Harriet Hyman Alonso, *Growing Up Abolitionist: The Story of the Garrison Children* (Amherst: University of Massachusetts Press, 2002), 313. For a list of the members of the Committee of One Hundred (which became Two Hundred by month's end) who organized the August parade, see *NYT*, Aug. 17, 1914, 5. Also MarchandAPM, 182–184.

7. Louise Carnegie quoted in Nasaw, *Carnegie*, 790.

8. *NY World,* Aug. 30, 1914, 10; *NY Journal,* Aug. 29, 1914; *NYT,* Aug. 30, 1914, 11; *NY Call,* Aug. 29, 1914, 6.

9. R.N. Page letter quoted in Arthur S. Link, *Wilson: The Struggle for Neutrality, 1914–1915* (Princeton, NJ: Princeton University Press, 1960), 7.

10. *NYT,* Aug. 26, 1914; *NY World,* Aug. 7, 1914, 7.

11. "Once Again!," *World,* Aug. 30, 1914, 4. On press opinion, see Kevin J. O'Keefe, *A Thousand Deadlines: The New York City Press and American Neutrality, 1914–1917* (The Hague: Nijhoff, 1972), and Albert Russell Buchanan, "European Propaganda and American Public Opinion, 1914–1917," PhD dissertation, Stanford University, 1935. Page quoted in Michael Kazin, *A Godly Hero: The Life of William Jennings Bryan* (New York: Alfred A. Knopf, 2006), 235.

12. From House's diary, Aug. 30, 1914, quoted in Link, *Struggle for Neutrality,* 51.

13. Hearst in *NY Journal,* Aug. 22, 1914, 12.

14. Link, *Struggle for Neutrality,* 81.

15. Quoted in Justus D. Doenecke, *Nothing Less Than War: A New History of America's Entry into World War I* (Lexington: University Press of Kentucky, 2011), 43. The treaties included no prohibition on building up a military during the one-year hiatus. Every major European nation had signed a "Bryan treaty" except, ominously, Germany and Austria-Hungary.

16. Ron Chernow, *The House of Morgan: An American Banking Dynasty and the Rise of Modern Finance* (New York: Atlantic Monthly Press, 2010 [1990]), 187–188. That winter, President Wilson proposed to create a federal merchant marine system, but a Senate filibuster defeated it.

17. *Nashville Banner,* Feb. 1915, quoted in Timothy Gregory McDonald, "Southern Democratic Congressmen and the First World War, August 1914–April 1917: The Public Record of Their Support for or Opposition to Wilson's Policies," PhD dissertation, University of Washington, 1962, 74. On the rights of neutrals at the time, see John W. Coogan's excellent essay "Wilsonian Diplomacy in War and Peace," in *American Foreign Relations Reconsidered, 1890–1993,* ed. Gordon Martel (London: Routledge, 1994), 79. Paolo E. Coletta, *William Jennings Bryan,* vol. 2: *Progressive Politician*

and Moral Statesman, 1909–1915 (Lincoln: University of Nebraska Press, 1969), 284.

18. Cong. Clyde H. Tavenner, "The War Trust: How Can We Beat It?," LFM, Aug. 15, 1914. On sentiment in Congress, see John Milton Cooper, Jr., *The Vanity of Power: American Isolationism and the First World War, 1914–1917* (Westport, CT: Greenwood Pub. Corp., 1969), 28–32; McDonald, "Southern Democratic Congressmen," 58–64; Clifton J. Child, "German-American Attempts to Prevent the Exportation of Munitions of War, 1914–1915," *Mississippi Valley Historical Review* 25 (Dec. 1938), 360.

19. Quoted in Cooper, *Vanity of Power*, 31.

20. Cecil Spring-Rice to Edward Grey (British foreign minister), Feb. 12, 1915. Quoted in Joseph Edward Cuddy, *Irish-America and National Isolationism, 1914–1920* (New York: Arno Press, 1976), 62.

21. Hexamer quoted in Child, "German-American Attempts," 355. For a sophisticated analysis of the views of the Irish-Catholics who essentially ran the American church, see Thomas J. Rowland, "From Neutrality to War: Irish-American Catholics and World War I, 1914–1917," PhD dissertation, George Washington University, 1992. The German-American Alliance also donated substantial amounts of money to the German embassy for use in propaganda. Reinhard R. Doerries, *Imperial Challenge: Ambassador Count Bernstorff and German American Relations, 1908–1917*, trans. Christa D. Shannon (Chapel Hill: University of North Carolina Press, 1989), 49–50.

22. John Carver Edwards, *Patriots in Pinstripe: Men of the National Security League* (Washington, D.C.: University Press of America, 1982), 8–9, 12, 213–217.

23. TR quoted in *NYT*, Oct. 31, 1914, 4; Kathleen Dalton, *Theodore Roosevelt: A Strenuous Life* (New York: Alfred A. Knopf, 2002), 447.

24. *Literary Digest*, Jan. 23, 1915, 137 and ff.

25. Quoted in Homer Larry Ingle, "Pilgrimage to Reform: A Life of Claude Kitchin," PhD dissertation, University of Wisconsin, 1967, 9. On the 1878 election, see Eric Anderson, *Race and Politics in North Carolina: The Black Second* (Baton Rouge: Louisiana State University Press, 1981), 61–79.

26. Kitchin quoted in Ingle, "Pilgrimage," 38. Kitchin never denied his involvement in these efforts. For one example, see "Red a Good Campaign Color," *WP*, Sept. 29, 1914, 6.

27. Anderson, *Race and Politics*, 312.

28. Kitchin quoted in Ingle, "Pilgrimage," 48, and in Anderson, *Race and Politics*, 310.

29. Sarasohn, *Party of Reform*, 20. Kitchin quoted in *WP*, March 26, 1904, 1.

30. Quotations from Arnett, *Claude Kitchin*, 27-28; Ingle, "Pilgrimage," 94.

31. Since the party that controlled the House had no more important duty than raising or lowering taxes, it had long been customary for the Chairman of Ways and Means to also be the Majority Leader.

32. http://www.presidency.ucsb.edu/ws/index.php?pid=29555.

33. Lodge quoted in William C. Widenor, *Henry Cabot Lodge and the Search for an American Foreign Policy* (Berkeley: University of California Press, 1980), 198.

34. Richard W. Fox, "The Paradox of 'Progressive' Socialism: The Case of Morris Hillquit, 1901-1914," *American Quarterly* 26 (May 1974), 127. The only book-length biography, short but indispensable, is Norman Fain Pratt, *Morris Hillquit: A Political History of an American Jewish Socialist* (Westport, CT.: Greenwood Press, 1979). Hillquit's first language was German. He learned Russian in school in Riga and both English and Yiddish in the United States.

35. Morris Hillquit, *Loose Leaves from a Busy Life* (New York: Rand School Press, 1934), 10; Hillquit, *Socialism in Theory and Practice* (New York: Macmillan, 1909), 11.

36. Haywood in 1912, quoted in Ira Kipnis, *The American Socialist Movement, 1897-1912* (New York: Columbia University Press, 1952), 412. Hillquit 1908 resolution on immigration, ibid., 284. Hillquit also occasionally acted as the American agent for Maxim Gorky, the Russian novelist and playwright who was a dedicated Socialist and, later, Communist.

37. Morris Winchevski, quoted in Pratt, *Morris Hillquit*, 29. On the X Club, see Hillquit, *Loose Leaves*, 68-69. On his credo as "practical idealism," see ibid., 10.

38. Hillquit, *Loose Leaves*, 91; Pratt, *Morris Hillquit*, 75. Reports of the live

debates were published in *NYT*, Jan. 24, 1910, 5; Jan. 29, 1912, 7; Feb. 28, 1912, 10 (Clark); April 28, 1912, 13. The debate with Ryan was published as *Socialism—Promise or Menace?* (New York: Macmillan, 1914).

39. MH, "Socialist Neutrality," *American Socialist*, Jan. 9, 1915. In Clippings, MHP-W. One of Hillquit's early articles that attempted to explain the outbreak of the fighting was reprinted in a San Francisco paper under the title "Murderous War in Europe Is Inevitable Culmination of Murderous European Capitalism." *San Francisco Bulletin*, Oct. 17, 1914.

40. MH, "Speech at Harlem River Casino," NYC, Sept. 21, 1914, Typescript, MHP-W, Reel 8; MH, "Socialism and War; I: The Causes of War," *Metropolitan Magazine*, Dec. 1914, Typescript, ibid.

41. Gardner, "Where Are Our Guns?" speech delivered in Congress, Jan. 21, 1915. http://archive.org/details/whereareourgunss00gard. On Gardner's efforts in 1914 and early 1915, see John Patrick Finnegan, *Against the Specter of a Dragon: The Camp for American Military Preparedness, 1914–1917* (Westport, CT: Praeger, 1974), 34–36.

42. Gardner, *Must We Arm?*, 9, 14, 10, 26.

43. Hillquit, ibid., 28, 31, 32-37.

44. Ibid, 32-37; 39-40

45. "I Didn't Raise My Boy to Be a Soldier," lyrics by Alfred Bryan, music by Al Piantadosi. On the popularity of the song, which one Englishman "found it sung wherever he traveled in America" that spring, see Mark W. Van Wienen, *Partisans and Poets: The Political Work of American Poetry in the Great War* (Cambridge, UK: Cambridge University Press, 1997), 54–59.

46. http://www.toxipedia.org/display/wanmec/Charlotte+Perkins+Gilman.

47. *WP*, Jan. 11, 1915, 1.

48. On the growth and strategies of women's groups during this period, see Elisabeth S. Clemens, *The People's Lobby: Organizational Innovation and the Rise of Interest Group Politics in the United States, 1890–1925* (Chicago: University of Chicago Press, 1997), 184–234.

49. A good source of biographical information on the two women is David S. Patterson, *The Search for Negotiated Peace: Women's Activism and Citizen Diplomacy in World War I* (New York: Routledge, 2008), passim.

50. Mrs. Pethick-Lawrence, "Union of Women for Constructive Peace,"

Survey, Dec. 5, 1914; Schwimmer quoted in Patterson, *Search for Negotiated Peace*, 42.

51. Louis Lochner, *Always the Unexpected: A Book of Reminiscences* (New York: Macmillan, 1956), 47.

52. Catt quoted in Degen, *WPP*, 51.

53. Spencer quoted in ibid., 40–41.

54. Ibid., 38.

55. The entire platform is reprinted in ibid., 41–42.

56. Wales, "Continuous Mediation Without Armistice," WPP, 1915, 5–6. On Wales's life, see Walter I. Trattner, "Julia Grace Wales and the Wisconsin Plan for Peace," *Wisconsin Magazine of History* 44 (Spring 1961), 203–213.

57. Julia Grace Wales, "Continuous Mediation Without Armistice," issued by Woman's Peace Party, 1915, 7–8, 9.

58. On the WPP's activities, see Degen, WPP, 50–51; "Peace Day," May 18, 1915, in WPPP.

59. Jane Addams, *Peace and Bread in Time of War* (New York: Macmillan, 1922), 10; Belle La Follette, quoted in Patterson, *Search for Negotiated Peace*, 49.

60. LFM, March and April 1915; RML, vol. 1, 518–19.

61. Degen, WPP, 156.

62. On TR's letter and his critics, see Degen, WPP, 70–73; Belle La Follette in LFM, May 1915, 5; McCulloch quoted in NYT, April 17, 1915, 6.

63. The term comes from the splendid history of this relationship, Thomas J. Knock, *To End All Wars: Woodrow Wilson and the Quest for a New World Order* (New York: Oxford University Press, 1992). The chancellor, Theobald von Bethmann Hollweg, is quoted on p. 44.

64. Quoted in Patterson, *Search for Negotiated Peace*, 49.

65. Quotes from Degen, WPP, 67; Jane Addams et al., *Women at the Hague: The International Peace Congress of 1915* (Amherst, NY: Humanity Books, 2003), 126–127.

66. Quoted in Karen Offen, *European Feminisms, 1750–1950: A Political History* (Stanford, CA.: Stanford University Press, 2000), 258.

67. Addams quoted in Patterson, *Search for Negotiated Peace*, 58.

68. Shaw quoted in ibid., 59.

69. Addams, *Peace and Bread*, 13. Degen, WPP, 69. For a full report on the voyage and the conference itself, see Emily Balch's narrative in *Women at the Hague*, 39–50.

70. Addams quoted in ibid., 107.

71. Vorse quoted in Patterson, *Search for Negotiated Peace*, 75–76; Lecher quoted in *Woman at the Hague*, 44.

72. *WP*, May 1, 1915, 4.

73. Hamilton quoted in Patterson, *Search for Negotiated Peace*, 80.

74. Schwimmer quoted in Ibid., 81.

75. Quotes from *Literary Digest*, May 15, 1915, 1139.

76. Balch in *Women at the Hague*, 47.

77. The anonymous critic, who may have been Mary Heaton Vorse, is quoted in Mary Chamberlain, "The Women at the Hague," *Survey*, June 5, 1915, 219.

78. On Zetkin's actions and views, see http://www.marxists.org/archive/cliff/works/1981/xx/zetkin.html; Offen, *European Feminisms*, 260; Patterson, *Search for Negotiated Peace*, 67–68.

79. *Rendezvous with Death: American Poems of the Great War*, ed. Mark W. Van Wienen (Urbana: University of Illinois Press, 2002), 94.

80. Wilson quoted by Addams, in Degen, WPP.

81. NYT, May 1, 1915, 3. By the end of the war in November 1918, an estimated 424,000 German civilians had died as a result of the British blockade. Adrian Gregory, *A War of Peoples, 1914–1919* (Oxford, UK: Oxford University Press, 2014), 159.

82. I have derived the casualty totals from http://historum.com/war-military-history/47949-world-war-i-military-casualties.html; on the *Lusitania's* cargo, see Thomas A. Bailey and Paul Ryan, *The Lusitania Disaster: An Episode in Modern Warfare and Diplomacy* (New York: Free Press, 1975), 96–113; http://www.rmslusitania.info/cargo/.

CHAPTER TWO: CRY PEACE AND FIGHT PREPAREDNESS

1. Ford, quoted in Barbara S. Kraft, *The Peace Ship: Henry Ford's Pacifist Adventure in the First World War* (New York: Macmillan, 1978), 50.

2. Jarboe to Claude Kitchin, Jan. 28, 1916, CKP, Reel 6.

3. From a speech given under AUAM auspices at Carnegie Hall. Quoted in Charles T. Hallinan, "Swinging Around the Circle Against Militarism," *Survey*, April 22, 1916, 95.

4. The exact number of Americans who died is disputed. The Cunard Line listed 123. Erik Larson, *Dead Wake: The Last Crossing of the Lusitania* (New York: Crown Publishers, 2015), 300, 403. Quotations from Bailey and Ryan, *Lusitania Disaster*, 192; Link, *Struggle for Neutrality*, 373; Doenecke, *Nothing Less Than War*, 72.

5. It is important to note that submarines by their nature were forced to operate outside the traditional rules of naval warfare. It was not necessarily cruel indifference that the U-boat failed to pick up survivors.

6. For a lengthy discussion of these negotiations and intra-administration debates, see Link, *Struggle for Neutrality*, 309–367.

7. For press reaction, see Bailey and Ryan, *Lusitania Disaster*, 234–5. Frederick Palmer, *Our Gallant Madness* (Garden City, NY: Doubleday, Doran and Company, 1937), 29.

8. http://www.presidency.ucsb.edu/ws/?pid=65388#axzz2jEiIVlLI.

9. TR quoted in Link, *Struggle for Neutrality*, 383; Wood quoted in Bailey and Ryan, *Lusitania Disaster*; NYT, May 12, 1915, 4.

10. Arthur S. Link, *Wilson: Confusion and Crises 1915–1916* (Princeton, NJ: Princeton University Press, 1964), 42–43.

11. John Patrick Finnegan, *Against the Specter of a Dragon*, 38; Herbert Barry, NSL Secretary to CK, Jan. 31, 1916, CKP, Reel 6; "The American Rights Committee," Bulletin No. 8, at https://archive.org/details/americanrights co00amer.

12. Eastman quoted in NYT, Nov. 16, 1915, 9. Beginning in the spring of 1915, smaller anti-war groups also proliferated; many were active in only a single state or region. They had such names as the Patriotic Peace League and the Ohio Anti-Militarist League.

13. *War Memoirs of Robert Lansing, Secretary of State* (Indianapolis, IN: The Bobbs-Merrill Company, 1935), 24. In a classic work about diplomacy during the neutral period, Ernest May shrewdly wrote that a majority of the public in the months immediately following the *Lusitania*

disaster espoused neither "pacifism" nor "chauvinism" but, instead, a rather "muddy" nationalism. Most Americans wanted the administration to threaten the Germans with strong actions but not so strong as to lead to intervention. Ernest R. May, *The World War and American Isolation, 1914–1917* (Cambridge, MA: Harvard University Press, 1959), 172.

14. La Follette quoted in Nancy C. Unger, *Fighting Bob La Follette: The Righteous Reformer* (Chapel Hill: University of North Carolina Press, 2000), 235.

15. Wales quoted in Patterson, *Search for Negotiated Peace*, 84.

16. Addams quoted in WP, June 27, 1915, 7.

17. Quotes from Patterson, *Search for Negotiated Peace*, 87, 88; WP, June 27, 1915, 7.

18. Addams, "The Revolt Against War," *Survey*, July 17, 1915, 355–359; Jane Bethke Elshtain, *Jane Addams and the Dream of American Democracy: A Life* (New York: Basic Books, 2002), 230–31.

19. Quotes from Sherry R. Shepler and Anne F. Martina, "'The Revolt Against War': Jane Addams' rhetorical challenge to the patriarchy," *Communication Quarterly* 47 (May 2009), 161–162; Marie Louise Degen, *The History of the Woman's Peace Party* (Baltimore: Johns Hopkins Press, 1939), 111–114. Later in July, Addams gave a well-received talk to a crowd of four thousand in Chicago. She omitted the references to drinking and bayonet charges. But the address drew little attention outside her hometown. *Chicago Examiner*, July 23, 1915, WPPP, Reel 3.

20. *The Norton Book of Modern War*, ed. Paul Fussell (New York: Norton, 1991), 32–33. After the war ended, Addams wrote that she and Dr. Alice Hamilton, a member of her delegation, "had notes" for all the "statements with the dates and names of the men who had made them, and it did not occur to me that the information was new or startling." Addams, *Peace and Bread*, 136.

21. Addams et al., *Women at the Hague*, 91.

22. Ford quoted in Patterson, *Search for Negotiated Peace*, 163; Robert Lacey, *Ford: The Men and the Machine* (Boston: Little Brown, 1986), 134.

23. Kraft, *Peace Ship*, 51.

24. Ford quoted in NYT, Nov. 25, 1915, 1. At lunch with Schwimmer, a Jew,

the industrialist did announce his belief that "German-Jewish bankers" had "caused the war"—"I have the evidence here. Facts! . . . I can't give out the facts now, because I haven't got them all yet, but I'll have them soon." Schwimmer, quoted in Victoria Saker Woeste, *Henry Ford's War on Jews and the Legal Battle Against Hate Speech* (Stanford, CA: Stanford University Press, 2012), 31.

25. David Starr Jordan, *The Days of a Man: Being Memories of a Naturalist, Teacher and Minor Prophet of Democracy*, vol, 2, 1900–1921 (Yonkers-on-Hudson, NY: World Book Co., 1922), 681; Kraft, *Peace Ship*, 83. Ford sent Hillquit both the same telegram he sent to all notable invitees and a personally signed letter. Ford to MH, Nov. 24, 1915; Nov. 27, 1915, MHP-W, Reel 2.

26. Louis P. Lochner, *America's Don Quixote: Henry Ford's Attempt to Save Europe* (London: K. Paul, Trench, Trubner and Company, 1924), 29.

27. Lochner, *America's Don Quixote*, 31.

28. For the most complete list of passengers, which included staff members, see Kraft, *Peace Ship*, 301–305

29. Quoted in Kraft, *Peace Ship*, 92.

30. Lochner, *America's Don Quixote*, 46.

31. For details, see Kraft, *Peace Ship*, 82–83; Patterson, *Search for Negotiated Peace*, 161.

32. CE to Jane Addams, December 3, 1915. WPPP, Reel 12.

33. Reverend Alfred W. Wishart, quoted in *Public*, Jan. 21, 1916, 64. Ford quoted in Kraft, *Peace Ship*, 85.

34. Quoted in Lochner, *America's Don Quixote*, 49.

35. Ford quoted in Patterson, *Search for Negotiated Peace*, 167; NYT, Dec. 21, 1915, 1. For a positive account of these debates, see "Aboard the Oscar II," letters from Florence L. Lattimore, a delegate and social worker from New York City, *Survey*, Jan. 15, 1916, 457–460.

36. Lochner, *America's Don Quixote*, 66.

37. Patterson, *Search for Negotiated Peace*, 172.

38 Lattimore, "Aboard the Oscar II," 460; Patterson, *Search for Negotiated Peace*, 168.

39. Quoted in Lochner, *America's Don Quixote*, 33; Cooper, *Vanity of Power*, 91.

40. Crystal Eastman Benedict, "To Make War Unthinkable," letter to *New Republic*, July 24, 1915, 313.

41. Quotations from John Milton Cooper, Jr., *Woodrow Wilson: A Biography* (New York: Alfred . Knopf, 2009), 304; Link, *Confusions and Crises*, 48, 23.

42. Baldwin quoted in Ross Wetzsteon, *Republic of Dreams: Greenwich Village: The American Bohemia, 1910–1960* (New York: Simon & Schuster, 2002), 193.

43. Crystal Eastman, *Work Accidents and the Law* (New York: Arno, 1969 [1910]), 13. There is no full biography of Eastman. But see the pioneering introduction by Blanche Wiesen Cook in her edited anthology, *Crystal Eastman on Women and Revolution* (New York: Oxford University Press, 1978), 1–38. Hereafter, *CE on Women and Revolution*.

44. NYT, Aug 6, 1910, BR4. She was the only female member of the state commission. For more detail on Eastman's life before World War I, see Amy Aronson's forthcoming biography.

45. Claude McKay, *A Long Way from Home* (New Brunswick, NJ: Rutgers University Press, 2007 [1937]), 28. CE quoted in *NYT*, May 22, 1912, 10.

46. CE quoted in http://vcencyclopedia.vassar.edu/alumni/crystal-eastman. html; NYT, Jan. 15, 1910, 16. On the consultations with Brill, see Max Eastman, *Enjoyment of Laughter* (New York: Simon & Schuster, 1936), 357.

47. NYT, Dec. 16, 1914, 13.

48. On the uncertain date, see "Crystal Eastman Married," NYT, Nov. 14, 1916, 11. The office was located at the Ginn building, at 70 Fifth Avenue. It soon became the headquarters of several other peace groups, both national and local.

49. NYT, Nov. 16, 1915, 9.

50. Crystal Eastman Benedict, "A Platform of Real Preparedness," *Survey*, Nov. 13, 1915, 160–161.

51. NYT, Nov. 13, 1915, 5.

52. See the leaflet "What the Woman's Peace Party of New York City Has Done in the Five Months, February 6 to July 5, 1916," WPPP, Reel 12–2.

53. For details, see WPPP, Reel 21; *Survey*, May 20, 1916, 197; AUAMP, Reel 10.2.

54. "What the Woman's Peace Party . . . Has Done"; Letter from "A.B.P." to NYT, May 31, 1916, 12.

55. The group changed its name several times throughout its relatively short history. It began, in March 1915, as the American League to Limit Armaments, then, in early 1916, became the Anti-"Preparedness" Committee. In April 1916, it was renamed the AUAM. The last title was suggested by Walter Fuller, Crystal's lover and, later, husband. CE to Amos Pinchot, March 30, 1916, APP, Box 15. After the United States declared war a year later, the group altered its name twice more.

56. For a glimpse of the weekly activities of the Anti-"Preparedness" Committee under Eastman's leadership, see its Minutes from January 17, 1916, AUAMP, Reel 10.1. Five of the six staffers were women; the only man, Charles Hallinan, received the highest salary: $125 a week. Eastman paid herself $75. Both totals were far higher than the average pay of that time. Minutes from May 8, 1916, ibid.

57. CookDiss, 3, 7, ii.

58. See various documents about the New York branch of the WPP in WPPP, Reel 12:4. The New York State bill was introduced by two Republican legislators and known as the Welsh-Slater Act. More conservative members of the WPP, particularly in the Massachusetts branch, complained that the New York contingent was too radical. From Boston, the veteran pacifist Lucia Ames Mead wrote to Jane Addams that Crystal Eastman was "such an extreme socialist that she cannot greatly help the movement." This sentiment would deepen after the U.S. declaration of war. Mead to Addams, July 13, 1915, quoted in MarchandAMP, 219.

59. Keller quoted in NYT, Dec. 20, 1915, 3. On the reception of Keller's talk, see Wm. Brushwacker to CK, 12/22/15, CKP, Reel 5.

60. The American Socialists and the War, ed. Alexander Trachtenberg (New York: The Rand School of Social Science, 1917), 14.

61. Hillquit in April 1915, quoted in Pratt, Morris Hillquit, 120. Hillquit also corresponded, in English, with Socialists in Cuba and Puerto Rico.

62. On Hillquit's prediction of a Russian revolution, see Atlantic City Review, Oct. 18, 1915, in MHP-W, Reel 5.

63. Knock, To End All Wars, 54–55; Robert William Iversen, "Morris Hillquit:

American Social Democrat: A Study of the American Left from Haymarket to the New Deal," PhD dissertation, University of Iowa, 1951, 161–162.

64. Elizabeth McKillen, *Making the World Safe for Workers: Labor, the Left, and Wilsonian Internationalism* (Urbana: University of Illinois Press, 2013), 108. On labor's opposition to preparedness, see ibid., 91–122.

65. Gompers address to Annual Meeting of the NCF, Jan. 18, 1916. *Papers of Samuel Gompers*, vol. 9 (Urbana: University of Illinois Press, 2003), 380, 378. To further his vision of a democratic military, Gompers wanted union members to be able to get military training at a series of camps set up by General Leonard Wood in Plattsburgh, New York, and other locations. Wood was dubious about men with little formal education being trained as potential officers. See Gompers to Wood, Oct. 6, 1915, *Papers of Gompers*, vol. 9, 329–331.

66. "Defense Hotly Discussed by Federation Delegates," *San Francisco Chronicle*, Nov. 19, 1915, in *Papers of Gompers*, ibid., 344–346.

67. Larson, *Labor and Foreign Policy*, 66–76, quote at 66.

68. In late May 1915, the Mine Workers convened a meeting of other strongly anti-war unions at its national office in Indianapolis. But Gompers ignored their vague call for a conference "of all labor organizations if the situation regarding war would seem to justify such action," and the group never met again. McKillen, *Making the World Safe*, 110.

69. The pamphlet can be found in AUAMP, Reel 10.1. The illustration was adapted from a drawing by Ray O. Evans in *Puck*.

70. CK, "The Nation's Preparedness," published in several North Carolina papers on Nov. 20, 1915, and printed in the *Congressional Record* on Dec. 14, 1915. CKP, Reel 4. A short excerpt appears in the pamphlet mentioned above, p. 3.

71. CK, ibid. For the 1915 budget, see http://federal-budget.insidegov.com /1/17/1915.

72. Kitchin also had a warm correspondence with Thomas Dixon, author of the novel that D.W. Griffith adapted for his brilliant and openly racist 1915 film, *Birth of a Nation*. At Dixon's urging, the congressman "persuaded" the chairman of the House Committee on Education "to abandon" a bill that would have allowed cities and states to censor the movie. Thomas

Dixon to CK, Feb. 2, 1916, CKP, Reel 6; CK to Dixon, Feb. 14, 1916, CKP, Reel 7.

73. CE to CK, Nov. 30, 1915, CKP, Reel 4. While Congress was in session, Kitchin continued to work fairly amicably with Wilson and his top advisors on domestic issues like the income tax, on which they substantially agreed.

74. James Parker Martin, "The American Peace Movement and the Progressive Era, 1910–1917," PhD dissertation, Rice University, 1975, 274–276; Tumulty to Wilson, Jan. 17, 1916, quoted in Link, *Confusion and Crises*, 45.

75. Wilson quoted in Link, *Confusion and Crises*, 46. On the "questionable" success of the tour, see Cooper, *Woodrow Wilson*, 310. A few days after the tour concluded, Kitchin wrote to William Jennings Bryan: "I see no real change in the attitude of the Members," and he added that even some preparedness advocates were saying "that the President was a little too war alarming in his speeches—They sounded too much like Roosevelt." CK to Bryan, Feb. 9, 1916, CKP, Reel 7; Baker quoted in CookDiss, 58.

76. Bryan quoted in my *Godly Hero*, 247–248.

77. Perhaps unaware that Eastman and other feminists were among the leaders of the group, Bryan addressed his letter to "Gentlemen." Bryan to Anti-"Preparedness" Committee, Feb. 26, 1916, AUAMP, Reel 10.1; Bryan to CK, Feb. 5 (?), 1916, CKP, Reel 7; Alvin E. Dyer to CK, Jan. 25, 1916, CKP, Reel 6.

78. Johnson, *Peace Progressives*, 44–45.

79. Quotation from La Follette's *Autobiography* (1913), quoted in Unger, *Fighting Bob La Follette*, 123–124. On La Follette's oratory, see Carl R. Burgchardt, *Robert M. La Follette, Sr.: The Voice of Conscience* (New York: Greenwood Press, 1992).

80. Lincoln Steffens quoted in *La Follette: Great Lives Observed*, ed. Robert S. Maxwell (Englewood Cliffs, NJ: Prentice Hall, 1969), 91.

81. George Middleton in 1947, quoted in Unger, *Fighting Bob La Follette*, 57.

82. *Literary Digest*, March 11, 1916, 617, 650.

83. W.T. Hefley to CK, Jan. 7, 1916, CKP, Reel 6; F.E. Davis to CK, March 6, 1916, CKP, Reel 8. For examples of petitions, see Mary E. Garbutt, from Los Angeles, to CK, Feb. 8, 1916, CKP, Reel 7; Mrs. Mary Wilson et al.,

from Stafford County, Kansas, to CK, Feb. 15, 1916, ibid; W.F. Rodoff, from Cottage Grove, Oregon, to CK, March 1, 1916, CKP, Reel 8.

84. Alexander to CK, Nov. 3, 1915, CKP, Reel 3; Gibson to CK, CKP, Reel 5.

85. Dodd to CK, May 27, 1916, CKP, Reel 10; John W. Mitchell to CK, March 15, 1916, CKP, Reel 8; Anonymous to CK, Feb. 24, 1916, CKP, Reel 7; Irving Winslow to CK, Jan. 14, 1916, CKP, Reel 6.

86. H.A. Davis to CK, Feb. 7, 1916, CKP, Reel 7. His brief letter was addressed only to "Hon. Claude Kitchin M.C., Washington, D.C."

87. Eleven copies of the petition, with 1,199 names, can be found in CKP, Reels 7 and 8. The first is dated Feb. 21, 1916; the last March 27 of that year. On the genesis of the document and the total of signers, see *The Church and International Relations*, vol. III, prepared by Sidney L. Gulick and Charles S. Macfarland (New York: Missionary Education Movement, 1917), 43–48. I computed the locations of the signers from the petitions in the Kitchin Papers, a large and probably representative sample.

88. George A. Lippincott et al. to CK, Jan. 14, 1916, CKP, Reel 6; *Church and International Relations*, 44.

89. William M. Walton, quoted in Andrew Preston, *Sword of the Spirit, Shield of Faith: Religion in American War and Diplomacy* (New York: Alfred A. Knopf, 2012), 247; Ray H. Abrams, *Preachers Present Arms* (Scottsdale, PA: Herald Press, 1969 [1933]), 37.

90. The best study of this subject is Thomas J. Rowland, "From Neutrality to War: Irish-American Catholics and World War I, 1914–1917," PhD dissertation, George Washington University, 1992.

91. NYT, March 6, 1916; Rowland, ibid., 215.

92. A.G. Stock, *W.B. Yeats: His Poetry and Thought* (Cambridge, UK: Cambridge University Press, 1964), 68. One diocesan paper, the *Brooklyn Tablet*, did run a column summarizing the convention and defending it against charges that the delegates were pro-German. P.J. Boylan, "The Irish Race Convention," *Tablet*, March 11, 1916, 6. Thanks to Caroline Kahlenberg for her excellent research into Irish nationalist and Catholic papers during World War I. Archbishop Ireland quoted in Rowland, ibid., 71.

93. Wilson to House, Feb. 16, 1916, quoted in Link, *Confusions and Crises*, 144.

94. Ibid., 163.

95. Kitchin quoted in Arnett, *Claude Kitchin*, 161; Bryan quoted in Kazin, *Godly Hero*, 248.

96. Stone quoted in Timothy Gregory McDonald, "Southern Democratic Congressmen and the First World War, August 1914–April 1917: The Public Record of Their Support for or Opposition to Wilson's Policies," PhD dissertation, University of Washington, 128.

97. Stone quoted in Cooper, *Woodrow Wilson*, 313.

98. Wilson quoted in NYT, 2/25/16, 1..

99. Mann quoted in Doenecke, *Nothing Less Than War*, 165.

100. An abridged version of the speech was published as "Congress Dodges Responsibility," LFM, March 1916, 1–2. On the atmosphere in the Senate, see RML, vol. 1, 556–560.

101. Kitchin quoted in CookDiss, 136; Bryan and von Bernstorff quoted in Link, *Confusions and Crises*, 193–194.

102. The submarine commander, Pustkuchen, quoted in Link, ibid., 228.

103. Ibid., 252.

104. Kenyon and Bryan quoted in Doenecke, *Nothing Less Than War*, 170, 171.

105. *Kolnische Zeitung*, May 5, 1916, quoted in Link, *Confusions and Crises*, 272.

106. For the full transcript of the meeting, see "A Colloquy with a Group of Antipreparedness Leaders," WWP, vol. 36, 634–48.

107. Charles T. Hallinan, "Swinging Around the Circle Against Militarism," *Survey*, April 22, 1916, 95–96.

108. "Colloquy," 641–642.

109. Ibid., 646, 648.

110. Ibid., 648; Max Eastman, "The Masses at the White House," *Masses*, July 1916, 6. The same issue of the magazine featured a two-page illustration by Boardman Robinson titled "The Deserter." It portrayed Jesus standing, blindfolded, against a wall, about to be executed by a firing squad composed of five soldiers, one from each of the main belligerent powers.

111. http://www.firstworldwar.com/features/aslowfuse.htm.

112. https://www.khanacademy.org/humanities/history/euro-hist/world-war -I-fighting/v/battles-of-verdun—somme-and-the-hindenburg-line.

113. Max Eastman, "What Is Patriotism and What Shall We Do with It?,"

Toward the Great Change: Crystal and Max Eastman on Feminism, Antimilitarism, and Revolution, ed. Blanche Wiesen Cook (New York: Garland Publishing, 1976), 248

CHAPTER THREE: KEEP US OUT

1. Quoted in Arthur S. Link, *Wilson: Campaigns for Progressivism and Peace, 1916-1917* (Princeton, NJ: Princeton University Press, 1965), 48.
2. AUAMP, Box 4.
3. Russell, "An Open Letter to President Wilson," *Survey,* Dec. 30, 1916, 372.
4. Quotations from Link, *Campaigns for Progressivism and Peace,* 42–46; WP, June 15, 1916, 1, 5; Kazin, *Godly Hero,* 251.
5. WP, June 15, 1916, 1.
6. Wilson quoted in CookDiss, 157–158.
7. Wilson quoted in WP, July 1, 1916, 1.
8. CE quoted in MarchandAPM, 243–244.
9. Gardner and TR quoted in Doenecke, *Nothing Less Than War,* 193. On the NSL's response, see Link, *Confusion and Crises,* 332.
10. On La Follette's amendment, which received only eight votes, and his speech, see RML vol. 1, 575–577.
11. CK quoted in Ingle, "Pilgrimage," 119; "Danger Ahead!," *SF Examiner,* Aug. 7, 1916, in CKP, Reel 11; CK to J. Malcolm Forbes, Aug. 19, 1916, ibid. Josephus Daniels may have signaled his own misgivings about military expansion that month when he had his private secretary send a personal note to Kitchin asking for copies of his "speeches and articles touching the subject of militarism and preparedness" and adding, "I have in mind sympathetic and not critical use of them." Private secretary [unnamed], Secretary of the Navy to CK, Aug. 10, 1916, ibid.
12. Maurer quoted in *Labor World,* Duluth, Minnesota, Feb. 19, 1916, 1.
13. For details on the 1916 Revenue Act and its legislative history, see Steven R. Weisman, *The Great Tax Wars* (New York: Simon & Schuster, 2002), 302–310. An excellent source on the tax system and World War I is David M. Kennedy's *Over Here: The First World War and American Society* (New York: Oxford University Press, 1980).

14. Wise to Amos Pinchot, Oct. 17, 1916, APP, Box 17. On the explosion at Black Tom Island in New York harbor that killed four, see Captain Henry Landau, *The Enemy Within: The Inside Story of German Sabotage in America* (New York: G.P. Putnam's Sons, 1937), 77–83. On the bombing in San Francisco, which killed ten, see Richard H. Frost, *The Mooney Case* (Stanford, CA: Stanford University Press, 1968). Convicted of the crime were Tom Mooney and Warren Billings, militant Socialists who served more than two decades in jail before receiving a gubernatorial pardon.

15. CE, "Suggestions for 1916–1917," AUAMP, Reel 1.

16. Hallinan to CE, Oct. 10, 1916, APP, Box 17.

17. On the finances of the NSL, see "National Security League Hearings, Special Committee of the House of Representatives, Sixty-fifth Congress, Third Session" (Washington, 1919), 17, 24, 25 and passim; "Notes Regarding the Security League of Pittsburgh," no date but internal evidence suggests spring 1916, APP, Box 73.

18. Quoted from "Joint Peace Effort," *Survey*, Nov. 11, 1916, 149. On the other activities, see Nellie M. Smith (AUAM) to Dr. James P. Warbasse, Sept. 22, 1916, AUAMP, Reel 1; Esther E. Baldwin, "War Relief and the American Contributor," *Survey*, Oct. 21, 1916, 63–70; Winthrop D. Lane, "The 'Militarist' Laws of New York," ibid., June 17, 1916, 313–314; Degen, *History of the Woman's Peace Party*, 168–170.

19. Richard Hofstadter, *The Age of Reform* (New York: Alfred A. Knopf, 1955), 205.

20. TR letter to Sir Horace Plunkett, July 9, 1916, quoted in Link, *Campaigns for Progressivism and Peace*, 142; Henry Morgenthau, quoted in S.D. Lovell, *The Presidential Election of 1916* (Carbondale: Southern Illinois University Press, 1980), 7.

21. Villard quoted in Michael Wreszin, *Oswald Garrison Villard: Pacifist at War* (Bloomington: Indiana University Press, 1965), 63.

22. Quotations from Knock, *To End All Wars*, 95, 93.

23. Quote from ibid., 95. A September *Literary Digest* poll of 457 union officials found that 73 percent believed their members were supporting Wilson, with Benson and Hughes drawing just 10 percent apiece. See Lovell,

Presidential Election of 1916, 164. On labor support for Wilson, also see Link, *Campaigns for Progressivism and Peace*, 126–127.

24. Leaflet in CKP, Reel 39. On the primary campaign, see Homer Larry Ingle, "Pilgrimage,"115–117.

25. "La Follette for President," LFM, March 1916, 14.

26. Ernest C. Bolt, Jr., *Ballots Before Bullets: The War Referendum Approach to Peace in America, 1914–1941* (Charlottesville: University Press of Virginia, 1977), 19.

27. NYT, quoted in Unger, *Fighting Bob La Follette*, 236.

28. Norris quoted in RML, 580. W.D. Mallett to RLF, Sept. 2, 1916, LFFP, Box 1, B-19.

29. "Morris Hillquit Accepts," *New York Call*, Sept. 1, 1916. On the excitement among Hillquit volunteers, see ibid., Oct. 13, 1916; Oct. 20, 1916; Oct. 24, 1916; Oct. 29, 1916. These and other clippings from the campaign can be found in MHP-W, Reel 8.

30. Quoted in *New York Evening Sun*, Oct. 18, 1916.

31. Ibid; NYT, Oct. 17, 1916; MH address at Harlem Star Casino, Oct, 22, 1916, 4. All in MHP-W, ibid. Two weeks before the election, the Socialist *Call* ran a story about Hillquit's race, headlined "Election to Office Almost Assured," *New York Call*, Oct. 24, 1916.

32. Hillquit, *Loose Leaves*, 117–118.

33. Ibid., 118. For the SPA's argument, see "Hillquit Count Ended; Frauds Clearly Shown," *New York Call*, Jan. 14, 1917.

34. Quoted in William M. Leary, Jr., "Woodrow Wilson, Irish Americans, and the Election of 1916," *Journal of American History* 54 (June 1967), 60.

35. TR in a private letter, June 23, 1916, quoted in Cooper, *Woodrow Wilson*, 339.

36. Hughes quoted in Lovell, *Presidential Election of 1916*, 130; Link, *Campaigns for Progressivism and Peace*, 135. For a more sympathetic account of the Republican campaign, see Merlo J. Pusey, *Charles Evans Hughes*, vol. 1 (New York: Columbia University Press, 1963), 335–359.

37. Barnes quoted in Betty Glad, *Charles Evans Hughes and the Illusions of Innocence: A Study in American Diplomacy* (Urbana: University of Illinois

Press, 1966), 78. On Hughes's blunders in California, see Lovell, *Presidential Election of 1916*, 136–147.

38. Quoted in Cooper, *Woodrow Wilson*, 348. On Bryan's tour, see Link, *Campaigns for Progressivism and Peace*, 109–110, and my *Godly Hero*, 251–252.

39. WP, Jan. 23, 1917, 4.

40. NYT, Nov. 13, 1916, 6; RLF quoted in RML, 585.

41. *Samuel Gompers Papers*, vol. 9 (Urbana: University of Illinois, 2003), 524–525; CE, "Fighting Pacifists in 1917," *Survey*, Dec. 30, 1916. Reprinted by the Woman's Peace Party of NY. WPPP, Reel 4.

42. Quoted in Patterson, *Search for Negotiated Peace*, 271.

43. CE, ibid; Program for "Conference of Oppressed or Dependent Nationalities," Dec. 10–11, 1916, WPPP, Reel 3.

44. Hamilton Holt to Amos Pinchot, Dec. 18, 1916, APP, Box 18. This letter includes the names of the large number of people who served, usually in an honorary capacity, as Vice-Chairmen or members of its Executive Committee or General Committee.

45. On this point, see Link, *Campaigns for Progressivism and Peace*, 109. The memo from Nov. 25, 1916, is quoted in Doenecke, *Nothing Less Than War*, 227.

46. Quotations from ibid., 218.

47. Bryan quoted in Paolo E. Coletta, *William Jennings Bryan*, vol. 3 (Lincoln: University of Nebraska Press, 1969), 47; Stone in Doenecke, *Nothing Less Than War*, 231; Rebecca Shelly to Amos Pinchot, Jan. 16, 1917, APP, Box 18.

48. Trevelyan quoted in Knock, *To End All Wars*, 108. On December 8, Wilson, referring to a supportive note from Trevelyan, remarked to Colonel House, "The time is near at hand for *something*!," ibid. Russell, "Open Letter to President Wilson," 372–373. On prior efforts by Trevelyan and other liberals in the small but vocal UDC to convince Wilson to begin a mediation effort, see Patterson, *Search for Negotiated Peace*, 275–282.

49. Quoted in Widenor, *Henry Cabot Lodge*, 251.

50. WP, Dec. 24, 1916, 4.

51. Lansing statement quoted in Link, *Campaigns for Progressivism and Peace*, 222. As Link wrote: "Lansing had in fact concluded that the national

interest and the good of mankind demanded that he do his best to sabotage the President's peace effort altogether, or at least make certain that it culminate in American belligerency on the Allied side." Ibid., 223.

52. Link, *Campaigns for Progressivism and Peace*, 236; Doenecke, *Nothing Less Than War*, 235. For a thoughtful, detailed account of the complex diplomacy between the United States and Great Britain and Germany during these crucial days, see May, *World War and American Isolation*, 305–415.

53. Circular letter from Jane Addams, Jan. 10, 1917, WPPP, Reel 3; "Socialist Party Makes Move to End World War," *Milwaukee Leader*, Jan. 11, 1917, MHP-W, Reel 8..

54. Wilson to Ellen Axson in 1884, quoted in Patterson, *Search for Negotiated Peace*, 108.

55. WP, Jan. 23, 1917, 1; WW to J.P. Gavit of the *New York Post*, Jan. 29, 1917. Quoted in Link, *Campaigns for Progressivism and Peace*, 271.

56. Knock, *To End All Wars*, 115.

57. Max Eastman quoted in ibid., 114; "An Interesting Comparison," late January 1917, WPPP, Reel 3; Addams quoted in Patterson, *Search for Negotiated Peace*, 299.

58. Quotations from "Congress Views on Wilson's Fateful Words," WP, Jan. 23, 1917, 4; NYT, Jan. 29, 1917; Link, *Campaigns for Progressivism and Peace*, 268.

59. France also compared a peace without victory to "bread without yeast, jugged hare without wine, brill without capers, mushrooms without garlic," as well as "love without quarrels" and a "town without brothel." Quoted in Link, *Campaigns for Progressivism and Peace*, 274.

60. Quoted in ibid., 276–277.

61. Quoted in Link, *Campaigns for Progressivism and Peace*, 247.

62. Memorandum from Henning von Holtzendorff, chief of the German Admiralty staff, Dec. 22, 1916, quoted in William Mulligan, *The Great War for Peace* (New Haven, CT: Yale University Press, 2014), 189; Doenecke, *Nothing Less Than War*, 221.

63. Doerries, *Imperial Challenge*, 220.

CHAPTER FOUR: DO THE PEOPLE WANT WAR?

1. "Do the People Want War?" *New Republic*, March 3, 1917, 145. The ad appeared in several newspapers as well. A copy of the galley proof is located in APP, Box 73.

2. Quoted in RML, vol. 1, 654.

3. CR, April 5, 1917, 385.

4. Quotes from Link, *Wilson: Campaigns for Progressivism and Peace*, 301, 303. On February 1, according to Agriculture Secretary David Houston, Wilson also told the cabinet that he feared that the supremacy of white people would be endangered if the United States entered the war. The president said that "in order to keep the white race or any part of it strong to meet the yellow race—Japan, for instance; in alliance with Russia, dominating China—it was wise to do nothing, he would do nothing, and would submit to anything and any imputation of weakness or cowardice." Quoted in Doenecke, *Nothing Less Than War*, 252.

5. NYT, Feb. 2, 1917, 7.

6. Ibid., Feb. 3, 1917, 11; WP, Feb. 13, 1917, 4. At the Chicago Coliseum, Representative Oscar Callaway, a Democrat from Texas who was close to Bryan, condemned the "munitions makers, capitalists, American Admirals, Generals, Captains, and so-called metropolitan newspapers . . . leagued together to force the United States into the European war." Quoted in Link, *Campaigns for Progressivism and Peace*, 306.

7. Paul U. Kellogg, "The Fighting Issues: A Statement by the Editor of the *Survey*," *Survey*, Feb. 17, 1917, 573. On the context of his statement, see Clarke A. Chambers, *Paul U. Kellogg and the Survey: Voices for Social Welfare and Social Justice* (Minneapolis: University of Minnesota Press, 1971), 57–60.

8. Kellogg, "Fighting Issues," 573.

9. Ibid., 574.

10. Ibid., 577.

11. Ibid., 576, 577. Kellogg was influenced partly by Bryan's plea "To the American People," which was widely reported in the press that month.

See copy in APP, Box 72. The editor also floated a proposal for a "league of armed neutrals" that would police the seas. This would soon be expanded in the pages of his magazine by Columbia professor Carleton Hayes, as discussed later in this chapter.

12. Kellogg, ibid., 574.

13. The only book-length treatment of this subject is Bolt, *Ballots Before Bullets*. Also helpful is James Parker Martin, "The American Peace Movement and the Progressive Era, 1910–1917," PhD dissertation, Rice University, 1975, 299–342.

14. Bolt, *Ballots Before Bullets*, 49; *Irish World and American Industrial Liberator*, Feb. 17, 1917.

15. NYT, Feb. 5, 1917, 7; Feb. 7, 1917, 8. The postcards also asked a second question, which their sponsors hoped would elicit a negative response: "Should we enter the war in order to uphold our legal right to go into the war zone?" Martin, "American Peace Movement," 316–317. The Committee for Democratic Control was headquartered at 70 Fifth Avenue, the same building where Crystal Eastman ran the AUAM and the WPP of New York. Leaders of the American Peace Society, who had been prominent in the movement before the war, opposed the referendum as "impractical and unnecessary" and likely to embarrass the president, whom they thought might still keep the nation out of war. See NYT, Feb. 23, 1917, 2.

16. Bryan quoted in Bolt, *Ballots Before Bullets*, 57. Lindbergh quoted in Doenecke, *Nothing Less Than War*, 269. Several of the referendum proposals would have allowed women to participate too.

17. Ibid., 63.

18. CDC, "Do the People Want War?" The editorial from March 3, 1917, was reprinted as "A Confession from Wall Street."

19. For the *World* cartoon and other accusations in the press along the same lines, see *Literary Digest*, Feb. 24, 1917. Correspondents to anti-war lawmakers heavily favored a referendum. For example, some 90 percent of Missourians who wrote to their congressmen did so. Christopher C. Gibbs, *The Great Silent Majority: Missouri's Resistance to World War I* (Columbia: University of Missouri Press, 1988), 29.

20. Jane Addams, *Peace and Bread*, 194–195.

21. The statement was titled "Democratic Defense." Quoted in Markku Ruotsila, *John Spargo and American Socialism* (New York: Palgrave Macmillan, 2006), 76. It included the millionaire J.G. Phelps Stokes and his wife, Rose Stokes, a Russian working-class immigrant, as well as the English-born writer John Spargo.

22. Victor Berger et al., telegram to CK, Feb. 2, 1917. CKP, Reel 15. On March 3, the SPA's National Committee dropped the embargo demand. NYT, March 4, 1917, 10.

23. "Socialists in U.S., Says Morris Hillquit, Opposed to War," *New York Times Magazine*, Feb. 11, 1917; http://www.marxists.org/archive/lenin/works/1914/sep/00.htm.

24. Louis Waldman, "Leon Trotsky on Second Avenue," in *Jewish Radicals: A Documentary History*, ed. Tony Michels (New York: New York University Press, 2012), 215, 218.

25. The final resolution called for opposing censorship and supporting "the workers in any concerted mass action against extortionate food prices and other sufferings of the war and against the tyranny of conscription and martial law." NYT, March 5, 1917, 11.

26. From Leon Trotsky, chapter XX of *My Life*, accessed at http://www.marxists.org/archive/trotsky/1930/mylife/1930-lif.pdf.

27. "She is very tired, and she ought to stop overworking at this time," Amos Pinchot wrote to Wald, who responded that "Miss Eastman is to have two months' vacation." Pinchot to Wald, March 10, 1917; Wald to Pinchot, March 14, 1917, APP, Box 19. On March 16 and 17, Eastman wrote to Pinchot about her plans and his part in them. Ibid.

28. Harriet Hyman Alonso, *Peace as a Woman's Issue: A History of the U.S. Movement for World Peace and Women's Rights* (Syracuse, NY: Syracuse University Press, 1993), 74–75; Patterson, *Search for Negotiated Peace*, 310.

29. The title came from a line in Magellan's *First Voyage 'Round the World*: "Then he showed four lights when he wished them to set full sail and follow in his wake." *Four Lights*, Jan. 27, 1917. All extant copies of the periodical can be found in WPPP, Reel 23.

30. Ibid., March 24, 1917; Feb. 6, 1917.

31. See MarchandAPM, 219–221. The previous December, CE had written to Harriet Thomas, an official of the national Woman's Peace Party, about attacks being made by WPP leaders in Boston: "These 'charges' and 'insinuations' you refer to are so ridiculous that they don't even make me angry—they just make me laugh." CE to Thomas, Dec. 4, 1916, WPPP. Reel 12:10.

32. He added, "Wilson will in no event enter into an alliance with our enemies." Quoted in Link, *Campaigns for Progressivism and Peace*, 324.

33. See Fred C. Russell (president of a hardware company in McAlester, Oklahoma) to CK, Jan. 25, 1917. CKP, Reel 15. That January, Kitchin received several other letters with this tone and message. A few days before the revenue bill passed, the House decided, by more than a 3–1 margin, to appropriate $62 million to fortify the nation's coasts. Kitchin voted against the bill. On the huge increase in corporate profits, see Ajay K. Mehrotra, *Making the Modern American Fiscal State: Law, Politics, and the Rise of Progressive Taxation, 1877-1929* (New York: Cambridge University Press, 2013), 333. For example, U.S. Steel's profits went up by 1,056 percent, Du Pont's by 1,597 percent, and that of General Motors by a mere 297 percent.

34. Hayes, "Which? War Without a Purpose? Or Armed Neutrality with a Purpose?" *Survey*, Feb. 10, 1917, 537.

35. http://wwl2.dataformat.com/HTML/30693.htm.

36. See the excerpts from fifty-four dailies from New York to San Francisco in NYT, Feb. 27, 1917, 4; Link, *Campaigns for Progressivism and Peace*, 349–350.

37. NYT, Feb. 28, 1917, 10. Irish nationalists opposed it too as a "step nearer war." *Irish World and American Industrial Liberator*, March 17, 1917.

38. Quotes from NYT, Feb. 27, 1917, 2; Doenecke, *Nothing Less Than War*, 269. The *Times* headline claimed inaccurately, "Pacifists Approve President's Action."

39. NYT and WP, March 1, 1917. For a survey of editorial opinion, see Thomas Boghardt, *The Zimmermann Telegram: Intelligence, Diplomacy, and America's Entry into World War I* (Annapolis, MD: Naval Institute Press, 2012), 163–166.

40. For several versions of the wording, see ibid.

41. Ibid., 180.

42. WP, March 2, 1917. On the vote, see Cooper, *Vanity of Power,* 179.

43. CK quoted in Ingle, "Pilgrimage," 131. London in CR, March 1, 1917, 4669.

44. Professor Edwin Borchard, quoted in Richard Drake, *The Education of an Anti-Imperialist: Robert La Follette and U.S. Expansion* (Madison: The University of Wisconsin Press, 2013), 168.

45. RML, vol. 1, 605.

46. Norris quoted in ibid., 609. CR, March 3, 1917, 4869.

47. CR, March 3, 1917, 4887.

48. CR, March 3, 1917, 4877–4878, 4886, 4888. Ruth Warner Towne, *Senator William J. Stone and the Politics of Compromise* (Port Washington, NY: Kennikat Press, 1979), 222. Lodge did not respond.

49. Quoted in RML, vol. 1, 613.

50. RML, vol. 1, 618.

51. Ibid., 620. Unger, *Fighting Bob La Follette,* 245.

52. Link, *Campaigns for Progressivism and Peace,* 362.

53. Quotes from correspondence in LFFP, Box 33; NYT, March 7, 1917, 3.

54. Unger, *Fighting Bob La Follette,* 246–247; Doenecke, *Nothing Less Than War,* 275–276. For a critique of Wilson's angry response, see Link, *Campaigns for Progressivism and Peace,* 363–364.

55. *New York Post,* March 17, 1917, quoted in Christopher Lasch, *The American Liberals and the Russian Revolution* (New York: Columbia University Press, 1962), 29.

56. For a summary of the U-boat attacks in March, see Doenecke, *Nothing Less Than War,* 278–280.

57. See the judgment of Arthur Link, *Campaigns for Progressivism and Peace,* 414.

58. Wilson quoted in Cooper, *Woodrow Wilson,* 382.

59. Quotes from Lansing's diary, as quoted in ibid., 404, 406. Ibid., 408.

60. May, *World War and American Isolation,* 427. The ship was the steamer *Aztec.* It was sunk off the coast of France; twenty-eight people on board died, including a navy gunner.

61. *New Republic*, Feb. 10, 1917, 38; John A. Fitch, "Will American Labor Fight?" *Survey*, March 24, 1917, 707–708. For examples of such ad hoc referenda, see the CR for April 3 and 4, 1917.

62. F.W. Calkins to CK, March 28, 1917; F.W. Kelsey to CK, March 29, 1917; Francis Joyner et al to CK, March 31, 1917, CK to Anna D. Graham, April 3, 1917. All in CKP, Reel 16. Growing up in Littleton at the time was fourteen-year-old Ella Baker, who would become an iconic civil rights leader after World War II. For Arthur Link, the "overwhelming sentiment" of the North Carolinians who wrote to Kitchin "shows that opposition to war was still very wide and deep . . . in a state that had virtually no German Americans." Link, *Campaigns for Progressivism and Peace*, 429.

63. Jordan, *Days of a Man*, 725–729.

64. Dewey to Pinchot, March 30, 1917, APP, Box 19. Robert B. Westbrook, *John Dewey and American Democracy* (Ithaca, NY: Cornell University Press, 1991), 202.

65. Link, *Campaigns for Progressivism and Peace*, 419; Cooper, *Woodrow Wilson*, 381.

66. NYT, April 3, 1917. Lodge had not, however, softened his feelings toward Wilson. Later that month, he wrote to Roosevelt, "He is a mean soul and the fact that he delivered a good message on April 2d does not alter his character." Quoted in Seward W. Livermore, *Politics Is Adjourned: Woodrow Wilson and the War Congress, 1916–1918* (Middletown, CT: Wesleyan University Press, 1966), 252.

67. Quoted in Walter Millis, *Road to War: America, 1914–1917* (Boston: Houghton Mifflin Company, 1935), 442–443.

68. Ibid., 434; "Lodge Knocks Down Pacifist Assailant," NYT, April 3, 1917. Bannwart was a Princeton graduate and the secretary of the Woodrow Wilson Independent League in his state. So he may have been kindling hostility toward Lodge long before they came to blows.

69. Stone quoted in CR, April 4, 1917, 210; Norris, ibid., 214. WP, April 5, 1917; Williams in Unger, *Fighting Bob La Follette*, 249.

70. Unger, *Fighting Bob La Follette*, 249; Sherwood in CR, April 5, 1917, 335, 337; Lundeen, in ibid., 362.

71. CR, April 5, 1917, 319; WP, April 6, 1917.

72. CR, April 4, 1917, 223–234; Pinchot and Williams quoted in Unger, *Fighting Bob La Follette*, 249–250.

73. CR, April 5, 1917, 332–333. La Follette was present in the House and joined in the applause for Kitchin's speech.

74. On Kitchin's impact, see WP, April 6, 1917. Quote from CR, April 5, 1917, 332.

75. Degen, *History of the Woman's Peace Party*, 191.

76. Paul Sothe Holbo, "They Voted Against War: A Study of Motivations," PhD dissertation, University of Chicago, 1961, 537. Holbo compiled brief but often vivid political biographies of all fifty-six lawmakers who voted against going to war.

77. For a full statement of this view, see the speech by Representative Henry Flood of Virginia, chair of the House Foreign Affairs Committee, CR, April 5, 1917, 307 and ff. On Ford's about-face, see Lacey, *Ford*, 155–156.

78. Fiorello H. La Guardia, *The Making of an Insurgent: An Autobiography, 1882–1919* (Philadelphia: J.B. Lippincott Co., 1947), 138.

79. Quoted in the eloquent family memoir written by his grandson: George Packer, *Blood of the Liberals* (New York: Farrar, Straus and Giroux, 2000), 79–80. In his own memoir, Hillquit also took the view that a Hughes victory would have led most Democrats to oppose going to war. Hillquit, *Loose Leaves*, 168–169.

CHAPTER FIVE: THE WAR—OR AMERICAN PROMISE: ONE MUST CHOOSE

1. Hallinan to Executive Committee of AUAM, April 5, 1917, AUAMP, Reel 10.1.

2. Bourne, "A War Diary," *Seven Arts*, September 1917, reprinted in Bourne, *War and the Intellectuals: Collected Essays, 1915–1919*, ed. Carl Resek (New York: Hackett Publishing Company, 1964), 38.

3. *Four Lights*, Sept 22, 1917. Quoted in CookDiss, 234.

4. Quoted in Theodore Kornweibel, Jr., "Apathy and Dissent: Black America's

Negative Responses to World War I," *South Atlantic Quarterly* 80 (Summer 1981), 327.

5. *Complete Report of the Chairman of the Committee on Public Information* (Washington, 1920), 1. The CPI was nearly as active abroad as at home—with bureaus all over the globe, producing documents in nearly every major language and several minor ones too.

6. On the enforcement of the Espionage Act of 1917 (which remains in force today) and the Sedition Act of 1918, see Geoffrey R. Stone, *War and Liberty: An American Dilemma: 1790 to the Present* (New York: W.W. Norton, 2007), 41–63; Christopher Capozzola, *Uncle Sam Wants You: World War I and the Making of the Modern American Citizen* (New York: Oxford University Press, 2008), 144–172; Lon J. Strauss, "A Paranoid State: The American Public, Military Surveillance and the Espionage Act of 1917," PhD dissertation, University of Kansas, 2012.

7. TR in July 1918, speaking to the convention of the New York State Republican Party, http://quotes.dictionary.com/There_can_be_no_fiftyfifty_Americanism_in_this.

8. Addams, "Patriots and Pacifists in Wartime," speech given in June 1917. Quoted in Allen F. Davis, *American Heroine: The Life and Legend of Jane Addams* (New York: Oxford University Press, 1973), 245.

9. Wilson's address on June 14, 1917, delivered in Washington, D.C. http://wwl2.dataformat.com/HTML/30696.htm.

10. Max Eastman quoted in William O'Neill, *Max Eastman: The Last Romantic* (New York: Oxford University Press, 1978), 63.

11. MH speech, delivered in Madison Square Garden, Sept. 23, 1917, in MHP-W, Reel 5; CE quoted in CookDiss, 213–214.

12. H.A. Partridge to RLF, April 30, 1917, LFFP, I: Box 33; W.B. Taylor to CK, Aug. 9, 1917, CKP, Reel 19. For examples of letters claiming that most Americans opposed the war, see R.J. Lewellyn, Elkin, North Carolina, to CK, April 9, 1917, CKP, Reel 17; James Arttey (?), Duluth, Minnesota, to RLF, April 12, 1917, LFFP, I: Box 27. As late as July, straw polls in Missouri and elsewhere in the Midwest reported overwhelming opposition to the war. Gibbs, *Great Silent Majority*, 38–39.

13. Excellent studies of the wartime state include Kennedy, *Over Here*; Capoz-
    zola, *Uncle Sam Wants You*; and Gary Gerstle, *Liberty and Coercion: The
    Paradox of American Government from the Founding to the Present* (Princ-
    eton, NJ: Princeton University Press, 2015), 125–142.

14. Buckley's line about conservatism, which appeared in the Mission State-
    ment of *National Review* in 1955, was: "It stands athwart history, yelling
    Stop, at a time when no one is inclined to do so, or to have much patience
    with those who so urge it." Randolph Bourne, "War Diary," originally pub-
    lished in September 1917, *The Radical Will: Selected Writings, 1911–1918*,
    ed. Olaf Hansen (New York: Urizen Books, 1977), 324, 329.

15. *Survey*, April 14, 1917. The magazine did occasionally try to balance pro-
    war and pacifist sentiments. In August, for example, Kellogg ran both "A
    Plea for the Conscientious Objector," by Norman Thomas; and a column
    by Edward T. Devine, a longtime staff member, which began: "Young men
    of military age and normal physique who are social reformers by instinct
    and conviction will ordinarily find their best occupation at the present
    time in military service." Thomas, *Survey*, Aug. 4, 1917, 391; Devine, ibid.,
    Aug. 18, 1917, 438.

16. Quotations from CookDiss, 218. On the group's troubles, see the minutes
    from executive committee meetings that summer, AUAMP, Reel 10:1.

17. Marie Louise Degen, *History of the Woman's Peace Party*, 202–203, 204;
    Louise W. Knight, *Jane Addams: Spirit in Action* (New York: W.W. Norton,
    2010), 218.

18. *Four Lights*, July 14, 1917, 1, 2. Blanche Watson to CE, Nov. 30, 1917,
    quoted in MarchandAPM, 221.

19. Ibid.

20. Quotations from Paolo E. Coletta, *William Jennings Bryan: Political Puri-
    tan, 1915–1925* (Lincoln: University of Nebraska Press, 1969), 57; Kazin,
    Godly Hero, 255; Eastman, "Religion of Patriotism."

21. Dewey quoted in Kennedy, *Over Here*, 50.

22. Bourne quoted in Kennedy, *Over Here*, 52; Bourne, "War Diary," http://
    fair-use.org/seven-arts/1917/09/a-war-diary.

23. 405. Bertrand Russell in April 1916, quoted in Ray Monk, *Bertrand Rus-
    sell: The Spirit of Solitude, 1872–1921*, vol. 1 (New York: Free Press, 1996),

458. For comparative histories of conscription during the Great War, see George Q. Flynn, *Conscription and Democracy: France, Great Britain, and the United States* (Westport, CT.: Greenwood Press, 2002); and Robin Archer, "Stopping War and Stopping Conscription: Australian Labour's Response to World War I in Comparative Perspective," *Labour History* (May 2014), 43–67.

24. TR quoted in John Whiteclay Chambers II, *To Raise an Army: The Draft Comes to Modern America* (New York: Free Press, 1987), 88. This book is the best and most complete study of its subject. Eastman in NYT, Jan. 14, 1917, 6; Green to Amos Pinchot, March 22, 1917, APP, Box 19. After Samuel Gompers died in 1924, Green became the president of the American Federation of Labor.

25. Capozzola, *Uncle Sam Wants You*, 21.

26. On Wilson's decision, see Chambers, *To Raise an Army*, 125–151; Cooper, *Woodrow Wilson*, 393–395. La Guardia, *Making of an Insurgent*, 140.

27. "Daniel Webster on the Draft," AUAM pamphlet, April 17, 1917. AUAMP, Box 73. On Addams's testimony, see Degen, *History of the Woman's Peace Party*, 195.

28. Quotations from Reverend W.O. Hart to CK, April 12, 1917, CKP, Reel 17; William Louis Poteat to CK, April 18, 1917, ibid; Chambers, *To Raise an Army*, 154.

29. Quotations from Chambers, *To Raise an Army*, 163.

30. On Dent's background and his politics, see Robert D. Ward, "Stanley Hubert Dent and American Military Policy, 1916–1920," *Alabama Historical Quarterly* (Fall/Winter, 1971), 177–189.

31. Hardwick and Clark quoted in ibid., 164, 165; La Follette in LFM, May 1917; RML, vol. 2, 734.

32. WP, April 29, 1917, 1, 4.

33. http://www.presidency.ucsb.edu/ws/?pid=65403. Arguably, Wilson was also speaking to a grander impulse. As David Kennedy wrote, calling the draft plan "Selective Service" was an effective way of appealing to the desire of many Americans to "substitute an ethos of cooperative nationalism for the obsolescent credo of narrow self-interest—without sacrificing the positive aspects of individualism." Kennedy, *Over Here*, 154.

34. AUAMP, Reel 10.1; Minutes of April 30 meeting, ibid; NYT, July 7, 1917, 6; H.C. Peterson and Gilbert C. Fite, *Opponents of War, 1917–1918* (Seattle: University of Washington Press, 1957), 31.

35. Frank Mason North from the FCC, quoted in Abrams, *Preachers Present Arms*, 58. "The Christian Patriot," May 12, 1917, in *Norman Thomas on War: An Anthology*, ed. Bernard K. Johnpoll (New York: Garland Publishing, 1974), 46–47. For an excellent summary of Christian responses to the war, see Preston, *Sword of the Spirit*, 253–274.

36. Cooper, *Woodrow Wilson*, 84.

37. The case before the Court was *Arver v. United States*. Quoted in Capozzola, *Uncle Sam Wants You*, 29. On the defense of draft resisters by the Bureau of Legal Advice, an ally of the AUAM located in the same Ginn Building, 70 Fifth Avenue, see Frances H. Early, *A World Without War: How U.S. Feminists and Pacifists Resisted World War I* (Syracuse, NY: Syracuse University Press, 1997).

38. On Madison's proposed addition, see Duane C.S. Stoltzfus, *Pacifists in Chains: The Persecution of Hutterites During the Great War* (Baltimore: Johns Hopkins University Press, 2013), 62.

39. For the statistics, see Chambers, *To Raise an Army*, 216–217.

40. Bourne, "War Diary," 329; Stoltzfus, *Pacifists in Chains*, 121; Evan Thomas quoted in his great-granddaughter Louisa Thomas's eloquent book *Conscience: Two Soldiers, Two Pacifists, One Family—A Test of Will and Faith in World War I* (New York: Penguin Press, 2011), 123.

41. Quoted in James R. Green, *Grass-Roots Socialism: Radical Movements in the Southwest, 1895–1943* (Baton Rouge: Louisiana State University Press, 1978), 359.

42. Ibid.,360.

43. On the IWW protests, see Gerald E. Shenk, *"Work or Fight!": Race, Gender, and the Draft in World War One* (New York: Palgrave Macmillan, 2005), 72, 145.

44. Chambers, *To Raise an Army*, 213. On the understudied "Mexican Exodus," see Jose A. Ramirez, *To the Line of Fire: Mexican Texans and World War I* (College Station: Texas A&M University Press 2009), 31–34. The

comparison with draft evaders during the Vietnam War is, of necessity, inexact. During the later conflict, it was harder to avoid registering but also somewhat easier for those who resisted openly to evade prosecution. The draft operated before U.S. military personnel were first dispatched to Vietnam in the late 1950s and was not abolished until 1973. Out of a total of 26.8 million men eligible for conscription in those years, only about 250,000 men failed to register, while about 360,000 broke the law in some way but were never indicted. See Lawrence M. Baskir and William A. Strauss, *Chance and Circumstance: The Draft, the War and the Vietnam Generation* (New York: Vintage Books, 1978), 69.

45. See the excellent summary of the APL's history in Capozzola, *Uncle Sam Wants You*, 41–53; quotes on 51, 49.

46. Jeanette Keith, *Rich Man's War, Poor Man's Fight: Race, Class, and Power in the Rural South During the First World War* (Chapel Hill: University of North Carolina Press, 2004), 197.

47. https://www.census.gov/population/censusdata/urpop0090.txt; Keith, ibid., 159. On Native American draft resistance, see Thomas A. Britten, *American Indians in World War I* (Albuquerque: University of New Mexico Press, 1997), 67–72.

48. For a fuller narrative of this incident, see Keith, *Rich Man's War*, 185–188.

49. In his splendid history of U.S. society in wartime, David Kennedy wrote that, by the spring of 1917, the SPA had become "the largest center of organized opposition to American participation" in the conflict. Kennedy, *Over Here*, 26–27.

50. Ruotsila, *John Spargo and American Socialism*, 77.

51. MH's keynote speech is posted at https://www.marxists.org/history/usa/parties/spusa/1917/0407-hillquit-convkeynote.pdf.

52. O'Hare quoted in James Weinstein, *Decline of Socialism in America, 1912–1925* (New York: Monthly Review Press, 1967), 126. Max Eastman, "The Religion of Patriotism," *Masses*, July 1917, at https://www.marxists.org/history/etol/writers/eastman/works/1910s/patriot.htm.

53. See "Who's Who in The People's Council," PCAP, Reel 1.

54. http://www.forgottenbooks.com/readbook_text/Approaches_to_the

_Great_Settlement_1000412392/213. On the paucity of veterans from prewar peace groups, see MarchandAPM, 384. The executive committee of the embattled AUAM did, however, vote to send a delegation to the council's ill-fated convention in September. CookDiss, 221.

55. Adam Tooze, *The Deluge: The Great War, America and the Remaking of the Global Order, 1916–1931* (New York: Viking, 2014), 73–4.

56. "L.W." in the *New York Call*, reprinted in *Four Lights*, June 2, 1917, 1.

57. MH Address, May 31, 1917, in MHP-W, Reel 5; Hillquit, *Loose Leaves*, 171–172; Harriet Hyman Alonso, "Gender and Peace Politics in the First World War United States: The People's Council of America," *International History Review* 19 (February 1997), 90.

58. Dr. J.L. Magnes, "For Democracy and Terms of Peace," 1, PCAP, Reel 2. Daniel P. Kotzin, *Judah L. Magnes: An American Jewish Nonconformist* (Syracuse, NY: Syracuse University Press, 2010), 93.

59. Magnes, ibid., 8.

60. NYT, June 1, 1917, 1.

61. Ibid., 2.

62. Wilson quoted in *The Cabinet Diaries of Josephus Daniels*, ed. David Cronon (Lincoln: University of Nebraska Press, 1963), 199; Alan Dawley, *Changing the World: American Progressives in War and Revolution* (Princeton, NJ: Princeton University Press, 2003), 169.

63. Frank L. Grubbs, Jr., *The Struggle for Labor Loyalty: Gompers, the A.F. of L. and the Pacifists* (Durham, NC: Duke University Press, 1968), 45, 35.

64. The July 23, 1917, letter to Lansing was signed by Hillquit, Magnes, Max Eastman, and Henry W.L. Dana, a well-known Columbia professor. PCAP, Reel 1; "How to Organize a Local People's Council," no date, ibid.

65. "The People's Council for Democracy and Peace," introductory pamphlet, no date, PCAP, Reel 1.

66. Hillquit, *Loose Leaves*, 173.

67. Peterson and Fite, *Opponents of War*, 76; Louis Lochner to Organizing Committee, Aug. 19, 1917, PCAP, Reel 1; Hillquit, *Loose Leaves*, 174.

68. Hillquit, *Loose Leaves*, 176–177; Lochner, *Always the Unexpected*, 71.

69. Stephen J. Whitfield, *Scott Nearing: Apostle of American Radicalism* (New York: Columbia University Press, 1974), 92, 84.

70. *Revolutionary Radicalism: Its History, Purpose, and Tactics* (Albany, NY: J.B. Lyon, 1920), vol. 1, 1040.

71. Quoted in Livermore, *Politics Is Adjourned*, 66. The title of the book, taken from a speech Woodrow Wilson gave in 1918, is ironic.

72. B.S. Whipple to CK, April 4, 1917, CKP, Reel 16.

73. Kitchin quoted in NYT, July 30, 1917, 4. A typical example of the support he received came from James A. Martin, a lumber dealer in Tennessee: "While millions of our best young men go freely to Europe to fight the battles for HUMANITY, the RICH are today laying there [sic] schemes to rob the great body of the people, and to escape all possible just taxation." Martin to CK, July 30, 1917, CKP, Reel 19. For good summaries of the tax legislation and the larger fiscal context, see Kennedy, *Over Here*, 106–110; and Ajay K. Mehrotra, *Making the Modern American Fiscal State: Law, Politics, and the Rise of Progressive Taxation, 1877–1929* (New York: Cambridge University Press, 2013), 293–348.

74. Johnson letter, Sept. 17, 1917, quoted in Kennedy, *Over Here*, 110. LFM, September 1917, 1.

75. Quoted in Robert L. Morlan, *Political Prairie Fire: The Nonpartisan League, 1915–1922* (Minneapolis: University of Minnesota Press, 1955), 252.

76. Drake, *Education of an Anti-Imperialist*, 194; For the most complete account of the Saint Paul speech, see RML, vol. 2, 761–770.

77. RML, 766–769.

78. Ibid., 769–70.

79. Quotes from ibid., 770; Drake, *Education of an Anti-Imperialist*, 197; Unger, *Fighting Bob La Follette*, 255. Louis Lochner mentioned seeing the grisly collection in his *Always the Unexpected*, 67.

80. "La Follette's Complete Speech," LFM, Nov. 1917, 5, 15.

81. WP, October 7, 1917, 7.

82. According to La Follette biographer Nancy Unger, a sample of the letters in late 1917 "ran 67:1 in his favor." Unger, *Fighting Bob La Follette*, 257.

83. Johnson quoted in William G. Jordan, *Black Newspapers and America's War for Democracy, 1914–1920* (Chapel Hill: University of North Carolina Press, 2001), 42–43; Calvin Chase of the *Washington Bee*, ibid., 41. Booker T. Washington, "A Statement Written for the Woman's Peace

Party," Sept. 15, 1915, *The Booker T. Washington Papers*, ed. Louis R. Harlan and Raymond W. Smock (Urbana: University of Illinois Press, 1984), vol 13, 365.

84. Stephen R. Fox, *The Guardian of Boston: William Monroe Trotter* (New York: Atheneum, 1970), 179–182.

85. According to A. Philip Randolph, Trotter was "the one individual in Boston who had the courage to preside at an anti-war meeting" there at which Randolph spoke. Ibid., 215–216, http://faculty.washington.edu/steptoe/afram%20270/Reading/DuBois%20in%20the%20Crisis%201917-1919.pdf. For a cogent analysis of black views toward the war, see Kornweibel, "Apathy and Dissent," 323 and passim.

86. Vardaman, August 1917, quoted in Adriane Lentz-Smith, *Freedom Struggles: African Americans and World War I* (Cambridge, MA: Harvard University Press, 2009), 37.

87. Ibid., 66.

88. Major Joel E. Spingarn, "Memorandum on the Loyalty of the American Negro in the Present War," in *Federal Surveillance of Afro-Americans (1917–1925)*, ed. Theodore Kornweibel, Microform (Frederick, MD.: University Publications of America, 1985), Reel 19; File 0313.

89. Kornweibel, "Apathy and Dissent,"325, 328. The poster, carried in a silent parade down Fifth Avenue on July 28, was "censored by police." On black religious pacifists, see ibid., 329–331.

90. Fox, *Guardian of Boston*, 214.

91. A. Philip Randolph and Chandler Owen, "Terms of Peace and the Darker Races" (New York, 1917). Thanks to Eric Arnesen for sharing this pamphlet with me, which is part of the research for his forthcoming biography of Randolph.

92. *Messenger*, November 1917, 2; Theodore Kornweibel, Jr., *"Investigate Everything": Federal Efforts to Compel Black Loyalty during World War I* (Bloomington: Indiana University Press, 2002), 45.

93. MH speech given on Oct. 30, 1917, MHP-W, Reel 5.

94. Hillquit, *Loose Leaves*, 184; Eugene Schoen, chairman, Hillquit Victory Fund, to all Friends of Liberty, October 1917, MHP-W, Reel 2.

95. In mid-August, Crystal Eastman wrote to Hillquit that the large field made

it possible that he could win and mentioned that she had recently spoken to a man, "far from radical," who "could pledge you fifty votes among his friends right now." She ended the letter: "Wouldn't that be a glorious joke on everybody?" CE to MH, Aug. 15, 1917, MHP-W, Reel 2.

96. *New York Tribune*, Oct. 27, 1917, 16.

97. Charles W. Wood, *New York World*, reprinted in *Freeman's Journal*, Oct. 13, 1917. Copy in MHP-W, Reel 8.

98. Thomas Watt Gregory to WW, Nov. 3, 1917, WWP, vol. 44, 504. Two days later, Wilson wrote back agreeing with his AG's "judgment . . . in this matter." Ibid., 512.

99. *New York World*, Sept. 21, 1917; TR quoted in *Boston Traveler and Herald*, Nov. 2, 1917; *Brooklyn Eagle*, Nov. 4, 1917.

100. *New York Tribune*, Oct. 27, 1917, 16; Hillquit, *Loose Leaves*, 185; circular letter by Joseph Yeska, chairman of Business Men's League, October 1917, in MHP-W, Reel 8; *New York Sun*, Nov. 1, 1917.

101. Hillquit, *Loose Leaves*, 198–199; *NYT*, Oct. 31, 1917, 6.

102. *NYT*, Oct. 23, 1917, 1; quotes from the *World* and *Herald* in Weinstein, *Decline of Socialism*, 153–154; *Detroit News Tribune*, Nov. 1, 1917, MHP-W, Reel 8.

103 *New York Tribune*, Nov. 7, 1917, MHP-W, Reel 8.

104. See results at http://en.wikipedia.org/wiki/New_York_City_mayoral_election,_1917. On the pivotal role of Socialists in the campaign for suffrage in 1917, see Mari Jo Buhle, *Women and American Socialism, 1870–1920* (Urbana: University of Illinois Press, 1981), 236–237.

105. *New York Post*, Nov. 10, 1917, MHP-W, Reel 8. The *Post* was then owned by Oswald Garrison Villard, Fanny's son. But he did not exert editorial control and sold it the following year.

CHAPTER SIX: A STRANGE SET OF CRIMINALS

1. Hillquit, *Loose Leaves*, 169.

2. Quoted in Wreszin, *Oswald Garrison Villard*, 101.

3. George MacAdam, "Ebb of Pacifism in America," NYT, Dec. 23, 1917, 56.

4. Clark A. Chambers, *Paul U. Kellogg and the Survey: Voices for Social*

Welfare and Social Justice (Minneapolis: University of Minnesota Press, 1971), 64–68.

5. "The Case Against Universal Military Training," PCA leaflet, no date but probably early 1918, PCAP, Reel 1; Degen, *History of the Woman's Peace Party*, 206, 213; Knight, *Jane Addams*, 218.

6. Hallinan to AUAM executive committee, April 17, 1918, AUAMP, Reel 10.1. At the head of the memo, Hallinan did type: "Please read this critically."

7. LFM, February 1918, 10; Unger, *Fighting Bob La Follette*, 259. He returned to the Senate in September in order to cast a vote in favor of the woman suffrage amendment.

8. Ingle, "Pilgrimage," 163–164; Steven R. Weisman, *The Great Tax Wars* (New York: Simon & Schuster, 2002), 332–334.

9. The large majority of Americans who served at least a year in prison for violating the Espionage or Sedition Acts or a federal conspiracy law were Socialists, anarchists, and/or members of the IWW. No complete list exists. But see the brief biographies of 474 prisoners in Stephen M. Kohn, *American Political Prisoners: Prosecutions Under the Espionage and Sedition Acts* (Westport, CT.: Praeger, 1994), 83–155.

10. Peterson and Fite, *Opponents of War*, 224, 227. Of course, not every antiwar utterance landed its speaker in jail for a long spell. In charge of registering enemy aliens, the twenty-three-year-old John Edgar Hoover, who would later run the FBI for almost half a century, called for lenient treatment toward Otto Mueller, a German immigrant, who had called President Wilson "a cock-sucker and a thief" and said about America, "fuck this god damned country." Richard Gid Powers, *Secrecy and Power: The Life of J. Edgar Hoover* (New York: Free Press, 1987), 53.

11. Peterson and Fite, *Opponents of War*, 225.

12. For these quotations and the context in which Debs gave the speech, see Ernest Freeberg, *Democracy's Prisoner: Eugene V. Debs, the Great War, and the Right to Dissent* (Cambridge, MA: Harvard University Press, 2008), 76–77 and passim.

13. "A Reminiscence of the Second Masses Trial," LIB, December 1918, 3.

14. Knock, *To End All Wars*, 145. Knock's book is, however, an excellent study of peace activists' long relationship with Wilson.

15. Quotations from ibid., 145–147; "Hillquit Approves President's Stand," *Christian Science Monitor*, Jan. 12, 1918 (in MHP-W, Reel 8); "Peace Terms," LFM, January 1918, 1; Eastman in LIB, May 1918, 21.

16. Eastman in LIB, May 1918, 22

17. My view of what Wilson hoped to accomplish with his big speech essentially agrees with what John Milton Cooper, Jr., writes in his *Woodrow Wilson: A Biography*, 423–424.

18. On the change in CO regulations, see Chambers, *To Raise an Army*, 216–217.

19. The best study of wartime worker militancy is Joseph A. McCartin, *Labor's Great War: The Struggle for Industrial Democracy and the Origins of Modern American Labor Relations, 1912–1921* (Chapel Hill: University of North Carolina Press, 1997).

20. Keller, "In Behalf of the I.W.W.," LIB, March 1918, 13; Max Eastman, *Love and Revolution: My Journey Through an Epoch* (New York: Random House, 1964), 70.

21. Keller, "In Behalf of the I.W.W.," LIB, 13; Max Eastman, LIB, March 1918, 3.

22. Lenin in LIB, Oct. 1918, 22; Debs at https://www.marxists.org/archive /debs/works/1918/canton.htm; MH quoted in Christopher Lasch, *The American Liberals and the Russian Revolution* (New York: Columbia University Press, 1962), 98. "U.S. Army of Reds Not Practicable, Hillquit Says," *New York Tribune*, Feb. 28. 1918, MHP-W, Reel 8.

23. Hillquit, *Loose Leaves*, 229, 234; MH, "Labor and the War," MHP-W, Reel 8; LIB, July 1918, 21.

24. Willam D. Haywood, "On the Inside," LIB, May 1918, 15–16; Emma Goldman, *Living My Life: An Autobiography* (Salt Lake City, UT: Peregrine Smith Books, 1982 [1931]), 664. On Wilson, see Max Eastman, "Wilson and the World's Future," LIB, May 1918, 19; on Lenin, Max Eastman, "A Statesman of the New Order," LIB, September 1918, 10.

25. Roger Baldwin, "Recollections of a Life in Civil Liberties: I," *Civil Liberties Review* 2 (Spring 1975), 56.

26. NCLB, "Who Are the Traitors?," pamphlet, 1918, reprinted in *Antiwar Dissent and Peace Activism in World War I America: A Documentary Reader*, ed. Scott H. Bennett and Charles F. Howlett (Lincoln: University of Nebraska Press, 2014), 253–255.

27. NCLB form letter, Jan. 3, 1918, ACLU Archives, Reel 1; Charles Edward Russell to L. Hollingsworth Wood (chair of the bureau's "directing committee"), Jan. 10, 1918, ibid. The rally on Jan. 13 filled the aptly named Liberty Theatre in midtown Manhattan (which had a capacity of about a thousand). According to the brief report in the *New York Times*, the crowd "cheered to the echo a remark made by . . . Lincoln Steffens, who declared that the 'Kaiser did not start the war.'" NYT, Jan. 14, 1918, 11.

28. Robert C. Cottrell, *Roger Nash Baldwin and the American Civil Liberties Union* (New York: Columbia University Press, 2000), 30; Goldman, *Living My Life*, 477; Roger Baldwin, "Recollections of a Life," 44–45. The bureau's records contain thousands of examples of Socialists and radical pacifists— with or without religious affiliations—whom its cooperating attorneys defended. In particular, see the ACLU Archives, Reels 5, 6, and 7.

29. The NCLB published the pamphlet in August. It can be accessed at: https://www.marxists.org/history/usa/groups/aclu/1917/0800-thomas-warshere tics.pdf.

30. Cottrell, *Baldwin*, 67; New York (State) Legislature. Joint Legislative Committee to Investigate Seditious Activities, *Revolutionary Radicalism* (New York: J.B. Lyon, 1920), vol. 2, 1091, 1088.

31. Baldwin's statement was printed in a pamphlet, with funds contributed by these allies—as well as by twenty-three other supporters, including Crystal Eastman, Oswald Garrison Villard, and Paul Kellogg. See Roger N. Baldwin, "The Individual and the State" (New York, 1918). The *New York Times* mistakenly believed Baldwin to be an academic: "Pacifist Professor Gets Year in Prison," NYT, Oct. 31, 1918,11. Goldman, *Living My Life*, 665.

32. Baldwin, "Recollections of a Life," 63–64. In the Tombs, he was housed in a tier with other war resisters and several gangsters. They shared their disgust for authority and argued at length about politics. One "little Bolshevik," a Jewish immigrant, predicted that the revolutionary government in

Russia would soon abolish all prisons. Baldwin, "The Seventh Tier Soviet," LIB, Dec. 1918, 10–11.

33. Quoted from federal government surveillance files, in Chapter Four of Eric Arnesen's forthcoming biography of Randolph. I am indebted to Eric for allowing me to read and borrow from what will be a path-breaking account of the life of one of the most significant figures in twentieth-century U.S. political and labor history.

34. Arnesen, ibid.; http://www.everydaycitizen.com/2008/08/democratic_left _hero_a_philip.html.

35. Chicago *Broad Axe*, July 13, 1918, 2; *Appeal*, Saint Paul, MN, Oct. 12, 1918, 2. Mia Bay, *To Tell the Truth Freely: The Life of Ida B. Wells* (New York: Hill and Wang, 2009). 304. The descriptions of Trotter are from R.H. Van Deman, the chief of Military Intelligence, to his Northeastern Department, Oct. 2, 1917, FSAA, Reel 19, p. 0369; and from Major W.H. Loving (a black officer) to Director of Military Intelligence, Aug. 6, 1919, ibid., p. 0613.

36. After the court meted out punishment to Fletcher and other IWW officials, the longshoremen's leader told Big Bill Haywood, "'The Judge has been using very ungrammatical language.' I looked at his smiling black face and asked: 'How's that, Ben?' He said: 'His sentences are much too long.'" http://en.wikipedia.org/wiki/Ben_Fletcher#Treason_arrest_and_sentence. Wells-Barnett quoted in Bay, ibid., 303–304; James Weldon Johnson, "What the Negro Is Doing for Himself," LIB, June 1918, 31.

37. Ludendorff quoted in John Keegan, *The First World War* (New York: Vintage, 2012), 393–394. Also see Christopher Clark, *Kaiser Wilhelm II: A Life in Power* (London: Harlow, 2000), 327.

38. Keegan, ibid., 393. As Keegan summarized the case: "Nowhere among Germany's remaining resources could sufficient force be found to counter the millions America could bring across the Atlantic, and the consequent sense of the pointlessness of further effort rotted the resolution of the ordinary German soldier to do his duty." Ibid., 412.

39. Robert H. Ferrell, *America's Deadliest Battle: Meuse-Argonne, 1918* (Lawrence: University Press of Kansas, 2007), xi. The overall number of American battle deaths is disputed. I have used the number cited by one of the

most respected students of the U.S. Army during the war: Jennifer D. Keene, *Doughboys, the Great War, and the Remaking of America* (Baltimore: Johns Hopkins University Press, 2001), ix. A total of over 116,000 servicemen lost their lives in the war; many succumbed to the flu epidemic of 1918: http://www.pbs.org/greatwar/resources/casdeath_pop.html.

40. George Seldes, *You Can't Print That* (Garden City, NY: Garden City Publishing Company, 1929), 36; http://oldmagazinearticles.com/General_Paul_von_Hindenburg_Interview_1918#.VMaAFv54qFE.

41. The horrific influenza epidemic of 1918 was cresting during the battle and also slowed the U.S. offensive. See Carol R. Byerly, *Fever of War: The Influenza Epidemic in the U.S. Army During World War I* (New York: NYU Press, 2005), 108–114.

42. Gabriel Chevallier, *Fear: A Novel of World War I*, trans. Malcolm Imrie (New York: New York Review Books Classics, 2014 [1930]), 277; Keene, *Doughboys*, 43. A white sportswriter for the *New York World* viewed the aggressiveness of black soldiers more positively—and framed it in racialist terms. About a black regiment in training, he wrote: "'Those boys certainly do love the bayonet,' said an officer to me one day when we were watching the darkies at work. And they certainly did. Cold steel is the natural weapon of the African. He has been bred to handling it in many centuries of hand-to-hand fighting with assagai and heavy knife. The negro [sic] regiment went through bayonet practice with all the fury of actual combat." R. Edgren, column in the *World*, no precise date but 1918. Scrapbooks in the William Monroe Trotter Papers, Boston University, Box 20.

43. John Dos Passos, *Three Soldiers* (Boston: Houghton Mifflin, 1921), 200. Donald Dinsmore, quoted in Keene, *Doughboys*, 77.

44. *Stars and Stripes*, April 12, 1918; Feb. 22, 1918; July 12, 1918. A Union Army paper of the same name had been briefly published in Missouri during the Civil War. On the creation of the World War I paper, see the detailed account of its founder and first editor by his granddaughter: Virginia G. Vassallo, *Unsung Patriot: Guy T. Viskniskki* (Danville, KY: Krazy Duck Productions, 2007). During the winter of the paper's birth, according to Viskniskki, a major in the AEF, "the morale of the American soldier in France was shot to hell," 57.

45. Adjutant General, Eastern Department, to [left empty], June 19, 1917. ACLU Archives, Reel 5. Ferrell, *America's Deadliest Battle*, 118.

46. Sgt. Louis H. Pontlock to Du Bois in Lentz-Smith, *Freedom Struggles*, 111–112; G.H. Hill [Sidney Wilson] to Dr. H.D. Everett, April 27, 1918, in Bennett and Howlett, *Antiwar Dissent*, 178.

47. York quoted in Capozzola, *Uncle Sam Wants You*, 67; Richard Slotkin, *Lost Battalions: The Great War and the Crisis of American Nationality* (New York: Henry Holt, 2005), 378. In November 1921, Whittlesey probably committed suicide by jumping into the sea while on a voyage to Cuba. Several days earlier, he, Alvin York, and the only other Medal of Honor recipient from World War I had been pallbearers at the Tomb of the Unknown Soldier at Arlington Cemetery.

48. Ludendorff quoted in Gideon Rose, *How Wars End: Why We Always Fight the Last Battle* (New York: Simon & Schuster, 2010), 24.

49. General Wilhelm Groener, quoted in Keegan, *First World War*, 419.

50. For a detailed account of the Democrats' problems, see Livermore, *Politics Is Adjourned*, 169–184.

51. Hays quoted in WP, Sept. 13, 1918, 5; Lodge quoted in Knock, *To End All Wars*, 169; TR quoted in Slotkin, *Lost Battalions*, 377.

52. WW quoted in NYT, Oct. 26, 1918, 1. Franklin K. Lane quoted in Knock, *To End All Wars*, 178.

53. WW quoted in Cooper, *Woodrow Wilson*, 435; Hays quoted in WP, Oct. 28, 1918, 2.

54. WW quoted in Knock, *To End All Wars*, 162.

55. Eastman concluded, "We must hold our own counsel, and, with the help of Russia and what other nations may with good luck establish the Republic of Labor, make our council more important than theirs. It is our task to make the world democratic before they make it safe." ME, "The League of Nations," LIB, Dec. 1918, 6–7.

56. Quotations from Knock, *To End All Wars*, 159, 160.

57. On the Newberry case, see https://www.senate.gov/artandhistory/history/common/contested_elections/102Ford_Newberry.htm.

58. A week before the election, the *Washington Post*, a Democratic paper, editorialized: "How Majority Leader Kitchin has not supported the President

is too well known to need amplification." WP, Oct. 31, 1918, 6. For lists of winners and losers among those who had voted against the declaration of war, see Paul Sothe Holbo, "They Voted Against War: A Study of Motivations," PhD dissertation, University of Chicago, 1961, 541–542. Twenty-seven anti-war congressmen retained their seats, while fourteen lost them. Jeannette Rankin ran for Senate in Montana but lost in the Republican primary. Only two of the six anti-war senators were on the ballot in 1918. George Norris, the Republican from Nebraska, was reelected by nine percentage points, but James Vardaman, the Mississippi Democrat, was defeated in his party's primary.

59. On this point, see Weinstein, Decline of Socialism in America, 170.

60. "'Hillquit is Kaiser's Ally,' Says La Guardia," New York World, Nov. 4, 1918, MHP-W, Reel 8.

61. "C.E.," "The Socialist Vote," LIB, Dec. 1918, 33. New York's Socialist daily paper was almost as cheerful about the results. See "The Election Results," New York Call, Nov. 11, 1918. Thanks to Eric Arnesen for this source.

62. La Follette quoted in RML, vol. 2, 897; New York Call, Nov. 8, 1918. Thanks to Eric Arnesen for this source.

63. MH, "New Year Greetings, 1919," in MHP-W, Reel 2.

CHAPTER SEVEN: LEGACIES

1. Colum McCann, TransAtlantic (New York: Random House, 2013), 299.

2. Stone quoted in RML, vol. 1, 654; Bourne, "War Diary," Seven Arts, September 1917: http://fair-use.org/seven-arts/1917/09/a-war-diary.

3. Keegan, First World War, 423.

4. H.G. Wells quoted in Erez Manela, The Wilsonian Moment: Self-Determination and the International Origins of Anticolonial Nationalism (New York: Oxford University Press, 2007), 3. Disguised as a merchant seaman, Monroe Trotter, Wilson's leading black critic, traveled to Paris to demand that the peace treaty include an endorsement of racial equality. Unsurprisingly, neither the president nor Colonel House agreed to meet with him.

5. Borah, Nov. 19, 1919, quoted in Christopher McKnight Nichols, Promise

and Peril: America at the Dawn of a Global Age (Cambridge, MA: Harvard University Press, 2011), 265; Harold Nicolson quoted in Tooze, *Deluge*, 516.

6. CE, "A Platform of Real Preparedness," *Survey*, Nov. 13, 1915. Reprinted in Cook, *Toward the Great Change*, 223; CK in CR, April 5, 1917, 332–333.

7. Quoted in Max Eastman, "The Chicago Conventions," LIB, Oct. 1919, 17.

8. Addams quoted in Davis, *American Heroine*, 261.

9. Addams, *Peace and Bread*, 142.

10. http://www.nobelprize.org/nobel_prizes/peace/laureates/1931/press .html. The prize was jointly awarded that year to Nicholas Murray Butler, the longtime president of Columbia University who headed the Carnegie Endowment for Peace but had supported America's entry into World War I. Wisconsin Democrats declined to run a candidate against La Follette, and only an independent and a Prohibition Party nominee opposed him. NYT, Dec. 20, 1931, Sunday Magazine 20.

11. Lisa M. Budreau, *Bodies of War: World War I and the Politics of Commemoration in America, 1919–1933* (New York: New York University Press, 2010), 101; Nye quoted in https://www.senate.gov/artandhistory/history /minute/merchants_of_death.htm.

12. Millis, *Road to War*, 460 For an excellent study of the writings of historians critical of U.S. entry during the 1920s and '30s, see Warren I. Cohen, *The American Revisionists: The Lessons of Intervention in World War I* (Chicago: University of Chicago Press, 1967).

13. Remarque, *All Quiet on the Western Front*, trans. A.W. Wheen (New York: Fawcett Crest Ballantine, 1982 [1928]), 194; Andrew Delbanco, "The Civil War Convulsion," *New York Review of Books*, March 19, 2015, 33.

14. *The Gallup Poll: Public Opinion, 1935–1971*, vol. 1 (New York: Random House, 1972), 54.

15. Quoted in Unger, *Fighting Bob La Follette*, 258.

16. Quoted in ibid., 285, 284.

17. La Follette, undated but 1923, quoted in Drake, *Education of an Anti-Imperialist*, 405.

18. Quote from RML, vol. 2, 1144.

19. WP, April 10, 1920. The resolution that passed formally ended U.S.

hostilities with Germany—but without agreeing to the treaty that established the League of Nations.

20. WP, June 2, 1923.

21. Quoted in Eastman, *Love and Revolution*, 504. For a healthy sample of her postwar writings, see *Crystal Eastman on Women and Revolution*, ed. Blanche Wiesen Cook (New York: Oxford University Press, 1978).

22. Hillquit, *Loose Leaves*, 329-330.

23. Hillquit made this damning comment about the USSR during a debate in 1928. Quoted in Pratt, *Morris Hillquit*, 239.

24. Kirchwey, *Nation*, August 4, 1928.

25. Samuel Eliot Morrison and Henry Steele Commager, *The Growth of the American Republic*, vol. 2 (New York: Oxford University Press, 1962), 564. This was the textbook assigned in my advanced placement class in U.S. history in 1965.

26. Lyndon Johnson, address at Johns Hopkins University, April 7, 1965. http://www.lbjlib.utexas.edu/johnson/archives.hom/speeches.hom/650407.asp. In 1967, the historian Barbara Tuchman, a relative of mine, compared the U.S. intervention in Vietnam with that in World War I. "How We Entered World War I," in Tuchman, *Practicing History: Selected Essays* (New York: Knopf, 1981), 158-172.

27. WP, Jan. 16, 1968, C1; Edwin Starr, "War," lyrics at http://www.metrolyrics.com/war-lyrics-edwin-starr.html.

28. Philip Caputo, *A Rumor of War* (New York: Henry Holt and Company, 1996), 347-348.

29. http://blogs.wsj.com/dispatch/2013/03/18/full-text-of-president-george-w-bushs-speech-march-19-2003/.

30. Michael Walzer, "A Foreign Policy for the Left," *Dissent* (Spring 2014), 17; Bourne, "War Diary," *Seven Arts*, September 1917: http://fair-use.org/seven-arts/1917/09/a-war-diary. On the growing popularity of "isolationist" views, see Nichols, *Promise and Peril*, 343.

31. Larry Schweikart and David Dougherty, *A Patriot's History of the Modern World: From America's Exceptional Ascent to the Atomic Bomb, 1898-1945* (New York: Sentinel, 2012), 114, 124; Oliver Stone and Peter Kuznick, *The Untold History of the United States* (New York: Gallery, 2012), 5, 13-14.

Also see the critical history by Burton Yale Pines, a former top official at the conservative Heritage Foundation: *America's Greatest Blunder: The Fateful Decision to Enter World War One* (New York: RSD Press, 2013).

32. William James, "The Moral Equivalent of War," widely available online.

33. Ebel, *Faith in the Fight*, 193.

34. However, see the controversial argument that the percentage of humans killed in war diminished over the course of the twentieth century in Stephen Pinker, *The Better Angels of Our Nature: Why Violence Has Declined* (New York: Viking, 2011).

ACKNOWLEDGMENTS

1. Michael Wood, *Alfred Hitchcock: The Man Who Knew Too Much* (Boston: New Harvest/Houghton Mifflin Harcourt, 2015), 23.

GOOD READING

Here is a short list of the books (and one dissertation) that were indispensable to my understanding of the United States during World War I and of the Americans who sought to prevent their nation from fighting it.

ON THE UNITED STATES AND THE WAR

CHRISTOPHER CAPOZZOLA, *UNCLE SAM WANTS YOU: World War I and the Making of the Modern American Citizen*

JOHN MILTON COOPER, JR., *THE VANITY OF POWER: American Isolationism and World War I, 1914–1917*

JOHN MILTON COOPER, JR., *WOODROW WILSON: A Biography*

JOHN WHITECLAY CHAMBERS II, *TO RAISE AN ARMY: The Draft Comes to Modern America*

KATHLEEN DALTON, *THEODORE ROOSEVELT: A Strenuous Life*

JUSTUS D. DOENECKE, *NOTHING LESS THAN WAR: A New History of America's Entry into World War I*

REINHARD R. DOERRIES, *IMPERIAL CHALLENGE: Ambassador Count Bernstorff and German American Relations, 1908–1917*

JONATHAN H. EBEL, *FAITH IN THE FIGHT: Religion and the American Soldier in the Great War*

JOHN PATRICK FINNEGAN, *AGAINST THE SPECTER OF A DRAGON: The Campaign for Military Preparedness, 1914–1917*

JENNIFER D. KEENE, *DOUGHBOYS, THE GREAT WAR, AND THE REMAKING OF AMERICA*

JEANETTE KEITH, *RICH MAN'S WAR, POOR MAN'S FIGHT: Race, Class, and Power in the Rural South during the First World War*

DAVID M. KENNEDY, *OVER HERE: The First World War and American Society*

THOMAS KNOCK, *TO END ALL WARS: Woodrow Wilson and the Quest for a New World Order*

ADRIANE LENTZ-SMITH, *FREEDOM STRUGGLES: African Americans and World War I*

ARTHUR S. LINK, *WILSON: The Struggle for Neutrality*; *WILSON: Confusions and Crises*; *WILSON: Campaigns for Progressivism and Peace*

ERNEST R. MAY, *THE WORLD WAR AND AMERICAN ISOLATION, 1914–1917*

JOSEPH A. MCCARTIN, *LABOR'S GREAT WAR: The Struggle for Industrial Democracy and the Origins of Modern American Labor Relations, 1912–1921*

ANDREW PRESTON, *SWORD OF THE SPIRIT, SHIELD OF FAITH: Religion in American War and Diplomacy*

RICHARD SLOTKIN, *LOST BATTALIONS: The Great War and the Crisis of American Nationality*

ROBERT W. TUCKER, *WOODROW WILSON AND THE GREAT WAR*

ON THE U.S. OPPONENTS OF THE WAR

HARRIET HYMAN ALONSO, *PEACE AS A WOMEN'S ISSUE: A History of the U.S. Movement for World Peace and Women's Rights*

ALEX MATTHEWS ARNETT, *CLAUDE KITCHIN AND THE WILSON WAR POLICIES*

ERNEST C. BOLT, JR., *BALLOTS BEFORE BULLETS: The War Referendum Approach to Peace in America, 1914–1941*

WARREN I. COHEN, *THE AMERICAN REVISIONISTS: The Lessons of Intervention in World War I*

BLANCHE WIESEN COOK, "WOODROW WILSON AND THE ANTIMILITARISTS, 1914–1917," PHD DISSERTATION, JOHN HOPKINS UNIVERSITY, 1970

ROBERT C. COTTRELL, *ROGER NASH BALDWIN AND THE AMERICAN CIVIL LIBERTIES UNION*

MARIE LOUISE DEGEN, *THE HISTORY OF THE WOMAN'S PEACE PARTY*

RICHARD DRAKE, *THE EDUCATION OF AN ANTI-IMPERIALIST:* Robert La Follette and U.S. Expansion

FRANCES H. EARLY, *A WORLD WITHOUT WAR:* How U.S. Feminists and Pacifists Resisted World War I

STEPHEN R. FOX, *THE GUARDIAN OF BOSTON:* William Monroe Trotter

FRANK L. GRUBBS, JR., *THE STRUGGLE FOR LABOR LOYALTY:* Gompers, the A.F. of L. and the Pacifists

ROBERT DAVID JOHNSON, *THE PEACE PROGRESSIVES AND AMERICAN FOREIGN RELATIONS*

LOUISE W. KNIGHT, *JANE ADDAMS:* Spirit in Action

BARBARA S. KRAFT, *THE PEACE SHIP:* Henry Ford's Pacifist Adventure in the First World War

SIMEON LARSON, *LABOR AND FOREIGN POLICY:* Gompers, the AFL, and the First World War, 1914–1918

CHRISTOPHER LASCH, *THE AMERICAN LIBERALS AND THE RUSSIAN REVOLUTION*

C. ROLAND MARCHAND, *THE AMERICAN PEACE MOVEMENT AND SOCIAL REFORM, 1898–1918*

CHRISTOPHER MCKNIGHT NICHOLS, *PROMISE AND PERIL:* America at the Dawn of a Global Age

DAVID S. PATTERSON, *THE SEARCH FOR NEGOTIATED PEACE:* Women's Activism and Citizen Diplomacy in World War I

H.C. PETERSON AND GILBERT C. FITE, *OPPONENTS OF WAR, 1917–1918*

NORMA FAIN PRATT, *MORRIS HILLQUIT:* A Political History of an American Jewish Socialist

DUANE C.S. STOLTZFUS, *PACIFISTS IN CHAINS:* The Persecution of Hutterites During the Great War

LOUISA THOMAS, *CONSCIENCE:* Two Soldiers, Two Pacifists, One Family—A Test of Will and Faith in World War I

NANCY C. UNGER, *FIGHTING BOB LA FOLLETTE:* The Righteous Reformer

JAMES WEINSTEIN, *THE DECLINE OF SOCIALISM IN AMERICA, 1912–1925*

ILLUSTRATION CREDITS

P. 83: Courtesy of Amy Aronson.

14. Public domain. Originally published in the *Masses*, 1916.
15. Public domain. Originally published in the *Masses*, 1916.
16. Public domain. Originally published in the *Masses*, 1916.
17. Artist: Lute Pease. Courtesy of the Library of Congress.
18. Photographer: C. T. Chapman. Courtesy of the Library of Congress.

INSERT 2

1. Harris and Ewing. Courtesy of the Library of Congress.
2. Bain Collection, Library of Congress.
3. Courtesy of the Library of Congress.
4. Bain Collection, Library of Congress.
5. Baldwin Papers, Princeton University.
6. Cartoonist: W. A. Rogers, the *New York Herald*. Courtesy of the Library of Congress.
7. Illustration by Rollin Kirby. Courtesy of the Library of Congress.
8. Photographer unknown, 1911. Courtesy of the Library of Congress.
9. Schomburg Collection, New York Public Library.
10. Public domain. Illustration by George Bellows in the *Masses*, July 1917.
11. Poster by Arthur William Colen, June 1917. Courtesy of the Library of Congress.
12. Public domain.
13. Photographer unknown, c. 1900. Courtesy of the Bain Collection, Library of Congress.
14. Photograph by Arnold Genthe, 1916. Courtesy of the Library of Congress.
15. Underwood and Underwood. Courtesy of the Library of Congress.
16. Photographer unknown. Courtesy of the Library of Congress.
17. Harris and Ewing. Courtesy of the Library of Congress.
18. Photograph by Alice Boughton, 1907. Courtesy of the New York Public Library.
19. Poster by the Committee to Help Unsell the War, 1971. Courtesy of the Library of Congress.

INDEX

abolitionism, 4, 9, 96
Adams, H. R., 170
Adams, John, 189
Adamson Act, 115, 125, 132
Addams, Jane, xiii, xiv, 2, 4–5, 10–11, 38,
    48–56, 76, 84, 93, 98, 100, 122, 123, 124,
    127–28, 136, 155, 157, 160, 176, 193,
    200, 243, 279, 283, 284, 286, 310n, 319n,
    322n
  European peace tour of, 66–69, 75
  on Fourteen Points, 248, 249
  on internationalism, 189–90
  Nobel Peace Prize awarded to, 279, 355n
  Peace Ship and, 71, 72, 73
  Woman's International Congress and, 140,
    215
  Woman's Peace Party and, 39–42, 45–48
Afghanistan, war in, 288, 291
African Americans, 18, 188, 354n
  draft evasion by, 211, 231
  Socialism and, 233–34, 239, 256–58
  voting and, 30, 92, 126
  in WCU, 207–8
  in WWI, 188, 191, 229–34, 256–60, 263,
    265–66, 351n
Allies, xv, 5, 22, 25, 27, 28, 103, 108, 129, 137,
    138, 139, 144, 147, 165, 216, 249
  American attitude toward, 60–62, 77, 88,
    100–101, 104, 110, 113, 116, 148, 156,
    162, 181, 182
  battle of the Somme and, 144–45
  Germany's surrender and, 267–68

  League of Nations and, 277
  trade with, 139
  Treaty of Versailles and, 273
  war loans defaulted by, 279
All Quiet on the Western Front (Remarque),
    280–81
American Civil Liberties Union (ACLU),
    xviii, 78, 285
American Expeditionary Force (AEF), xv
  African-American soldiers in, 263, 265–66,
    352n
  impact of, on Great War, 260–67, 351n
American Federation of Labor (AFL), 12, 13,
    88–90, 135, 174, 219, 250, 283
American Neutral Conference Committee
    (ANCC), 136–37
American Peace Society, 2, 6–7
American Protective League (APL), 209–10
American Rights Committee, 62, 175
American Union Against Militarism
    (AUAM), xii, 79–85, 90, 92, 93, 101,
    108–10, 112, 119, 120, 124, 134, 148,
    149, 150, 154–55, 176, 208, 214, 235,
    243–44
  as Anti-"Preparedness" Committee, 90,
    95, 322n
  conscription opposed by, 198, 200, 203–5
  departures from, 193–95
  Hensley amendment and, 136
  Mexican conflict and, 116
  National Defense Act opposed by, 117
  referendum promoted by, 152–53

Anarchist Exclusion Act, 206
anarchists, 206, 254, 348n
Angell, Norman, 8, 10, 45, 85
anti-militarism, anti-militarists, xi–xv, xvii–
    xix, 13, 28–29, 62, 85, 127, 164, 242, 275,
    287–88
    arguments against preparedness by, 63–64
anti-Semitism, 22
anti-trust laws, 94
arbitration, 39, 149
Arlington National Cemetery, 280
armed neutrality, 162–74, 182–83, 184
Armistice, xvi–xvii, 87, 242, 265, 268, 271,
    276
arms embargo, proposed, 26–27
Army, U.S., 240, 245
    conscription and, 2, 28, 93, 117
    "preparedness" and size of, xii–xiii, 23, 35–
        36, 62–63, 80, 89, 94, 97–98, 117, 126
    segregation in, 231
Arnold, Nathan, 170
Asquith, Herbert, 51
Associated Press (AP), 227, 229
Association for International Conciliation,
    2, 3
Atherton, Gertrude, 19
Atlantic Ocean, xiv, 20, 25, 56, 67, 104, 162,
    172, 174, 180
Augspurg, Anita, 52
Australia, conscription vote in, 197
Austria, 274
Austria-Hungary, xi, 21, 51, 52, 67, 102, 140,
    186, 247, 267, 312n
    anti-war feeling in, 250

Bailey, Hannah Johnston, 9
Baker, Newton D., 93, 199
balance-of-power diplomacy, 140
Balch, Emily, 54, 55, 71, 148, 149, 279
Baldwin, Roger, 78, 205, 242, 253–57,
    350n–51n
Balkan war of 1912, 6, 8
Balkan war of 1913, 6, 8
Baltimore Sun, 135
Bannwart, Alexander, 179, 337n
Barnes, William, 133
Baruch, Bernard, 28
"Battle Cry of Mothers, The" (Morgan), 50,
    55–56
Beard, Mary, 19
Belarus, 249, 251
Belgium, 8, 51, 52, 199, 229–30, 274
    German invasion of, 22
    trenches of, xvii

Benedict, Wallace, 78–79
Benedict XV, Pope, 66
Benson, Allan, 81, 125, 127, 133, 328n
Berger, Victor, 87, 125, 215, 272
Berle, A. A., 109
Berlin, 66, 107, 111, 184, 219
Bernstorff, Johann von, Count, 26, 56, 107,
    135–36, 145, 161
Bethmann-Hollweg, Theobald von, 66, 145
Blatch, Harriot Stanton, 19
Boissevain, Inez Milholland, 72
Bolshevik Party, xvi, 240, 243, 247, 248, 251,
    252, 262, 270, 274, 351n
Borah, William, 277
Boston, Mass., 195, 197
Bourne, Randolph, xv, 187, 190, 195–96, 207,
    222, 235, 287, 289
    on American promise, 193
Brandeis, Louis, 70, 115, 128
Breckinridge, Sophonisba, 50
Brest-Litovsk, Treaty of, 249, 251
Briand, Aristide, 280
Brill, Abraham A., 79
British Empire, 144, 182, 197, 247–48, 277
Bryan, William Jennings, 14–15, 84, 100,
    113–14, 127, 138, 152, 173, 185, 227,
    242, 312n, 324n, 332n–33n
    as agrarian populist, 124
    as anti-militarist, 24–25, 29, 104, 105,
        107–8, 137, 149, 153
    influence of, in 1916 campaign, 94–95,
        133
    Kitchin's collaboration with, 94–95
    Peace Ship and, 72
    as presidential candidate, 30, 94
    resignation as secretary of state by, 63, 94,
        139
    as secretary of state, 24–25, 45, 46, 47, 226
    in wartime, 195–96
Buckley, William F., Jr., 192, 340n
Bureau of Investigation, xviii, 209, 232, 255,
    256, 257–58
Burleson, Albert, 173, 246, 253
Burnquist, Joseph, 221, 227
Bush, George W., 288
businessmen, 8
    peace supported by, 5, 7
Business Men's League, 237
Butler, Nicholas Murray, 355n

California, 9, 132–34
Calkins, Franklin, 175
Camp Logan riot, 231–32
Camp Upton, 236–37

Canada, 51, 160
  conscription in, 197, 202
capitalists, capitalism, 11, 13, 35, 71, 81, 86,
  156, 180, 239, 252, 278, 280, 283, 289
Carnegie, Andrew, 4, 10, 76, 89, 163, 311*n*
  endowment given by, 2, 6–7
  1907 Peace Conference organized by, 13
  on outbreak of war, 19
Carnegie, Louise, 19, 50
Carnegie Endowment, 2, 7, 10, 355*n*
  Woman's Peace Party and, 45
Carnegie Hall, 32–39, 67, 86, 91
Catt, Carrie Chapman, 19, 41, 46, 50, 159, 176
censorship, 272, 323*n*, 334*n*
  military, 263–64
  by post office, 194, 243, 246–47, 254–55
Central Powers, 5, 22, 113, 137, 139, 165, 186,
  246
  Petrograd Soviet and, 216
Cherokee County, Ga., 211–12
Chicago, Ill., 39, 40, 42, 90, 124, 150, 174, 194,
  221–22, 239, 252, 258
Chicago, University of, 99
child labor, 115
Children's Bureau, 160
China, 332*n*
  Japanese invasion of, xvi, 281
Chomsky, Noam, 287
Christianity:
  pacifism and, 204–5
  see also Protestants; Roman Catholicism
Churchill, Winston, 8
civil liberties, 176, 276
civil rights, 28, 258, 290, 292
Civil War, U.S., 9, 47, 114, 123, 147, 166, 197,
  200, 271, 308*n*
Clark, Champ, 105, 202, 203
Clark, John Bates, 7–8, 309*n*
Clay, Henry, 228
Cobb, Frank, 173
Cohan, George M., 260
College League of Common Sense, 67
Collier's, 72
Cologne, 108
Columbia University, 6, 162, 176, 227, 253,
  355*n*
Commager, Henry Steele, 287
Commission on Industrial Relations, 34
Committee for Democratic Control, 152, 154
Committee on Public Information (CPI),
  188–89, 264, 339*n*
Communism, 287
  Red Scare and, 278–79
Communist Labor Party, 278

Communist Manifesto (Marx and Engels), 11
Confederate Army, 29
Conference for Progressive Political Action
  (CPPA), 282–83
Conference of Oppressed or Dependent
  Nationalities, 136
Congo, 229
Congress, U.S., xii, 23, 29, 44, 60, 115, 164,
  237
  anti-war members of, 242, 243, 244, 354*n*
  Conscription Act in, 202–3
  declaration of war in, xiii, xiv–xv, 1, 155,
  173–74, 179–86, 200, 223, 280
  Great War ended by, 355–56*n*
  lead-up to war in, 161–71
  neutrality of, before WWII, 281
  peace process and, 269–70
  preparedness and, 15, 65, 90–109, 117–18,
  120, 160, 260, 269
conscientious objectors (COs), 198, 203, 206,
  254, 266
conscription, 138, 167, 186, 191, 197–212,
  223, 237, 242, 254, 283, 334*n*
  campaign against, 202, 203–4
  pacifists and, 191
  see also draft resisters
conservatives, 8, 192, 289, 292, 340*n*
  on Great War, 290
Constitution, U.S., 106, 167
  First Amendment to, 191, 228, 253–54, 256
  Fourth Amendment to, 253
  Nineteenth Amendment to, 239
  Second Amendment to, 206
  Thirteenth Amendment to, 205
  Twentieth Amendment to, 138
Continental Army, U.S., 77, 91, 93
"Continuous Mediation Without Armistice"
  (Wales), 43–44, 48
Coolidge, Calvin, 283
Cooper, John Milton, Jr., 177
Cooper Union, 81, 116
corporate taxes, 225, 244, 272
corporations:
  excessive power of, xiv, 5
  war profits of, 191
Creel, George, 188, 219, 221
Croly, Herbert, 77, 196
Cuba, 1, 353*n*

Daniels, Josephus, 104, 171, 173, 327*n*
Daughters of the American Revolution, 39
Davis, Richard Harding, 68
Debs, Eugene V., 12–13, 133–34, 170, 246–47,
  248, 252, 257, 266, 279

Delbanco, Andrew, 280–81
democracy, 5, 87, 149, 154, 182, 185, 190, 193,
    217, 247, 248, 259, 279, 282, 287
  industrial, 189
  socialism and, 33
Democratic National Convention, of 1916,
    113–14
Democratic Party, 27, 28, 59, 90, 91, 96, 105,
    117, 128, 130, 131, 138, 163, 169, 181,
    182, 183, 185, 198, 201, 228, 292
  anti-militarism in, xii, 14–15, 29, 94–95,
    112, 122, 124, 139
  businessmen opposed by, 30–31
  military finance and, 161
  as minority party, 123–24
  in 1918 election, 268–73
  progressives in, 5, 15, 119, 268
  Southern, xii, 26, 29, 31, 92, 94, 123–24,
    126, 153, 200, 231, 284
  TR and, 15
Detroit Free Press, 53
Dewey, John, 70, 129, 176, 196, 243, 289
Dies, Martin, 91
Dodd, William, 99
Dos Passos, John, 263, 308*n*
"Do You Advocate Peace or War" (Kitchin
    and Bryan), 94–95
draft, *see* conscription
Draft Registration Day, 208
draft resisters, 207, 208–12, 231, 232–33, 255,
    343*n*
Du Bois, W.E.B., 230–31, 259, 265, 283

Eastman, Annis, 41, 79
Eastman, Crystal, xiii, 39, 41, 64, 69, 77, 92,
    98, 109–10, 115–17, 124, 132, 148, 163,
    214, 216, 222, 235, 238, 261, 277, 288,
    307*n*, 324*n*, 334*n*, 346*n*–47*n*, 350*n*, 353*n*
  at AUAM, 79–82, 95, 110, 112, 120–23,
    152, 191, 194, 204, 333*n*
  background and activism of, 78–80, 84
  death of, 282, 284, 286
  at *Liberator,* 251–53
  at National Civil Liberties Bureau, 243
  on 1916 elections, 135, 185
  on 1918 elections, 273
  Peace Ship and, 71, 73
  in postwar politics, 284–85
  pregnancy and childbirth of, 158–59, 160
  "Truth about Preparedness" campaign of, 159
  at Woman's Peace Party, 45, 79, 81, 85–86,
    123, 191, 195, 322*n*, 333*n*, 335*n*
  on Zimmermann Telegram, 165

Eastman, Max, xi, 79, 81, 109–11, 146, 148,
    160, 190, 196, 213, 243, 246–49, 251–53,
    266, 285
  Bolsheviks supported by, 270
  on conscription, 198
  and 1916 election, 125
East St. Louis, Ill., 232, 250
Ebel, Jonathan H., 291, 308*n*
Edison, Thomas Alva, 28, 70
elections:
  of 1832, 123
  of 1852, 123
  of 1896, 30
  of 1900, 14, 30
  of 1904, 28
  of 1906, 15, 129
  of 1908, 30, 129
  of 1912, 9, 11, 15, 28, 85, 93, 115, 133, 235,
    266, 272, 310*n*
  of 1914, 31
  of 1916, 95, 108, 113–16, 120, 122, 123–37,
    149, 150, 181, 183, 266, 270, 282, 328*n*,
    329*n*, 330*n*
  of 1917, 191, 234–40
  of 1918, 268–74, 283
  of 1920, 279
  of 1922, 279, 282, 355*n*
  of 1924, 282–83, 285
  of 1932, 285
Emergency Peace Federation, 149, 152, 163,
    170, 176
Engels, Friedrich, 11
England, 66, 68, 88, 284
Equal Rights Amendment, 284
Espionage Act of 1917, xviii, 79, 188–89, 190,
    194, 205, 223, 225, 227, 236, 245–46,
    247, 257, 339*n*, 348*n*
Europe, 3, 162, 252
  Great War and collective memory of, xvii
  House in, 48, 56
  manufacturing centers of, 250

Farewell to Arms, A (Hemingway), xvii, 280
farm loans, 115
Federal Bureau of Investigation (FBI), xviii,
    209, 255
Federal Council of Churches, 100, 204
Federal Reserve Board, 201
feminism, xii, xiii, xiv, 5, 40, 78, 183–84, 214,
    284, 286, 292, 324*n*
  anti-militarism in, 9–10, 11, 63
  division in, 159
  in European peace tour, 66–69

International Women's Congress and, 53–54
   motherhood and, 20, 38, 40, 55–56
   peace movement and, 20, 287
"Fighting Issues, The" (Kellogg), 150–51
Finland, 49, 156
Fletcher, Ben, 259, 351n
Ford, Clara, 69, 70, 73, 75
Ford, Henry, xiv, 58, 69, 98, 127–28, 164, 184,
   242, 271
   anti-Semitism of, 319n–20n
   Peace Ship of, 70–76, 214, 215
   presidential primaries won by, 120
Four Lights, 159–60, 195
Fourteen Points, 247–53, 277
France, xv, 21, 51, 68, 108, 111, 140, 197, 199,
   200, 240, 260, 262, 263, 272, 274, 280,
   336n
   American Expeditionary Force in, xv,
     265–66
   anti-war strikes in, 250
   empire of, 144, 247, 277
   feminists in, 49
   Socialists in, 215, 248
   Taft's arbitration treaty with, 6–7
   as trading partner, 24–25
   trenches of, xvii
   Wilson's arrival in, 276–77
France, Anatole, 144, 331n
Freeman, Elisabeth, 250
Frick, Henry Clay, 28
Friends of Irish Freedom, 102, 152
Fuller, Jeffrey, 158, 284
Fuller, Walter, 80, 82, 152–53, 284, 322n

Gardner, Augustus Peabody, 17, 55, 62, 115,
   117, 124, 139, 181
   in Carnegie Hall debate, 33, 35–37, 86, 91
Garrison, William Lloyd, 18, 125, 251
Gerard, James W., 253–54
German-American Alliance, 152, 313n
German-Americans, 20, 25–27, 95, 101, 114,
   128–29, 164, 166, 184, 253, 337n
German Social-Democratic Party (SPD),
   11–12
Germany, xi, xviii, 11–12, 36, 37, 47, 51, 56,
   62–63, 64, 66, 68, 100, 108, 120, 139,
   140, 160, 177, 182, 189, 190, 197, 198,
   200, 204, 227, 240, 244, 246, 247, 259,
   267, 274, 282, 312n
   anti-war feeling in, 172, 215, 250
   attacks on nonmilitary vessels by, 59–63,
     103–9, 144–45, 161–72, 174, 180, 182,
     184

Belgium invaded by, 22, 229–30
   brutal settlement on, 271
   declaration of war against, 186
   diplomatic ties severed with, 147–52, 154,
     161
   feminists in, 49, 51, 52
   leftists in, 33
   Lusitania sunk by, see Lusitania
   militarism in, 8
   Operation Michael of, 261
   peace sought by, 267–69
   public opinion against, 100–101
   trade impossible with, 24–25
   Wilson's opinion of, 23
   Zimmermann Telegram and, 164–65
Germany, Nazi, xvi, 99, 276, 286
   militarization of, 281
Germany, Weimar, bankruptcy of, xv
Germer, Adolph, 89–90
Gilman, Charlotte Perkins, 19, 38
Glynn, Martin H., 113–14
Goldman, Emma, 206, 253, 254, 256
Gompers, Samuel, 13–14, 34, 88–90, 125, 135,
   198, 236
   war supported by, 174, 219, 323n
Gore, Thomas P., 105–6, 151
Great Britain, xv, 21, 51, 56, 108, 140, 182,
   200, 260, 263, 274
   anti-war groups in, 45
   armaments of, 262
   armed forces of, 21
   conscription in, 111, 197–98
   feminists in, 49
   German attacks on nonmilitary vessels of,
     59–63, 103–9, 144–45
   Irish-American opposition to, 14, 22,
     101–2
   Labour Party in, 215
   parliamentary government in, 22–23
   Taft's arbitration treaty with, 6–7
   as trading partner, 24–25
Great Depression, 276
Great Illusion, The (Angell), 8
Great War:
   AEF's impact on, 260–67, 351n
   death toll in, xii
   draft resisters in, 209
   foreign trade and, 23, 24
   as forgotten war, xvi–xvii, 280, 308n
   imperialism and, 216
   origins of, xii
   outbreak of, 18–19
   profiting from, 23

Great War (cont.)
    revisionism and, 280, 281, 286–87,
        289–90
    and subsequent wars, 276
    Vietnam War and, 287–88
    Western front in, 111
Grey, Edward, 66, 104
Griffith, D. W., 323n
Grimké, Archibald, 232–33
Grimké, Francis, 232–33
Gronna, Asle, 168–69, 182–83
"Group of Letters from Women of the
    Warring Nations," 45
Guest, Edgar, 73–74

Hague, The:
    1899 peace conference at, 5–6, 10, 13
    International Congress of Women at,
        48–56, 67, 69, 215
    Socialist International in, 140
    World Court at, 5
Haiti, American troops in, 122
Hallinan, Charles T., 84, 121, 187, 244, 348n
Hamer, Eugénie, 52, 53
Hamilton, Alice, 50, 53, 319n
Hanna, Louis B., 72, 74
Hanna, Mark, 89
Harding, Warren G., 153
Harlem, N.Y., 129–31, 233, 238–39, 274
Harvard Law School, 266
Harvard University, 6, 10, 35, 176, 231, 254
Hayden, Carl, 117
Hayes, Carleton J. H., 162, 164, 333n
Hays, Will, 268–71
Haywood, Big Bill, 87, 252, 255, 351n
Hearst, William Randolph, 19, 23, 127, 184
Hearst newspapers, 118, 201, 237, 282
Hemingway, Ernest, xvii, 280
Hensley, Walter, 118, 120
Hexamer, Charles John, 26, 27
Hillquit, Morris, xiii, xiv, 18, 46, 54, 69, 71,
        76, 115–16, 123, 136, 241, 252, 274, 278,
        285, 314n, 315n, 356n
    in Carnegie Hall debate, 33–38, 86, 91
    death of, 282
    on Fourteen Points, 248, 249
    New York mayoral campaigns of, 191,
        234–40, 285, 346n–47n
    in 1916 Congressional election, 129–31,
        237, 329n
    in 1918 election, 270, 272–73
    and People's Council, 217, 220–21
    in response to impending war, 156–58

in SPA, 86–87
    at SPA emergency conference, 212–14
    Wilson criticized by, 108
Hillquit, Vera, 33
Hindenburg, Paul von, 262
Hitler, Adolf, xv–xvi, 99, 111
Hofstadter, Richard, 123
Holocaust, 286
Holt, Hamilton, 71, 84, 85–86, 136
Hoover, Herbert, 195
House, Edward, 23, 48, 56, 70–71, 103–4, 107,
        330n, 354n
House of Commons, British, 137
House of Representatives, U.S., 30, 31, 35,
        106, 115, 138–39, 153
    anti-militarists in, xiii, 94, 115–16
    declaration of war in, 183–84
    Education Committee of, 323n
    Foreign Affairs Committee of, 105, 153
    Military Affairs Committee of, 92–93, 94, 201
    in 1918 election, 271
    Rankin as first woman in, 134
    Socialists in, 129
    Ways and Means Committee of, 31–32,
        118–19, 224, 244
Houston, Tex., uprising in, 232, 259, 265
Howells, William Dean, 70
Hughes, Charles Evans, 78, 115, 120, 129,
        131–33, 185–86, 328n
Hull, William, 4, 6, 15–16, 84, 85
Hungary, 51, 53, 250
Hutterites, 207
Hylan, John, 237, 238

"I Didn't Raise My Boy to Be a Soldier"
    (song), 38–39, 134
immigrants, 114, 129, 136, 189, 246
    radical, 157, 213
    Russian, 156
    as Socialists, 158
income tax, 94, 119, 210, 324n
Independent Social-Democratic Party
    (USPD), German, 142, 215
industrialists, 89, 98, 119, 185
    military spending and, 15, 27
Industrial Workers of the World (IWW), 12,
        208, 246, 250, 252, 254, 255–56, 258,
        259, 348n, 351n
influenza epidemic of 1918, 352n
International Congress of Women, 48–56,
        67, 69
internationalism, 20, 47, 135, 149, 160, 163,
        188–90, 248

International Ladies' Garment Workers'
Union (ILGWU), 88, 214, 235
International Women's Day, 54
interventionists, interventionism, 147, 148,
161, 177, 181, 184
Iraq War, xvi, 188, 288, 291
Ireland, Easter Rising in, 102
Irish-Americans, 14, 22, 27, 63, 101–2, 114,
129, 131, 235, 313n, 335n
in New York City draft riots, 197
isolationism, 20, 184, 287, 289–90, 307n
anti-militarism vs., xiv
anti-preparedness vs., 95
Italy, xvi, 250, 274, 282
empire of, 144, 277
Ethiopia conquered by, 281

Jackson, Andrew, 123, 124
Jacobs, Aletta, 49, 50
James, Ollie, 113, 169
James, William, 1–4, 8, 10, 37, 267, 290–92
Japan, 36, 37, 64, 198, 332n
attack on Pearl Harbor by, 59, 286
China invaded by, xvi, 281
in World War II!, 276
Zimmermann Telegram and, 164–65
Jefferson, Thomas, 14, 127, 182
Jews, 22, 67, 84, 115, 201, 217, 234, 237, 238,
319n–20n
anti-war, 100
Hillquit as, 33, 34
Jim Crow laws, xiv, 92, 96, 230, 231–32, 258,
259
Johnson, Hiram, 133, 209, 225
Johnson, James Weldon, 229, 259
Johnson, Lyndon, 287
Jones, Mary Harris "Mother," 125
Jordan, David Starr, 71, 176, 179, 214, 222
J.P. Morgan & Co., 6, 24, 25, 168, 207
Justice Department, U.S., 209, 211, 232, 236,
246, 255, 257, 272

Kahn, Julius, 202
Kautsky, Karl, 33
Keegan, John, 261, 276
Keep Out of War Committee, 152
Keith, Jeanette, 210–11
Keller, Helen, 86, 125, 250–51, 283
Kellogg, Frank, 280
Kellogg, Paul, 79, 84, 109, 123–24, 148,
150–51, 155, 160, 164, 242, 332n–33n,
340n, 350n
pacifism abandoned by, 193–94

Kennedy, John F., 59–60
Kenyon, William, 95, 108
Keppel, Frederick, 253–55
Kirchwey, Freda, 286
Kitchin, Claude, 29, 63, 64, 84, 96, 134,
139, 153, 163, 175, 200–201, 216,
307n, 324n, 327n, 335n, 337n, 338n,
353n–54n
and battle against preparedness, 91–92,
94–95, 98–99, 100, 103, 104–7, 122,
161
and corporate taxes, 244–45, 283–84
death of, 282, 283
and declaration of war, 181–83, 185,
277–78
as House majority leader, 31–32, 91, 224
as House minority leader, 283, 285
National Defense Act and, 117–18
in 1916 election, 126–27
in 1918 election, 272
popularity of, 95, 98, 272
as populist, 29–31, 46, 289
Revenue Act and, 118–19, 223–24,
244–45
in wartime, 191–92, 244
woman suffrage and civil rights opposed
by, xiv, 29–30, 92, 230, 323n
Korean War, 291
Ku Klux Klan, 259

Labor Department, U.S., 99
labor movement, xii, 46, 63, 78, 115, 119, 132,
149, 170, 184, 198, 214, 242, 250–52,
274, 278–79, 328n
war protested by, 174–75
labor unions, xiii, 5, 9, 12–14, 28, 33, 89, 97,
125, 152, 278
Labour Party, British, 142, 215, 248
La Follette, Belle Case, 45–47, 97, 167,
226–27, 282
La Follette, Fola, 167, 214
La Follette, Robert, xiii, xiv, 15, 45, 63, 65, 70,
115, 139, 152, 153, 216, 235, 237, 248,
261, 273–74, 307n, 338n, 348n
in anti-preparedness movement, 95–97,
103, 106
and armed neutrality, 166–71, 174
arms embargo supported by, 26–27
conscription opposed by, 202, 203
death of, 282, 283
and declaration of war, 179, 181–83, 185,
223–24
influence of, 95, 285–86

La Follette, Robert (*cont.*)
   in 1916 election, 126–29, 135
   in 1922 election, 279, 282, 355*n*
   1924 presidential candidacy of, 282–83, 285
   NPL speech and attempt to expel, 225–29, 243, 244
   in wartime, 191–92
   and Wilson's war speech, 83, 179
La Follette, Robert, Jr., 169, 229, 244, 282
La Follette's Magazine, 84, 97, 167, 225
La Guardia, Fiorello, 185, 199–200, 273
Lane, Harry, 169, 182–83
Lansing, Robert, 64–65, 103–5, 107–8, 139, 145, 173, 216, 219, 330*n*–31*n*
Lasch, Christopher, 287
League of Nations, 270, 277
   American refusal of, 277–78, 283, 356*n*
   prototypes for, 43, 138, 141, 149, 243
league of neutral nations, proposed, 162, 163
League to Limit Armaments, 93
Lee, Robert E., 29
Lenin, Vladimir Ilyich, 12, 157, 213, 240, 248, 250, 251, 253
Leopold, King of Belgium, 229
Liberator, 243, 251–53, 259, 270, 273, 284
Liberty Bonds, 188, 233, 238, 244, 245
Liebknecht, Karl, 11
Lincoln, Abraham, 81, 228, 287
Lindbergh, Charles A., 153, 166
Link, Arthur, 24, 62, 104, 177, 337*n*
Lippman, Walter, 196
Literary Digest, 26, 28–29, 59, 97
Lloyd George, David, 139–40, 248, 250
Lochner, Louis, 40–41, 70–71, 73–76, 149, 214, 221, 242, 243
Lodge, Henry Cabot, 28, 32, 33, 62, 115, 122, 124, 127, 138, 139, 168, 199, 223, 224, 270
   League of Nations opposed by, 277
   on peace treaty, 269
   on Wilson's war speech, 179, 185, 337*n*
London, 24, 66, 104, 139, 165, 234
London, Meyer, 67, 87, 129, 166, 183, 272
Louisville Courier-Journal, 59
Lowden, Frank, 221–22
Ludendorff, Erich, 261–62, 267
Lusitania, 57, 59–63, 65–66, 68, 79, 86, 100, 103, 108, 116, 124–25, 144, 172, 180, 226–27, 229, 318*n*–19*n*
Luxemburg, Rosa, 54
lynching, 229, 230, 234, 257, 258

McAdoo, William Gibbs, 24, 224–25
McClure, Samuel S., 72, 74

McKellar, Kenneth, 201–2
McLemore, Jefferson, 104–6, 151
Macmillan, Chrystal, 49
Madison, James, 206
Madison Square Garden, 137, 149, 152, 216–18
Magnes, Judah L., 217–19, 222, 256
Malone, Dudley Field, 235–36
Mann, James R., 106, 139
manufacturing, 119
   war and profits for, 161
Marx, Karl, 11
Marxism, 212, 233, 234, 285
   on imperialism, 156
Marxists, 86, 89, 170
Masses, 79, 81, 110, 129, 160, 213, 243, 246–47, 249, 251–52
Maurer, James, 85, 87–88, 119, 214
Mead, Lucia Ames, 160, 195, 322*n*
Medal of Honor, 266, 353*n*
mediation, 47–48, 50, 54, 56, 88, 104, 148
   Peace Ship and, 73, 74
merchant marine, U.S., 23, 312*n*
   armed neutrality and, 162–74, 182–83, 184
Messenger, 233–34, 257–58
Meuse-Argonne, battle of, 262, 266–67
Mexican-American War, 188, 291
Mexico, 209
   hostilities with, 116–17, 120
   Zimmermann Telegram and, 164–65
Michigan, 69, 120, 271, 272
Midwest, xiii, 15, 26, 29, 94, 95, 106, 132, 153, 166, 184, 283
   agrarian, xii, 85, 184
   Socialists in, 272
   urban, 53, 124, 126, 184
militarism, isolation and, xiv
military censorship, 263–64
military intelligence, xviii, 255
military preparedness, 62–64, 85
   debate over, 32–38
Minneapolis, Minn., 90, 150, 220–21
Minnesota, 15, 227, 272
Mitchel, John, 22, 234, 237, 238–39
Mitchell, Clingman W., 126–27
Monroe Doctrine, 141
Moore, Thomas E., 245
"Moral Equivalent of War, The" (James), 1–4, 290–91
Morey, Lewis S., 116
Morgan, Angela, 50, 55–56
Morgan, J.P., 81, 94, 127, 157
Morgan, J.P., Jr., 24

munitions makers, tax on, 119
Mussolini, Benito, xvi
Muste, A. J., 288

Nation, 59, 84, 124, 271, 286
National American Woman Suffrage
  Association (NAWSA), 42
National Association for the Advancement of
  Colored People (NAACP), 42, 229–30,
  232, 258, 259
National Civil Liberties Bureau (NCLB), 205,
  243, 253–56
National Colored Liberty Congress, 258–59
National Defense Act, 117–18
National Equal Rights League, 230, 258–59
National German-American Alliance, 26
National Guard, U.S., 93, 117, 204, 211, 231
nationalism, 67, 151, 319n, 341n
National Peace Congress, 2
National Security League (NSL), 28–29, 62,
  64, 77, 101, 117, 121–22, 175, 198, 201,
  230, 260, 269
National Socialist Party (Nazis), xv–xvi
Native Americans, 36, 207
Navy, German, 91, 108, 144–45, 267
Navy, U.S., 181, 199
  proposed expansion of, 2, 14–15, 62–63,
    77, 80, 89, 94, 97–98, 118, 121, 126
Navy Department, U.S., 81, 171, 173
  shipbuilding and, 32
Navy League, 14, 62, 91, 110, 198, 201
Nearing, Scott, 222, 243, 256, 274
Netherlands, 51
neutrality, 177, 182, 192, 230
  conference on, 46, 52, 75–76
  Wilson and, see Wilson, Woodrow
New Deal, 278, 283
Newer Ideas of Peace (Addams), 10
New Republic, 72, 77, 196
New Willard Hotel, 39, 41–43, 69
New York, N.Y., 28, 69, 101, 121, 124, 149,
  175, 181, 216, 252
  anti-draft rallies in, 206
  AUAM in, 85
  draft riots in, 197, 204
  Hillquit's mayoral campaigns for, 191,
    234–40, 285, 346n–47n
  Trotsky in, 157–58
  Women's Peace Parade in, 18–22
New York Call, 20, 86
New Yorker, 264
New York Gaelic American, 131–32
New York Herald, 238
New York Journal, 19

New York Post, 84, 172, 239, 347n
New York State, 34, 78, 272, 322n
New York Times, 19–20, 53, 61–62, 68, 78, 81,
  128, 130, 148, 156, 161, 164, 179, 218,
  227, 238, 242–43, 279, 350n
New York World, 19, 22, 154–55, 173, 236,
  238, 271
Nicholas II, Tsar of Russsia, 5, 22, 158, 172
Nobel Peace Prize:
  of Addams, 279, 355n
  of Balch, 54
  of Roosevelt, 2
No-Conscription Fellowship (NCF), 197–98
No-Conscription League, 135, 204
Nonpartisan League (NPL), 225–29, 268,
  283
Norris, George, 15, 128, 167–68, 170, 180,
  182–83, 354n
North Atlantic, 24, 118
North Carolina, xiii, 21, 29, 30, 98, 99, 126,
  175, 245, 337n
North Dakota, 72, 133
North Sea, 21, 24, 51, 59, 162, 180, 267,
  317n
Norway, 49, 70, 75, 76, 279

Obama, Barack, 291
O'Reilly, Leonora, 19, 50
Orwell, George, 249
Oscar II, 70–76
Ottoman Empire, 247, 267
Outlook, 28
Owen, Chandler, 233–34, 239, 256–58

pacifists, pacifism, 63, 66, 76, 95, 191, 243,
  254, 279, 292
  Christianity and, 204–5
  definition of, 4–5, 10
  liberal, xiii
Page, Robert Newton, 21
Page, Walter Hines, 21, 22, 51, 165
Palmer, A. Mitchell, 278
Paris, xv, 21, 24, 66, 261
Pasternak, Boris, xvii
Paterson, N.J., 204
Patriot's History of the Modern World, A,
  289–90
Peace Congress of 1907, 13
Peace Day, 9, 45
peace movement:
  internationalism in, 20
  paternalism in, 19
Peace Ship, 70–76
Peace Week, 122

Pearl Harbor, 59, 286
Pennsylvania Federation of Labor, 85, 214
People's Council of America for Democracy
  and Peace (PCA), 214–23, 228, 235, 243,
  245, 250
Perkins, Frances, 19
Pershing, John J., 116, 260, 262, 264
Pethick-Lawrence, Emmeline, 39–40, 42, 48,
  79
Petrograd, 172, 222
Philippines, 1, 14, 30, 124, 152, 231
Pierce, Franklin, 123
Pinchot, Amos, 70, 109, 124, 176, 182, 235,
  271, 334n
  on Mexican conflict, 115
Poland, 21, 249, 274
populism, 29–31, 46, 69, 126, 203, 211
  referendum and, 154
Post, Alice Thatcher, 42, 50
postal authorities, anti-war activists punished
  by, 194, 243, 246–47, 254–55
preparedness, 32–38, 62–64, 74, 76, 85, 89,
  114, 119–23, 127, 134, 161, 185, 198,
  204, 224
  Congress on, 15, 65, 90–109, 117–18, 120,
  160, 260, 269
  industrial and financial interests and, 119
Presbyterians, 135, 204, 205, 233
press:
  African-American, 229–30, 258
  feminists opposed by, 68–69
  on foreign policy, 127–28
  La Follette criticized by, 227–29
  on Mexican conflict, 116
  Selective Service Act endorsed by, 201
  war and, 180
Princeton University, 28, 85, 99, 176, 205,
  337n
Progressive Era, 46
Progressive (Bull Moose) Party, 9, 11, 115,
  124, 133
Progressive Party (La Follette's), 282–83
progressives, xiv, 8, 119, 123, 161, 196, 227,
  242, 270, 286, 292
  anti-militarism and, xiii
  in Democratic Party, 5, 15, 119, 268
  lawmakers as, 5
  in New York City, 19
  referendum and, 154
  in Republican Party, 5, 15, 115, 119, 132,
  163, 182, 185
  wealthy, 33
  of Wilson, 115, 161

prohibition, 92
Protestants, 175, 232
  liberal anti-war, 63, 73, 99–101, 122, 214
  pro-war, 100–101, 204
Prussianism, 100, 151, 198, 252

Quakers, 4, 9, 84, 122, 204–5, 206

racism, 29–30, 289
Railroad Brotherhoods, 283
Randall, Charles, 183
Randolph, Asa Philip, 233–34, 239, 256–58,
  274, 288, 346n
Rankin, Jeannette, 134, 183, 288, 354n
Rauschenbusch, Walter, 101, 170
Red Scare, 278–79
Reed, John, 251, 253, 278
referendum, on war, 148–55
Remarque, Erich Maria, xvii, 280
Republican National Convention, of 1916,
  133
Republican Party, 26, 29, 31, 72, 89, 106, 108,
  128, 134, 138, 139, 180, 181, 185, 199,
  200, 272, 292
  anti-militarists in, xiii, 6, 15, 153
  conservatives in, 15, 96, 127, 163
  in 1916 election, 115, 130–33
  in 1918 election, 268–73
  in 1920 election, 279
  progressives in, 5, 15, 115, 119, 132, 163,
  182, 185
  support for war in, 153, 168, 185; see
  also Lodge, Henry Cabot; Roosevelt,
  Theodore
  war profiteers and, xiv, 15, 28, 224–45
  wealth in, 124, 133
Reserve Officers' Training Corps (ROTC),
  117
Revenue Act, 119
revenue bill, 126
Robinson, Joseph, 170, 228
Rochester, N.Y., 176, 239
Rockefeller, John D., 121, 245
Roman Catholicism, 313n
  attitudes toward war in, 101–2, 204
Roosevelt, Franklin D., 283, 286–87
Roosevelt, Theodore, xiii, 32, 68, 96, 127, 190,
  227, 246, 270, 271, 311n
  on Americanism, 189
  conscription supported by, 198, 199
  Fourteen Points condemned by, 249, 269
  Hillquit opposed by, 236–38
  on La Follette, 171

military intervention supported by, 28, 55, 124, 149, 160, 171
in 1912 election, 9, 11, 15, 28, 115, 133, 310n
in 1916 election, 115, 122, 124, 282
Nobel Peace Prize won by, 2
preparedness supported by, 2, 14–15, 36, 62, 93, 110, 117, 260
progressive domestic policies of, 15
on self-preservation, 1–2
on Wilson, 61, 114, 124, 132, 147, 185, 269
Woman's Peace Party opposed by, 47, 53
Ross, Harold, 264
Royal Navy, British, xii, 14, 24–25, 51, 57, 91, 165, 180, 267, 317n
Russell, Bertrand, 45, 112, 138, 198
Russell, Charles Edward, 155, 176, 234, 236–37, 254
Russia, 8, 12, 21, 51, 56, 140, 214, 217, 248, 253, 332n, 353n
  Bolsheviks in, xvi, 240, 243, 247, 248, 251, 252, 262, 270, 274, 351n
  Goldman and Berkman's deportation to, 206
  Jewish and Polish resistance to fighting for, 14
  Socialism in, 223
  surrender by, 219, 247, 249, 251, 262
  see also Soviet Union
Russian Revolution of 1905, 156
Russian Revolution of 1917, 172, 239–40, 270, 274

St. Louis, Mo., 174, 212
Saint Paul, Minn., 225–26
San Francisco, Calif., 89, 94, 120
Saranac Lake, 272–73, 274
Scandinavian-Americans, 22, 166, 184
Schlesinger, Benjamin, 214
Schneiderman, Rose, 19
Schurz, Carl, 152
Schwimmer, Rosika, 39–40, 42–43, 45, 48, 52–53, 319n–20n
  Peace Ship and, 70–71, 73–76
Second Amendment, 109
Second International, 33, 34
Sedition Act of 1918, xviii, 188, 245–46, 339n, 348n
Seldes, George, 262
Selective Service Act, 199, 203, 341n
  Supreme Court challenge to, 205–6
self-determination, 247, 248, 249, 277
  national, 87

Senate, U.S., 280
  anti-militarists in, xiii, 115
  armed neutrality in, 166–71
  Finance Committee of, 225
  Foreign Affairs Committee of, 167
  Foreign Relations Committee of, 46, 105, 137
  La Follette's filibuster in, 167–71
  Military Affairs Committee of, 92–93, 119, 201
  in 1918 election, 271
  Privileges and Elections Committee of, 228–29
  proceedings to expel La Follette in, 228–29
  war resolution in, 181–83
September 11, 2001, 288
Shaw, Anna Howard, 42, 50
Shelly, Rebecca, 137, 214, 217
Sherwood, Isaac, 91, 166, 181
shipping:
  Allied, 51, 59–60
  neutral, 50–51
  transatlantic halt in, 161–64
  U-boats in attacks on, see U-boats
Siberia, 270
Siegel, Isaac, 131, 181
Sinclair, Upton, 125, 212, 242
slavery, 4, 9
Social-Democrats, German, 87
Social Gospel, 100–101, 109, 170, 235
socialism, Socialists, xii, 3, 6, 8, 11, 14, 40, 46, 50, 63, 64, 67, 71, 75, 76, 79, 85, 95, 119, 127, 130, 149, 152, 232, 233, 236, 246, 248, 270
  African Americans and, 233–34, 239, 256–58
  democracy and, 33
  Fourteen Points and, 249
  Hillquit on, 34
  internationalism and, 11–12
  on potential intervention, 155–61
  pro-war, 155, 176
  Wilson supported by, 125
Socialist International, 140
Socialist (Second) International of 1907, 11–12, 13
Socialist Labor Party, 239
Socialist Party of America (SPA), xiii, xiv, 12–13, 28, 33, 36, 86, 125, 129–31, 133, 140, 152, 166, 251–52, 254, 258, 278, 283, 343n
  and anti-war movement, 86–90
  Committee on War and Militarism, 213

Socialist Party of America (SPA) (*cont.*)
  and Hillquit as NYC mayoral candidate of,
    191, 234–40, 285, 346*n*–47*n*
  in 1918 election, 270, 272–73
  Trotsky and, 157–58
  wartime emergency convention of,
    212–13
  Women's Committee of the, 39
Somme, battle of the, 111, 144
South, xii, 26, 29, 94, 210–12
Soviet of Workers and Soldiers, Petrograd,
    214–17, 222–23, 248, 251
Soviet Union, 158, 276, 282, 285, 356*n*
Spanish-American War, 1, 30, 35, 114, 291
Spanish Civil War, 281
Spargo, John, 212, 334*n*
Spencer, Anna Garlin, 41–42, 73, 159
Spingarn, Joel, 232
Springfield Republican, 53
Springfield State Journal, 163
Stalin, Joseph, 158, 276
Stanton, Elizabeth Cady, 9, 11
Stars and Stripes, 264–65
State Department, U.S., 25, 106
Stedman, Seymour, 246–47, 257
Steffens, Lincoln, 97, 350*n*
Stokes, Rose Pastor, 256, 334*n*
Stone, Oliver, 290
Stone, William J., 105–6, 127, 137, 145, 167–
    68, 170, 180, 182–83, 276
strikes, 140, 246, 250, 278
Stuttgart, Second International in, 11–12, 35
submarines, 108
  see also U-boats
suffrage parade of 1913, 72, 79
Sumner, Charles, 228
Sumner, Charles P., 57
Supreme Court, U.S., 115
  Selective Service Law affirmed by, 205–6
Survey, 84, 135, 150, 162, 164, 193–94, 242,
    340*n*
Sussex, 107–9, 144
Sweden, 8, 75–76
Switzerland, 21, 54, 66
Sykes-Picot Treaty, xvi

Taft, William Howard, 6–7, 10, 96, 178
Tavenner, Clyde H., 26, 91, 134
taxes, 186, 244
  corporate, 225, 244, 272
  income, 94, 119, 210, 324*n*
  inheritance, 161
  on war profits, 224–25, 283

Teamsters Union, 175
Ten Days That Shook the World (Reed), 251
terrorism, 120
Texas, 26, 90, 164
Thomas, Norman, 135, 204–7, 235, 255, 256,
    288, 340*n*
Three Soldiers (Dos Passos), 263
Tobacco Merchants Association, 126
Tocqueville, Alexis de, 39
Tolstoy, Leo, 10, 25
Tomb of the Unknown Soldier, 280, 353*n*
Trevelyan, Charles, 137–38, 330*n*
Trotsky, Leon, 157–58, 213, 240, 250
Trotter, William Monroe, 230–31, 258–59,
    346*n*, 354*n*
"Truth about Preparedness" campaign, 159
Tumulty, Joseph, 93, 179
Turkey, 186, 247, 267

U-boats, 59, 60, 73, 103–5, 107–8, 144–45,
    147–50, 153, 180, 199, 267, 318*n*, 336*n*
  armed neutrality and, 161–64, 166, 171–72,
    174
unemployment, 23, 25
Union of Democratic Control (UDC), 45,
    137, 142
United Kingdom, *see* Great Britain
United Mine Workers (UMW), 13, 88–89,
    175, 198, 323*n*
United Mine Workers Journal, 89
United States, 3
  economic and demographic expansion in,
    148
  economic recession in, 23–24
  neutrality of, xiii
  popularity of peace advocacy in, 4
  wartime manufacturing boom in, 25–26
  as world military power, xvii–xviii, 276,
    286–92
Universal Peace Congress, of 1901, 2, 4
Untold History of the United States, The
    (Kuznick and Stone), 290

Vanderbilt, Cornelius, 28
Van Lear, Thomas, 220–21
Vardaman, James, 180–81, 182–83, 231, 289,
    354*n*
Verdun, battle of, 108, 111
Versailles, Treaty of, xv, 273, 277, 283, 354*n*
Vienna, 66–67
Vietnam War, xii, xvi, xvii, 188, 287–88, 291,
    308*n*, 356*n*
  draft resisters in, 209, 212, 343*n*

Villard, Fanny Garrison, 38, 42, 47, 55, 59, 149–50, 163, 347n
  Women's Peace Parade and, 18, 20, 21, 141
Villard, Oswald Garrison, 59, 67, 72, 84, 124–25, 148, 241, 271, 347n, 350n

Wald, Lillian, 19, 79, 84, 93, 109, 124, 155, 158–59, 164, 194, 242, 243, 334n
  on Mexican conflict, 116
Wales, Julia, 43–44, 45–46, 48, 50, 52, 56, 136
  Peace Ship and, 71
  Wisconsin Plan of, 66, 74, 88
Wall Street, 61–62, 82, 180, 184, 209, 210, 237, 283
Walzer, Michael, 289
Wanamaker, John, 70
"War Against War" exhibit, 82, 83, 160
War Department, U.S., 208
  Military Intelligence branch of, 257–58
  morale division of, 264
War of 1812, 148, 200
war profiteers, xiv, 15, 28, 224–25, 243, 268, 280, 283
"War's Heretics" (Thomas), 255
Washington, Booker T., 230
Washington, D.C., 26, 30, 84, 89, 121, 150, 174, 232–33
Washington, George, 141
Washington, Margaret, 230
Washington Post, 39, 67, 114, 142, 164, 169, 203, 284, 353n
Washington Star, 53
Washington State, 9, 133
Watson, Tom, 211
Webster, Daniel, 200, 228
Wells, H. G., 277
Wells-Barnett, Ida Bell, 258–59
West, xiii, 26, 124, 132
Western Front, 189, 261, 267, 276
White, Edward D., 178, 205–6
White, George Henry, 30
White House, 87
white supremacy, 29–30, 233, 332n
Whittlesey, Charles, 266–67, 353n
Wilhelm II, Kaiser, xii, xv, 22, 26, 56, 59, 87, 103, 104, 139, 160, 164, 165, 172, 177, 184, 223, 227, 232, 251, 267–68, 350n
  abdication of, 268
Will, George, 289
Williams, John Sharp, 169, 178–79, 180, 182
Wilson, Edith, 93

Wilson, Woodrow, xi, 17, 36, 64, 146, 155, 196, 205, 207, 218, 223, 226, 227, 230, 236, 238, 239, 241, 260, 287, 290, 312n, 335n, 347n, 353n–54n
  AAUM meeting with, 108–10
  AUAM and, 85, 92
  Anglophilia of, 22–23, 103, 139
  anti-militarists prosecuted by, xv, 189–91, 209, 244–47, 271
  April 2 wartime speech of, 177–79
  armed neutrality and, 162–64, 166–68, 171–74, 182
  aspirations of, 140–41
  at peace conference, 276–77
  conscription and, 198–200, 201–3, 207–8, 341n
  declaration of war and, xiii, xiv–xv, 172–77, 184–86, 198, 212, 261
  diplomatic ties with Germany severed by, 147–52
  domestic agenda of, 32
  Flag Day speech of, 190, 219
  Fourteen Points of, 247–53, 267, 269, 270, 271, 277
  German surrender and, 267–70
  League of Nations and, 277–78, 283, 356n
  National Defense Act and, 117–18
  neutrality supported by, xvi, 21–22, 24, 27, 32, 40, 103, 106–7, 133, 138, 162–63, 164, 236, 332n
  in 1912 election, 15, 85, 93, 125
  in 1916 election, 95, 108, 113–16, 120, 122, 123–26, 128–29, 131–37, 149, 150, 186, 266, 270, 328n, 330n
  peace negotiations promoted by, 137–41, 144, 331n
  peace speech of, 61–62
  "peace without victory" speech of, 141–44, 147, 190, 194, 215, 217, 220, 236, 247–48, 331n
  preparedness and, 74, 77, 80, 85, 91, 94–95, 98, 114, 125, 136
  as progressive, 115, 161
  and response to German U-boat attacks, 103–9
  second inaugural address of, 168, 171–72, 177
  Treaty of Versailles and, 273
  U-boat sinkings and, 60–62, 149–50, 161–64
  war declared inevitable by, 107, 155, 157, 165, 229
  wartime legislation of, 188–93
  Woman's Peace Party and, 47–48, 56, 92
Zimmermann Telegram and, 165–66

Wilson administration, 24, 25, 29, 161, 173, 190, 232
Wisconsin, xiii, 15, 26, 44, 96, 127–29, 135, 139, 279
Wisconsin, University of, 43, 228
Wise, Stephen, 58, 70, 84, 85, 109, 120, 124, 217, 237
Woman's Christian Temperance Union (WCTU), Department of Peace and Arbitration of, 9
Woman's Peace Party, xii, 17, 20, 39–48, 63, 67, 72, 90, 92, 122, 124, 127, 148, 152, 167, 183, 187, 208, 214, 230, 243, 248, 279, 288
　divisions within, 159, 194–96, 322n, 335n
　and Hague conference, 48–56
　New York branch of, 45, 79, 81, 85–86, 123, 191, 195, 322n, 333n, 335n
　paper vs. active membership of, 121
　Wilson and, 47–48
women, in anti-militarism movement, 18–22, 38–48
Women's International Congress, 140
Women's International League for Peace and Freedom, 279

Women's Peace Parade, 18–22, 141
women's suffrage, xii, 9, 18, 40, 42, 46, 78, 79, 96–97, 123, 183
　national, 239, 348n
　in New York State, 239, 273
women's suffrage movement, peace movement and, 159
Women's Trade Union League, 39, 50, 67
Wood, Leonard, 61, 62, 115, 198, 260, 323n
working class, 55, 86, 157, 278
Working Class Union (WCU), 207–8
workmen's compensation laws, 78, 132
World Trade Center, 60
World War I, see Great War
World War II, xvii, 276, 286, 308n
　as justified war, 286, 291
　memorials for, xvi
　neutrality in lead-up to, 281
　in wake of Great War, xvi, 276n

York, Alvin, 266, 353n

Zimmermann, Arthur, 164–65
Zimmermann Telegram, 164–66, 167, 184

ABOUT THE AUTHOR

MICHAEL KAZIN is a professor of history at Georgetown University and co-editor of *Dissent*, a magazine of politics and culture founded in 1954. He is the author of several books on U.S. politics and social movements, contributes frequently to publications both popular and academic, and is a recipient of a Guggenheim Foundation fellowship, among others. He lives in Washington, D.C., with his wife, Dr. Beth Horowitz.